UN-AMERICAN

LEFT TO RIGHT: Tang Ming-chao, undersecretary of the United Nations; Ting Hsi-lin, vice-chairman of the Chinese People's Association for Cultural Relations; Anna Louise Strong; Mao Tse-tung; W.E.B. Du Bois; Shirley Graham Du Bois; Chu Poshem, direct descendant of the last Chinese emperors; and an unidentified figure in Wuhan, People's Republic of China, 1959. *(Used with permission of the Special Collections and University Archives, W.E.B. Du Bois Library, University of Massachusetts Amherst.)*

UN-AMERICAN

W.E.B. DU BOIS AND
THE CENTURY OF WORLD REVOLUTION

BILL V. MULLEN

TEMPLE UNIVERSITY PRESS
Philadelphia • Rome • Tokyo

TEMPLE UNIVERSITY PRESS
Philadelphia, Pennsylvania 19122
www.temple.edu/tempress

All reasonable attempts were made to locate the copyright holders for the poetry excerpts published in this book. If you believe you may be one of them, please contact Temple University Press, and the publisher will include appropriate acknowledgment in subsequent editions of the book.

Library of Congress Cataloging-in-Publication Data

Mullen, Bill, 1959–
  Un-American : W.E.B. Du Bois and the century of world revolution / Bill V. Mullen.
       pages cm
  Includes bibliographical references and index.
  ISBN 978-1-4399-1109-9 (hardback : alkaline paper) — ISBN 978-1-4399-1110-5 (paper : alkaline paper) — ISBN 978-1-4399-1111-2 (e-book) 1. Du Bois, W. E. B. (William Edward Burghardt), 1868–1963—Political and social views. 2. Revolutions—History—20th century. 3. Revolutionaries—History—20th century. 4. World politics—1945–1989. 5. Cold War. 6. Anti-imperialist movements—History—20th century. 7. Peace movements—History—20th century. 8. Working class—Civil rights—History—20th century. 9. Democracy—History—20th century. 10. Internationalism—History—20th century. I. Title.
  E185.97.D73M85 2015
  321.09'4—dc23

                                                                                2015000680

∞ The paper used in this publication meets the requirements of the American National Standard for Information Sciences—Permanence of Paper for Printed Library Materials, ANSI Z39.48-1992

Printed in the United States of America

9 8 7 6 5 4 3 2 1

For Tithi, Shayari, and Max

and

For the comrades everywhere

CONTENTS

ACKNOWLEDGMENTS

In a book about happy endings, it is fitting to begin these acknowledgments where most conclude. The better ideas here owe to long thinking and conversation with Tithi Bhattacharya, the best historian I know and the person who keeps alive my daily hopes for world revolution and a better planet. This book is dedicated first and foremost to her.

Student colleagues helped see this work to fruition in a variety of ways. While Cathryn Watson was a graduate student at the University of Texas, San Antonio, we worked together as co-editors of an earlier book on Du Bois's writings on Asia, which nurtured chapters herein on China, Japan, and India. Ernest Gibson assisted in the production of that book before moving on to his own position in the academy. Mark Bousquet was an expert research assistant at an early stage of this project. Na'eemah Webb talked with me for two years, in two seminars, about Du Bois. Her questions and queries about Du Bois's Marxism and Pan-Africanism have sharpened my reflections. Annagul Yarieva provided remarkable translations of Du Bois's late essays in the Soviet press while guiding me through the archives at the Russian State Library. I cannot thank her enough for her assistance. Students in my W.E.B. Du Bois seminar in American studies at Purdue University—Michelle Campbell, Jonathan Freeman, Ivan Jackson, Keturah Nix, Deena Varner, Na'eemah Webb, Jeff Wimble, and Lisa Young—created a collective space and sounding board for remarkable discussion and debate on Du Bois's legacy.

Comrades and friends in common struggle inside and outside the university, too many to name, have shaped this book's optimistic trajectory in the face of twentieth- and twenty-first-century state violence against movements for national liberation and working-class emancipation. They include Joe Allen, Sofia Arias, Becca Barnes, Tithi Bhattacharya, Bridget Broderick, Candace Cohn, Paul D'Amato, Angela Dillard, Wael Elasady, Sue Ferguson, Lauryn Flizer, Joel Geier, Shaun Harkin, Brian Jones, Deepa Kumar, Paul LeBlanc, Phil Marfleet, David McNally, Elizabeth Schulte, Alan Sears, Ahmed Shawki, Snehal Shingavi, Ashley Smith, Sharon Smith, Lee Sustar, Alan Wald, Sherry Wolf, and Keeanga Yamahtta-Taylor. This book also evolved through three major political movements on the Purdue University campus, where some of our ideas on the theory and practice of social change were shaped. Among the leaders in the Occupy Purdue, Trayvon Martin, and Black Lives Matter protests were April Burke, Tyrell Connor, Casarae Gibson, Aria Halliday, Steve Horrocks, Josh Iddings, Tiffany Montoya, Fernando Tormos, and Na'eemah Webb. Their organizing galvanized students and community members into sustained struggle against racism and catastrophic economic inequality that students and working people in Indiana experience daily.

This book begins its own reflections on world revolution with the Arab Spring of 2011. A cadre of scholars and activists dedicated to Palestinian liberation have been heroic in keeping alive the idea and spirit of self-determination both in Occupied Palestine and in the pages of this book. Most are members of the U.S. Campaign for the Academic and Cultural Boycott of Israel. They helped push the American Studies Association to vote for a boycott of Israeli universities during the composition period of *Un-American*. They include Rabab Adulhadi, Kristian Davis Bailey, Rana Barakat, Omar Barghouti, Nora Barrows-Friedman, Ashley Dawson, Haidar Eid, Nada Elia, Cynthia Franklin, Moira Geary, Salah Hassan, Sami Hermez, Cheryl Higashida, Lena Ibrahim, Charlotte Kates, J. Kehaulani Kauanui, Rahim Kurwa, David Lloyd, Alex Lubin, Sunaina Maira, Rima Najjar Merriman, Fred Moten, David Palumbo-Liu, Jordana Rosenberg, Bob Ross, Steven Salaita, Malini Johar Schueller, Magid Shihade, Neferti Tadiar, Lisa Taraki, Salim Vally, and Phil Weiss. These friends and fighters prove that the university can still be a place of radical social change, despite uphill struggles everywhere.

I am also indebted to a number of scholars whose writing and thinking about world revolution, and Du Bois, have shaped my own, though not always to the same political conclusions. Some of these people are recognized in my final chapter. Here I acknowledge especially Ali Abunimah, Aijaz Ahmad, Dohra Ahmad, Tariq Ali, Perry Anderson, Benjamin Balthaser, Tithi Bhattacharya, Carol Boyce-Davies, Alex Callinicos, Kunal Chattopadhyay, Neil Davidson, Michael Denning, Barbara Foley, Dayo Gore, Sobhanlal Datta

Gupta, the late Duncan Hallas, Adam Hanieh, Cheryl Higashida, Gerald Horne, Robin D. G. Kelley, Clarence Lang, David Levering Lewis, Alex Lubin, Soma Marik, William Maxwell, Erik S. McDuffie, Pankaj Mishra, Yuichiro Onishi, Eric Porter, Vijay Prashad, Ruth Price, Paula Rabinowitz, John Riddell, Cedric Robinson, Sumit Sarkar, Marika Sherwood, James Smethurst, Etsuko Taketani, Alan Wald, and Mary Helen Washington.

This book has been written with indispensable institutional and library support. My thanks go to Purdue's College of Liberal Arts for a Purdue Center for the Humanities Research Grant, which enabled me to take a full term off to write. The library staffs at Purdue and the University of Massachusetts Amherst have been crucial to the success of this project. The staff at Jawaharlal Nehru University helped direct me to important material in the collection that I used in the chapter on India. My gratitude goes to Frederick T. Courtright for assistance in obtaining permission to use materials from the Du Bois papers. At an early stage in the conception of this book, LeAnn Fields at the University of Michigan Press helped advocate for my work on Du Bois's "Russia and America: An Interpretation." I extend my thanks to her for her tireless confidence. A portion of this book was published in different form in *Lineages of the Literary Left*, a University of Michigan Press book dedicated to the work of Alan Wald. Howard Brick, Paula Rabinowitz, and Robbie Lieberman, editors of that volume, provided keen feedback that made that work stronger. Readers of early proposals on this project, Roger Buckley, Brian Jones, and James Smethurst, provided essential support and input that sharpened my focus. My thanks also go to the anonymous reviewers for Temple University Press.

I have not known a better editor advocate than Janet Francendese. Janet reached out to me long ago to inquire about this project. A single phone conversation convinced me that she and Temple were the right place for the book. I am fortunate to be one of the last writers to work with Janet; she retired just as the manuscript was entering production. I thank Janet for her knack for knowing what this book could be and for her patient stewardship of the project through the entire process of writing and editing. Joan Vidal spirited production along beautifully. Bruce Gore produced a killer cover. Susan Deeks was an amazing and gracious copyeditor.

The world at home has been filled with love and sometimes loss since I long ago started this project. My mother, Lynn, passed during the writing of this book, as did her brother, Barry, and my father-in-law, Somir. So, too, did my aunts, Gertrude and Dot. My dear friend and collaborator Fred Ho also succumbed to cancer. I offer oceans of love and appreciation to longtime and new friends who helped me live my life and keep the book breathing: Megha Anwer, Becca Barnes, Mandira Bhattacharya, Bridget Broderick, Kazumi Chino, Steve Chino, Candace Cohn, Susan Curtis, Chuck Cutter,

Paul D'Amato, Joel Geier, Shaun Harkin, Sally Hastings, Eliza Hilton, Dennis Kosuth, Marlene Mergenthaler, Mike Mergenthaler, Lindsey Miles, Bhumika Dogra Mukherjee, Kamalika Mukherjee, Leo Mukherjee, Pablo Mukherjee, Jack Mullen, Jean Niemann, Louis Niemann, Juno Parmer, Bill Roberts, Deborah Roberts, Kirstin Roberts, Achin Vanaik, and Anish Vanaik.

My love and appreciation go to the children who came after them, as well: Oliver, Sean, Maggie, Teo; Caitlin; Brad; Jill; Kelsey; Claire, Audrey; Arkady; Neo. My world beats faster every day because of two: Max, who has grown wise during the composition of this book, and Shayari, who lives with her fist in the air. So much love. Choose your own circumstances; make your own history.

Author's Note: All royalties from the sale of this book go to support the U.S. Campaign for the Academic and Cultural Boycott of Israel.

THE FORETHOUGHT

History is the object of a construction whose place is formed not in homogenous and empty time, but in that which is fulfilled by the here-and-now [*Jetztzeit*]. For Robespierre, Roman antiquity was a past charged with the here-and-now. . . . The French revolution thought of itself as a latter day Rome. It cited ancient Rome exactly the way fashion cites a past costume. Fashion has an eye for what is up-to-date, wherever it moves in the jungle [*Dickicht*: maze, thicket] of what was. It is the tiger's leap into that which has gone before. Only it takes place in an arena in which the ruling classes are in control. The same leap into the open sky of history is the dialectical one, as Marx conceptualized the revolution.

    —WALTER BENJAMIN, "ON THE CONCEPT OF HISTORY," 1940

Judge Mansart began to learn what most men learn slowly and some never—namely, that when we live through a great series of human events, we do not necessarily see them, even less do we really understand them, nor can we arrange them to fit logically into the world we already know. Perhaps (and this complicates understanding even more) current events clearly show us that our interpretation of the past has been wrong, that only through the present can we see the past. Time, in other words, shifts—future is partly the past and the past is future.

    —W.E.B. DU BOIS, *WORLDS OF COLOR*, 1961

The violent conflicts of our age enable our practiced vision to see into the very bones of previous revolutions more easily than before.

    —C.L.R. JAMES, PREFACE TO *THE BLACK JACOBINS*, 1938

—an American, a Negro . . .

    —W.E.B. DU BOIS, *THE SOULS OF BLACK FOLK*, 1903

When the twenty-six-year-old Tunisian fruit vendor Tarek al-Tayeb Mohamed Bouazizi set himself aflame in January 2011 to protest police efforts to confiscate his livelihood, protestors took up the ringing denunciation of French colonial rule by the poet Aboul-Qacem Echebbi a century earlier: "If one day, a / people desire to live, / then fate will answer their call / And their night will then begin to fade, / and their chains break and fall." Weeks later, Egyptian revolutionaries shouting down neoliberal state policies and the high cost of daily goods invoked the nation's deposition of British colonial rule in 1952 and bread riots of 1977 en route to toppling the autocrat Hosni Mubarak. In Greece, in the months after Mubarak's fall, workers protesting wage and employment cuts carried out a series of general strikes, reviving a tactic instrumental to the Russian Revolution of 1905, the decolonization of India in 1947, and the Solidarność (Solidarity) movement in Poland in the 1980s. By the summer of 2012, some fifty years after launching pickets against the fascist government of Francisco Franco, Spanish mine-workers in the northern village of Ciñera blockaded roads and hurled rocks—slingshot-style—at police dispatched to quell protests against austerity. As the battle waged on the ground, the forty-two-year-old coal miner Miguel Angel Iglesias told the *New York Times*, "I don't preach violence, but I guess it's turn-ing into our version of the intifada. . . . When somebody is determined to take away your job and what has kept families living here for over a century, you fight to the end."[1]

The twenty-first century and its dissidents are haunted by the specter of one of the twentieth century's most ambitious and unrealized projects: world revolution. When on its last day the Nobel Prize–winning poet Rabindranath Tagore wrote the epitaph for a hundred years of nineteenth-century imperial conquest—"The century's sun has set in blooded clouds. / There rising in the carnival of violence / from weapon to weapon, the mad music of death"[2]—he limned the dawn of a new century marked out by interdependent serial strug-gles for global emancipation. The first to apprehend this vector in full was Leon Trotsky. In his book *Results and Prospects* (1906), written in the wake of the failed Russian Revolution of 1905, Trotsky argued that the "combined and uneven" development of capitalism across the world could create conditions where a revolution in one "backward" country could help initiate another in a more advanced industrial nation, a process Trotsky called "permanent revolution."[3] Trotsky was not alone in conceiving world-system change as the new century's historic task. In 1900, conveners of the first Pan-African Con-gress in London, the largest gathering of African diasporic descendants to date, proclaimed, "Let the nations of the World respect the integrity and inde-pendence of the first Negro States of Abyssinia, Liberia, Haiti, and the rest, and let the inhabitants of these States, the independent tribes of Africa, the Negroes of the West Indies and America, and the black subjects of all nations take courage, strive ceaselessly, and fight bravely, that they may prove to the world their incontestable right to be counted among the great brotherhood of mankind."[4] Five years later, after a Japanese fleet commanded by Admiral Togo Heihachiro destroyed much of the Russian Navy in a territorial war in Manchuria, future revolutionary leaders of the coming century, from Mu-stafa Kemal (Turkey) to Mohandas Gandhi (India), were positively stricken by the prospects of chain decolonization across the globe.[5] Japan's victory also helped to inspire China's Republican Revolution of 1911, an event that was nearly concurrent with the Mexican Revolution of 1910, which helped draw the African American Lovett Fort-Whiteman first to Mexico and then to Russia, becoming the century's first black Bolshevik.[6]

In 1916, the Polish communist Rosa Luxemburg, repelled by social democrats backing German imperial ambitions in World War I, posited a formal political movement for global emancipation. "The founding of a new workers' international has become a living question of socialism," she wrote, "which would undertake the task of guiding and coordinating revolutionary class struggle against imperialism in all countries."[7] By October 1917, world revolution had become both iteration of possibility and historical fact. "The fall of Petrograd," Tariq Ali has quipped, "was . . . a universal event."[8] In the wake of their victory, the Bolsheviks formed the Communist International (Comintern) to build revolutionary communist parties and movements in every country of the world and to link liberation struggles in the global South to proletariats in industrial nations. World revolution became an official Bolshevik program to end Russia's internal civil war through global communist victory and to put into practice what Trotsky had first described and Vladimir Lenin had endorsed as the central objective of the new Third International. Indeed, the year 1919 saw an explosion of global struggle that seemed to bring the world to the brink: a May 4 anti-imperialist movement in China motivated by lost Chinese concessions in the Treaty of Versailles; a new communist movement in Korea; nationwide *hartals*, or labor strikes, in India in response to the Rowlatt Act, events Sumit Sarkar calls "the biggest and most violent anti-British upsurge which India had seen since 1857"—the year of the Sepoy Mutiny.[9] In Germany and Italy, new communist parties led by Luxemburg and a young Antonio Gramsci were flooded with members, heralding enthusiasm in the Soviet Union that world revolution was a matter of when, not whether. In 1920, the Dutch astronomer and council communist Anton Pannekoek published the essay "World Revolution and Communist Tactics" in *Kommunismus*, the Vienna-based theoretical organ for southeastern Europe.[10] In 1923, the radical poet Herman Gorter published an article in the London journal *Workers' Dreadnought* asking whether England might be the starting point of the world revolution.[11] Between 1919 and 1929, workers' uprisings across the United States, Asia, and Europe especially were undertaken in the name of the world revolution, anticipating the massive strike waves after the global crash of 1929.[12] By the mid-1930s, in the midst of world depression and emerging fascism, the Trinidadian expatriate, Bolshevik, and newly won Trotskyist C.L.R. James would both canonize and mourn the prospects for world revolution, assessing the surge and crest of events in the first third of the still new century as *World Revolution 1917–1936: The Rise and Fall of the Communist International.*

These movements and moments constitute a provisional genealogy of the history of world revolution forged from the twentieth-century left's contradictory aspirations, achievements, and failures. Among Marxists, this genealogy was first given flesh most brilliantly by the German communist Walter Benjamin in the essay "On the Concept of History" (1940). Written, likes James's *World Revolution*, in the flow tide of ongoing revolutions in Europe and Asia, Stalin's takeover of the Communist International, and the rise of European dictators, the essay seeks to create a mode of historical materialism in which revolution is not incidental but typological. "The tradition of the oppressed teaches us that the 'emergency situation' in which we live is the rule," wrote Benjamin. "We must arrive at a concept of history which corresponds to this." In response, Benjamin famously evoked a "messianic" theory of revolution that acknowledged the cyclical imminence of historical eruption. "On the Concept of History" proposed a temporal dialectics in which the present (*Jetztzeit*) inhabits history as the potential to rehabilitate *all revolutions* that had come before but not yet arrived in the here and now. It conceives the historical materialist, in turn, as the caged bird of history necessarily taking a leap of faith toward the "open sky" of revolutions past and present. For Benjamin, she or he is like the "Angel of History" in Paul Klee's famous painting, blown by the storm of past human failures and misery "irresistibly into the future." As Alex Callinicos astutely notes, Benjamin's essay transforms the apocalyptic doubts of revolutionary failures—"midnight in the century"—into a prophetic mode of recovery and restoration.[13]

Benjamin's typological reading of prospects for world revolution with and against the grain of the twentieth century also illuminates the long arc of the political thought and political life of W.E.B. Du Bois. In the summer of 1961, the year he joined the Communist Party of the USA and exiled himself to Ghana, Du Bois wrote a seldom studied essay for *Freedomways* magazine that provided, with abrupt clarity, an inordinately self-reflexive synopsis of what might be called his cumulative historical method, or "concept of history." The essay, titled "Africa and the French Revolution," begins with Du Bois imagining someone (the reader) approaching a senior on an American Ivy League college campus and asking what influence Africa had on the French Revolution. The answer "None" provokes the interlocutor's fantasy of approaching the student's teacher of "historiography," who, Du Bois avers, would give the same answer: "You would be told that between African slavery in America and the greatest revolution of Europe, there was of course some connection, since both took place on the same earth; but nothing causal, nothing of real importance, since Africans have no history."[14] Here, Du Bois conflates and animates the "ancient" problem of Hegel's (and Hume's) imperial erasures of Africa from Western timelines as an ongoing dilemma of writing history, as Benjamin has it, in an "arena in which the ruling classes are in control." The "leap" Du Bois insists on is historical materialism as an antidote to the hegemony of capitalist scripture. Thus, Du Bois proclaims, "It is a perfectly defensible thesis of scientific history that Africans and African slavery in the West Indies were the main causes and influences of the American Revolution and of the French Revolution. And when after long controversy and civil war, Negro slavery and serfdom were not suppressed, the United States turned from democracy to plutocracy and opened the path to colonial imperialism and made wide the way for the final world Revolutions in the 20th century."[15]

Like Benjamin, Du Bois here solves a crisis of *historicism* with the recovery of revolutionary agency. The recurring absence of Africa *from* world history is resolved by making Africans the subject *of* history. Revolution thus becomes the hermeneutic engine of both history writing and history making. The twentieth century's dream of world revolution discloses itself not just as a latent topic of Du Bois's nearly one hundred-year life but as a main leitmotif of that life's self-consciousness. As Benjamin puts it, "The subject of historical cognition is the battling, oppressed class itself."[16]

Fittingly, Du Bois's resolution of a world revolution typology in "Africa and the French Revolution" retrospectively drew together the totality of his life. Embracing communism and leaving America for Africa, Du Bois in 1961 reconciled a tension endemic to his most famous and oft-repeated archetype of African American experience: double-consciousness. Shopworn assertions about the dilemma of being "an American, a Negro" have typically failed to register the passage as antecedent and seed of Du Bois's eventual alienation from the U.S. nation-state and what Eric Porter has called Du Bois's "disidentifactory Americanism."[17] For example, in *The Souls of Black Folk*, Du Bois describes the problem of trying to become "both an American and a Negro" as particular to one "who has never been anything else, save perhaps in babyhood and in Europe."[18] This qualification offers exile and exilic consciousness as a variant antithesis to what Orlando Patterson calls "natal alienation," reminding us that *Souls* was written on the heels of Du Bois's first extended period abroad as a fellow of the John F. Slater Fund for the Education of Freedmen in Germany.[19] Describing in the posthumously published *Autobiography* his first journey south to take a teaching position at Fisk University, Du Bois rewrites the primal scene of double-consciousness as a precondition for national disidentification: "So I came to a region where the world was split into white and Black halves, and where the darker half was held back by race prejudice and legal bonds, as well as by deep ignorance and dire poverty. But facing this was not a lost group, but at Fisk, a microcosm of a world and civilization in potentiality. Into this world I leapt with enthusiasm. A new loyalty and allegiance replaced my Americanism: hence-forward I was a Negro."[20]

Du Bois here clearly presents his coming to race-consciousness as a leap outside the *nation* and into what he calls a "world and civilization in potentiality." He retrospectively applies Cold War terminology ("Americanism") to describe an oppositional consciousness formed (or forming) some sixty years earlier (the "Un-American"). We can now begin to understand more clearly, more dialectically, the contours of affiliation between Du Bois's embrace of a typology of world revolution and lifelong traumas of disidentification with the U.S. nation-state. Thus, when he finally assembled his *actual* autobiography in the late 1950s, Du Bois's reordered the chronology of his development. Part I begins not with his biological birth in the United States but with an account of his travels abroad, starting in 1951 in Europe, including his trips to the Soviet Union and China. This time of exile is antecedent to the "Interlude," titled "Communism," where he declares famously and emphatically, "I now state my conclusion frankly and clearly: I believe in communism."[21] This a priori section of the book is itself a conglomerate of earlier writings that point to his eventual formal embrace of world revolution politics. *The Autobiography of W.E.B. Du Bois* re-presents wholesale passages from Du Bois's account in *The Crisis* of his inaugural trips to both the Soviet Union and China in 1926 and 1936. The "Communism" declaration also recasts Du Bois's "Basic American Negro Creed," first enunciated in a column in *The Crisis* in 1936 and repeated as the closing pages of *Dusk of Dawn* in 1940: "We believe in the ultimate triumph of some form of Socialism the world over; that is, common ownership and control of the means of production and equality of income."[22] Structurally and thematically, then, *Autobiography* symbolically resolves the original sin of natal/national alienation by foregrounding both the totalizing capacity of world revolution Du Bois declares possible and the unitary or merged autobiographical self forged outside the United States as the agent of that historical possibility: "Only through the present can we see the past."

For Du Bois, then, the capacity to think, live, and write "a world and civilization in potentiality" necessitated a morphological break of time and space. Racial identification with and as the "Negro" is not a static identification with identity but, as Paul Gilroy has argued, a mode of passage into a counterculture of modernity. This is the true meaning of what in 1939 Du Bois called the "race concept." Yet Gilroy, like much Du Bois scholarship, founders there on Du Bois's political praxis, denying the obvious trajectory of his thought toward international revolutionary Marxism and mystifying Du Bois's practice of diaspora as a diffuse engagement with a corpus of *non-Marxist, anti-Marxist*, or *Pan-African sources*.[23] As should be clear by now, I argue instead that Du Bois's most useful analogues for thinking his relationship to modernity and its dark shadows were those thinkers like himself (James, Benjamin, Karl Marx, for starters) who were both exiled from its dominant currents and wholly committed to tearing down its prevailing apparatus of exploitation, immiseration, racism, and inequality. Put another way, I argue that Du Bois's diasporic identification was a necessary condition for transcending a capitalist hegemony in the United States that sought to incarcerate his mind, if not his body, to hold him captive within discursive limits of the possible, to make him a hostage to a legacy of "ruling class" history to which un-Americanness and exile became both a political necessity and a passport to global solidarity.

It is this aspect of Du Bois's life that I track in this book as the baseline of his political and intellectual development across the twentieth century, the century of world revolution. The central contention of this study is that Du Bois's political and intellectual life lived *outside* the United States and his body of writing in support of world revolution beyond the real and ideological borders of the United States constitute a counter-narrative to what might called the American Du Bois. Put another way, Du Bois's life may best be understood as the evolutionary political embrace of the Un-American years before the political label became the Cold War cloak designating his marginalization and dishonor. Indeed, Du Bois, I argue, came to himself as a committed global revolutionary thinker and typologist of world revolution as a means of shedding the historical excrescence of political failure and reformism within the United States: the structural and political limits of racial uplift theory and Second International reformism; Fabian socialism; cooperative economics; Jim Crow; structural racism and violence; liberalism and reaction; a relentless, elephantine, and repressive state apparatus. In time, Du Bois came to equate the totality of this U.S. history with the American "counterrevolution" read forward and backward in both his brilliant analysis of the Civil War and its aftermath, *Black Reconstruction*, and the "Propaganda of History," his postscript to that book on U.S. historiography. In the end, Du Bois had no choice, as a world revolutionary, but exile from both.

Thus, I argue, Du Bois's most deeply affecting political lessons and analysis of twentieth-century history were drawn primarily—though not exclusively—from sources and events outside the United States. The century of world revolution was lived elsewhere than America; across the course of his long life, Du Bois, to the best of his ability, insisted on living, thinking, and working on that stage of history. But if it was a life increasingly alienated from American soil, American thought, it was not one lived alone. Indeed, Du Bois's first encounter with Marxism "beyond the shores" of the United States as a Slater Fund fellow in Berlin in 1896 was the symbolic entry point into his participation in what in this study I call a diasporic international. This dynamic and fluid constellation may be defined as a cognate group of communist, socialist, anticolonial, and anti-imperial writers and thinkers who both contributed to and participated in many of the century's most important struggles for worldwide emancipation. The group itself is made visible and coherent by two characteristics I have already marked as fundamental to Du Bois's evolving political temperament and practice: a dedication to the concept of world revolution as drawn by Pan-African, Pan-Asian, and communist worldwide organizing movements and exilic wanderlust committed to intellectual and political formations beyond the boundaries of the nation-state. These attributes are dialectically linked by affiliation with internationalist organizations and political movements synchronically arranged to encompass the "combined and uneven" development of both capitalism and revolutionary struggle across the globe. Voluntary and involuntary diasporic movement across and between nation-states earmark members of the diasporic international, whose political biographies were necessarily shaped—like Du Bois's—coincident with the prospects for political realignment worldwide.

The members of the diasporic international include a range of Du Bois's friends, collaborators, correspondents, comrades, intimates, and familiars, each of whom acted as confidante, interpreter, or political mentor unto his own grasp of World Revolution theory and practice. Among them are Jawaharlal Nehru, Lajpat Rai, and Mohandas Gandhi from India; the Trinidadian Comintern member and Pan-Africanist George Padmore, perhaps Du Bois's most companionate member of the diasporic international; the aforementioned C.L.R. James and his fellow Trinidadian Claudia Jones, also exiles from the United States in 1953 and 1955, respectively; Agnes Smedley, Esther Cooper Jackson, and Anna Louise Strong, Americans who like Du Bois had committed early support for the Russian Revolution of 1917 and, later, China's 1949 revolution; Vladimir Ilyich Ulyanov (Lenin) and Joseph Stalin, leaders of the Russian Revolution of 1917; and Kwame Nkrumah, Du Bois's early mentee and later mentor in Pan-Africanism and Ghanaian decolonization. More directly—or closer, ironically, to home—Shirley Graham Du Bois functioned as Du Bois's navigator and amanuensis through the field of the diasporic international, entering Du Bois's life at a moment of personal consolidation over the meaningful relationship between communism as theory and practice and his own relationship to the non-U.S. world. Indeed, Graham Du Bois was a personal and calendrical tipping point for Du Bois not just in confirming his confidence in Marxism as a method for grasping and changing history, but in companionship that enabled him to resolve the dilemma of becoming (or embracing) Un-Americanness by not going it alone.

The trajectory of this group and its constituted network of relationships encompasses the entire course of Du Bois's life: many (Nehru, Gandhi, Rai, Lenin, Stalin) were born within a few years of him in 1868; others, slightly younger, came to revolutionary commitment through similar passages—World War I, the Russian Revolution, Pan-Africanism—and would include Strong,

Smedley, Padmore, and James. Still others, including Jones and Graham Du Bois, were turned toward revolutionary politics later by events such as the Italian invasion of Ethiopia in 1935, the fight against fascism, and mid-century anticolonial struggles. All, however, were bonded by the series of revolutionary upturns, successes, near-misses, and deferrals that constitute the expansive timeline of world revolution with which I began this study. As I show in chapters to come, they are the archetypal figures of the typology of world revolution with whom Du Bois conjoined, from whom he learned to stay the course and whose solidarity, even when at great distance, kept him moving always in the direction of revolutionary affirmation, even, banally, hope.

At the same time, Du Bois's diasporic international was, like Benjamin's Angel of History, buffeted and impelled by defeat, betrayal, contradiction, misjudgment, and fatal lapse. Its members are the children of both the midnight of Indian decolonization and the "midnight hour" of fascism and revolutions betrayed. Paramount to this bidirection was Stalinism, the twentieth century's dark hijacking by what Isaac Deutscher has called the "mongrel offspring of Marxism and primitive magic."[24] This study emphasizes world events between companionate poles of twentieth-century revolutionary foment: the formation of the Communist International in 1919 and of the Pan-African Congress of 1945 in Manchester, England. These events were shaped, and at times directed, by Stalin's tragic influence on the world-revolutionary left. Consequential throughout were the disastrous turns in the Soviet Union toward famine and genocide in the Ukraine; mass starvation from failed collectivization; internal repression of dissidents; alliance with fascism; purges, exile, and murder— events to which members of the diasporic international at times lent tacit support, denial, defense, or, in the best of cases, critical dissent. *Politically* most damaging and significant to the diasporic international's aspiration for world revolution was Stalin's dedication to Socialism in One Country, prioritizing the defense of the Soviet "socialist homeland" over the building of workers' revolutions in industrialized capitalist states and their colonies. While the Soviet abandonment of the Communist International in 1943 signaled the formal demise of Soviet leadership for the world revolution, its protracted dissipation can be traced to the earliest years after 1917. Its tragic traces are thus everywhere to be examined here: in Germany's failed revolution of 1923; Chiang Kai-shek's attack on Shanghai's working class in 1926; the Comintern's redirection of world communist parties away from class struggle; the destruction of Soviet democracy in the U.S.S.R.; lapses and cycles within the Pan-African movement; and tensions between anticolonial nationalism and internationalism within the world-revolutionary left.

Thus, members of the diasporic international elicited contradictory adherence to a Stalinist Soviet Union claiming a mantle of world revolution while simultaneously repressing, eroding, and destroying the capacity of workers' states. Indeed, the Soviet revolution, in part because of its isolated singularity, became not just typological but archetypal for the diasporic international, even its distant mistakes and distortions templates for the world revolution conception. Ideologically, comprehension of the world revolution idea after 1917 was also produced through a filter of conflicting events on the ground where members of the diasporic international found themselves: Beijing, Shanghai, Delhi, London, Paris, Manchester, Berlin, New York, Accra. Physical diffusion, differentiated nationalisms, uneven class struggles, inconsistent or truncated understanding of Marxist thought—itself distended by Stalinist rule—mercurial shifts and starts in political conditions, and political lines: each of these traumas of the revolutionary left tore at and challenged allegiance to Stalinism in practice even as *in name* Stalinism and the Soviet Union remained synonymous with the world revolution concept. For figures such as Strong, Smedley, James, Padmore, and Nehru, for example, this meant often sharp disagreement with specific turns in Stalinist policy—the Popular Front strategy; support, or lack thereof, for African decolonization and the Chinese communist movement; liquidation of the kulaks—mediated by overarching support for the Russian Revolution itself. Thus, what Alan Wald has noted of recent scholarship on members of the African American left is even more strikingly true in assessment of the diasporic international—namely, that "despite its clarifying potential when used in a sophisticated manner to treat an ideology, social system or political organization, 'Stalinism' can be an oversimplifying lens through which to evaluate the thinking, personalities and life activities of diverse individuals." And yet, contradictorily again, even as the prospects for both the Soviet revolution and world revolution had dimmed by World War II, *Stalinism* was burnished as a historical marker of each by the very tragedies it helped to create. As Tariq Ali has noted, Red Army battles with Hitler's troops at Leningrad and Stalingrad "provided Stalinism with a legitimacy it had hitherto established over the corpses of old Bolsheviks."[25]

Nowhere were the contradictions of world revolution in the Stalin era more acute than in the political work and thought of W.E.B. Du Bois. Because he came to full support for the Russian Revolution after Stalin's ascent to leadership, Du Bois was a particularly vulnerable prisoner of Stalinism's dark magic. In his unpublished manuscript "Russia and America," Du Bois acknowledged directly his orientation to a "Stalinist" conception of world revolution from which he, like many of the diasporic international, was unable fully to break. "The World Revolution for which the Communists hoped did not materialize," he wrote about the 1920s. "Even Lenin had doubted if a single Socialist agricultural state could stand alone in a capitalistic industrial world: and Trotsky had insisted that the Russian Revolution could only succeed if it was prelude to a European uprising. Only Stalin, slowly but with ear to ground, came to believe that Russia not only could but must prepare to stand alone in the world as a socialist state."[26] For Du Bois, as for many members of the diasporic international, defense of Socialism in One Country doctrine and the world revolution concept came to be paradoxically synonymous—Du Bois referred to the Soviet revolution as a "part" of the world-revolutionary whole—even while Stalin's leadership of the former generated massive roadblocks to the latter. This explains Du Bois's increasingly strident public proclamations for Stalin's leadership, especially after the successes of Indian and Chinese decolonization, and much of his refusal to recognize the material disasters and persecutions under Stalinism in his written record. At the same time, especially as we shall see in Chapters 2 and 4, Du Bois's staggered and incomplete understandings of Marxism, his lifelong aversion to political violence, and the congruent pull of competing ideological influence on his thought (from Pan-Africanism and Pan-Asianism to cooperative economics) evince marks of doubt, hesitation, and deviation from Stalin's Russian program up to the end of his life.

Hence, a judicious accounting of Du Bois's relationship to Stalin's influence on the world revolution must take heed of and refine both Robin D. G. Kelley's assertion that Du Bois, like Paul Robeson and others on the procommunist left, had "nothing to say" about Stalin's atrocities, and Eric Porter's more recent assertion that "we must avoid the problem of making leftist ideas and affinities overly determinative of his thought . . . in either positive or negative ways. Du Bois might have praised Stalin, for example, but he was not a Stalinist in any systematic way."[27] Indeed, to return to an example discussed earlier: Du Bois's essay "Africa and the French Revolution" of 1961 reconciles what, contemporarily or in hindsight, would seem to be two radically oppositional conceptions of world revolution itself: C.L.R. James's Trotskyist-influenced conception of black self-activity as part of the worker's vanguard with the unremitting Communist Party loyalism of Herbert Aptheker. Five years after Du Bois made Aptheker his literary archivist, James had savagely attacked Aptheker's scholarship on Negro slave revolts.[28] He accused Aptheker of producing a "Stalinist" historiography that diminished black self-activity in the creation of the abolitionist movement, thereby replicating white chauvinism as a feature of the Communist Party to which Aptheker belonged. Du Bois, for his part, had viciously attacked Trotsky (though not James) in several places during the 1950s, including in his unpublished manuscript "Russia and America: An Interpretation," discussed later. But in both the 1950 manuscript and the 1961 essay, Du Bois evinces a desire to preserve and enunciate what I have been calling a typology of revolutionary reading and writing that supersedes political sectarianism and specifically identifiable political traditions.

The burden of revolutionary aspiration—or, in other words, the Benjamin-ian impulse to animate the messiah of revolution—eclipses what might be called political "orthodoxy" even in the high moment of Du Bois's publicly professed Stalinist loyalties. Supporting world revolution in the Stalin era for Du Bois came to mean the intellectual survival of an idea—human self-emancipation—even in the objective face of its own distorted meanings and often depleted prospects. Put another way, world revolution for Du Bois was also a version of Benjamin's angel: a figure of contradiction constantly chased forward by counterrevolution and defeat—the brooding, ever present shadow of historical and political foreclosure Benjamin called "progress."

ON REVOLUTION AND REVOLUTIONARY TYPOLOGY: A NOTE ON METHOD

In the same year in which he published "Africa and the French Revolution," W.E.B. Du Bois published *Worlds of Color*, the last of his Mansart trilogy of novels. The Mansart trilogy, according to Brent Edwards, is Du Bois's most neglected major work. Yet it is arguably an explanatory key not only to his life's self-evaluation but also to the historical method he offered readers for explicating that life. The trilogy is a collective autobiography in which Du Bois both represents and is represented by figures across the time and space of twentieth-century history. In his preface to the trilogy, Du Bois explains that fiction serves the purpose of giving history (and fact) a shape and meaning it otherwise cannot achieve. The generic slippage is a clue to an anxiety and assertion about political conclusions and political consequences in a world where epistemic reach exceeds political grasp, where "pessimism of the intel-lect and optimism of the will" are in dialectical interplay, if not at war. Man-sart's internal soliloquy on time is key to this: the refusal of history and lived experience to conform to what we already know necessitates recognition that "our interpretation of the past has been wrong, that only through the present can we see the past. Time, in other words, shifts—future is partly the past and the past is future." Here Du Bois again challenges "historicist" time, what Ben-jamin called "Once upon a time," to comprehend dialectically the dialectics of history. In Benjamin's words, "The historical materialist cannot do without the concept of a present which is not a transition, in which time originates and has come to a standstill."[29] In 1961, time stood still for Du Bois as epiphany that the making of human struggle, of class struggle, was the only means of making and comprehending human history. The aforementioned moment, cited in an epigraph from *Worlds of Color*, is thus a gloss on Marx's famous dictum from "The Eighteenth Brumaire of Louis Bonaparte": "Men make their own history, but they do not make it as they please; they do not make it under self-selected circumstances, but under circumstances existing already, given and transmitted from the past."[30] For Marx, as for the late Du Bois, accepting the forfeit is the burden of historical struggle and interpretation.

We thus risk comprehending the totality of Du Bois's concept of history by ignoring the totality of Du Bois's life, a risk all too often fulfilled by Du Bois scholarship. Too commonly, the "late Du Bois" is configured by scholars as a veering or departure from a life lived in general disciplined dedication to humanist ideals.[31] At times, this departure is described as a crude embrace of communism or of decrepit alienation from earlier commitments. This mechanical and stagist view of Du Bois carries with it an attempt to rescue Du Bois's radicalism from serious scrutiny. It shuns and censors that which it implicitly condemns. Against this grain and in the interval, this study reads the self-evident traces and tracks of Du Bois's commitment to the theory and practice of world revolution to argue for revolutionary typology as the key-note of Du Bois's political life and political thought. Here, I borrow from the literary scholar Mary Frances Fahey's interpretation of Benjamin's "On the Concept of History" as a pursuit of the idea that the past "bears with it a secret index through which it is directed towards deliverance." The task of the historical materialist, writes Fahey, is to discover the "monadological structure within configuration of data and events, in order to liberate the past so that it may be put in service of the future."[32] Indeed, this book argues here and in subsequent chapters that the most productive way to read the life and work of Du Bois is backward: as the retrospective fulfillment of a conception of human history best understood as its capacity for world revolution. I claim, first, that Du Bois's own retrospective and "revisionist" method, in which iterations of recurring tropes and ideas (the color line, double-consciousness, souls of black folk,) and textual reassemblage (the regeneration and recycling of prior themes, words, and ideas across texts) is the materialization or practice of Du Bois's late revelation that "future is partly the past and past is future." Second, I argue that only by seeing his thought and work in this perspective can we grasp the long arc of Du Bois's highly secularized aspiration for a "messiah" of world revolution and the century that made it so alluring and elusive for him.

As an example of this reading method to come, I return again briefly to "Africa and the French Revolution." Du Bois's essay tracks citationally to three prior historical texts and three historical epochs, each of them constitutive of Du Bois's typology of world revolution. The first is C.L.R. James's *The Black Jacobins* (1938). The central argument of Du Bois's essay derives directly from James's magisterial thesis that the consolidation of black labor in Haiti and the Caribbean constituted at once the world's first wholesale proletariat and nascent rebellion against proletarian status and that the "colonial question" itself was a singular spur to France's revolution: "It was not the Mulattoes they feared[;] it was the slaves. Slavery corrupted the society of San Domingo and had now corrupted the French bourgeoisie in the first flush and pride of its political inheritance."[33] This historical causality is, in turn, repeated in the French Revolution's aftereffects in San Domingo. As James puts it, "What of the slaves? They had heard of the revolution and construed it in their own image."[34] James's book, composed while reading Du Bois's *Black Reconstruction* (1935), inhabits the typology of revolution for Du Bois in two ways: first, as texts that "reorder" ruling class historiographical past and present by placing a history of Caribbean slave rebellions *prior to* the revolution of the French, and second, by adopting Du Bois's own typological reading of black slaves in *Black Reconstruction* as primary historical agents in the making of revolution. In *Jacobins*, James provides what might be called a "globalized" historiographical complement to Du Bois's final chapter of *Black Reconstruction*, "The Propaganda of History," his excoriation of "historicist" U.S. history that eliminates black agency in self-emancipation in the Civil War and Reconstruction. Indeed, speaking about the Haitian Revolution specifically but the arc of world revolution more generally, James averred in 1939: "The only place where Negroes did not revolt is in the pages of capitalist historians."[35] James's *Black Jacobins*, like Du Bois's *Black Reconstruction*, was also written in the self-conscious aftermath of the Russian Revolution of 1917—the crucial event in their respective "Bolshevization" of history—and within the grain of ongoing anticolonial movements in Pan-Africa and Asia (the former being the special subject of their contemporary political commitments, as I show later). Thus, James's prefatory comment to the *Black Jacobins*—"The violent conflicts of our age enable our practiced vision to see into the very bones of previous revolutions more easily than before"—was a double-voiced, or dialectical, iteration of a typological historiographical method he and Du Bois were collaboratively developing in the mid-1930s—not so coincidentally, the age of Benjamin. The years 1935–1940, then, were something like the "midnight hour" of their own advance in world-revolutionary theory.[36]

The second text to which Du Bois's 1961 essay tracks is Herbert Aptheker's *American Negro Slave Revolts*, first published in 1943. The book derives from Aptheker's doctoral dissertation, written at Columbia University, and like *Black Jacobins* it is a companion and intertext to Du Bois's own typological method. Like *Black Reconstruction*, which it cites, *American Negro Slave Revolts* assaults consensus school scholarship on the history of slavery, particularly the work of Ulrich B. Phillips, which, Aptheker notes, held that "slave revolts and plots very seldom occurred in the United States."[37] Laying the groove of his own dissident historiographical method, Aptheker cites C.L.R. James's then obscure (to American readers) book *A History of Negro Revolt* (1938), published in London the same year as *Black Jacobins*. Aptheker's own typology of slave rebellions, beginning with a panic in Virginia in 1673 about possible uprisings between slaves and indentured servants and ending with Civil War–era insurrections, was an affirmation and defense of James's (and Du Bois's) earlier revisionist historiography. Like James, Aptheker argued for the symbiotic influence of rebellion in San Domingo on African American slavery and on prior slave rebellions in the United States. Significantly, like Du Bois's *Black Reconstruction*, *American Negro Slave Revolts* expanded its analysis of black self-emancipation to demonstrate its relationship to wider working-class struggle: "The anti-slavery struggle broadened into a battle for the security of the democratic rights of the white people."[38] This reference is not just to the support from white workers in the United States for the abolitionist movement but also to what Aptheker knew to be the support cast by the International Workingmen's Association in London, headed by Karl Marx. That support elicited letters on behalf of the association from Marx to President Abraham Lincoln urging him to end slavery and became the kernel of Marx's most famous dictum on both race and the Civil War: "Labor cannot emancipate itself in the white skin wherein the black it is branded."[39] It was those letters from Marx that became an important source of Du Bois's *Black Reconstruction*.

The third, and culminating, source of the 1961 essay is Du Bois's oft-neglected *Black Folk Then and Now: An Essay in the History and Sociology of the Negro Race* (1939), a text that, I argue, stands as the crossroads in Du Bois's historiographical typology of world revolution. The book began in conception as a sequel to Du Bois's *The Negro* (1915), a study of African history. It ended as a synthesis of Du Bois's mobile and frantic self-education in shifting scholarship on Africa (the work of Melville Herskovitz, for example, which induced last-minute revisions) and his decade-long investment in the study of Marxism precipitated most significantly by his visit to the Soviet Union in 1926. This dual orientation is registered in the structure of the book: the first six chapters are ethnographic descriptions of African history, geography, demographics, and culture; the nine later chapters interpret modern world history as the interdependence of capitalist development and the slave trade. Of all of his books, *Black Folk Then and Now* is most emblematic of Du Bois's efforts to negotiate the midnight hour of midcentury, or what the text deems "fascist capitalism."[40] The term signals Du Bois's evolving grasp of Marxist theory, as well as his attempts to verify a method that can legitimate what he calls "the magnificent and apostolic fervor of Karl Marx and the communists."[41] Du Bois's sketch of capitalism's rise, for example, attributes Marx's description of the emergence of wage labor to the institution of slavery. Marx argued in addition that the exploitation of Africa produced "primitive accumulation" (what Du Bois calls "primary accumulation") that generated wealth necessary to capitalist development as a system. Du Bois also interprets colonialism and imperialism as intended to "keep the majority of people in slavish subjection to the white race"—the kernel of his conception of "fascist capitalism," an argument Marx never made.[42]

At the same time, Du Bois's interpretations were consistent with the endeavor of *Black Folk Then and Now* to consummate the *intention* of Marxist historiography—from the *Manifesto* of 1848 through the Russian Revolution of 1917—to foment world revolution. The "typology" and resolution for this was set clearly in the book's final chapter, "The Future of World Democracy." Producing a progressive timeline of Africa's own twentieth-century workers' rebellions—in the Belgian Congo in 1904, the railway workers' strikes in Sierra Leone in 1919, the anti-imperialist dockworkers' strikes in Dahomey in 1923, in South Africa again and again—Du Bois concludes the book with these words: "The proletariat of the world consists not simply of white European and American workers but overwhelmingly of the dark workers of Asia, Africa, the islands of the Seas and South and Central America. These are the ones who are supporting a superstructure of wealth, luxury, and extravagance. It is the rise of these people that is the rise of the world. The problem of the twentieth century is the problem of the color line."[43]

Several aspects of Du Bois's revolutionary typology are at work in this paragraph. First is its analysis of capitalism's "combined and uneven" development and proletarian global formation, a perspective owing to both the Communist Third International's support for colonial self-determination, as we shall see, and Du Bois's long-standing Pan-Africanist emphasis on the consequences of imperialism. Second is the embrace of a presentist (in the Benjaminian sense) temporality averring that the current moment of history can redeem failed revolutions past: "It is the rise of these people that is the rise of the world." Third is the "tiger's leap" into reassessment of Du Bois's own personal and textual history of thinking about the predicament of history and writing about it. "The problem of the twentieth century is the problem of the color line" is a recasting of that sentence's inaugural iteration—not, most famously, in *The Souls of Black Folk*, but as the concluding sentence of the "To the Nations of the World," the statement collectively constructed by participants in the Pan-African Congress of 1900.[44] Indeed, "The problem of the twentieth century is the problem of the color line" was a sentence fluid and repetitive—typological even—in space and time for Du Bois. He also invoked it in the essays "The Color Line Belts the World" (1906) and "The World Problem of the Color Line" (1914), among other usages.[45] Du Bois's self-citation is thus itself part of a dialectical typology in which "objective conditions" of historical change can be measured through a mode of historical and textual repetition. In *Black Folk Then and Now*, Du Bois's dramatic "color line" finale stands in, objectively and subjectively, for the closing lines of the *Communist Manifesto*: "The proletarians have nothing to lose but their chains. They have a world to win. Working men of all countries unite!"[46] In sympathetic answer to C.L.R. James's lament that black workers are rebelling everywhere but in the pages of capitalist history, Du Bois rewrites both Marx and himself as a leap of faith into the "open sky" of revolution both in the world and in the book.

————

Chapter 1 of this study, "From Comintern to the 'Colonial International': Making the Diasporic International, Making World Revolution," provides a historical framework for the people and events that the rise of the diasporic international and world revolution comprised. It bookends the formation of the Communist International in 1919 and the Manchester Pan-African Congress of 1945 as emblematic of two dominant currents in the world revolution conception: proletarian internationalism and national self-determination struggle. These currents organized the political aspirations of the diasporic international and drew them into oscillating relationship, especially to the Russian Revolution after 1917. By the end of World War I, Stalin's Socialism in One Country policy had tipped the balance of world revolution forces in the direction of anticolonial struggle and reshaped revolutionary communism to suit national liberation struggles during the Cold War and Bandung era during which decolonizing Asian and African countries allied themselves in common struggle, highlighted by their conference in Bandung, Indonesia, in 1955.

Chapter 2, "'Experiments of Marxism': W.E.B. Du Bois and the Specter of 1917," offers a close reading of Du Bois's engagement with the Russian Revolution and especially Leninist conceptions of self-determination. It argues that the major works of Du Bois's life written after his 1926 visit to the Soviet Union and deep study in Marxist thought oriented every phase of his political development thereafter. The chapter pays special attention to *Black Reconstruction* (1935) and Du Bois's unpublished "Russia and America: An Interpretation," arguing for it as a key text in his continually self-revised typological conception of world revolution and the place of African Americans within it.

Chapter 3, "India, the 'Indian Ideology,' and the World Revolution," examines Du Bois's relationship to the place of India in both his own conception of world revolution and the contradictory ideological lineaments cast out by India's decolonization. Here, Du Bois's emotional and intellectual affiliations with the Indian anticolonial leaders Lajpat Rai, Mohandas Gandhi, and Jawaharlal Nehru are used as a template for measuring the tensions between nationalism and proletarian internationalism embedded in India's freedom struggle. The chapter also explores affinities between Du Bois's view of India and that of Agnes Smedley, with whom he shared important intellectual and political influences.

Chapter 4, "World Revolution at the Crossroads: Japan, China, and the Long Shadow of Stalinism," argues that Japanese imperialism and China's gradual emergence as a Stalinized communist state was a pivot in Du Bois's thinking about the world revolution concept. Both events reflected the influence of the Soviet Union's increasingly Stalinized and bureaucrat conception of Socialism in One Country, which significantly damaged the chances for China's first revolution of the 1920s and later imprinted Mao's replication of features of Soviet Stalinism. The chapter constellates Smedley, Anna Louise Strong, and Du Bois as similarly influenced by these developments into hard advocates for Asian liberation struggles, especially during the Cold War era.

Chapter 5, "Making Peace: Gendering the World Revolution/Reckoning the Third World," describes Du Bois's concomitant turn to international peace activism and his negotiation of Cold War currents as final stages in his revised typology of world revolution. Pushed by his new life partner, Shirley Graham Du Bois, toward peace politics and membership in the Communist Party, Du Bois embedded himself in a network of black female radical activists who were simultaneously reassessing their own place in the world revolution. Stalin's death in 1953 and the Soviet invasion of Hungary in 1956 elicited a final stage of Du Boisian reflection, "revolutionary nostalgia," evident in late stagings of his thought. Legacies of the diasporic international are also the subject of Chapter 5.

Finally, "The Afterthought" considers the legacy of the diasporic international and world revolution for scholars seeking to de-Stalinize and decolonize their work and its relationship to social and political struggle in our time.

1

FROM COMINTERN TO THE
"COLONIAL INTERNATIONAL"

Making the Diasporic International,
Making World Revolution

Out of the murderous division of war, there came to all the earth a knowledge
of the oneness of our planet; no land could stand aloof, no ports but were swept
by participation in the ruthless struggle—China, Japan, and the islands of the
Pacific, no less than the trench-scarred fields of Europe. But if World War broke
forever for us Americans the fetish of our uniqueness and peaceful isolation, we
had our recompense; we also became joint heirs of the World Revolution.
       —Anna Louis Strong, *I Change Worlds*, 1935

As, then, a citizen of the world as well as of the United States of America, I claim
a right to think and tell the truth as I see it. I believe in Socialism as well as
Democracy. I believe in Communism wherever and whenever men are wise and
good enough to achieve it; but I do not believe all nations will achieve it in the
same way or at the same time.
       —W.E.B. Du Bois, *In Battle for Peace*, 1952

Today there is only one road to effective action—the organization of the masses.
And in that organization the educated Colonials must join. Colonial and Subject
Peoples of the World—Unite!
    —Kwame Nkrumah, "Declaration to the Colonial Workers, Farmers and
       Intellectuals," Manchester Pan-African Congress, 1945

W.E.B. Du Bois's biographer David Levering Lewis has argued that
his subject's epiphany on his first visit to the Soviet Union in
1926—"If what I have seen with my eyes and heard with my ears
is Bolshevism, then I am a Bolshevik"—was a climactic moment of dialectical tension in his political thought: "The teleology of global class revolution,"
Levering Lewis writes, "now began to vie powerfully with the concept of the
superordinate power of race in Du Bois's thinking."[1] I argue in this chapter
that Du Bois's conflict was endemic to and representative of the two dominant
political currents that formed not only his political biography up to 1926 but

also those in the larger constellation I am calling the diasporic international. These are, first, Communist Internationalism, including the Second International (1889–1919) and Third International (1919–1943), and second, the global anticolonial movement that formally began at the Pan-African Conference in London in 1900 but by 1926 had become a many-headed Hydra of Asian, Arab, African, and African American activists, ambitions, and programs for national self-determination. This chapter proposes that these political narratives were braided into an inchoate but monumental (and in some ways fatal) resolution at the Pan-African Congress of 1945 in Manchester, England. They constituted the double strands of what is best understood not as teleology but as a *typology* of world revolution: a variant mode of historical materialism interpreting global events of the past as templates for a revolutionary present. The chapter also argues that the diasporic international conjoined these currents to internal contradictions, conflicts, and problems that inhered in efforts to develop from them a theory and practice of world revolution. Along the way, the diasporic international drew together into an expanding orbit many of the world's brightest anticolonial, anti-imperialist, and communist stars. It manifested a creative dynamism of theoretical innovation and political practice that was a historical juggernaut for both reform and revolution, the Scylla and Charybdis of political debate in this period. These tensions produced a contradictory trajectory, yet one that in the main was dedicated to the demolition of what Marx in 1853 called the "inherent barbarism of bourgeois civilization,"[2] and what the diasporic international understood Marx rightly to mean as the capitalist-colonialist complex.[3] The degree to which this project was fulfilled, deferred, and derailed by political misstep—most prominently, Stalinism—is also the subject of this chapter. Thus, the first portion of the chapter describes the historical confluence of figures who constituted the diasporic international, and the second describes events that largely shaped their conception of world revolution.

Many scholars have identified W.E.B. Du Bois's essay "The African Roots of War" (1915) as his most incipient statement of what over time would become a radical synthetic interpretation of global history. The essay ascribes motivation for European countries' participation in World War I to the perennial "scramble for Africa" inaugurated at the Berlin Conference of 1884–1885. Its interpretation anticipates, as scholars have also noted, Lenin's "Imperialism: The Highest Stage of Capitalism" (1917), an essay that advanced for his contemporaries the most totalized blueprint yet for turning "imperial war into civil war"—that is, urging the world's working classes to rise up against their masters rather than become cannon fodder in a ruling class war.[4] Yet the two essays are also uncannily alike in constellating key events between the formation of the Second International in 1889 and the nascent anticolonial struggles arising in Asia and Africa during the same period. It is the "braiding" of these events that indexes watershed moments in the formation of the diasporic international and its conceptions of world revolution.

Both Du Bois and Lenin refer to the division of Africa by the European nations as the starting point of modern imperialism; both refer to the "monopolizing" trend of capital through extraction from the global south to the global north as a direct engine for and consequence of imperialism. Both, too, perceive the European working class as directly imbricated in this development: for Du Bois, modern democracies are reconstituted as national units "composed of united capital and labor" based on the exploitation of Asia and Africa.[5] For Lenin, colonialism has produced a new "stratum" of the European proletariat whose compliance with capital buttresses ruling-class power and profits. As he wrote in a preface to the essay in 1920: "This stratum of workers-turned-bourgeois, or the labour aristocracy, who are quite philistine in their mode of life, in the size of their earnings and in their entire outlook, is the principal prop of the Second International, and in our days, the principal *social* (not military) *prop of the bourgeoisie*. For they are the real *agents of the bourgeoisie in the working-class* movement, the labour lieutenants of the capitalist class, real vehicles of reformism and chauvinism. In the civil war between the proletariat and the bourgeoisie they inevitably, and in no small numbers, take the side of the bourgeoisie, the 'Versailles' against the 'Communards.'"[6]

Here, however, Du Bois and Lenin deviate in their analysis. Du Bois invests aspiration for overthrowing colonial capitalism in the insurgent leadership (largely intelligentsia) in the colonies of Asia and Africa: "In this great work who can help us? In the Orient, the awakened Japanese and the awakened leaders of New China; in India and Egypt, the young men trained in Europe and European ideals, who now form the stuff that Revolution is born of." This vanguard, Du Bois argues, might then spread revolution to "twenty-five million grandchildren of the European slave trade" scattered around the world.[7] For Lenin, the most advanced (meaning non-opportunist) section of the working class remains the tip of the revolution's spear: the proletariat of both colonized and colonizing countries must seize the initiative against "philistine" labor and capital to begin the dismantling of capitalism and colonialism. "Imperialism," he wrote, "is the eve of the social revolution of the proletariat."[8]

Yet despite their differences, two ideas bind the interpretations of Lenin and Du Bois into a theoretical totality. The first is their overarching political project, however unfulfilled: prospects for global emancipation. The second is the project's shared genesis in a single event that resonated across the diasporic international until at least 1945—namely, the 1904–1905 Russo-Japanese War and its political aftermath. It is *this* event, rather than his trip to Russia in 1926, that instantiated Du Bois's participation in wider world-revolutionary struggle. Dialectically, the Russo-Japanese War also became a pivotal moment of transition for the Communist International between Second and Third Internationalism and Third Internationalism's much sharper analytics of both colonial capitalism and the "color line."

John Steinberg has helped to develop a recent interpretation of the Russo-Japanese War as "World War 0," the inaugural prototype for later inter-imperialist wars.[9] Japan's defeat of Russia in a territorial skirmish over Manchuria indeed crafted two distinct political trajectories. First, as Pankaj Mishra has written, it brought to fever pitch and released simmering resentments across the Asian and Arab colonial worlds; the Egyptian nationalist leader Mustafa Kemal declared Japan the "Rising Sun" of anticolonial struggle in a book of that name; radical nationalists in Calcutta and Dhaka began sponsoring Bengali student trips to Tokyo, while Jawaharlal Nehru called the victory a "great-pick-me-up for Asia."[10] Thousands of Chinese, meanwhile—including a young writer named Lu Xun and the future Republican President Sun Yat-sen—incubated ideas for national self-determination in Japanese exile inspired by the war. For his part, Du Bois described Japan's victory as an apocalyptic breach of the "color line" trope he had installed as a descriptor of the obstacle facing not just African Americans but Pan-Africa in 1900: "The Russo-Japanese war has marched an epoch. The magic of the word 'white' is already broken, and the Color Line in civilization has been crossed in modern times as it was in the great past. The awakening of the yellow races is certain. That the awakening of the brown and black races will follow in time, no unprejudiced student of history can doubt."[11]

Du Bois here invokes a preliminary and transitory "typology" of colored nationalisms as engine of world-historic change. This natal 1906 conception based on anticolonial struggles would inform subsequent generations of radicals in the African Blood Brotherhood and Ethiopian Pacific League and act as an intellectual retainer on Du Bois's sympathies for Japan's nationalist mythologies up to and through the period of its imperial aggression in China, as I show in Chapter 4. At the same time, Japan's "forward-leaning" national profile made it a vanguard state for incipient black internationalists seeking a model for Pan-African emancipation. In both "The Color Line Belts the World" (1906), from which the above passage is taken, and "The World Problem of the Color Line" (1914), Du Bois invokes "the looming race disturbances all over Africa, the wide-spread unrest in India and the so-called 'Yellow Peril' of China and Japan" as challenges to ancient racial hierarchies portending a potential "great coming war of Races"[12]—rhetoric, Yuichiro Onishi notes, that united turn-of-the-century Pan-Asian and Pan-Arab nationalism and that swept up in its wake African American internationalists from Marcus Garvey to Cyril Briggs.[13]

The second idea linking Du Bois to Lenin, one which ultimately prevailed in Du Bois's thinking, was the Russo-Japanese War as a spur to twentieth-century Communist Internationalism. As has been well documented, Russia's defeat in the territorial war over Manchuria signified for both Bolsheviks and Mensheviks in Russia the weakening of tsarist rule and the imminent collapse of feudal autocracy. Both were trip wires for the first incomplete Russian Revolution in 1905–1907. Lenin himself took two urgent lessons from Russia's defeat by Japan and the Bolshevik response of 1905. The first was that the Bolsheviks were the true embodiment of the legacy of German social democracy, which, as his mentor Karl Kautsky had convinced him, was to bring a workers' revolution forward. The Bolsheviks, Lenin argued, were the true leaders of the *narod*, or people, and symbolized what Lars Lih calls Lenin's "heroic scenario" of workers' self-activity leading the class to victory.[14] The second is that Japan was destined to join the Western imperialists as a competitor for global domain, a thread to which I return, especially in Chapter 4.

Du Bois's appreciation of *this* interpretation of 1904–1905 was gradual. One might even say it was repressed by the flush of anticolonialism's first victory in Asia since the Haitian Revolution and by his self-acknowledged unfamiliarity with details of Russian history. Yet its *centrality* to the long arc of his thought can be appreciated by consideration of the influence on Du Bois of William Walling. Walling, Du Bois's close intimate and a Second International socialist, traveled through Russia in 1905–1907 with his wife, Anna Strunsky. He was in Russia during the whole of the first Russian Revolution. There he met many notable figures, including Lenin, whom he called "perhaps the most popular leader in Russia."[15] As Lih notes, Walling strongly advocated for "peasant socialism" and sided with the Bolsheviks against the Mensheviks. Walling believed that it was the *narod*—the workers and the peasantry—who carried Russia's "message" of world revolution. Walling set all of this down in *Russia's Message: The True World Import of the Revolution* (1908), written just two years before he helped to found and join the Board of Directors of the National Association for the Advancement of Colored People (NAACP) along with Du Bois. In a headnote to *Russia's Message* (a title that echoes Du Bois's "message" for the black world in *Souls of Black Folk*), Walling dedicated the book to men and women battling contending forces "trying to introduce into America the despotism and class rule of Eastern Europe" and who "in the traditional, revolutionary American spirit" were leading the country "to its great democratic and social world-destiny."[16] Walling's interpretation of events in Russia helped persuade Du Bois to join the Socialist Party of the United States in 1911 and shaped the political conclusions in his 1909 biography of John Brown, whose martyrdom Du Bois saw as a harbinger of uprisings across the colored world.[17] Longer term, Du Bois would more directly align his interpretation of events in Russia of 1905 with Walling's. In the essay "Worlds of Color" (1925), he would consider the Russian Revolution part of a new historical configuration that makes "the Color Problem and the Labor Problem to so great an extent two sides of the same human tangle."[18] In his unpublished manuscript "Russia and America: An Interpretation" (1950), Du Bois writes that it was the Russo-Japanese War and Russia's subsequent first revolution that inspired him to consider for the first time the historical parallels between Russia's peasantry under the tsar and African American slaves, peasants, and sharecroppers in the American South—the subject of his flurry of economic studies at Atlanta University between 1903 and 1910. In the aftermath of Russia's *successful* revolution of 1917, Du Bois, like C.L.R. James, moved quickly to the argument for African American slaves and former slaves as "black Bolsheviks," agents in their own attempts at American Reconstruction, if not revolution. In short, Du Bois, like Walling and Lenin, came to see the events of 1905–1907 as a historical turning point in which workers of the world—not Mensheviks, reformists, or mere race agitators—could not just conceive but make a revolution.[19]

The dynamic tensions generated in his thinking around 1905 thus prepared Du Bois for the baptism by fire that produced the diasporic international. World War I would serve as the cauldron and the inferno for a wave of creative destruction in internationalist thought about the prospects for world revolution. Indeed, this period of Du Bois's life—his disavowal of Socialist Party membership in 1912 and a series of essays over ten years on the unlikelihood of *American* socialism's appeal to the Negro[20]—is best understood as a gradual break from the limits of Second International socialist reformism in which Du Bois sided with the "leftist" current that became the Third International. The war itself famously divided the socialist globe, with Kautsky and other former leaders of the German Second International refusing to condemn the war as fundamentally capitalist in nature on one side, and Lenin, Luxemburg, Trotsky, Stalin, and others declaring the war imperialist and forming the Communist International on the other. To this break, Lenin's "Imperialism: The Highest Stage of Capitalism" was a central theoretical testament, just as Du Bois's "African Roots of War" signaled his sharp turn toward a programmatic anti-imperialism. Fittingly, the physical "road" that members of the diasporic international traveled was one of mutual displacement from the security of national borders and nationalist ideologies that were under siege from the blitzkrieg of inter-imperialist war. World War I jostled domestic and global positionings by making race contact, colonial machinations, working-class repression, and brute imperialist violence part of a new lingua franca simultaneously if differentially experienced by aspirant educated radicals of the global North and global South. World War I thus produced something like a *class* of political refugees from the old capitalist-colonial order who over the next forty years found themselves in new mutual relations via compulsory dedication to revolutionary thought and practice. Du Bois was a citizen-subject of that class. Inspired particularly by the Russian Revolution of 1917 and the formation of the Communist International in 1919, revolution replaced reform in the shared consciousness of diasporic international subjects; self-determination replaced national belonging; a tacit commitment to an idea of permanent revolution—the global liberation of humanity from both capitalism and colonialism—became the leitmotif of their shared political work and political lives. They became, to use Anna Louise Strong's poetic trope, "joint heirs of the World Revolution."[21]

To begin with Anna Louise Strong: a photograph of Du Bois taken in Mao Tse-tung's Wuhan villa garden in 1959, during Du Bois's penultimate visit to China, shows him with Strong, Tang Ming-chao, Ting His-lin, Chu Poshem, and Mao. Strong had first come to China in 1925 as a young journalist and newly minted world revolutionary. In 1921, she had left the United States for the Soviet Union, where, inspired by Lincoln Steffens's personal reports on the Russian Revolution, she threw herself into the task of supporting it by sending favorable reports to U.S. publishers. She lived in a state of impermanent exile from 1925 to 1959, in and out of Mexico, Germany, China, and Russia, "roving to revolutions," as she described it in her autobiography *I Change Worlds* (1935).[22] As with Du Bois, it was World War I, the violent incursion onto an erstwhile progressive consciousness neither fully socialist nor comprehensibly internationalist, that shot her into solidarity with anticolonial and anticapitalist revolutions worldwide. She recalls "signals from Moscow" arriving in Seattle in 1918, including translations of Lenin's 1918 address to the Congress of Soviets published by workers' organizations in Seattle joined to the Industrial Workers of the World (IWW), Strong's first formal political association. On Wednesdays, she would attend Seattle Central Labor Council meetings until midnight, listening to "emissaries of suppressed and rebelling peoples: Indians, Irish, Chinese, Koreans," and absorbing stories of mutinies by French troops in Odessa and rising Soviets in Russia.[23] Strong quickly deduced that "the revolution has begun in Moscow, but was not in Moscow alone. It was world revolution which took us in. . . . Workers all over the world were rising to rule; it would be our turn soon."[24] Strong's voluntary exile to the Soviet Union in 1921 culminated a process of national disidentification begun earlier with President Woodrow Wilson's declaration of war and the "Everett massacre" of IWW workers in Seattle in 1919.

That chapter of her life, and book, titled "I Lose 'My America'" was also the beginning of her long, overlapping life with W.E.B. Du Bois, which culminated at Mao's villa in Wuhan. In 1934, she would assist in the production of a special issue of *The Crisis* on segregation, a year David Levering Lewis asserts Du Bois could hear "the locomotive of world changes approaching."[25] In 1948, Du Bois and Strong would speak together at Carnegie Hall at an event organized by the National Conference on American Policy in China.[26] During the Cold War and Du Bois's internal exile, they would become close friends and mutual supporters. By the time Du Bois arrived in China in 1958, where Strong was living, both had perceptibly shifted their aspirations for world revolution to China's lead over and against oscillating doubts about what Strong called the "Stalin Era." The photograph taken in 1959 thus not only symbolizes their conjoined fate as members of a diasporic international but is totemic of the retrospective hermeneutic—"only through the present can we see the past"—that is explanatory of Du Bois's lifelong association with global radicalism.

The same is true of Du Bois's relationship to Agnes Smedley and Lajpat Rai. Smedley's relationship to Du Bois is thought so incidental that she does not merit a mention in Levering Lewis's two-volume biography. But the two corresponded and shared a durable set of collaborators and ideas that stretched across the diasporic international. According to her account, Smedley first met Du Bois in 1920 when he lectured at the Civic Association, or Civic Club, a group Du Bois had helped form in 1916 with the Russia sympathizers James Weldon Johnson and John Reed and to which Smedley belonged. In 1925, Smedley was living in exile in Berlin when she wrote to Du Bois. Smedley was there with the Marxist nationalist Virendranath Chattopadhyaya, her lover and partner whom she had met in the San Francisco Bay Area during World War I. Chattopadhyaya, too, was in exile, seeking to raise funds and build support for decolonization at home. Through her work with the Bay Area Ghadr Party, an expatriate Indian nationalist movement, Smedley became a committed anticolonialist and supporter of the Russian Revolution. Her letter to Du Bois in June 1925 sought materials about U.S. lynching for use in a course Smedley was teaching on "problems in America" in Berlin. Du Bois responded by sending Smedley copies of *The Crisis* of 1924 and 1925, the NAACP pamphlet *Thirty Years of Lynching in the United States*, and Du Bois's book *The Gift of Black Folk*.[27] In 1928, Du Bois's novel *Dark Princess* would render in fictional form his second-hand knowledge of Smedley and Chattopadhyaya's work on the "Berlin Committee," a group of Asian and Arab radicals inspired by both the Communist International and anticolonial struggle to try to foment world revolution.[28] Indeed, the novel, discussed in more detail later, is best understood as Du Bois's ode to the diasporic international and a sign of his conjoined status to it.

Dark Princess is also a homage to Du Bois's affiliation to the Indian nationalist Lajpat Rai, who served as a mentor to both he and Smedley in their early educations in Indian anticolonialism.[29] Like Smedley, Du Bois met Rai during his period of political exile from India to the United States between 1914 and 1919 as he attempted to build support for anticolonial struggles at home and escape persecution by colonial authorities. He would appear as the character Sardar Ranjit Singh in the novel *Daughter of Earth* (1929), Smedley's own fictional ode to the diasporic international.[30] Rai helped Du Bois to form the Civic Club and lectured with him in 1917 at a meeting sponsored by the Intercollegiate Socialist Society. Rai also read in full the manuscript for *Dark Princess*. When Rai was murdered by police in India for his part in a protest after his return, Du Bois wrote in the April 13, 1929, edition of Rai's newspaper *The People*, "When a man of this sort can be called a Revolutionist and beaten to death by a great civilized government then indeed revolution becomes a duty of all right-thinking men."[31] Yet because of Rai's premature death and their shared network of influences, it was Smedley whose participation in the diasporic international came to mirror Du Bois's, writing on behalf of revolutions in China, India, and Russia while living in and out of real and political exile in the United States during the Cold War. In 1949, Smedley would join Du Bois in 1949 as a featured speaker at the Scientific and Cultural Conference for World Peace held by the Communist Party of the USA (CPUSA) at the Waldorf Astoria Hotel in New York City, a culminating point of intersection in their long dedication to diasporic internationalism. Smedley's career radicalism, including her strange turn in Comintern espionage, was beleaguered, as was Du Bois's, by an overdetermined and ambivalent relationship to Stalinism; her better-informed doubts were shaped by the early stages of the Russian Revolution, his were shaped by the later stages. Their shared fate in the United States was to be cast as Cold War apparatchiks for the Soviets, despite wildly unorthodox, even maverick, relationships to a regime for which their support was sometimes ambivalent.

Smedley and Rai also index Du Bois's considered relationship to more prominent leaders of Indian anticolonial struggles—namely, Jawaharlal Nehru and Mohandas Gandhi. Du Bois's excessive historiographical enthusiasm for Indian decolonization—he referred to August 15, 1947, as the "greatest historical date of the nineteenth and twentieth centuries"[32]—reflect his hagiographic relationship to its two most eminent leaders. "There is today in the world but one living maker of miracle," Du Bois wrote in 1932, "and that is Mahatma Gandhi."[33] Du Bois's strategy for affiliation to these two anticolonial giants was to include them in his collective biography of revolutionary leaders to which he hoped his own would correspond. In his retrospective essay "Gandhi and the American Negroes" (1957), Du Bois noted that Gandhi has been born "nineteenth months after my birth"; that he had published his first book on the African slave trade in 1896, "while Gandhi was in South Africa"; and that the formation of the NAACP reflected Du Bois's first contact with Gandhi's work through his co-worker John Haynes Holmes. "Indeed," Du Bois wrote, "the 'Coloured People' referred to in our name was not originally confined to America."[34] In 1921, Du Bois and Jessie Fauset co-edited a special issue of the *Brownies Book* featuring two articles on Gandhi: "Saint Gandhi," by Hubert Harrison, and the editorial "The Brown Man Leads the Way."[35] In 1929, stunned by the economic impact of Depression-era conditions on black America, Du Bois asked Gandhi for a message for American Negroes, which he published in *The Crisis*. In turn, Du Bois's shift during the Depression to black "cooperative economics" as a bulwark against capitalist ravages was, as I later show, modeled in part on Gandhi's *swadeshi* strategy of peasant cooperatives and localized production. The Gandhian exemplar was thus for Du Bois part of an evolving "race concept" in which Indian decolonization occupied a centripetal place in building anticapitalist forms of world revolution: "If now the coloured people—Negroes, Indians, Chinese and Japanese, are going successfully to oppose these assumptions of white Europe, they have got to be sure of their own attitude toward their laboring masses. Otherwise they will substitute for the exploitation of coloured by white races, an exploitation of coloured races by coloured races."[36] The key to India's successful anticolonial struggle was to end "industrial exploitation" for all men. By 1936, India had thus become a singular touchstone as an anticapitalist alternative for Du Bois, an idea pursued to full conclusion in Chapter 3.

Yet despite his efforts at concordance to the Mahatma, Du Bois's political biography maps far more intimately to the life of Jawaharlal Nehru, a perspective both of them haltingly tried to develop. In his review of Nehru's *Autobiography* (1941), Du Bois wrote, "In comparison with the Negro problem in America one sees in Nehru's career astonishing resemblances: the violence, the stress upon religious submission, the inner difficulties within the Indian race and the way in which these difficulties have been played upon to the advantage of the English."[37] Nehru meanwhile used Du Bois's writings on race as a leveraging point for his open avowals of support for black liberation in the United States,[38] and the two endeavored to sustain a correspondence—and to meet in person—through the years immediately after India's decolonization. Yet their real proximity within the diasporic international was ideological. Both moved significantly to the left through World War I; the anticolonial upturn in India and the Soviet Revolution of 1917 hardened their commitment to what became known, and popularly identified with Nehru, as "Third World" liberation. For both Du Bois and Nehru, this politics took the form of support for national self-determination struggles that at times was independent of Washington and Moscow, coupled to an often mediated, compromised, and ultimately degenerate conception of socialism differentially distorted by Stalinism itself. For Nehru, this incurred a commitment to bureaucratic capitalism in India after decolonization; for Du Bois, it meant a defense of the same. Indeed, their mutual misrepresentations and misrecognitions of socialism follow a nearly exact path of conversion based on personal visits to the Soviet Union (by Du Bois in 1926 and by Nehru in 1927) and written interpretations of the "meaning" of Russia's revolution for world-revolutionary practice. To demonstrate this, my chapter on India pays special attention to Nehru's seldom studied first-person account, *Soviet Russia: Some Random Sketches and Impressions* (1929). Examined in relation to Du Bois's writings based on visits to the Soviet Union in 1926, 1936, and 1949, it helps to disclose precisely how Stalinism became both a delusional hope and the greatest misstep of the diasporic international.

Nehru also connects to the figure who is arguably both the avatar of the diasporic international and Du Bois's doppelgänger and closest collaborator within it. George Padmore, born Malcolm Nurse in 1902 in Trinidad, was like Nehru an active member of the League against Imperialism, the Communist International body formed in 1927 in Brussels. He also served alternatively as Du Bois's mentor, foil, counselor, and formal link to both currents of world revolution theory and practice under study here, international communism and Pan-Africanism. Through each of those turns, he served as a political amanuensis to Du Bois. Their relationship even in outline here merits extended consideration.

Like Du Bois, Padmore passed into the world-revolutionary left through the American crucible. He joined the CPUSA in 1927—the year after Du Bois's "I am a Bolshevik" proclamation—while attending law school at New York University. For political reasons, Nurse changed his name to Padmore and began writing for the *Daily Worker* in 1928; in 1929, he became editor of the party newspaper in Harlem, the *Negro Champion*. Significantly, Padmore entered the Communist Party on the cusp of its "Third Period" initiated at the Communist International's Sixth Congress in 1928. Third Period policy was the first major theoretical reorientation of the Comintern after Lenin's death in 1924 and Stalin's consolidation of power as general secretary of the Communist Party. Politically, the Third Period reversed the "United Front" policy of the 1922 Comintern, which proposed that communists should build national parties and working-class movements internationally through alliance with trade unions and "reformers" without liquidating revolutionary politics. After 1928, the Comintern deemed reformers, including social demo-crats, "social fascists." Communists in trade unions were no longer to work with reformers; hard sectarianism and "class and against" struggle ruled the day. The Third Period also consecrated a shift in Comintern orientation in which the primary objective of building communist parties worldwide was sacrificed for the priority of shoring up the new Soviet state bureaucracy—the term given this process was "Bolshevization"—within the Soviet Union. As Duncan Hallas succinctly puts it, "The bureaucracy became a self-conscious ruling class. Bureaucratic state capitalism was firmly established—its ideology being, of course, 'Socialism in One Country.'"[39]

Padmore would serve first as lieutenant and then as rebel to this theory and practice of world revolution; in turn, both he and the world revolution concept would hang from its historical cross. Padmore's entry into the sphere of inter-national communist activity came via his participation in the Second Con-gress of the League against Imperialism in Frankfurt, Germany, in 1929 and, one year earlier, attendance at the Fourth Congress of the Profintern, or Red International of Labour Unions (RILU). During the Third Period, the RILU existed to indicate the autonomy of communist trade unions from "reformist" unions. Padmore applied this ultra-leftist strategy to his work, planning the First International Conference of Negro Workers for the Comintern in Ham-burg on July 7–9, 1930.[40] In 1931, RILU passed a "Special Resolution on Negro Work among Negroes in the U.S. and the Colonies." The resolution applied to labor organizing the Third Period's Black Belt thesis, which argued for the uniqueness of African Americans as an oppressed national minority within U.S. borders. In the same year, Padmore published *The Life and Struggles of Negro Toilers*. There, he grouped Du Bois with Oscar DePriest as "Ameri-can Negro petty-bourgeois reformists" distracting the Negro from the task of revolution.[41] Not long thereafter, Padmore generated a special pamphlet titled "Negro Workers and the Imperialist War—Intervention in the Soviet Union." In it, Padmore attacked Du Bois for his "reflexive anticommunism," a reaction to Du Bois's continuing string of attacks on the American communist and socialist movement for failing to recruit black workers and failing to focus on reversing chauvinism and racism among white workers.[42]

Padmore's attack on Du Bois reflected related weaknesses and contradic-tions in the global revolutionary left's political perspectives that would shape not only their personal relationship but also the contours of anticapitalist and anticolonial struggles to come. On the one hand, Padmore's "ultra-leftist" criticism of Du Bois reflected the isolating effects of Third Period Stalinism, which weakened communism's ability to intervene in the very same workers' struggles it sought to advance. Indeed, Du Bois himself rejected the Third Period Black Belt thesis as both isolating African Americans in the United

States and alienating potential allies. At the same time, Padmore remained dedicated to the Third Period's continued commitment to "self-determination" for oppressed nations and colonies, a position more generally shared by Du Bois. Thus, in 1934 the two collaborated across their political divide to try to raise $5 million to bail out Liberia's rulers, a move Padmore justified to Du Bois by saying he wanted to save "the black baby from the white wolves."[43] In the same year, Padmore left the Comintern. Reasons for Padmore's leaving are disputed. Padmore claimed he quit the Comintern for its liquidation of the Negro Trade Union Committee and halting of the publication of the *Negro Worker*, as well as for its failure to pay attention to Africa, especially in Liberia.[44] Padmore's biographer says he was expelled from the Comintern by the International Control Commission for working openly with a national bourgeoisie formation in Liberia.[45] After his departure, Padmore wrote to Du Bois seeking support to organize a Negro World Unity Congress, a first gesture of collaboration in what would become a close twenty-year working relationship dedicated mainly to Pan-African politics.

How are we to understand both the volte-face in Padmore and Du Bois's relationship and their subsequent partnership within the diasporic international? Fundamentally, we should view it as synecdochical of tensions between what Levering Lewis called the "teleology of class revolution" and the superordinate power of race—or, in this case, its surrogate, nation. As Barbara Foley has noted, the central debate within the twentieth-century global left about nationalism hinged on its class character. For Lenin, as Foley notes, "Just as the proletariat in the 'advanced' countries must become class-conscious to abolish itself as a class, Lenin theorized, oppressed peoples in the colonized part of the globe must become nation-conscious to abolish nationalism."[46] It was this doctrine in part that first drew Du Bois, Nehru, Padmore, and many other African Americans to support the Soviet position on colonial self-determination. Conversely, Foley notes, because the Comintern posited nationalist self-consciousness as a necessary step in building proletarian internationalism, the door remained open for what she calls "metonymic nationalism," a "project of claiming that one group had as much right to stand for, and belong in, the nation as any other."[47] In Padmore's case, metonymic nationalism prevailed in two significant ways: first, in a direct way by accepting national bourgeoisies as representative of the "national" interest; and second, and more significant for this study, indirectly by positing that it was the working classes of oppressed colonial nations whose task it was to foment world revolution. They were to be the vanguard "part" of the international proletarian "whole." Indeed, after his break from the International Trade Union Committee of Negro Workers, as James R. Hooker notes, Padmore never again joined a non-Negro organization and prioritized his work so that "a socialist Africa might co-operate with a federated, socialist Britain and Europe" in precisely that order.[48]

This critical moment of political impasse helps to illuminate several related aspects of diasporic international thought and its subsequent place in twentieth-century history. First, it indicates the rapid degeneration of Soviet credibility on the global left after Stalin's ascent to power in 1924. Padmore's departure from the Communist International is symptomatic of how by 1934 the international's own "Bolshevization" strategies were nurturing sectarian conflicts and fault lines that were more serviceable to protecting the Soviet state bureaucracy than to generating international communist movements. The Soviet Union's decision to provide material supplies to Italy even throughout its invasion of Ethiopia in 1935—a move that also hastened Padmore's retreat from international communism—is yet another example. Second, Padmore's split in 1934 foretold rising problems and resentments across the colonial world with ever erratic leadership from the Communist International as it sought to relate to national liberation struggles. The Communist Party's reversal of course again in 1935 to a "Popular Front" strategy would hasten another level of crisis around this, as we shall see. Third, Padmore's own contradictory and competing allegiances to both national colonial bourgeoisies and oppressed "workers of the world" would envelop the anticolonial movement as it cajoled, à la Nkrumah's plea for "educated Colonials" to join with the masses.[49] This problem would only widen as both the Communist International and emergent anticolonial movements struggled to sustain faltering working-class movements in the face of counterrevolutions, uneven economic development, tactical errors, erratic support for communist parties in colonizing states, fascism, and world wars. Finally, the conflictual circumstances that produced Padmore's "shift" from "communism" to "Pan-Africanism" (most famously articulated in his book *Pan-Africanism or Communism?*) became metonymic of the struggle with Stalinism that characterized diasporic international politics. Even as he publicly excoriated Stalin's management of the Communist International, for example, Padmore would continue to extol the Soviet Revolution of 1917 and its dedication to colonial self-determination, as he did, for example, in his book *How Russia Transformed Her Colonies: A Challenge to the Imperialist Powers*, published in 1946, more than a decade after his "break" with Stalinism. More dramatically ironic still, at the very moment of Padmore's split and newfound alliance with Du Bois, Du Bois himself was in the midst of a major reconsideration of his own relationship to Marxism and communism that would lead him, contrapuntally, toward Communist Party membership and public support for Stalinism, even as his political alliance and working relationship with Padmore deepened. How this set of conflicts, crossroads, and contradictions mapped to world events and

the theory and practice of the diasporic international across the long twentieth century is the remaining subject of this chapter.

———————

If the fall of Petrograd in 1917 was, as Tariq Ali asserts, a "universal event,"
then world revolution was its universal subject. For members of the diasporic
international, history itself provided the typology of revolution whose meaning was discernible by those who went looking. A conception of "world-historical events" simultaneously interacting across the globe—what Du Bois in
1925 called the "shadow" effect of economic imperialism and colonialism—
produced a dialectical timeline in which the capitalist-colonialist complex
threw up both newly exploitative social relationships and institutions and
their "grave-digging" others. These events both constituted and were constituted by participants in the diasporic international who perceived the new
typology of world revolution as their own coming to historical consciousness.
As Du Bois aptly said of the Russian Revolution, "It explained me."[50]
    The first of these simultaneities was the formation of the Indian National
Congress in 1885 and the development of the Second Socialist International
in 1889 in Paris. Both events came on the heels of the Berlin Conference of
1884, which produced the partition of Africa (and formal anticolonial struggle), on one hand, and the rise of new working classes and class struggles
advanced by worldwide strikes in the 1870s in the United States, Europe,
and India, on the other.[51] The Indian National Congress was a bid by Indian
(and British) elites to ameliorate the effects of colonialism and capitalist economic immiseration, if only for the elect. The Second International committed itself to an anticolonial politics despite the absence of global South
states. Yet the upturn of anticolonial and labor militancy in their wake was
pronounced. The fifteen years between 1885 and the first Pan-African Congress were marked by the Matabele uprising in Rhodesia, the defeat of Italy
by the Abyssinian army near Adowa, the Boxer Rebellion in China, and the
formation in 1898 of the U.S. Anti-Imperialist League in response to the
U.S. annexation of the Philippines, Cuba, and Hawaii. This prototype of the
League against Imperialism would draw in Nehru and Padmore. Du Bois
would later conjoin to these events in his historiography of world revolution
the Madhist revolt in Sudan. The 1890s also saw widening strikes globally
for the eight-hour workday; bitter worker uprisings in Homestead, Pennsylvania; and popular labor explosions that, as Nell Irvin Painter has written,
"seemed to be harbingers of revolution."[52] The Pan-African Conference, held
in 1900 in London, and its "Message to the World" were a first enuncia-
tion of the "two-sided" nature of this nascent world-revolutionary struggle.
The conference's public petition to Queen Victoria for interrogation of labor

conditions in South Africa and Rhodesia, the "indenture" of black workers by white colonists, and compulsory labor in public works brought to bear on the capitalist-colonialist complex pressures that were building through widespread organizing by workers of the world.

As Du Bois and Lenin both noted, the Japanese victory over Russia in 1905 and the first failed Russian Revolution jump-started, temporarily, the optimism and confidence of a nascent global left. Yet the geographically narrow, ideologically diffuse nature of early anticolonial Second Internationalism was also an inheritance. Between 1905 and the explosion of 1917—despite sudden revolutions in Mexico and China—something like a reformist interregnum occurred in both the Pan-African Movement and the Second International. The causes were similar. Both movements were dominated by privileged bourgeois intelligentsias removed from mass struggles; both were handicapped by aggressive attacks on white and black labor by well-armed capitalist states from Johannesburg to East St. Louis, a vector Du Bois himself drew in his magisterial *Darkwater*. The Bolshevik defeat of 1905 also emboldened tsarists and imperialist states globally, contributing to the making of World War I, while in the United States, Second International socialism's tepid commitment to antiracism and black recruiting undermined its credibility to advance an anti-imperialist perspective more complementary to than distinct from that announced at the Pan-African Conference of 1900. International organizing during the reformist interregnum also reflected ideological weakness and organizational disunity. The Pan-African Conference failed to realize plans to hold meetings in the United States in 1902 and Haiti in 1904. The Universal Races Congress of 1911 in London was something of a surrogate for these Congresses, but featured primarily academic and scientific discussions of race unmoored from a clear anticapitalist or anticolonial agenda (Du Bois and fellow NAACP member and socialist Mary White Ovington's approving participation in the Races Congress is also symptomatic of the reformist drift of the period). Meanwhile, the competing leadership roles of Eduard Bernstein and Karl Kautsky in the Second International, their downplaying of colonialism and imperialism as new capitalist forms, and their insistence on the withering away of capitalism without the necessity of working-class takeover of state power all worked to stay the hand of the Second International in working-class struggles, despite internal dissent from Lenin, Trotsky and Luxemburg and splits within the Second International itself from 1903 to 1915.[53] The same reformist perspectives also triggered division in the Second International during World War I in which some European socialist parties—most famously the German Social Democratic Party—backed their own imperialist state. Indeed, no two documents in the Du Bois oeuvre better capture the ambivalence and contradiction of *his* place in the reformist interregnum than his two best-known essays from it: the aforementioned "The African Roots of War," a prophecy of both his and the diasporic international's future, and "Close Ranks," his reactive editorial in *The Crisis* in 1918 calling for African American support for U.S. (and African American) participation in the war. "Close Ranks," a vintage artifact of Second International thought, not surprisingly would also become an important exemplar of Du Bois's revisionist typology: as part of his sharpening anti-imperialist opposition to World War II in 1941, he would sign an "open letter" written by the socialist Norman Thomas condemning President Franklin D. Roosevelt's decision to inter Japanese Americans. "We close ranks again," he would write, "but only, now as then, to fight for democracy not only for white folk but for yellow, brown, and black."[54]

Yet the true tipping point between the reformist interregnum and what I am calling the age of the diasporic international was without question the year 1919. The simultaneous death that year of the first great inter-imperialist war and the birth of the first global body to enunciate world revolution as its goal—the Comintern—dialectically telescoped into a single yearlong conflagration the potential and promise of overthrowing the capitalist-colonialist complex. On March 4, 1919, thirty-five delegates in the Kremlin voted to create the Third, or Communist, International. Where the Second International had been a loose federation of national parties, as Hallas notes, the Third International "was to be a centralized world party with national sections."[55] The Third International immediately dedicated itself to two tasks that were consensus failures of the Second International: building communist leadership within international labor struggles and foregrounding the historic role of peasants and proletarians in colonial states in advancing international communism. The formation of the Comintern had an immediate impact on both realms. In the United States, two new communist parties appeared within the year: Charles Ruthenberg's Communist Party and John Reed's Communist Labor Party. In China, a student movement known as "May Fourth," inspired by the Bolsheviks' promise to repudiate tsarist claims on China's territory, erupted in Beijing and soon allied itself with working-class struggles in the city; two years later, twelve participants in May Fourth would be among the founders of the first Chinese Communist Party in Shanghai.[56] In India in March 1919, the notorious antisubversive Rowlatt Act placing wartime restrictions on civil rights and detention without trial was rushed through the Imperial Legislature.[57] Rowlatt was in part a jittery imperial response to huge industrial strike waves begun in India in 1918, but as Sumit Sarkar notes, "Most far-reaching of all ultimately was the impact of the Bolshevik Revolution of November 1917. . . . In a panic reminiscent of that caused by the French Revolution, official reports from 1919–1920 onwards discovered Bolshevik ideas and Soviet agents everywhere" with even people such as the determinedly non-Marxist Gandhi "not above suspicion."[58] By the end of 1919, Indian revolutionary nationalists such as Mahendra Pratap, Manabendra Nath Roy, and Virendranath Chattopadhyaya had turned to Moscow as the epicenter of new colonial self-determination struggles; in 1920, Roy, Abani Mukhetji, and Santi Devi would draft an "Indian Communist Manifesto" en route from Mexico to Moscow for their first Comintern meeting. Meanwhile in the United States, labor competition in the postwar economy produced both massive anti-black backlash (seventy-six lynchings in the notorious Red Summer of 1919, memorialized by Claude McKay's extraordinary sonnet "If We Must Die") and unprecedented strike waves. During the year, approximately one in seven workers went on strike, one in four in New York City.[59]

The Comintern and new communist parties worldwide also indicated a dialectical tipping point between reformist interregnum and world revolution regarding the nature of geopolitical institutions and organizations. In addition to boosting new communist movements and parties in India, China, the United States, Japan, and Korea, 1919 advanced new working-class radical nationalist organizations such as the U.S. African Blood Brotherhood and radical black socialist leaders such as Hubert Harrison, whose call for "A Colored International" was also a response to the Comintern's model of a federated world revolution. Even Marcus Garvey's nationalist Universal Negro Improvement Association was not averse to the world revolution virus, with Garvey himself predicting in 1921 that Lenin and Trotsky would join Indian, Japanese, and Chinese nationalists in fighting for "Africa for the Africans."[60] Thus, as Barbara Foley notes, "The proposed League of Nations offered an imperialist version of self-determination that parodied the cosmopolitan proletarian internationalism that, for many, held out the only possibility for a nonexploitative world order."[61] Likewise, the three-day Pan-African Congress hastily arranged and attended by Du Bois in February 1919, calling for direct League of Nations supervision of the former German colonies, was an effort by the excluded colonial states to gain some semblance of "anticolonial" commitment after the Treaty of Versailles. A second resolution calling for the "international protection of the natives of Africa" was drafted but never advanced.[62] Hindered still by reformist conceptions of colonial paternalism most clearly articulated by the French diplomat Blaise Diagne, the Pan African Congress of 1919 was largely a failure but, as Levering Lewis notes, "a powerful idea to bind up the wounds of the world had been launched in Paris."[63]

Yet by the end of the bloody Red Summer of 1919, after his return from Paris and confrontation with U.S. lynchings and strikes of that year, Du Bois would prophetically commit himself to more than binding wounds. In the September *Crisis* he would publish the essay "Let Us Reason Together," an apocalyptic restatement of his assessment of the world conflagration. Noting the rampant labor strife and concurrent racist backlash worldwide, Du Bois wrote, "In this fight for Justice in Labor the Negro looms large. In Africa and the South Seas, in all the Americas and dimly in Asia, he is a mighty worker and, potentially, perhaps, the mightiest."[64] He continued, "There lies the most stupendous labor problem of the twentieth century—transcending the problem of labor and capital, of the Equality of Women—for it is the problem of the Equality of Humanity in the world as against white domination of black and brown and yellow serfs."[65] With the "cry of oppressed India" ringing in his ears, Du Bois turned full force for the first time since 1917 to revolutionary interpretation of history's new direction: "The one new Idea of the World War—the one which may well stand in future years as the one thing that made the slaughter worthwhile—is an Idea which we are like to fail to know because it is today hidden under the maledictions hurled at Bolshevism. It is not the murder, the anarchy, the hate which for years under Czar and Revolution have drenched this weary land, but it is the vision of great dreams that only those who work shall vote and rule."[66]

Du Bois's new typology of world revolution coupled to a newfound urgency toward global solidarity—"Brothers, we are on the Great Deep. We have cast off on the vast voyage which will lead to Freedom or Death"—may stand as epigraph and epitaph for his fellow travelers in the diasporic international, who in different iterations, national contexts, and political struggles also "cast on the vast voyage" based on events of 1919.[67]

Those events, in turn, shaped Du Bois's political development and direction. After organizing the Ahmedabad hunger strike of 1918, his first use of that weapon, Gandhi responded to the Rowlatt Act uprising by organizing the first all-India protest, or *hartal*, on March 30, 1919. The event formally launched Gandhi's Indian Satyagraha, pulling together three types of political networks: the Home Rule League, Pan-Islamist groups, and a Satyagraha Sabha.[68] The *hartals* were sporadic but largely successful; they advanced unity among Hindus, Muslims, and Sikhs and pushed Gandhi to such prominence in the national movement that he was externed by the British, provoking massive rioting and burning of government buildings that culminated in the Amritsar massacre, a moment David Arnold has called the turning point in the Indian national movement.[69] Both the anticolonial struggle and Gandhi's place in it were changed utterly; for both, he would earn his first public recognition by Du Bois in *Brownies Book*.

Sumit Sarkar likewise notes that it was the nationalization of struggle in 1919 that prompted Jawaharlal Nehru's implantation to the anticolonial leadership of the 1920s. Gandhi's Satyagraha moved him to action. Nehru, who describes a meandering political ambivalence and rootlessness dominating his years of study in London prior to the war, was also shell-shocked into political awakening by the significance of the "Russian Experiment" of 1917. As he describes it in *The Discovery of India*, in language redolent of Du Bois's contemporary musings on revolutionary typology:

> A study of Marx and Lenin produced a powerful effect on my mind and helped me to see history and current affairs in a new light. The long chain of history and of social development appeared to have some meaning, some sequence, and the future lost some of its obscurity. The practical achievements of the Soviet Union were also tremendously impressive. Often I disliked or did not understand some development there and it seemed to me to be too closely concerned with the opportunism of the moment or the power politics of the day. But despite all these developments and possible distortions of the original passion for human betterment, I had no doubt that the Soviet Revolution had advanced human society by a great leap and had lit a bright flame which could not be smothered, and that it had laid the foundations for that new civilization towards which the world could advance.[70]

What one might call the ripple effects of India's 1919 convulsions were shared, closer to home for Du Bois, by his friend and colleague Lala Rai. In the same year, as the two men spoke together at the Civic Association and likely met Agnes Smedley, Rai made the fatal decision in response to the upturn in national struggle to return to India. In 1920, he would lead the Indian National Congress, which would provide formal authorization of the home rule movement and start on the long road toward his imprisonment and death at the hands of British police in 1929. Before leaving the United States, Rai sent a telegram to Woodrow Wilson appealing for Indian freedom after the war's end.[71] In the same year, he published the essay "Bolshevism and Anti-Bolshevism." In it, Rai, like Du Bois, sided not with the party but with the class: the revolution had demonstrated "that the world is for all and not for the few who happen to be in possession at this minute."[72] In a footnote indicative of the heterodox nature of world-revolutionary theory, Rai also praised Trotsky's contributions to the revolution, particularly for his position on the liberation of Persia. Of even more immediate importance to Du Bois, Rai left the United States committed to the argument partly shaped by his mentor that African Americans were the American "untouchables," a perspective that would help shape much of Du Bois's subsequent efforts to analogize caste to race and to pull African American attention to Indian decolonization.[73]

Events of 1919 also recast the world revolution and her place in it for Anna

Louise Strong. Her personal tipping point into the diasporic international was the five-day general strike in her hometown of Seattle on February 6–11. Already persuaded by World War I to "expose and lash the capitalists who had caused it and who lied about it still,"[74] Strong immediately perceived the events of February as "our local 'revolution'" symmetrical to events in Russia and evidence of its global inevitability. "We had a majority in Seattle," she wrote. "The tide was starting to give us a majority in the world."[75] Thus, like Du Bois, Strong perceived attacks on black workers in the summer of 1919, the Red Summer, as an attack on that emerging minority, what the socialist daily *The Call* called "pogroms." Published under the pen name "Anise," Strong's poem "The Negro Worker" (1919) appeared in the *Seattle Union Record*. The poem describes a black worker job hunting in shipyards "from some of these patriots / Who made a lot of money / From the war." Turned away, the narrator concludes:

> *i do know*
> That I can't get into
> The UNION I belong to . . .
> I wonder why
> They are so shortsighted
> As not to realize
> That every time
> They keep ANY WORKER
> Man or woman
> White, yellow, or black
> OUT OF A UNION
> They are forcing a worker
> TO be a SCAB
> *To be used against them.76*

Like "If We Must Die," Claude McKay's better-known paean to working-class racial division, fighting back, and revolution published the same year, Strong's poem helps to explain why she turned directly from writing to voluntary exile to Russia. (McKay and Strong would arrive in Moscow within months of each other.) Strong put it as follows in her own version of "pressed to the wall / dying but fighting back": "The general strike put into our hands the organized life of the city—all except the guns."[77]

Finally, the most enduring and immediate effects of 1919 among members of the diasporic international were cast onto the figure of Agnes Smedley. As the year began, Smedley was living in New York working with Chattopadhyaya to raise funds for India through the Friends for Freedom of India committee formed within the Rand School and working as a reporter for the socialist *New York Call*. The formation of the Comintern in February determined both the ideological and structural relationship Smedley was to have to its world-revolutionary aspiration until its disbanding in 1943. Specifically, Chattopadhyaya and Smedley were to become employees, liaisons, contacts, organizers, and emissaries for Comintern policy in four "centers" of world-revolutionary implantation: New York, Shanghai, Moscow, and Berlin. Smedley's diasporic movements within the world-revolutionary international were also determined by shifting lines in Comintern policy and thought, shifts that implicated her in fundraising, propaganda, and spying on behalf of the Stalinist Soviet Union, as exposed in Ruth Price's essential biography, *The Lives of Agnes Smedley* (2005). Yet although her biography was different in almost every detail from Du Bois's, their continuously overlapping, intersecting political responses to and evaluations of prospects for world revolution are nearest in parallel to those among the diasporic internationalists, with the possible exception of Padmore. Indeed, their "novels" of the Communist International—Du Bois's *Dark Princess* (1928) and Smedley's *Daughter of Earth* (1929)—are, as we shall see, fictional masterworks of the diasporic international, fractured reflecting mirrors from across the world of the prospects for the "romance" of world revolution to become real.

While 1919 gave institutional form to world revolution as a theoretical concept, it also immediately generated political contradictions and problems that were to shape its application. Two are stressed here as emblematic of chapters and analyses to come. The first was political misjudgment about the nature and potential success of global working-class struggles, especially after Stalin's seizure of power in 1924; the second was political dependence, oscillation, and reaction to shifting conceptions of colonial self-determination within the Communist International by the Pan-African Movement and across Asia. Structuring both fault lines was the success of capitalism and fascism in setting back each movement in both aggressive attack on the Soviet Revolution of 1917 and on a tightening grip on colonial states. The result was a further narrowing of Stalinist communism into a doctrine of Socialism in One Country and increasing distance and fractured solidarity among working-class struggles in the colonies, the Soviet Union, and the advanced capitalist states. Duncan Hallas has provided the clearest exposition of how between 1917 and 1922 the Communist International and Russian Revolution lost the titanic momentum generated across the international left. The siege of the revolution by fourteen outside invading capitalist states (including the United States, Great Britain, and Japan), internal Civil War, economic underdevelopment, and inherited difficulties in transforming a peasant agricultural economy were all instrumental in both setting back working-class power in Russia and strangling a national economy attempting to sustain the world's first communist state. These regressions also coincided with failures in working-class struggles tied to new communist revolutionary parties outside the Soviet Union on which revolutionary confidence of 1919 had been built—in particular, the failure of the working-class uprising led by the Communist Party of Germany in 1919 and 1923; the Kuomintang's destruction of the workers' movement in Shanghai between 1925 and 1927; and the uneven success of large railway strikes in northwestern India beset by conflicts among communist revolutionaries, nationalists, noncooperators, and labor and peasant activists.[78] I discuss these moments as they relate to individual national movements in subsequent chapters. Here, it is important to register their composite effect on the concept of world revolution, particularly as it relates to the exemplar of class struggle in the Soviet Union. As Hallas notes, "The more the influence of the Russian was reinforced [on global revolutionary movements], the greater became the dependence of the international movement on the outcome of the post-revolutionary struggle for power in a backward and isolated country in which the working class was itself disintegrating."[79] He continues: "Herein lies the tragedy of the subsequent development of the Comintern. The complex process of uneven and combined development of both capitalism and of the workers' movements had not only falsified the assumption made by Marx and Engels that the workers' revolution would occur first in what were, in their day, the most economically and politically developed countries—Britain, France and Germany—it had also led to Russian dominance of the revolutionary movement at the very moment with workers power was dying of atrophy in Russia itself."[80]

The story of the diasporic international is in many ways a story of historical compensation for the conditions Hallas describes. Alliance of the state bureaucracy in Stalin's Russia with the petty bourgeoisie and its assumption of the role of a "self-conscious ruling class"; Soviet commands to subordinate the Chinese Communist Party to the Kuomintang in China; the Stalinization of the Indian Communist Party; the ultra-leftism of the Third Period and its assault on "social fascists"; and the volte-face of the Popular Front, Stalinism's last-ditch effort to accommodate the Soviet revolution to reformist strategies in the face of the revolution's stagnation—these turns and fits would become the obstacle course for members of the diasporic international trying to carry through what Nehru called a "new civilization towards which the world could advance" and Du Bois called the "idea [that] only those who work shall vote and rule." At the same time, the serial faltering of proletarian internationalism after 1919 that Hallas describes led to compensatory emphasis within and outside Soviet Russia on the fate of the world's colonies. Especially after Stalin's assumption of power in 1924, the Comintern's defense of national self-determination became totemic of the Soviet commitment to world revolution and a mask for failures in other areas. Dialectically, this meant a hardening conception of anticolonial political autonomy and a weakened conception of how national self-determination struggles could advance, in theory and practice, proletarian internationalism.

The itinerant development and zigzagging path of the Pan-African Congress in the years after 1921 is most emblematic of this and serves here as a parable for things to come. Emboldened by the "self-determination" thematic of 1919, the congress held in 1921 in London released a "Declaration to the World" demanding the "establishment of political institutions among suppressed peoples."[81] It also called for "self-government for the Africans in Africa."[82] The congress, however, was still encumbered by both paternalistic reformism and an anti-Bolshevik animus that constrained dedication to the working classes of the continent (or the world) as the tip of change. Du Bois was further along than his contemporaries in his class analysis, noting the "cleft between our incipient social classes"—the "privileged and exploited"— was a divide still had to be overcome within Pan-Africanism.[83] Yet the 1923 congress in Lisbon was nearly a total bust; the congress was hamstrung by a winnowing of elites, a separation of the movement from concurrent anticolonial movements (e.g., no one from the congress had attended the important Baku Conference held by the Soviets in 1920, where representatives of Chinese, Arab, and Indian parties could be found), and a low level of worker and trade union representation. This led to quixotic and narrowly nationalist projects, such as support for the resettlement of Liberia, a particular focus of Du Bois up through his 1925 visit there, where he misread Western imperialist recapitalization of the rubber industry as the potential "self-determination" of Pan-African peoples. This debacle was followed by another small Pan-African Congress in New York in 1927, with 208 delegates from eleven countries; only three—Liberia, Sierra Leone, and Gold Coast—represented Africa.

The years 1926–1928 constituted a reorientation in both Du Bois's outlook and the Pan-African Movement, mostly related to events in Russia and the Communist International. Indeed, Immanuel Geiss has argued that the period after 1927—the year of the last Pan-African Congress until Manchester—constituted another interregnum on the global left in which communism filled a "vacuum" in the Pan-African Movement.[84] What were the ingredients of that shift and merger? First, the stalled internal dynamics of Russia's revolution put precedent—and compensatory emphasis—on its anticolonial work. The successful formation of the University of Toilers of the East (KUTVU), attended by anticolonial leaders such as Liu Shaoqi (China), Ho Chi Minh (Vietnam), M. N. Roy (India), and Khalid Bakdash (Syria), and the Baku Congress of 1920 gave the Soviets a platform of international legitimation of one aspect of United Front work. These events earned the Soviets the designation "champion of the darker races" even as, in the case of China, as we shall see in Chapter 3, Comintern policy was setting back working-class struggles there. In 1927, the Communist International formed the League against Imperialism as a second apparatus of that legitimation. Its founding conference in Brussels, as noted earlier, attracted the widest pantheon of anticolonial leaders yet assembled in world history. The conference was dedicated to three main tasks: anticolonial struggle in China, U.S. imperialism in Latin America, and "Negro revendications"—namely, the fight against European imperialism in South Africa and the Congo. The league issued a manifesto to all "colonial peoples, workers and peasants of the world"—a slogan to be echoed later by Pan-Africanism—to engage in anti-imperial struggle. Finally, the league initiated a new wave of Africa-centered work by the Comintern: renewed efforts were made to bring African representatives to the KUTVU; the Black Belt thesis of 1928 underscored African slavery and colonialism in the historical composition of capitalism; and the U.S. Communist Party increased efforts to recruit black members, eliminate white "chauvinism," and generate publishing organs that would address black liberation domestically and internationally, such as the *Negro Worker* and *The Liberator*.

Within a decade, the world communist movement would recruit to its ranks, as members or fellow travelers, these members of the diasporic international, each of whom was also dedicated to Pan-Africanism: George Padmore, C.L.R. James, Claudia Jones, Jomo Kenyatta, and W.E.B. Du Bois. Not long after, Kwame Nkrumah would begin a collaboration with James and Padmore that would last until the end of their lives. Cumulatively, these figures rebalanced the wheel of Africa's place in the conception of world revolution—and of the conception itself. In the main, they evolved the Comintern's support for anticolonial struggle into a theory of black vanguard leadership as a substitute for what was perceived as the failures of United Front strategies and interracial working-class unity. African and black participation in world revolution was conceived as both "national" in character, as defined by Lenin and Stalin in their writings on the national question, and dissident in its increasing bid for autonomy from the Communist International project. The result was a newly minted conception of the black working class as the revolutionary vanguard of both national self-determination struggles and proletarian internationalism. This revision of the world revolution conception would have far-reaching consequences within and outside the Pan-African movement and global left; it would, in effect, "globalize" Pan-Africa, sowing the seeds for new alignments, such as the Bandung Conference of 1955, and the creation of a postcolonial "Third World" politics. At the same time, it would index the fatal consequences of the Stalinization of the communist left in carrying out a credible policy of world revolution, consequences that would survive well into the era of decolonization. The struggle with Stalinism would, in turn, result in a conception of world revolution that was autonomous to its own tradition, a "break" typical of the diasporic international's revisionist typology.

Du Bois's own monumental evolution in this period provides a quintessential example. The path to *Black Reconstruction*, a bellwether text of this period and one to which, by need, we repeatedly return, was constituted by events internal and external to the global crisis of the 1930s. On the heels of his epiphanic trip to Russia, Du Bois began his methodical study of Marx's writing, preparing courses on "Karl Marx and the Negro" at Atlanta University (also the title of an article in the March 1933 issue of *The Crisis*) and publicly referring to Marx as the "greatest figure in the science of modern industry."[85] Simultaneously, Du Bois continued to berate the American communist movement for threatening to use blacks as "shock troops," especially in the Scottsboro South—a specific feature of his opposition to the Stalinist Black Belt thesis—and persisted in his denunciation of American efforts at socialism: "No [American] Soviet of technocrats would do more than exploit colored labor in order to raise the status of whites."[86] It was this deep skepticism about U.S. imperial nationalism—"The South is not interested in freedom for dark India," as he famously put it—that prompted Du Bois to imagine the Reconstruction-era black working class as both a tragic synecdoche of the American "counterrevolution" after Reconstruction and as herald of a newly conceived *world revolution*: "The unending tragedy of Reconstruction is the utter inability of the American mind to grasp its real significance, its national and world-wide implications. . . . We are still too blind and infatuated to conceive of the emancipation of the laboring class in half the nation as a revolution comparable to the upheavals in France in the past, and in Russia Spain, India and China today."[87] Here Du Bois reveals the typological conception: that all past revolutions inhere in the present and all present revolutions portend in the past. In this context, Du Bois's notorious designation of slave rebellions as "general strikes" resonate logically to their anachronistic sources—New Orleans of 1892, Seattle of 1919, England of 1926—as retrospective prototypes of the present. *Black Reconstruction* also formalized two unfolding typological ideas in Du Bois's thought: that the black working class, beginning with slavery, was what he had first called in *John Brown* in 1909 the cornerstone of the modern global "proletariat" and that Reconstruction was the prototypical anticipation of all twentieth-century revolutions—its revolution, or dream deferred. Hence, in anticipation of his Mansart thesis, Du Bois discovered in *Black Reconstruction* the historical subject—or historiographical method—of world revolution for the first time.

The most important (if overlooked) theoretical companion to Du Bois's originary contribution to both Pan-Africanism and world-revolutionary theory from this period is C.L.R. James's *World Revolution 1917–1936: The Rise and Fall of the Communist International.* Undertaken like Du Bois's *Black Reconstruction* during a major reappraisal—one might say, crisis—of his relationship to Marxism, James settled in his book on the concurrence of ongoing contemporary revolutions (in Spain, France, and Russia) as a litmus test of the Communist International's theory and practice of world revolution. Specifically, the book was written out of James's engagement with a dozen or so members of the Communist League, the first British Trotskyist organization. The members formed something called the Marxist Group inside the Independent Labour Party of England. James's book predicted the imminent collapse of the Third International under Stalin for failing adequately to support both workers' movements and anticolonial struggles in Europe, Asia, and Africa, foretelling an imminent new stage in world revolution: the Fourth International of Trotsky. "We may well see, especially after the universal ruin and destruction of the coming war," James wrote, "a revolutionary movement which, beginning in one of the great Europeans cities, in the course of a few short months, will sweep the imperialist bourgeoisie out of power, not only in every country in Europe, but in India, China, Egypt and South Africa."[88] James's bitter abandonment of Stalinism in *World Revolution* is significant in two ways for my larger argument and in relationship to Du Bois: first, it heralded the gradual sharp turn toward a theory of black working-class autonomy he would articulate in discussions with Trotsky in Mexico in 1939, a crucial moment of confluence in the history of Pan-Africanism; and second, it followed the pattern of the diasporic international left after 1927 of seeking to recover the rational kernel—working-class self-emancipation—of Marxism inside the mystical shell of Stalinism. It was this "latent" aspect of their work that Du Bois would recognize, revisionistically, in his essay "Africa and the French Revolution" (1961). Finally, James would self-consciously "merge" his revisionist Pan-African typology for world revolution with Padmore and Du Bois in his book *A History of Pan-African Revolt* (1938). James's argument there that "Africans must win their own freedom" was influenced by two texts in particular: Padmore's *The Life and Struggles of Negro Toilers* (1931), a classic Third Period Stalinist text, and Du Bois's *Black Reconstruction.* As Robin D. G. Kelley notes, James's analysis of slave rebellions in the U.S. South "is taken straight from . . . *Black Reconstruction* in America, from his invocation of the 'general strike' to his description of the slaves' hesitant responses towards the Union soldiers."[89]

Padmore undertook the third and most practical turn in Pan-African orientation after 1927. As had been hinted at earlier in his correspondence with Du Bois, Padmore was the cook who governed the larger historical arc of Pan-Africa's globalization and its revision of world revolution typology. A year after his departure from the Communist International in June 1934, Padmore moved to London, where he was reunited with James. From there, Padmore began to cast out what became the formal ideological lineaments of both global Pan-Africanism and "new" world revolution theory. In 1937, he published *Africa and World Peace*, criticizing the Soviet Union for refusing to fight on behalf of Ethiopia because it was a "race war," while simultaneously urging colonials to support the Soviet Union as the "peaceable" alternative to both Western imperialism and fascism. In the same year, he and James established the International African Service Bureau from the remnants of the Ethiopian Defense Committee, which James had established but had gone defunct.[90] In 1938, the bureau became the "colonial section" of the International Labor Party, publishing the essay "Hands Off the Colonies!" for the *New Leader*. Significantly, Padmore anticipated in his essay what would become recognizable during the postwar period as Third World politics, accusing the Communist Party of creating a "false dichotomy between so-called good and bad imperialisms" for failing to stand up for Ethiopia. Shortly thereafter, he joined the Centre against Imperialism, a successor to the League against Imperialism "minus the communists," Hooker notes.[91] The league had itself collapsed under the weight of Stalinist misdirection—for example, helping to foster civil war in China by backing the Kuomintang.

Padmore thus was ironically positioned by both personal history and ideological hostility to Stalinism to generate a new typological model of world revolution that would bear its influence, if not its name. The results emerged in the period 1939–1945, culminating in the Pan-African Congress in Manchester. In 1939, Padmore attended a meeting of European socialist parties as a representative of the Pan-African Movement, endorsing a scheme for an autonomous black-controlled economy that eventually would become socialist, a variation of the Black Belt thesis. The idea reflected Padmore's gradual move toward what Barbara Foley calls metonymic nationalism. Here, I affirm Foley's definition and extend it to indicate the related phenomenon of national liberation struggles coming to represent the "whole" of proletarian internationalism, a Stalinist variant of Socialism in One Country and a tendency that Trotsky differentially identified as "national messianism."[92] Indeed, Padmore would gradually build Pan-African conceptions of world revolution both circumscribed by and deviating from his loyalty to the original Leninist perspective on national self-determination. In 1943, he would write in *The Crisis* that the Soviet Union "has done more to liquidate illiteracy and raise the cultural level of the former subject races of Central Asia within twenty-five years, than the British government has accomplished in India or Africa in two centuries."[93] In February of that year, in an essay published by George Orwell in the weekly *Tribune*, Padmore attributed the Soviets' military success in resisting fascism to their colonial policy: "Without a doubt, Soviet unity in resisting the invader is due to the policy of self-determination which the Soviet Government undertook in relation to the national minorities and communities which before 1917 formed what might be called the colonial territories of the Czarist Empire."[94] Padmore here subtly reverses the historical causality of world revolution of 1917 and 1919 to conform to what I have been calling a Stalinist corrective after 1924: Soviet unity and the success of the revolution depend first on a policy of colonial self-determination rather than on seizure of the means of production through workers' power. Like Du Bois and James, Padmore tips the balance in the formula of world revolution toward emancipating "black hands" of the darker nations.

In 1946, in his book *How Russia Transformed Her Colonial Empire: A Challenge to the Imperialist Powers*, Padmore more generally codified this conception. "Whatever criticism or charges one might level against Stalin's policy in relation to socialism and world revolution and his programme of 'Socialism in a single country,'" he wrote, "he has in the main adhered to the fundamental principles laid down by Lenin as far as concerns of the Right of Self-Determination for the Soviet national minorities."[95] Padmore's criticism mediated failings of the Communist International under Stalin as a means of explaining the necessary transformation and new vanguard leadership of the Pan-African Movement. It implicitly reminded readers of the failed Popular Front strategy, which had subordinated class struggle in the name of saving capitalist regimes in the fight against fascism; of the fatal Stalin-Hitler Pact of 1939, which had resulted in the partition of Poland and the absorption as "colonies" of the Baltic states by the Soviet Union; and, most lethal, of Stalin's collaboration with an imperial United States and Britain at the Tehran Conference of 1943, a precursive step to Stalin's disbanding of the Communist International in that year to appease the Western imperialist powers. Although he hedged his formulation—"He has *in the main* adhered to the fundamental principles laid down by Lenin"—for those who, like Padmore, were assessing Stalin's policy "in relation to Socialism and world revolution," these steps were nothing less than catastrophic abandonment. "At its foundation," writes Hallas, "the Comintern had declared its opposition to all imperialisms and proclaimed the right of self-determination for all peoples. By 1943, indeed earlier, it had come to oppose the national struggle in the colonies and 'spheres of influence' of Russia's allies."[96]

Consequently, Padmore's affirmation in 1946 of the Leninist "self-determination" thesis for its internal colonies was meant primarily to indicate why the Pan-African Movement now had to strive to carry its torch at the global level. The liquidation of the Comintern in 1943 thus was a trip wire for the century's turn in the theory and practice of world revolution. It began the slow descent of Communist Internationalism and Stalinism as a historical force on the global left while inaugurating the gradual autonomization of the anticolonial movement. In 1944, using the International African Service Bureau as its nucleus, Padmore formed the Pan-African Federation (PAF). Its implicit mission was to fill the vacuum left by the Comintern's demise. Its organizational work focused on two objectives: forming a new global labor alliance dedicated to building socialism and reanimating the dormant Pan-African Movement as the tip of the anticolonial spear. Peter Milliard and T. Ras Makonnen of British Guiana were named president and general secretary, respectively. Representatives included a cluster of figures soon to become emergent national leaders of Africa's decolonization: Jomo Kenyatta for the Kikuyu Central Association of Kenya; Isaac Wallace-Johnson from the West African Youth League of Sierra Leone; and the Friends of African Freedom Society, Gold Coast. Within the United Kingdom, the PAF also enrolled leading African labor associations, such as the Negro Association (Manchester), the Coloured Workers Association (London), and the African Union (Glasgow).

Two immediate tasks were undertaken by the PAF: first, to find ways to ensure that the third clause of the new Atlantic Charter on "self-determination" would be applied to colonial states; and second, to induce colonial representatives to attend the inaugural World Trade Union Conference (WTUC), to be held in London in February 1945. Like the PAF, the WTUC's history can be traced to the aspirations and failures of the global left since 1919. It was formed at the behest of the International Labor Organization (ILO), which was also founded in 1919, and was a successor to the International Federation of Trade Unions (IFTU), or Amsterdam International, itself brought into existence in the year of the Comintern's founding. Between 1919 and 1945, the Communist International stood in hostile opposition to the socialist and social-democratic IFTU. The collapse of the Comintern in 1943 thus produced a realignment within the new WTUC, drawing partly on its old constituents. In February 1945, representatives from the Soviet Union and, for the first time in the history of the IFTU, seven delegates from colonial countries, including those in the British West Indies and British West Africa, met in London. They included Ken Hill of the Jamaica Trade Unions Council and Wallace-Johnson. Among their actions was an appeal to British trade unions to support decolonization. In practice, though, the WTUC would function as a kind of United Nations of labor; "A Call to All the Peoples," its founding statement at its meeting in London on February 6–17, stressed labor unity to close out the war against fascism: "To achieve these ennobling aims and purposes, our World Conference pledged the organized millions we represent to support the heroic armed forces of the United Nations in the battles still to be fought to secure full and final victory."[97] In an effort to more strongly realign WTUC labor to anticolonial struggles, members of the PAF invited West African and Caribbean delegates to the WTUC to meet in Manchester immediately after the conference ended to attend the first Pan-African Congress in sixteen years. October was selected for the congress, to succeed the scheduled follow-up meeting of the WTUC. This would enable West African and Caribbean delegates to the WTUC to attend more easily.

A flurry of preparatory activity ensued throughout the remainder of 1945. In March, a provisional organizing committee for the Pan-African Congress that included Kenyatta, Milliard, Wallace-Johnson, James, and Padmore (and, later, just arrived from the United States, Nkrumah), met in London and produced a "draft manifesto" calling for African participation in the upcoming United Nations, international coordination against discrimination, an end to the "present system of exploitation" in the colonies, and a general statement of the need for African self-determination.[98] The committee also agreed tentatively to invite "observers" to the Pan-African Congress from Arab countries, China and India—a whiff of the emerging Bandung era. In May 1945, the PAF met to consider a statement by Soviet Foreign Minister Vyacheslav Molotov asking delegates at the upcoming United Nations meeting in San Francisco to back colonial independence and for an open reading of the recently completed PAF "manifesto" on Africa in the postwar world. As Hakim Adi notes, the event made clear that "there was now a growing black anticolonial movement in Britain which could present its own anti-imperialist analysis and demands to the embryonic UN organization."[99] On June 10, 1945, the PAF organized the first All Colonial Peoples Conference in Holborn Town Hall, London. The meeting was organized in collaboration with the London-based West African Student Union, the Federation of Indian Associations in Britain, the Ceylon Students Association, and the Burma Association. There, a charter of demands was established modeled in part on the "Charter of Coloured Peoples" drawn up in 1944 at the meeting of the League for Coloured Peoples, a largely reformist organization headed by Harold Moody and established in 1931, a clear precursor to the PAF.[100] Momentum for the All Colonial Peoples Conference was also advanced by the outbreak the same month of a fifty-two-day general strike in Nigeria supported by more than seventeen unions representing more than 150,000 workers. The strike generated a massive rally at Conway Hall, London, on July 15 organized by the PAF and West African Student Union.[101]

It was the All Colonial Peoples Conference in June, an assortment of forty delegates and twenty-five observers, trade union delegates, and "left-wing parties "that became what Adi calls "something of a dress rehearsal for the Manchester Pan-African Congress."[102] More important, the conference ended with the establishment of a small committee whose aim was to create a program and constitution to "bring into being as early as possible a 'Colonial International.'"[103] This term was clearly a revisionist turn on the Communist International, now in the dustbin of history, and Pan-Africa's vanguard conception of a new typology of world revolution. What was it to be? In April 1945, just two months earlier, Padmore had written to Du Bois to describe his vision for the congress. He underscored the role of trade union delegations that were "primarily concerned with the workers and peasants, who must be the driving force behind any movement which we middle class intellectuals may establish. Today, the African masses, the common people, are awake and not blindly looking to doctors and lawyers to tell them what to do."[104] For Padmore, the Pan-African Congress was to be the "Africanized" iteration of the Leninist thesis on both colonial self-determination and the vanguard role of the working class within it, the only "salvageable" aspect of the Comintern's—and, by implication, Stalin's—legacy. It was this conception that became the consensus in the newly revitalized Pan-African left and drove the ideological agenda of colonial delegates to the WTUC's follow-up meeting in Paris from September 25 to October 8 and to the Pan-African Congress in Manchester in October.

Indeed, at the Palais de Chaillot, where the chairman introduced the conference location as the "Paris of 1789, of the taking of the Bastille, of the revolutions of 1830 and of 1848, of the Commune of 1871," colonial delegates argued for the working classes of the *colonized world* as the new typological vanguard of world revolution.[105] They advocated for the creation of a "Colonial Council" or "Colonial Department" within the WTUC and for the exclusion of trade unions that practiced racist discrimination and argued that "the system of colonies is the thin end of the wedge of capitalism, and therefore, the arch enemy of the working class."[106] In the face of what must have seemed like a feeble description from the Soviet delegate of a new five-year plan to rehabilitate the Soviet wartime economy—more evidence of Socialism in One Country Stalinism—delegates from Syria, Lebanon, Palestine, China, Jamaica, and India pressed for the withdrawal of colonial forces as the first step in worldwide working-class emancipation. As J. S. Annan, an electrical engineer representing the Gold Coast African Railway Employees Union (and, later, a delegate to the Pan-African Congress in Manchester) put it, "How, in particular, are we to make the imperialist governments of America, Belgium, Britain, France, etc. recognize the decision of the World Federation of Trade Unions on matters affecting labour, wages, social security, working hours, etc. . . . Are we to leave these helpless colonial organizations at the mercy of imperialistic capitalism?"[107]

This drive toward the real and ideological "proletarianization" of the Pan-African Congress was consummated in industrial Manchester. In the heart of the British textile empire that had once spun slave cotton into imperial gold, mass emancipation from at least the colonial form of capitalist empire was set rocketing forward. As Nkrumah, who thereafter would lead the Gold Coast out of its colonial moorings, later wrote, "We shot into limbo the gradualist aspirations of our African middle classes and intellectuals and expressed the solid down-to-earth will of our workers, trade unionists, farmers and peasants who were decisively represented at Manchester, for independence."[108] Hakim Adi and Marika Sherwood's useful and comprehensive catalogue of delegates and organizations to Manchester lists, among others, the Colored Workers Association of London, the Federation of Indian Organizations of Great Britain, the Gold Coast Farmers Association, the Workers League of British Honduras, the Nigerian Trade Unions Congress, the Gambia Trades Union, the Trade Union Congress of Trinidad, the St. Lucia Seamen's and Waterfront Workers' Union, the Saint Kitts and Nevis Trades Union, the Workers' Association of Bermuda, and the Trinidad Oilfields Workers Union. Political organizations presented included the African National Congress, the Grenada Labour Party, the Independent Labor Party of the United Kingdom, the Lankda Sama Samajist Party of Ceylon, the People's National Party of Jamaica, the Universal Negro Improvement Association of Jamaica, and the National Association for the Advancement of Colored People of the United States.[109]

The representation at Manchester of delegates from India and Ceylon reflected a carryover of affiliate organizing between West African and Indian student and workers' groups in London preceding October and, more directly, from a "Subject People's Conference" held in the short interval between the WTUC follow-up meeting and Pan-African Congress. There, the focus was on colonial liberation in Indochina, India, and Malaya and Afro-Asian unity, a harbinger of things to come. The Pan-African Congress included statements of fraternal greetings "to the masses of India" read by Padmore on behalf of the Standing Orders Committee to the "toiling masses of India through the Indian National Congress"—an echo of the KUTV and a homage to ongoing strikers in India in 1945, as had just been reported at the WTUC.[110] It also included messages of solidarity sent directly to the Dutch and French embassies in London on behalf of the Javanese and Indonesian independence struggle. These more global solidarity gestures would blossom in time. The main business of the meeting was affirming Pan-African labor unity as the basis of a new proletarian internationalism. Amy Ashwood Garvey chaired the first session, "The Color Problem in Britain." It reported on black soldiers from the Gold Coast to Liverpool and Cardiff living in below subsistence conditions after fighting the first war of empire (1914) and the second (ongoing), while Peter Abrahams reported on black poverty in the East End of London. In a second session, "Imperialism in North and West Africa," G. Ashie Nikoi, chair of the West African Cocoa Farmers Delegations of Gold Coast, blamed "British imperialism" for black labor troubles and noted that the Aborigines Rights Protection Society had been the first in black West Africa to champion the cause of labor.[111] Chief A. Soyemi Coker of the Trade Union Council of Nigeria thanked the PAF for moral and financial aid during the recent general strike there and called for living wages for the working classes, "co-operative societies" throughout Africa, and the nationalization of industry. F.O.B. Flaie of the West African Student Union, noting the "remarkable rise of the Soviet Union," called for general strikes in Africa and the implementation of boycotts. Significantly, while recognizing the context of imperialist war and the role of the Soviet Union in advancing anticolonial movements, the reports emphasized the interdependent autonomy of black labor struggle and self-determination as ingredients of the "colonial international."

These politics were enshrined in a series of resolutions passed at the congress. They included condemnations of the "systematic exploitation of the economic resources of the West Africa territories"; enforced uneven development produced by obstruction of West African industrialization by the indigenes; restrictions on independent trade unions; lack of legal enforcement of trade unions' rights in the West Indies; foreign monopolies of mining; and control of the West African government by a "merchants' united front"—an ironic nod to the Comintern's legacy.[112] Resolutions specific to decolonization included a demand for the removal of British armed forces from Egypt and the abolition of the Condominium over Sudan; "full equality of rights for all citizens, without distinction of race, colour and sex" in South Africa; and "justice and social equality for the Indian Community" in South Africa.[113] Demands were also made for the destruction of the "colour bar" in Britain and the recognition of democratic rights of indigenous citizens of Tunisia, Algeria, Morocco, and Libya independent from French and Italian rule. The conference closed with fraternal greetings from the district secretary of the Communist Party Lancashire and Cheshire District and the Socialist Vanguard Group, among others, including a portentous greeting from Surat Ali of the Federation of Indian Associations in Great Britain, "a working man . . . and Indian" and longtime comrade of African seamen: "This common struggle should bring Indians and Africans closer to realizing their ancient relationships, so that coloured people would no longer be oppressed."[114]

Most symbolic of all, the congress concluded with a "Declaration to the Colonial Workers, Farmers and Intellectuals," written by Nkrumah, a longtime associate of Padmore who was quickly becoming his most intimate collaborator and friend, and the gathering's rising star. Nkrumah gave voice, literally, to Padmore's reconstruction of the twentieth century's deferred dream of a "colonial international":

The object of imperialist powers is to exploit. By granting the right to Colonial peoples to govern themselves that Object is defeated. . . . The Fifth Pan-African Congress therefore calls on the workers and farmers of the Colonies to organize effectively. Colonial workers must be in the front of the battle against Imperialism. Your Weapons—the Strike and the Boycott—are invincible.

Today, there is only one road to effective action—the organization of the masses. And in that organization the educated Colonials must join. Colonial and Subject Peoples of the World—Unite!"[115]

Nkrumah's typological recasting of the *Communist Manifesto*—like Du Bois's revisionist iterations cited earlier—articulated an anticapitalist (and postcolonial) future from the archetype of a revolutionary past. Interred within it was the marriage of, and break between, the Leninist self-determination thesis of Communist Internationalism and its utility for the new colonial international; between Stalin and Padmore; between the KUTV and Baku and Moscow as epicenters of world revolution and its newly emerging coordinates of London, New Delhi, Port-au-Prince, Shanghai, and Accra. This geographical "map" writ larger traced the roots and routes of many of the figures in the diasporic international who had contributed to the arc of "world revolution" between 1919 and 1945 and now existed at a political and ideological crossroads that in many ways replayed the challenges of the earlier period in a new register: how to advance the "teleology of class struggle" (better understood now as a typology of the twentieth century) with the superordinate weight of race—and nation. Manchester had resolved these dilemmas—in resolution form, at least—as an assertion of a *colonial* international dedicated to emancipation along national lines, a metonymic nationalism produced by interpretive variation in Leninism, on one hand, and contradictory traces of the Stalinist legacy, on the other. Not surprisingly, these tendencies would carry forward well into the postcolonial era and determine the form and content of "socialism" in the century's ongoing world revolutions.

———

Finally, and significantly, Manchester indexed and foreshadowed a contradictory crossroads in Du Bois's relationship to both individual members of the global left and the world revolution concept. Du Bois played a marginal role in the planning and execution of the Manchester conference. In 1944–1945, he was out of London, mainly in New York, where his participation in the newly developed Council of African Affairs, a Marxist front group that would soon splinter under Cold War pressure, was instantiating his hardening support for communism as a political idea, even as Stalin was abandoning the Comintern.

Ironically, these contradictory events, in addition to the coming end of the war and emergence of the United Nations as an international body, reanimated Du Bois's hopes for a renewal of the Pan-African Congress. He corresponded eagerly with Padmore throughout 1945, debating locations (they both wanted Africa) and strategies. Despite Du Bois's minor role, Padmore made sure his legacy in the movement was clear in Manchester. Du Bois was unanimously voted international president of the congress on its first day, and he chaired four sessions at the meeting. When Padmore gathered and edited *Colonial and Coloured Unity: A Program for Action*, a history of the Pan-African Congress published after its end, Du Bois was given pride of place, his autobiography a typological link to the history of world revolution itself. The frontispiece, a tribute to "William Edward Burghardt Du Bois: 'Father of Pan-Africanism,'" provided a biographical sketch of his life and an epigraph from his book *The Negro* (1915): "The future world will, in all reasonable possibility, be what coloured men make it."[116] In an essay titled "The Pan-African Congress in Perspective," Peter Abrahams paid tribute to Du Bois's *Dusk of Dawn* (1940) as an inspiration for the congress and ended with an appeal to the establishment of the "Century of the Common Man: Foreword to the Socialist United States of Africa! Long Live Pan-Africanism!" Du Bois's "history" of the Pan-African Congress that led the book was a self-serving but characteristic biographical framing, describing Pan-African unity as an idea that "stems naturally from the West Indies and the United States."[117] Du Bois's emphasis on his role in forming the congresses of 1919, 1921, and 1927 was perhaps a rejoinder to a sense of having been slighted in the planning of the Manchester meeting. It also, however, indicated tension and variance developing politically among Du Bois, Padmore, and members of the PAF. Du Bois was *deepening* his dedication to a Soviet-centric ideal of world revolution just as members of the federation were moving closer to a "neither Washington nor Moscow" perspective. As Joe Appiah, a delegate to the congress later wrote, "By the end of the conference we had taken very serious and far reaching conclusions. We had rejected both the capitalist and the communist solutions to our problems, adopted Pan-African socialism, and pledged to set our countries free as quickly as possible."[118] For Du Bois, Pan-African socialism would never come entirely into focus. Rather, his own shifting conceptions of world revolution before and after Manchester—from Leningrad and Beijing to Delhi—would sustain a sympathy for both "pure" Leninism (and Stalinism) that would survive many tests, even while forcing him to seek new middle grounds.

Perhaps most symbolic of the 1945 "crossroads" for this member of the diasporic international was his immediate post-Manchester turn: Du Bois traveled straight away to London, where he met with young black American communists to discuss a "founding meeting of the World Youth Conference," an antifascist youth group that in the same year formed the World Federation of Democratic Youth, itself a communist front organization.[119] One of the people he met was a young Esther Cooper Jackson, a recent graduate of Oberlin College and a member of the Southern Negro Youth Congress (SNYC), which had been founded at Howard University under the auspices of the communist National Negro Congress (NNC). Almost a year to the date later, on October 20, 1946, Du Bois would give one of his most memorable speeches to the SNYC, "Behold the Land," at Cooper's invitation, the beginning of a relationship that would carry to the end of his life. Du Bois's open relationship with Jackson—and the NNC—had already ruffled feathers with the NAACP and would continue to do so after his return home, as would alliances with new players on the American left, including the young, energetic, and rising Claudia Jones. But Du Bois's direction in London in 1945 was full speed ahead: into a long postwar dedication to a highly Stalinized American Communist Party. This road, too, would eventually lead him forward to membership and exile and backward, self-reflexively, to yet another revised typology of world revolution.

2

"EXPERIMENTS OF MARXISM"

W.E.B. Du Bois and the Specter of 1917

I am not interested in working out a perfect system on the basis of the Marxism brand of Hegelianism. What I want is a realistic approach to a democratic state in which the exploitation of labor is stopped, and the political power is in the hands of the workers.

—W.E.B. Du Bois, "Letter to George Streator," April 24, 1935

The unending tragedy of Reconstruction is the utter inability of the American mind to grasp its real significance, its national and world-wide implications. We are still too blind and infatuated to conceive of the emancipation of the laboring class in half the nation as a revolution comparable to the upheavals in France in the past, and in Russia, Spain, India and China today....

If the Reconstruction of the Southern states, from slavery to free labor, and from aristocracy to industrial democracy, had been conceived as a major national program of America, whose accomplishment at any price was well worth the effort, we should be living today in a different world.

—W.E.B. Du Bois, *Black Reconstruction in America*, 1935

I can interpret the Soviet Union today through my experience with two million American Negroes in the last half of the nineteenth century.

—W.E.B. Du Bois, "Russia and America," 1950

W.E.B. Du Bois's support for the Russian Revolution of 1917, the Soviet experiment in fostering world revolution, and the betrayal of the revolution by Joseph Stalin embody many of the contradictions that produced both the century's most successful communist revolution and the diasporic international that was its offspring. The arc of Du Bois's life and political thought is circumscribed by these contradictions: prior to 1917, Du Bois was beholden to reformist views of capitalism denuded of the Leninist conception of worker takeover of the state apparatus and of the state's role in sustaining class society, conceptions that Du Bois embraced belatedly, only after both had been corrupted into state capitalism under Stalin. In 1921, when the revolution was at its emancipatory crest, Du Bois was most cautious in his support, distilling his doubts about working-class sovereignty

in the new Soviet Union through the myopic lens of failed interracial cooperation in the U.S. labor movement. In 1926, upon visiting the Soviet Union
for the first time, Du Bois looked straight past the signs of the revolution's
betrayal—economic collapse, degeneration of workers' soviets, repression of
political dissidents—to claim he was a Bolshevik. Du Bois enacted a kind
of negative dialectics in relation to the Russian Revolution, often misappre-
hending its best moments and embracing its worst. This misreading discloses
strengths and limits to the "revolutionary typology" I have been describing
in his life and work: in his manuscript "Russia and America: An Interpretation" (1950), for example, Du Bois invoked the American Revolution as a war
against the exploitation of "colonial labor" to commemorate it retrospectively
as a template for what became the workers' uprisings in 1917 Russia. Faced
with the obvious paralysis of Russian Cold War state bureaucracy in 1949, Du
Bois attempted to reanimate it by injecting it with typological meaning that
sutured from a broken whole both the "teleology" of class revolution and the
superordinate power of race—a gesture equally hopeful and futile.

This retrospective reading strategy is essential to understanding Du Bois's
relationship not just to Russia's revolution but also to his theory and practice
of world revolution. By fits and starts, Du Bois came to embrace, against his
own inclination, the idea of revolution not as a "lowering of ideals," as he
protested in the first edition of his biography of John Brown, but as a fulfillment of his own, idiosyncratic conception of permanent revolution "whose
accomplishment at any price was well worth the effort." As he wrote in 1952,
"I believe in Communism wherever and whenever men are wise and good
enough to achieve it; but I do not believe all nations will achieve it in the same
way or at the same time."[1] Indeed, the aspirational typology of revolution cited
above—anticolonialism, the French Revolution, Russia, the United States—
ultimately braided itself into Du Bois's analysis of the archetypal event of his
intellectual and political life: *Black Reconstruction in America*. The events of
1865–1877 became Du Bois's template, as we shall see, for *all* world revolutions before and after. This chapter diagnoses in particular the manner in
which Du Bois's master text *Black Reconstruction in America* (1935) is itself
a rewriting and reinterpretation of the Russian Revolution of 1917 and how
his manuscript "Russia and America: An Interpretation" (1950)—still unpublished—is a sequel to that book. Du Bois sought in writing both to justify
each to the other, co-constituting the interracial working class and peasantry
of the late nineteenth century with the self-emancipating industrial workers
and farmers of the twentieth. Du Bois's autodidactic and textual overlay of
Marxian categories onto *Black Reconstruction in America*—the dictatorship
of the proletariat, the general strike—is his superimposition of one successful
revolution onto another deferred, his own strategic "experiment of Marxism,"

Figure 2.1. W.E.B.
Du Bois and Shirley
Graham Du Bois
viewing the May Day
Parade in Moscow's Red
Square, May 1, 1959.
*(Used with permission
of the Special Collections
and University Archives,
W.E.B. Du Bois
Library, University of
Massachusetts Amherst.)*

the phrase he coined to describe the rebellion of black peasants and workers
against slavery. The dialectical interplay of revolutionary achievement and
failure in both works—the very practice of making revolutionary surrogates
in the text—bespeaks once more the Benjaminian dilemma in Du Bois's work
of locating the Angel of History just as the doors of possibility move toward
closure. The Russian Revolution of 1917—and its failures—was for Du Bois
the specter that haunted everything, including his interpretation of the past,
his lived experience of the present, and his typology of a future world. It is the
ineluctable moment that tragically defines both the horizons of the century of
world revolution and Du Bois's place in it (see Figure 2.1).

———

Du Bois's career as what Adolph Reed calls a "Fabian" socialist prior to 1917
was as shot through with contradictions as his later attachment to Stalinism.[2] Two conceptual weaknesses in Second International socialism contributed to Du Bois's uneven engagement with socialist politics and his delayed
response to the historical significance of Russia's revolution. The first was
the Second International position associated with Eduard Bernstein and to a

lesser extent Karl Kautsky that capitalism was fundamentally reformable, that socialism was historically inevitable, and that the attainment of socialism did not necessitate removal of the capitalist state. That view has been summarized by Mark Van Wienen as the belief that "social equality could be achieved by gradual, parliamentary, and peaceful means."[3] In June 1921, four years after the Russian Revolution, in a *Crisis* editorial titled "The Class Struggle," Du Bois wrote, "We do not believe in revolution. We expect revolutionary changes to come mainly through reason, human sympathy and the education of children, not by murder."[4] In Du Bois's case, the Fabian impulse was undergirded by visceral horror and shock at the frequency of lynching in the United States (seventy-six hangings alone in the summer of 1919), which fostered a lingering phobia that a U.S.-based revolution would require African Americans as what he later called "shock troops." Aversion to violence—in 1935, Du Bois would call himself a "pacifist"—also dovetailed with a protective (if not paternalistic) attitude toward "black masses." The specter of black slaughter at the hands of counterrevolution (a theme to be fully explored in *Black Reconstruction in America*) likewise forestalled and delimited Du Bois's conception of the working class as an agent of its own emancipation. Thus, the Leninist argument decided as the Bolshevik course of action after 1905, and codified in Lenin's "The State and Revolution" in 1917, did not penetrate his early thought.[5]

Du Bois's political doubts about workers' self-emancipation were buttressed by a second major flaw in Second Internationalism—namely, its weakness in recognizing racism and black workers' oppression as a constituent part of the fight against capitalism. Du Bois was first drawn to socialism not as a theory of working-class emancipation but as a possible antidote to American racism. In his article "The Negro and Socialism" (1907), Du Bois wrote of African Americans, "We have been made tools of oppression against the workingman's cause—the puppets and playthings of the idle rich."[6] Salvation, he argued, lies in a "larger ideal of human brotherhood, equality of opportunity and work not for wealth but for Weal—here lies our shining goal."[7] In a letter to C. C. Owens in April 1908, Du Bois argued, "I believe the Negro problem is partly the American Caste problem & that caste is arising because of unjust and dangerous economic conditions."[8] In 1911, Du Bois wrote that U.S. socialists "rung truest" on race questions, a confidence gained in part by the fact that five founding members of Du Bois's beloved National Association for the Advancement of Colored People (NAACP) were active members of the Socialist Party of America: John Haynes Holmes, Mary White Ovington, Charles Edward Russell, William Walling, and Florence Kelley.[9]

Yet by October 1911—the same year he joined the Socialist Party—Du Bois was already abandoning the socialist ship for its tepid reaction to American racism. In an editorial for *The Crisis* titled "Forward Backward," Du Bois complained that the socialists were failing to organize black workers, especially in the Dixiecrat South.[10] In 1912, after leaving the party and supporting Woodrow Wilson for president, Du Bois wrote that he would "scarcely describe [himself] as a socialist."[11] The declaration would begin a roughly ten-year period featuring a slew of published essays on common themes: American socialism and socialists were failing to fight for racial equality, to challenge racism in the white working class, and to recognize how U.S. racism was integral to the racist logic of colonialism.[12] Du Bois was right about all of this. As has been well documented elsewhere, individuals within the socialist Second International and the Socialist Party of America adopted the same rearguard attitude toward racism as they did toward taking state power: in the best of cases (Eugene Debs, a hero of Du Bois), socialists refused to speak to segregated audiences; in the worst of cases, they refused to organize unions where challenging racist ideas might slow the task of building the party or make it vulnerable to attacks by racist white workers.

Here in microcosm, then, were the coordinates for the eventual making of Du Bois's revolutionary typology: the simultaneous challenge of racism and oppression against nonwhite workers of the world and the prospect of class unity that might undo the chains for them and their putative white allies. But it is the particularly *American* nature of their confluence that must be understood as the impetus for Du Bois's eventual leap into "open sky" of world revolution after 1917. Du Bois described his slowness to embrace Marxist method as a "provincialism" best understood as an enduring frustration with U.S. racial and class dynamics.[13] Here, the best account of the mechanics of transformation to world-revolutionary perspective is the unpublished one: in the introduction to the "Russia and America," Du Bois describes the outbreak of Russia's revolution as an event about which he "scarce knew what it meant to [him] and to the world."[14] Du Bois begins, typically, by giving the reader a biographical sketch of his political genealogy. He describes casual interest in a tsarist Russia as a "semi-civilized and tryanneous [sic]" civilization through his time as a student in Germany in the 1890s, all of "passing interest until Russia and Japan went to war in 1904–1905."[15] Suddenly, in addition to admiring the "temerity" of one of the "Darker peoples" to wage war against a "great white power," Du Bois writes, "My concept of Russia began to gain body and clearness":

> Already my contact with socialism in Germany had made me critical of Czarism, and there was now added the race problem in the conflict of white and colored people. After that I followed from afar the Russians' struggle for emancipation and drew parallels between Russian peasants and American Freedmen, emancipated at nearly the

same moment and both kept in slavery by denial of land. I read of the pogroms against the Jews and likened them to our lynchings, which were ominously increasing.

Then came the unthinkable First World War, which tore at the moorings of all my historical knowledge and economic foresight; and at its edge, the Russian Revolution of 1917. I was bewildered at what was happening and tried for ten years to withhold final judgment. . . . I certainly believed Russia needed radical reform and was encouraged at the Menshevik effort under Karensky [sic]. When the Bolsheviks came to power, I hesitated; was this the Thermidor or something more permanent and fundamental? Was Marxian Communism possible or a wild, perverted dream?[16]

Several things deserve underscoring in this retrospective account. First, Du Bois explains the birth of his "typological" impulse with Russia's 1917 upheaval: the studied comparison of Russia's peasantry and American freedmen are the first inklings of Du Bois's search for a proletarian takeover in *Black Reconstruction in America*. Second, Du Bois describes the Russian Revolution as the "edge" of World War I and its "unmooring" of his political analysis of the world, suggesting the explanatory retrospective role it came to play in his thought. Third, Du Bois's rhetorical conception of the Bolshevik revolution as either "Thermidor" or human salvation indicates the Angel of History prodding Du Bois from 1917 onward to conceive of the Russian Revolution, and revolution itself, as the central historiographical problem of the century still to come.

From 1921 to 1926, Du Bois tended the "wild dream" of Soviet communism like a hothouse plant, cultivated by an absence of fact and lingering Second Internationalist doubts. In a response to Claude McKay, who was exhorting him from Moscow to support the revolution, Du Bois wrote in 1921, "Time may prove . . . that the Russian Revolution is the greatest event of the nineteenth and twentieth centuries, and its leaders the most unselfish prophets. At the same time, *The Crisis* does not know this to be true."[17] Du Bois also wrote that while "social control of wealth" was needed, he did not "know just what form that control [was] going to take," nor was he prepared to "dogmatize with Marx or Lenin"—his standard euphemism for workers' takeover of state power. Second, Du Bois asked, "How far can the colored people of the world, and particularly the Negroes of the United States, trust the whole working classes?"[18] Du Bois here exhibits a distinct anti-internationalism fractured by the provincialism of American racism: it would take recurring visits to the Soviet Union to comprehend, as he later put it, how the revolution bespoke Russia's "refusal to be white," a phraseology that in shorthand emancipated Du Bois from an entire lifetime of whips and lashes via the American color line. Yet even in 1921, the specter of a future socialist world was in clear enough focus for Du Bois to reset the political agenda for African Americans: "Our task, therefore, as it seems to *The Crisis*, is clear: We have to convince the working classes of the world that black men, brown men, and yellow men are human beings and suffer the same discrimination that white workers suffer. We have, in addition to this, to espouse the cause of the white workers, only being careful that we do not in this way allow them to jeopardize our cause."[19]

In addition to lingering aftereffects of the Second International, Du Bois's contradictory responses to 1917 Russia bespoke the reactionary tendencies of a late Victorian patriarch and the realities of the revolution's struggle to survive in its first ten years. While openly receptive to reports by McKay and the Japanese communist Sen Katayama about the revolution's successes, Du Bois confessed, "I was upset by the current newspaper stories about Russia: Community of women; easy divorce and systematic abortions; collapse of industry, slave toil and continued incipient revolt; famine, hunger, homelessness and despair."[20] Du Bois does not date this observation in "Russia and America," but it seems to coincide with the civil war between White Russians and Bolsheviks that was being widely reported in the U.S. press and the massive economic catastrophes that beset the revolution after 1917 as a result of war, external attacks, crop failures, economic stagnation, and political misjudgments by the Comintern in China, Germany, and Italy. The New Economic Policy of 1921 was the Soviets' admission of some of these failures, what Duncan Hallas describes as the "Thermidor" of "industrial decline, desperately low productivity of labour, cultural backwardness and general scarcity."[21] By 1924, the Communist International had become less the imagined agent of world revolution than a fiefdom for Grigory Zinoviev.[22] Simultaneously, the economic blockade imposed on the Soviet Union by capitalist antagonists gravely weakened the economy. As Tariq Ali observes, "The preponderance of the peasantry, the weakness of the working class, the total lack of democratic traditions, the failure of the revolution to spread to even one advanced country in the West, the death of Lenin and Sverdlov: all these factors became inextricably linked to each other."[23] Finally, as David Levering Lewis notes, a month before Du Bois landed in Kronstadt in 1926, Leon Trotsky officially joined the "United Opposition" to Stalin with Zinoviev, Kemenev, and others; by mid-July 1926, Stalin would strip them and their allies of Politburo membership and party titles.[24] The impact on the revolution was devastating. By 1927, Bolshevik Party membership had dropped to 135,000, from 430,000 in 1920; Nikolai Bukharin had begun to oversee the "rightward turn" of the Comintern away from world revolution and toward Socialism in One Country; Stalin was beginning campaigns against Trotsky, Zinoviev, and a long list of political enemies; and the secret police were well in place.

Several standard narratives exist in Du Bois scholarship to explain how, in the face of these beleaguered counterrevolutionary facts, Du Bois returned from his first visit to the Soviet Union in 1926 to declare, "If what I have seen with my eyes and heard with my ears in Russia is Bolshevism, I am a Bolshevik."[25] The first is experiential conversion based on eyewitness account, a tempting narrative that dovetails with scholarship about confessional testimonies by African Americans (e.g., Paul Robeson and Langston Hughes) who, like Du Bois, were struck by the sweep of Russia's change, and the reduction or absence of racial animus. The second is comparative: Du Bois returned again and again to the Soviet Union as a touchstone of contrast between failing Western capitalist democracy and socialist ideals. Third, still, is the insight as blindness narrative: Du Bois is imagined as history's dupe, transformed from a reasonable statesmen for racial uplift into a caricature of the revolutionary hack. This third perspective especially conjoins to the circle of U.S. expatriates (e.g., Smedley and Strong) who, like Du Bois, were vilified during the Cold War for their support of Stalin and Stalinism, a matter to which I return.[26]

A correct assessment of the question requires a measured encounter with all three of these interpretations and careful consideration of the full record of Du Bois's written reflection on the Soviet Union and the Russian Revolution. In totality, Du Bois's writings on Russia are a précis of his most important political thought over the critical juncture of his life between 1926 and 1961; they are the deepest political imprint of internationalist politics on his mind, the most coherent record of his uneven development as a Marxist, and the best and most thorough evidence we have of his changing conception of world revolution. They are also the single most agonizing testament to his private struggle with Stalinism and its legacy. As such, they must also be read as both intertexts and counternarratives to his shifting domestic political views around such crucial historical events as the Great Depression, the New Deal, and World War II, as well as to shifts in African American economic life during these years. A primary argument in my analysis of Du Bois's Soviet writings is that they attempt to translate the Soviet revolution and Soviet communism into a workable hermeneutic for black self-activity and self-determination up through and including the years of World War II. The lingering appeal of the Lenin/Stalin thesis on self-determination, as well as Soviet support for autonomous national cultures, I argue, remained the ideas with the greatest determining pull on Du Bois's sympathetic expropriation of the Russian Revolution; they ultimately enabled his rereading of nineteenth-century Reconstruction through the revolution, and in dialectical reverse. They also help explain how, by the time the Pan-African Congress took place in Manchester in 1945, Du Bois had become overcommitted to a Stalinist conception of how African Americans (and Pan-Africa) should advance politically in the postwar world.

———

Levering Lewis has written that Du Bois returned from his two-month visit to the Soviet Union in 1926 "breathing anticapitalist fire."[27] Abroad, he landed first in Kronstadt in the late summer, traveling mostly with a single Russian-speaking friend, notebook in hand, where he was to write, "Here was a people seeking a new way of life through learning and truth."[28] He traveled by rail from Kronstadt to Moscow, where he spent a month and may have met Karl Radek, and afterward to Nizhni Novgorod, Kiev, and Odessa. Radek looms large in the explanation of Du Bois's emergent evaluation of Stalin and Stalinism. A founder of the German Communist Party, secretary to the Comintern after his entry into the Soviet Union in 1919, and, after 1924, a member of the opposition to Stalin, Radek was a touchstone for Du Bois's understanding of the revolution until at least 1940. Radek initially backed Trotsky in his battle for power with Stalin, publishing the article "Leon Trotsky: Organizer of Victory" in 1923 after Lenin's stroke. In 1927, Radek was expelled from the party, only to return to Stalin's good graces in 1929 after signing a statement of reconciliation. In 1936, preparing for his second Soviet and Asian trip, Du Bois wrote to Radek, hoping to arrange a meeting with him in the Soviet Union. By the time Du Bois arrived, Radek was under accusation of counter-revolution again and eventually accused of treason as part of the Great Purges. Du Bois wrote little about the purges themselves, even after his visit in 1936. In February 1940, reflecting on the state of the revolution, Du Bois wrote, "I never considered the Russians even after the Revolution as supermen. I expected them to stagger on in blood and tears toward their magnificent goal with many a stumble and retreat. I love the victim Radek more than the tyrant Stalin; but back of them all is the vast might of the Russian people."[29] Those people, Du Bois wrote, "have exercised out of a sodden, ignorant and enslaved mass of people, extraordinary leaders and thinkers. For me this is not all but it is enough. I care not if in the face of this accomplishment, they have murdered, suppressed thought and made ruthless war. With all they have accomplished more than that they have destroyed"—-a judgment about the Soviet vox populi and mechanics of revolution that we have reason to revisit in our consideration of "Russia and America."[30]

Du Bois published his initial reports of his 1926 expedition in two pieces: "Russia, 1926" for *The Crisis* and, shortly thereafter, "I Am a Bolshevik." He would republish both pieces, plus supplementary writing, in the unpublished "Russia and America: An Interpretation." Yet if Du Bois was "breathing anticapitalist fire" on his return from Russia, his first impressions were icily vivid: Russia, he wrote in his first account, was not a "picture of happiness and success":

> There was stark poverty. I remember the hordes of incredibly dirty, ragged and wild children of war and famine who were hiding in the sewers and stealing like beasts through the streets at dusk. I remember the long lines of ragged people, waiting to buy a loaf of bread. . . . A poor land, but a land of enthusiasm and one which to my astonishment had not emerged from war in 1918, on Armistice Day, but was beginning just in 1926 to breathe air free from Civil War and invasion, promoted and participated in by my own nation.[31]

Du Bois's chiaroscurist account belies, for starters, caricatured criticism of his visit and reportage as Panglossian accounts of the revolution. In fact, the opening pages of the narrative oscillate between protestations of ignorance that seem to reveal ominous details they mask—"I know nothing of political prisoners, secret police and underground government"[32]—and elegies for the toll of centuries of feudal decline, revolution, civil war, and economic catastrophe. Kronstadt is described as a "ghost city of a dead Empire," while a stroll past the Winter Palace elicits a description limned with reactionary nostalgia: "It loomed red-brown and the statues and chimneys above it were as ghosts. It must have been a brilliant and wonderful city in the day of Czars for those who could enjoy it."[33] Yet immediately, as if in color counterpoint, Du Bois draws attention to the conditions of differently lived ethnic nationals in the new Russia, what he calls the "faces of its races—Russians, Ukrainians, Jews, Tartars, Gypsies, Caucasians, Armenians and Chinese."[34] He describes seventy-two nationalities attending the Communist University for Eastern Peoples and three hundred to four hundred students at the Chinese University in Moscow, sixty of them women. In the theater, he sees a production of Vsevolod Meyerhold's "Hail China!" (a play that commemorates workers' uprisings in Shanghai that year, to which, in factual detail, Du Bois seems oblivious). Du Bois then sets out what appears to be almost an archetypal account of racial tolerance that momentarily passes as the greatest achievement of the great Soviet experiment: "Russia seems to me the only modern country where people are not more or less taught and encouraged to despise and look down on some group or race. I know countries where race and color prejudice show only slight manifestations but no country where race and color prejudice seems so absolutely absent. In Paris, I attracted some attention; in London I meet elaborate blankness; anywhere in America I would get anything from curiosity to insult. In Moscow, I pass unheeded."[35]

This essentially sentimental passage is largely abstracted from specific comment on the "faces of races" Du Bois enumerates elsewhere and is meant to incite the American reader to understand the difference Russia makes to his or her own racial biography. It merely intimates a socialist response to the liberal American dilemma and does not take us very far in understanding Du Bois's lifelong commitment to the Russian Revolution. *That* insight comes elsewhere in "Russia and America" in a visit to the State Printing Office, where workers are printing books in "one hundred or more languages."[36] The printing office has an attached school with a "hundred apprentices—Jewish, Chinese, Tartar, Arabic—a dozen more people, boys and girls." The students are sent by trade unions at public expense. As they work, "school books, new alphabets, cards, placards, all sorts of things in black and white [are] scattered about." Du Bois then describes the collective tower of meaning they seek to build: "They are fixing and comparing letters of the alphabets by all sorts of devices. They have German, English and American equipment, but German is cheapest and English and German firms give credit terms. They spend 250,000 rubles a month on the work. They spent 500,000 rubles on equipment last year and will spend 400,000 next. They set type here, print, out and bind, photograph and make plates, repair and build machines. It is a little nation of nations, working happily together."[37]

Here for a rare time in his writing (we shall see another in his writing on India), Du Bois reveals the explicit influence of Lenin's thesis on national self-determination in forging his sympathy for Soviet proletarianism. Lenin's "The Right of Nations to Self-Determination" (1914) would become the basis for the Communist International's 1919 program in support of anticolonial struggle and of autonomous succession for Russian ethnic minorities. Lenin's key insight, and a departure from his contemporaries Kautsky, Luxemburg, and Bauer, was that national self-determination, the right to secede from what he called the "Greater Russia nation," was an essential step in building proletarian internationalism. As Lenin put it:

> The proletariat, of Russia is faced with a twofold or, rather, a two-sided task: to combat nationalism of every kind, above all, Great-Russian nationalism; to recognise, not only fully equal rights, for all nations in general, but also equality of rights as regards polity, i.e., the right of nations to self-determination, to secession. And at the same time, it is their task, in the interests of a successful struggle against all and every kind, of nationalism among all nations, to preserve the unity of the

proletarian struggle and the proletarian organisations, amalgamating these organisations into a close-knit international association, despite bourgeois strivings for national exclusiveness.

Complete equality of rights for all nations; the right of nations to self-determination; the unity of the workers of all nations—such is the national programme that Marxism, the experience of the whole world, and the experience of Russia, teach the workers.[38]

In his description of the print shop, Du Bois presents ethnic autonomy and interdependence as the basis of proletarian harmony and workers' productivity. The "totality" of the revolution is best expressed by its collective parts working independently but together. Yet the "nation of nations" trope, more than just an idyllic interpretation of Soviet harmony and support for anticolonial movements, was also to become Du Bois's primary mediating expression of the relationship between African Americans and the Comintern's world-revolutionary scheme. The first indication of its special valence in his political imagining was the book he ran to write immediately upon his return from Russia: the fictional romance *Dark Princess*. The book is Du Bois's Comintern novel, a conceptual meditation of the Soviet experiment in the politics of national self-determination as the gateway to world revolution. The brief account of his trip to Russia in 1926 recounted here helps sets the stage for the book: an African American medical student (and proletarian), Matthew Town, is thrust into the making of global revolution when he encounters an aristocratic Indian Princess, Kautilya, in Berlin, where both are in exile. The novel introduces Matthew to an international constellation of anti-imperialist anticolonial elites under the leadership of the princess, who has recently returned from Moscow "breathing anticapitalist fire." Kautilya is the novel's Leninist avatar of self-determination, "inoculated with Bolshevism of a mild but dangerous type" who imagines independent anticolonial upsurge as the key to capitalism's demise.[39] The novel's epic and archetypal tableau brings together world revolutionaries who index at once the KUTVU, or University of Toilers of the East in the Soviet Union (Chinese, Tartar, Arabic) referenced by Du Bois during his visit, and the student body at the Moscow printing office seeking to produce from the helter-skelter of materials that constitute the nation—language, culture, history—an edifice of freedom for the "darker worlds." For example, early in the story, a global cadre of Egyptians, Indians, Chinese, and Arabs meets over dinner. Princess Kautilya articulates their mission that "Pan-Africa belongs logically with Pan-Asia," but it is she alone among the group who recognizes the special urgency of Matthew's (and African Americans') representation in the movement.[40] "Some of us think these former slaves unready for cooperation," says Kautilya, "but I just returned from Moscow last week. At our last dinner I was telling of a report I read there that astounded me and gave me great pleasure—for I almost alone have insisted that your group was worthy of cooperation."[41] The "report" in reference is likely Claude McKay's speech to the Comintern in 1922, published in the Soviet Union as "Negro v. Ameriki," in which the Caribbean poet argued for the special and distinct nature of black experience of oppression and its potential contribution to the Comintern's world revolution. It was, in fact, McKay's report back to Du Bois from Moscow in 1922 that began to entice Du Bois's deeper interest in matters Soviet. In December 1923, McKay published the essay "Soviet Russia and the Negro" in *The Crisis* in which he argued that "the Negro, as the most suppressed and persecuted minority, should use this period of ferment in international affairs to lift his cause out of his national obscurity and force it forward as a prime international issue."[42] By 1928, McKay, along with Harry Haywood, would provide the substantive arguments for the Soviets' Black Belt thesis of 1928 describing African Americans as an oppressed "nation within the nation." In *Dark Princess*, initially, the princess's enthusiasm for a black vanguard in the United States compels her to want to use Matthew as a political emissary to a "widespread and carefully planned uprising of the American blacks" that includes carrying a letter and money to help them buy explosives or arms. Members of the anticolonial cadre see the plot as giving "dynamite to children" and threaten Matthew against taking part in it.[43]

Du Bois here conflates several moments of Comintern politics and high drama. The princess is a metaphorical stand-in for the so-called Berlin Committee of Indian (mainly Bengali) nationals in exile there during and after the World War I period seeking to use the city as a hub for "treason" against British rule, including using raised funds to purchase arms. Her attraction to modes of "revolutionary terrorism" indirectly references armed struggles, bombings, and assassinations that had the putative, and sometimes even financial, support of nationalist exiles. One of those was Virendranath Chattopadhyaya, a figure who would have been well known to Du Bois through his relationships to Agnes Smedley and Lajpat Rai, his mentee on the Indian anticolonization struggle and who since 1919 had been directly lobbying Comintern officials to support Indian self-determination (as I discuss further in Chapter 3). Rai had already passed through his own period of nationalist ferment and pro-Bolshevism, while Chattopadhyaya was a founder of the Berlin Committee in 1915, which sought to provide arms to rebels back home. Indeed, a notorious case on which Du Bois may have based the plot for *Dark Princess* was the Kokoris conspiracy of 1925, in which members of the Hindustan Republican Association attempted to rob a train on the Northern Railway lines to raise funds to overthrow British rule. German-made Mauser pistols were used in the robbery, which resulted in the death of one passenger, numerous arrests, and a notorious trial and execution by hanging of four participants. Du Bois thus provides in the princess's early enthusiasm for "revolutionary terrorism" in black America his own trope of metonymic nationalism traversing, like railway lines, the diasporic international. Town, in this instance, meanwhile is most likely a stand-in for two figures: the revolutionary communist Harry Haywood, recruited into the Communist Party after his stint as a train porter in Chicago, a road that took him directly to Moscow and participation in the Comintern, and Agnes Smedley.[44] Smedley was indicted for "treason" in New York in 1919 for contributing material support to the Indian home rule movement in the United States. (Smedley's trial would have been well known to Du Bois. So would her reprising of that role in 1920 with her lover, Chattopadhyaya, in Berlin, from where she corresponded with Du Bois.) Like Matthew Town, Smedley was a willing "recruit" to Indian nationalism from the working classes. Her "romance" with Chattopadhyaya, like Matthew's with Princess Kautilya, was an entry point into diasporic radicalism. Smedley, meanwhile, would write her own Comintern novel, *Daughter of Earth*, just one year after Du Bois published *Dark Princess*, narrating in thinly veiled fictional guise her participation in the Ghadr Party, her involvement with Chattopadhyaya, and the role of political exile in building international anticolonial struggles. The novel in fact ends with its protagonist, Marie Rogers, heading into an exile that, by the time the book was published, would retrospectively include Smedley's wanderings through Berlin, Moscow, and revolutionary Shanghai. The "ending" of *Daughter of Earth*, in other words, signals the beginnings of Smedley's full-time immersion into life as a Comintern agent.[45]

The plot of Du Bois's novel, meanwhile, surges toward a full flowering of Comintern principles of national self-determination. The union of "Pan-Asia" and "Pan-Africa" initially suggested in Matthew's pairing with the princess leads dramatically and schematically toward proletarian internationalism. Toward the end of the novel, the two main characters, having passed through a separation and joint "proletarianization"—Kautilya as a box factory worker and domestic; Matthew, a la Harry Haywood, as a train porter—are reunited in the symbolic cradle of Matthew's birthplace, Virginia, where his mother, descended from slaves, resides. Du Bois crafts a remarkable passage from one of their final dialectical debates about how best to bring about world revolution. Kautilya speaks:

> You are not free in Chicago, nor New York. But here in Virginia you are at the end of a black world. The black belt of the Congo, Haiti, and

Jamaica, like a red arrow, up into the heart of white America. Thus I see a mighty synthesis: you can work in Africa and Asia right here in America if you work in the Black Belt. . . .

I have seen slaves ruling in Chicago and they did not do nearly as bad as princes in Russia. . . . How truly you have put it! Workers unite, men cry, while in truth always thinkers who do not work have tried to unite workers who do not think. Only working thinkers can unite thinking workers.[46]

In the Soviet print shop, Du Bois marveled at proletarian internationalism taking the form of united hands laboring to create a language and cultural tools of self-emancipation. Such a "text" is Du Bois's Comintern novel: the princess and Matthew develop a Sovietized language of human liberation—"Only working thinkers can unite thinking workers"—in the locus classicus of the Comintern's self-determination thesis: the Black Belt. The novel, as with so many of Du Bois's texts, deploys an existing typology of world revolution ("Workers unite!") in slightly modified form. *Dark Princess* is also Du Bois's Comintern novel insofar as it takes the measure of world revolution in 1928 after his Soviet excursion, transposing it back into a Pan-African schema merged to a new conception of Asia's (including Soviet Asia's) place in the new global map. In so doing, the book also foreshadows debate about application of the Soviet self-determination line to the colonies, played out through the Pan-African Congress in Manchester in 1945, as discussed in Chapter 1. Indeed, the novel ends with a harbinger of the "colonial international" brought into being in Manchester. The child delivered by Kautilya and Matthew is described as "messiah to all the darker races," and the novel's final prophecy—"The Dark World goes free in 1952"—misses the anticolonial mark at Bandung by inches while laying down a marker for Du Bois's anticipation of Third World revolutions to come. At the same time, what might be called the state form of workers' uprisings remains disarticulated in *Dark Princess*. Neither the Soviet Union nor "America" is rendered habitable as a site for the "little nations" seeking emancipation.

Thus, we can perceive both truth and limits to Mark Van Wienen's argument that the ending of *Dark Princess* indexes Du Bois's shift from "Second" to Third International politics.[47] The 1926 visit *did* indicate for Du Bois the centrality of labor power and workers' self-organizing and centered a single question that would dominate much of his work for the rest of life: "Can you make the worker and not the millionaires the center of modern power and culture?"[48] At the same time, Du Bois returned to a United States in 1926 that he described as "seething with prosperity," a general labor pool and trade union world still divided by race, and still reluctant about advocating a sequel to 1917, even if the results were now immaculately desirable: "If Russia fails, reason in industry fails. If Russia succeeds, gradually every modern state will socialize industry and the greater the Russian success, the less revolution."[49] These co-constituent questions and possibilities became the new "riddle of the sphinx" for Du Bois in his assessment of the prospects for both Soviet and world revolution. Not surprisingly, the stock market crash of 1929 and global depression that followed were catalysts that forced his reinvention as a student of Marx, Marxist theory, and the history of human emancipation struggles. It set the world revolution before him again as a topical conception in need of intellectual re-tooling. The fundamental challenge offered by his eyewitness to Russia's revolution was whether it could happen again after 1929, and if it could, what role African Americans and workers would play in it. For reasons to be enumerated here, Du Bois resolved this set of problems by revising his typology of revolution once again, seeking to confer on African Americans a revolutionary role that would seem to fill a historic destiny now opened to history by events in 1917 and by casting that role within a self-determination framework that was still dominant in theory (if not in practice) in the age of the Comintern.

As the Depression neared, Du Bois's new Russian compulsion took immediate form. On February 15, 1929, he wrote a letter to Algernon Lee, chairman of the New York State Socialist Party, urging him to air publicly the Socialist Party's acceptance of racially segregated union locals in the South and to take up resolutions on the special problem of racism in the labor movement that Du Bois knew had been written (then tabled) nearly thirty years earlier. Du Bois's looking backward was a means of looking forward: "If the Negro does not embrace the doctrines of socialism," he wrote in the same letter to Lee, "his advance will increase difficulties of the labor movement."[50] The letter followed a proposal Du Bois had made just months earlier for an Interracial Labor Commission of the American Federation of Labor, NAACP, and Brotherhood of Sleeping Car Porters that never came to fruition.[51] By February 1930, six months after the stock market crashed and with conditions spiraling downward for black workers, Du Bois would write to Edward P. Clarke, "I have entirely lost faith in the American Federation of Labor and its attitude towards Negroes."[52] Meanwhile, in August of the same year, the Communist International's Negro Commission would pass its "Equal Rights and Self-Determination" resolution,[53] while the Red International Labor Union Committee of Negro Workers demanded that the U.S. Workers Party (to be renamed the Communist Party in 1929) ramp up its organizing of southern black workers, part of its new Third Period line.[54] In 1931, the Communist Party would organize more than eight hundred black farmers into the Croppers and Farm Workers Union and form the League of Struggle for Negro Rights in the South.[55]

Du Bois's steadfast skepticism about prospects for American socialism breaking through the Maginot Line of racism soon collided head on with the Communist International's commitment to smash it via the Scottsboro case. James Miller has written the best account of the political infighting between the Communist Party and legal teams of the International Labor Defense and NAACP that sought to represent the Scottsboro Boys. Du Bois's outrage that the Communist Party would use the trial "to foment revolution in the United States" was ironically of a piece with his cynicism expressed in the same-year essay "The Negro and Marxism" that southern and northern white workers would never cooperate with black labor, the conjunction coming home to roost in the use of the Russian Revolution as an example of what was *not* possible in the United States: racism was so deeply ingrained in American workers that "even when the lines of the class struggle are closely defined and the Russian experience is so definite that it does not disprove but rather strengthens my belief."[56] Indeed, Du, Bois even blamed the Soviets indirectly for Scottsboro, saying the NAACP deserved "from Russia something better than a kick in the back from the young jackasses who are leading communism in America today."[57]

Still, politically starstruck by the print shop miracle of the Soviet Union, Du Bois went burrowing more deeply for answers in Marxism, a course of self-study that included *Capital*, the *Manifesto*, and most likely *The German Ideology* and the *Eighteenth Brumaire*. With the help of his friend Abram Harris, Du Bois developed a collection of Marxist writings and included in his circle of friends Marxists such as Will Herberg, a disciple of Jay Lovestone, and Benjamin Stolberg. In early 1932, his readings became syllabus fodder for new lectures at Atlanta University titled "Imperialism in the Sudan, 1400 to 1700" and "The Economic Future of Black America" and the courses "Karl Marx and the Negro" and "Economic History of the Negro."[58] In 1933, he announced intention to publish twelve articles on monthly topics for *The Crisis* to be a "rapprochement between black America and socialism" with featured articles on work and income, with several planned: "The 'Class Struggle of the Black Proletariat and Bourgeoisie,' Punishment, Charity and the Black Proletariat," and "The Dictatorship of the Black Proletariat."[59] The articles were intended to answer two questions posed by Du Bois in his 1926 report on the Soviet Union: "Visioning now a real Dictatorship of the Proletariat . . . [i]s it possible today for a great nation to achieve such a worker's psychology? And secondly, if it does achieve it, what will be its effect upon the world?"[60]

Du Bois answered both questions with a headstrong new schematic program—cooperative black economics—recognizable as an answer to those questions only within the framework of his Russian analysis and experience. His call for black control of "producers' cooperation" of goods, black consumerism of black production, and "increased economic independence" for African Americans was, on one hand, a rejection of U.S. capitalism, but more significantly, on the other, an application of the Soviet doctrine of national self-determination for ethnic minorities at the U.S. national level.[61] Indeed, Van Wienen has described Du Bois's plans for cooperative economics as a "strategy of self-directed social democracy for black America, and by extension for people of color throughout the world."[62] He notes that Du Bois's editorial "Segregation" (1934), in which he chides mainly black readers (and the NAACP) for their sneering dismissal of the concept, echoes Joseph Prokopec's articles in the 1930 for the communist U.S. journal *Negroes as an Oppressed National Minority*.[63] These loose applications of Soviet influence are amplified in Du Bois's theory and practice of cooperative black economics between 1933 and 1936. They reveal Du Bois struggling to reconcile contradictions in his own thought specific to U.S. race and labor conditions, ultimately incorporating a version of the national self-determination thesis as a means of transcending national parameters themselves. The tactic is an example of what Barbara Foley again calls metonymic nationalism, perceiving a single oppressed national minority—or a portion of it—as an index to the global "whole."

For example, in his first issue of *The Crisis* featuring his new research on "black America and socialism," Du Bois notes increasing gaps in black social wealth and asks, "Can this class-building technique of civilization be ignored in our case and something better substituted?"[64] The essay was nearly contemporary with Du Bois's public jettisoning of his own "Talented Tenth" thesis elsewhere, which he argued was leaving "the black laborer poor, ignorant and leaderless save for an occasional demagogue."[65] His essay "Marxism and the Negro Problem" (1933) endeavored to excavate this problem further. In it, Du Bois argues that racism remains the single barrier to class unity in the United States. "Colored labor has no common ground with labor," he writes, and "this black proletariat is not part of the white proletariat."[66] Du Bois goes as far in the essay as to assign the white working class (not the ruling class) the role of primary oppressor of black labor: "The lowest and most fatal degree of [their] suffering comes not from capitalists but from fellow white workers."[67] Du Bois here traffics in an aspect of self-determination discourse that is supremely contentious in the Marxist tradition, assigning white workers a role in the "labor aristocracy" that privileges their position over that of nonwhite (and Third World) workers of the world. The labor aristocracy was what Lenin referred to in "Imperialism the Highest Stage of Capitalism" as a "layer" of the global proletariat that sided with capital over the working class because of its privileged position within it and referred in particular to the European working class that thus might be coopted against struggles for colonial self-determination. Du Bois's embrace of the "labor aristocracy" view of the white working class here is an index to the essentially internationalist framework for thinking through black economic cooperatives. That is, his metonymic nationalism perceives independent black economic activity as a resistance to "white nationalism" in the U.S. context and hence as a *form* of proletarian internationalism. That Du Bois is conceiving economic cooperatives in relationship to "national self-determination" is also evident in his invocation of communal movements and sources on which his is modeled: the Jewish kibbutz, Indian *swadeshi*, and what he called later in *The World and Africa* African "primitive communism"—that is, non-exploitative social and economic relations that are noncapitalist or precapitalist in nature. Indeed, in an essay for the *Pittsburgh Courier* in 1937, Du Bois listed cooperative movements in Estonia, Latvia, Portugal, Mexico, Japan, China, Palestine, and India as means of raising living standards and national autonomous movements through "the equitable distribution of wealth."[68] He even cited the Bolshevik consolidation under government control of a growing cooperative economics movement in 1919 as an important potential "transitional" program that might yet bring about a yet unfulfilled "classless Russian state."[69]

Yet because Du Bois's cooperative economics totally abandoned Marxist categories such as surplus value, labor exploitation, and—important for Abram Harris and other contemporaries—Marx's argument that "white workers may not be free while wherein the Black is branded," his plans for economic cooperatives were subject to heavy criticism—especially from the left, not to mention from his NAACP colleagues, who saw his scheme as antiintegrationist and apocalyptic about working-class unity. Few comprehended that the program was part of a continuing move from Du Bois in the direction of new conception of world revolution, no matter what violence Stalinism was doing to its fundamental tenets. Though he claimed in 1934 that "no [American] Soviet of technocrats would do more than exploit colored labor in order to raise the status of whites,"[70] he continued to advocate for economic cooperatives as a global solution for nonwhite workers of the world: "Colored peoples *of the world*, and first of all those of Negro descent, should begin to concentrate upon this problem of economic survival," he wrote. "What can we do? We can work for ourselves. We can consume mainly what we ourselves produce, and produce as large as proportion as possible of that which we consume."[71]

Significant to his long-term thought, one of the sharpest contemporary critics of Du Bois's economic cooperative program was also one of the few figures to underscore his incomplete interpretation of the Leninist self-determination thesis. George Streator was an organizer with the Amalgamated Clothing Workers whom Du Bois had brought onto the staff of *The Crisis* at the end of 1933. In 1925, Streator had helped organize a student strike at Fisk

University, where he earned his bachelor's degree, and prior to joining *The Crisis* staff had worked as an organizer in New York City for the Amalgamated Clothing Workers. In 1934, he had seen Du Bois deliver a paper on economic cooperatives titled "A Pragmatic Program for a Dark Minority" at the Problems, Programs, and Philosophies of Minority Groups Conference. The "dark minority" of Du Bois's title was a nod to the "darker races" designation used in internationalist rhetoric in the post-1919 period. In an exchange of letters in 1935, Streator, with increasing vigor, criticized Du Bois's program for black economic cooperatives partly because of its racial veiling—"There is no such thing as a Negro loving his race in the matter of capital and investment."[72] But more significant, he criticized the program for its misreading of Lenin. Streator argued that Du Bois was stopping short at national self-determination as a step toward proletarian internationalism achieved through *class struggle.* "I was particularly chagrined at your complete turning to the notion that a minority group can save itself," he wrote. "If so, why does not the majority group of Chinese save themselves from the minority Japs? [*sic*] Or the minority English? . . . [N]o one group can pull apart from world economy, no matter how spiritual and how resolved."[73] In his response, dated April 24, 1935, Du Bois reiterated both his confidence in Marxism as method and his doubts about the symmetry of objective conditions between Russia and the United States, saying that while revolution may have been necessary in the former, "I do not think it is true in the United States in 1935." At the same time, Du Bois professed, "I regard Russia as the most promising modern country" and described his primary task, once he had left the NAACP, as assembling a "growing group of young, trained, fearless and unselfish Negroes to guide the American Negro in this crisis, and guide him toward the coming of socialism throughout the world."[74] Streator's reply dated five days later was terse, but, I argue, lasting: "As I get your program: Socialism is coming. We will work for it separately. We will work for a socialist Negro to be handed over to the movement when fully developed."[75]

The exchange of letters with Streator discloses both the narrowness—literally, provincialism—of Du Bois's economic cooperative conception and its skewed relationship to both Soviet Russia and its germinal self-determination thesis. Reading the letters also helps one to understand in proper historical and political context three seminal essays by Du Bois on cooperative economics that serve as an entrée to and, eventually, an exit from this phase of this thought: "The Negro and Communism" (1931), "A Nation within a Nation" (1935), and "Basic American Negro Creed" (1936). "The Negro and Communism," as I have noted, enumerated Du Bois's dire pessimism about the possibility of white workers' dropping their racist guard and joining in interracial class struggle. Yet throughout the essay, socialism and communism are negative foils for Du Bois's self-determination argument. The Negro is left "sympathetic with Russia and hopeful for its ultimate success in establishing a Socialistic state" but, in the meantime, forced to take matters into his own hands.[76] The author acknowledges that capitalism has failed; cooperative economics is Du Boisian "socialism" to the rescue:

> Present organization of industry for private profit and control of government is doomed to disaster. It must change and fall if civilization survives. The foundation of its present world-wide power is the slavery and semi-slavery of the colored word including the American Negroes. Until the colored man, yellow, red, brown, and Black, becomes free, articulate, intelligent and the receiver of a decent income, white capital will use the profit derived from his degradation to keep white labor in chains.[77]

Du Bois here shows the ceiling of his cooperative economic conception as a successful strike against racism while leaving capitalist relations fundamentally intact. It also shows him struggling to conceive an *international* program for economic cooperation. It was into the breach of this ambition he waded again on June 26, 1934, delivering the conspicuously titled "A Negro Nation within the Nation" as his departing address to the NAACP. The speech is popularly read as Du Bois's break with the organization over the question of integration. I argue, instead, that it signaled again his endeavor to apply a Third International self-determination perspective to the Negro problem. In the speech, Du Bois applies the logic of metonymic nationalism to schematize his provisional Marxism. Noting that the voting, consumer, and labor power of the American Negro "probably equals that of Mexico or Yugoslavia" and per capita wealth "about equals that of Japan,"[78] Du Bois argued that "separate Negro sections will increase race antagonism, but they will also increase economic cooperation, organized self-defense and necessary self-confidence."[79] "When all these things are taken into consideration," Du Bois wrote, "it becomes clearer and clearer to more and more American Negroes that, through voluntary and increased segregation, by careful autonomy and planned economic organization, they may build so strong and efficient a unit that twelve million men can no longer be refused fellowship and equality in the United States."[80] The result, Du Bois concludes, will be a nonviolent revolution in the United States:

> With the use of their political power, their power as consumers, and their brainpower . . . Negroes can develop in the United States an economic nation within a nation, able to work through inner coopera-

tion, to found its own institutions, to educate its genius, and at the same time without mob violence or extremes of race hatred, to keep in helpful touch and cooperate with the mass of the nation. *This has happened more often than most people realize, in the case of groups not so obviously separated from the mass of people as are American Negroes.* It must happen in our case, or there is no hope for the Negro in America.[81]

Du Bois's conception of a "consumerist" socialism is strikingly devoid of both the work and workers whose labor enables consumption at all. Its faith in cooperative economics transcribes optimism about the Soviet experiment and self-determination into a volunteerist politics largely more dependent on "cooperation" than class struggle. Yet by 1936, in the wake of his exchange with Streator and having completed his massive study of U.S. slavery, labor history, and the Civil War, Du Bois showed evidence of what his ongoing reeducation in Marxism both compelled and foretold. On June 20, 1936, what Du Bois called his "creed for American Negroes" today was published in the *Pittsburgh Courier*. The creed enumerated, in the style of an eleven-point manifesto or internal party bulletin, a number of assertions about the centrality of the black working class. It urged black workers to join the labor movement and argued, "We believe that Workers' Councils organized by Negroes for interracial understanding should strive to fight race prejudice in the working class." It also argued, "We believe in the ultimate triumph of some form of Socialism the world over; that is, common ownership and control of the means of production and equality of income." The creed was later republished, in a slightly revised version, as part of the final chapter (titled "Revolution") in *Dusk of Dawn: An Essay toward an Autobiography of a Race Concept*.[82] The creed's invocation of black "soviets" (worker's councils)—the Bolshevik heart of the 1905 and the 1917 revolution, of Chinese industrial strikes of 1926 and 1927, and of Spanish workers in the 1936 uprisings he cited in *Black Reconstruction in America*—added for the first time what might be called "labor value" to Du Bois's primarily consumerist cooperative model. It was also the first time in this period that Du Bois invoked "control of the means of production" as an objective of black economic self-activity. The creed thus constituted a significant and self-conscious refinement of what he called in his letter to Streator "a realistic approach to a democratic state in which the exploitation of labor is stopped, and the political power is in the hands of the workers."[83]

Du Bois's experimental yet methodical attempts here to "internationalize" and proletarianize his conception of black economic cooperatives, even in outline, is important to understanding the revolutionizing turn of his thought in the "midnight hour" of both a global Great Depression, and the specter of capitalist alternatives from which he was taking his cues. Levering Lewis's dismissal of Du Bois's cooperative economics musings of this period as merely "black nationalist nostrums" can now give way again to Van Wienen's more astute and nuanced reading of Du Bois's "strategy of self-directed social democracy for black America, and by extension for people of color throughout the world."[84] Indeed, between "The Negro and Communism," "A Negro Nation within a Nation," and "Basic American Negro Creed" (1936), Du Bois sketched out horizons and limits of a vernacular theory of world revolution. Russia and the Comintern incubated these dreams; Lenin and Stalin watered them; the Soviet print shop's "nations within nations" working in proletarian harmony and the lives of American Negroes were the dialectical coordinates of this new typology of world revolution. These coordinates were also influential to Du Bois's thinking as he wrapped up work on his next idiosyncratic manifesto, *Black Reconstruction in America.*

> As the Negro laborers organized separately, there came slowly to realization the fact that here was not only separate organization but a separation in leading ideas, because among Negroes, and particularly in the South, there was being put into force one of the most extraordinary experiments of Marxism that the world, before the Russian revolution, had seen.
>
> —W.E.B. Du Bois, *Black Reconstruction in America*

Black Reconstruction in America is a book that posits historical materialism as an elastic, emancipatory, and superior tool to bourgeois historiography. It intends to do for U.S. history what *The Communist Manifesto* did for world history: interpret its hidden or secret transcript of class struggle. In this regard, it is a prehistory, or retelling of U.S. historiography itself, relishing anachronism as a sign of exclusion. For example, the book reinterprets the Civil War by ascribing agency to African Americans, for whom, in the master historical narrative of that event, agency did not manifest. The book describes workers' self-activity in the American South of the 1850s in categorical terms—"general strike"—that would not have been used contemporaneously. Du Bois sought to name Reconstruction a "proletarian dictatorship" in the post–Civil War period, even though, as the Trotskyist journalist Benjamin Stolberg, his consultant to the book, pointed out, "Socialist conceptions did not exist" in the United States in 1863.[85] When the book was published, Du Bois's friend Abram Harris called it "the most completely fantastic attempt at applying Marxian dogma to history," mainly because it referred to Reconstruction as an American "revolution" when it fact it was not one.[86] Du Bois himself intimated that history had been both reversed and leaped over in the time of Reconstruction: the self-organizing of black and white workers was an "experiment of Marxism" prior to their consciousness of Marxist ideas or the Russian revolution itself.

Legitimating this string of irreconcilabilities is a single unifying anachronistic subtext to *Black Reconstruction in America*: it *is* Du Bois's book about the Russian Revolution. It is to this fact that Cedric Robinson, one of the most astute readers of Du Bois's book, points in his ambitious study *Black Marxism*. The "processes of the Russian Revolution," Robinson writes, "were a framework for this interpretation of Reconstruction because it, too, had begun among an agrarian, peasant people. It was a characteristic shared by all the revolutions that Du Bois linked in significance to the American Civil War and its Reconstruction: that is, France, Spain, India, and China."[87] Robinson here renders his own "typology" of Du Boisian revolution to argue that *Black Reconstruction in America* reversed history primarily by ascribing an originary revolutionary consciousness to African American (and white) workers to extend Marxist conceptions of revolutionary vanguards from industrial proletariats to the black peasantry. Building on Robinson's insight, I argue here that *Black Reconstruction in America* seeks to conceive an originary narrative of world revolution from the ashes of American history. *Black Reconstruction in America*, I argue, is best understood as Du Bois's historic and historical companion to his "Comintern novel" *Dark Princess*, published seven years earlier, and his manuscript "Russia and America," published fifteen years after. The three works in combination express Du Bois's titanic effort to wrest from the Russian Revolution and its aftermath a conception of world revolution that both deviates from the "template" of a Soviet (and, by implication, Stalinist) original by reinterpreting it as a part of a typology of world revolution in which nonwhite actors play the leading role. In this, *Black Reconstruction in America* is perhaps Du Bois's single most extended consideration of the Leninist and Stalinist self-determination thesis retrofitted to history, so that history may in turn change course even with, and because of, "after the fact" events.

Significantly, Du Bois announces the political and temporal theme of *Black Reconstruction in America* not in the beginning but at the end of his study. The retrospective inversion of statement mirrors the theme of backward glance. "The unending tragedy of Reconstruction," he writes, "is the utter inability of the American mind to grasp its real significance. . . . We are still too blind and infatuated to conceive of the emancipation of the laboring class in half the nation as a revolution comparable to the upheavals in France in

the past, and in Russia, Spain, India and China today."[88] Du Bois here argues
that the beginning and potential "end" of capitalist history, past and present,
coexist in the moment of *Black Reconstruction in America* as event and as text.
The book is a dialectical expression of history remade by historical events,
or what Marxists call "objective conditions." The historiographical challenge
of rewriting capitalist history discussed in "The Forethought"—the so-called
"Propaganda of History"—is resolved once a method of writing history itself
is disclosed. That method in *Black Reconstruction in America* was historical
materialism, its first deployment in Du Bois's career.

A primary source or template of that method is one that few scholars have
noted: Herman Schlüter's *Lincoln, Labor and Slavery: A Chapter from the
Social History of America*, first published in 1913. Schlüter was a German-
born immigrant to the United States won to socialism in Chicago as a laborer
in 1872. His books include a history of the beginnings of the German labor
movement in the United States and the Chartist movement in England, both
in German; a study of production and labor conditions in the U.S. brewery
industry, his first book in English; and a study of the U.S. Civil War, also
in English.[89] In "The Price of Disaster," chapter 9 of *Black Reconstruction in
America*, Du Bois cites Schlüter's book as the source of two letters written
under Karl Marx during the Civil War: one from the General Council of the
International Workingmen's Association (IWA) to Andrew Johnson, and the
second to the president of the National Labor Union. Both were written after
the assassination of Lincoln, the former an appeal to carry through the "new
era of the emancipation of labor," and the latter documenting the effects of
the war on prices, with a caution to avoid future wars that "would forge chains
for the free workingmen instead of surrendering those of the slaves."[90] But it
is less the citational than the methodological imprint of Schlüter's study on
Du Bois that is important. In his preface, Schlüter describes his perspective
on the Civil War as "historical materialist," adding, "The writer of this work
takes the position of the most advanced section of the labor movement."[91] The
text proper attributes the impetus for abolition in part to "antagonistic interests between ruling classes of American society, between the manufacturers
of the North and the planters of the South." More important, it emphasizes
the role of industrial workers in the U.S. North—and in London, where Marx
was stationed among the IWA—in resisting slavery in the name of workers'
rights. Schlüter, for example, cites the resolution passed at the convention of
New England workingmen in January 1846 that declared, "We will not take
up arms to sustain the Southern slaveholders robbing one-fifth of their coun-
trymen of their labor," as well as opposition among the Chartists and the IWA
to slavery as expressed in letters and resolutions. Schlüter underscores in his
study one central theme: that whereas the U.S. war of independence "initiated

a new era of ascendancy for the middle class"—the "bourgeois revolution"—
"so the American Anti-Slavery War will do for the working classes."[92]

In the latter instance, Schlüter, it might be said, introduced into historiography of the Civil War the preoccupying questions in Marxism and historical materialism: what are the conditions that give rise to a proletarian revolution, and how is that revolution to be executed? More important still, by writing from the perspective of the "most advanced" section of the working class, Schlüter implicitly centered the question of who *makes* a revolution. These are the central preoccupations of *Black Reconstruction in America*. Yet where Du Bois deviates from Schlüter is most obviously in the question of revolutionary agency. Schlüter follows what might be called standard Marxist historiography in examining the role of the industrial working class. Du Bois, more capaciously, conceives the "rebelling class" in *Black Reconstruction in America* as the maligned, thwarted, and repressed interracial U.S. working class, slaves and peasantry. As Cedric Robinson notes, Du Bois's famous description of the "general strike" that led to emancipation and war includes not just 200,000 fugitive slaves withholding their labor by fleeing the plantation, or joining the Union army, but thousands of poor whites who joined them in abandoning the plantation system. Robinson's citation of this aspect of *Black Reconstruction in America* is worth quoting at length:

> In the midst of the Civil War, it was these two peoples, the Black and white workers, who had mounted the rebellions, the "General Strike," which had turned loose the revolutionary dynamics that Du Bois would describe as 'the most extraordinary experiments of Marxism that the world, before the Russian revolution, had seen.' . . . One hundred thousand poor whites had abandoned the plantations. It was the same pattern, indeed, that would come to fruition in Russia. Like the American slaves and the poor whites, in the midst of war the Russian peasantry would desert their armies in the field. Their rebellion, too, marked the beginnings of revolution.[93]

Robinson's is an atypical reading of *Black Reconstruction in America* that foregrounds several aspects critical to this study. First, Robinson perceives the book as Du Bois's study in the typology of revolution heavily influenced by his interpretation of the Russian Revolution. Indeed, Robinson helps confirm my argument that Du Bois embraces anachronism and simultaneity in the study—that 1863 and 1917 are instantiations of historical dialectics. *Black Reconstruction in America* was Du Bois's experimental deviation from the self-determination thesis of the Comintern—the "nation within the nation" formulation—under pressure of the historical example of interracial working-class unity discovered fleetingly during the American Civil War. The book's emphasis on the potential (and centrality) of interracial collaboration in the American South was in fact the touchstone for a new *metonymic internationalism* in Du Bois's thought and work. This conception bookends the book. Chapter 1, "The Black Worker," describes the eponymous laborer as the "founding stone of a new economic system in the nineteenth century and for the modern world, who brought war in America. He was its underlying cause, in spite of every effort to base the strife upon union and national power."[94] Du Bois here casts the international slave trade as locus classicus of the modern labor system, the "pivot" as Marx described it of modern capital. "Black" American labor thus becomes metonymic of colonial exploitation— "That dark and vast sea of human labor in China and India, the South Seas and all Africa . . . that great majority of mankind, on whose bent and broken backs rest today the founding stones of modern industry" and that undergirds the "resultant wealth" and "resultant world power" of the advanced capitalist world.[95] Du Bois here lays out in 1935 what would become lineament arguments for the Manchester conference—"Colonies of the World, Unite!"—and the subsequent Third World. Yet significantly, Du Bois pulls back from a gestural reading of a "labor aristocracy" benefiting from dark exploitation and oppression to a brand new, revisionist typology of one of Marxism's most esteemed tenets: "Here is the real modern labor problem. Here is the kernel of the problem of Religion and Democracy, of Humanity. Words and futile gestures avail nothing. Out of the exploitation of the dark proletariat comes the Surplus Value filched from human beasts which, in cultured lands, the Machine and harnessed Power veil and conceal. The emancipation of labor is the freeing of that basic majority of workers who are yellow, brown and black."[96]

In this passage, Du Bois reverses the primacy but not the premise of Marx's famous conception, "White skin labor will not be free wherein the black it is branded." That rallying cry for IWA support for the end of slavery imagined the industrial working class as the historical engine of world revolution. Here, Du Bois invokes the "dark sea," or rising tide of colored labor, as the agentive angel of history itself. Once stirred, it will pull forward the train of white labor toward self-emancipation. As in Du Bois's conception of the "general strike," white workers are to be minority members, but essential members nonetheless, in this process. In conceiving this formula, Du Bois imagines not only the black worker throwing off the "mental provincialism" of exploitation and oppression but also world revolution as the transcending of "union and national power." Writ large, this is Du Bois's own transcendent reconception of his "nation within the nation" argument from his 1926 visit to the Soviet Union: national consciousness here *does* overcome itself as class consciousness en route to proletarian revolution. This is the real meaning of Du Bois's complaint that the tragedy of Reconstruction is the American mind's inability to grasp its significance and his retrospective, retroactive comparison of Reconstruction to ongoing revolutions in other nations. Each of these iterations of national liberation struggles connotes a chain of equivalence that resolves the tensions of metonymic nationalism and metonymic internationalism into a braided, totalized whole. Robinson is again one of the few readers of *Black Reconstruction in America* to recognize this dimension of the book: "The shocks to Western imperialism, *which in the previous century had appeared to European radicals to be at the margins of the world revolution, were by the 1930s occupying center stage.* The Indian mutiny, the Boxer Rebellion, the nationalist struggles that had erupted in the Sudan, Algeria, Morocco, Somalia, Abyssinia, West and southern Africa, and carried over into the twentieth century—the "people's wars"—had achieved major historical significance in the revolutions in Mexico, China, and Russia."[97]

Here, I share Robinson's premise but differ in political conclusion. Robinson argues that Du Bois venerated *Black Reconstruction in America* mainly as an instance of "peasants and agrarian workers" as the social bases of rebellion and revolution, without the precondition of a bourgeois order or industrial proletarian leadership. He concludes that this indicates Du Bois's deviation from essential Marxist (and Leninist) analysis. "Revolutionary consciousness had formed in the process of anti-imperialist and nationalist struggles," he writes, "and the beginnings of resistance had often been initiated by ideological constructions *remote from the proletarian consciousness* that was a presumption of Marx's theory of revolution."[98] As I have argued, Du Bois instead applied retroactively the single most important theoretical breakthrough of the Communist International—national self-determination—as a necessary step toward proletarian unity. As Du Bois concluded from his analysis of Reconstruction, "The emancipation of *labor* is the freeing of that basic majority of workers who are yellow, brown and black." White workers who joined the "general strike" in *Black Reconstruction in America*, as Robinson acknowledges, were following, not resisting, the lead of self-determining fugitive slaves. Armed with the "nation within a nation thesis" in 1935, Du Bois could creatively interpret black liberation struggle of the nineteenth century as antecedent to, prototypic of, the Marxist revolution in Russia of 1917. This conclusion bears out the full meaning of Du Bois's statement, "I can interpret the Soviet Union today through my experience with two million American Negroes in the last half of the nineteenth century."[99]

These latter words, from "Russia and America," also help underscore why Du Bois wrote *Black Reconstruction in America* as a surrogate for 1917 and returned in 1950 to writing about the Russian Revolution as a sequel to Reconstruction. The spook that sat by the door of Du Bois's consciousness as he drafted *Black Reconstruction in America* was Stalinism. In "Russia and America," Du Bois wrote that he was disposed throughout the 1930s to believe "all the liberal magazines" reporting Trotsky's criticisms of Stalinism. "I found myself at the time wavering in mists of knowledge," he wrote, "and I was upset by Trotsky's exile; by the treason trials and by the repeated assurance that the whole Soviet system was on the verge of collapse."[100] In 1938, after his second visit to the Soviet Union and in the teeth of the midnight hour of emerging fascism, Du Bois would say in a convocation address at Atlanta University on the occasion of his seventieth birthday, "When now the realities of the situation were posed to men, two radical solutions were suddenly resorted to: Russian communism and fascism. They both did away with democracy, and substituted oligarchic control of government and industry of thought and action. Communism aimed at eventual democracy and even elimination of the state, but sought this by a dogmatic program, laid down ninety years ago by a great thinker, but largely invalidated by nearly a century of extraordinary social change."[101] Here, still, linger Du Bois's doubts about the application and relevance of the Soviet Union to the history of American Negroes, about the violent extremities of Soviet state bureaucracy, and his deep-seated skepticism about interracial working-class unity in the United States.

These hesitation marks also constitute in hindsight definitive coordinates of Du Bois's struggle with the legacy of Stalinism in *Black Reconstruction in America*. The book was truly both an affirmation *and* a negation of Russia, 1917; the book rewrites the Russian Revolution as both black liberatory potentiality and dream deferred. Du Bois's last-minute changes to the text—removing the title "Dictatorship of the Proletariat" from his chapter on Reconstruction in South Carolina and willfully revising the national self-determination thesis—were other marks of his oscillating understanding of and empathy for Marxism and its application via a legacy of Stalinist rule. Indeed, Du Bois's gnawing worries over the Russian Revolution's stalled capacity, repressions, and mistakes found compensation in his overdetermined relationship to his black agency thesis, a contradiction that ran aground in history of the Civil War, much as Russia had "run aground" as a verifiable worker's state by 1935. *Black Reconstruction in America* thus conjoins to C.L.R. James's *World Revolution* (1935) and Padmore's Comintern exit as markers of "world revolution betrayed" but also reborn in black Jacobinage, Manchester, and the general strike of slavery.

Du Bois's "itch" to resolve doubts and rumors about the Soviet Union, he later admitted, drove him throughout his writing of *Black Reconstruction in America*. Despite the dire reports and predictions of the U.S. liberal media, he wrote, "My former visit to the Soviets did not let me believe all I heard. I was the more eager to see the Soviet Union again, and, also, to see the world—this side and beyond it."[102] Thus, immediately after completing the manuscript, Du Bois set out for Germany, his first stop intended to lead him back to the Soviet Union. The visit culminated fourteen years later in the completion of the unpublished "Russia and America: An Interpretation." That book was to be both a sequel to *Black Reconstruction in America* and a consummation of Du Bois's renewed commitment to the world revolution concept. It was also a tortured resolution and codification of his struggle with Stalinism.

————

"Russia and America: An Interpretation" is the only book-length manuscript Du Bois completed that to this day remains unpublished. Du Bois's prospective publisher Henry Giroux responded to the manuscript, finished in New York in June 1950, with a rejection letter stating that it was "an uncritical *apologia* for Soviet Russia and an excessive condemnation of the United States."[103] Du Bois scholars, with few exceptions, have ignored the manuscript or argued that its unpublished status is a gift to Du Bois's reputation. Levering Lewis, for example, says that Harcourt Brace "rendered Du Bois's legacy a favor by declining to publish."[104] He decries the "venom and bad taste" of Du Bois's characterization of Trotsky in the manuscript and his "adjusted . . . Russian casualty tables" as downplaying the calamities of the Soviet Union under Stalin's rule. His five-sentence reflection on the 317 page manuscript concludes, "To Du Bois, the degradation of the communist ideal in Soviet Russia was philosophically irrelevant to the expiation of the sins of American democracy, whose very possibility he now deeply doubted."[105]

Levering Lewis codifies in one fell swoop *Russia and America* as a metonym for Du Bois's late career as a dupe or demagogue on behalf of Soviet communism. I argue, instead, that the book is part of late Du Bois's revisionist "trilogy" on the U.S. Civil War and Reconstruction begun with *Black Reconstruction in America* and including the 1962 edition of his biography of John Brown, discussed briefly here and again in Chapter 5. That trilogy is dedicated to the potentiality of a workers' revolution in the United States and is united by this simple theme, "If American Negroes had been given the chance that the Russian peasant has had since 1917 his contribution to the uplift of the world might easily have been startling."[106] In *Black Reconstruction in America*, Du Bois restates this theme by asking whether U.S. history would have changed course had black self-emancipation succeeded as a "national program." In "Russia and America," Du Bois applies this thesis to include all citizens of Russia and the United States living in the era of a Cold War, which is imagined as a historic brake on human prosperity and freedom. The stalemate between the Soviet Union and the United States is conceived as a braided chain of modern capitalist history that can be solved only by a popular revolution from below undertaken by American and Soviet workers. The manuscript criticizes both the excessive violence of the Stalinist regime and the failure of the United States to continue a New Deal path to social welfare during the Cold War as conditions necessitating popular revolt. Completed less than a year after news of the Soviet Union's first testing of its atomic bombs on August 29, 1949, an event that challenged his adoration of the Soviet regime, and four years after the United States dropped atomic bombs on Japan, "Russia and America" also implicates both superpowers in a global arms race to the bottom destined to inflict violence and poverty on citizens of both nations. In response, Du Bois imagines a united front of citizens of the United States and Russia bringing about a revolution in the name of joint peace and prosperity.

By the time Du Bois sat down to compile "Russia and America," the spirit of what he called in *Black Reconstruction in America* "counterrevolution" was everywhere. With its victory in World War II, the United States had entered a period of political lockdown. Stalin and the Soviet Union had flipped from ally to mortal political and military enemy; Roosevelt's New Deal—once a bright hope of progressive reform for Du Bois and African Americans—had given way to unfettered capitalist boom, consumption, and backlash against labor. This stalemate was underscored for Du Bois by the deeply repressive domestic atmosphere. As he wrote "Russia and America," his close friend Paul Robeson was attacked at Peekskill, New York, by anticommunists for proclaiming at the Paris Peace Conference that African Americans would never take up arms against the Soviet Union. Thus, in his final chapter of the manuscript, Du Bois endeavored to interweave the national histories of Cold War adversaries into a "third way" path toward freedom for both peoples based on democratizing strategies for peace and disarmament.

———

The framing argument of Du Bois's historiographical project comes midway through "Russia and America." Chapter 5, titled "The Reign of Roosevelt," commences the second, comparative half of the manuscript, wherein Du Bois endeavors to weigh U.S. history between the start of the Depression in 1929 and the present, a framing roughly congruent with the years of the Russian Revolution. The comparative structure and timeline of the book are meant to demonstrate the effects of the global depression on both countries and to ponder whether the two national histories might be transposed, dialectically, into a single, unitary frame. The chapter also commences the American section of the book's odd autobiographical matrix: the first four chapters describe Du Bois's first, second, and third visits to Russia, in 1926, 1936, and 1949, from which he compiled his writings into manuscript form. The second half begins with the declaration "I am an American":

> I can thus at once look on the United States as an outsider and continuous visitor, integrated into this culture and yet knowing and sharing it. I can see as few others can, the way in which the presence of a depressed class of human beings has distorted and still distorts our social development. . . .
>
> Meanwhile my full and unstinting loyalty and service went to my fellows of Negro descent, not simply in the United States, but in the West Indies and in Africa. Thence by logic I gave my friendship to all colored folk, in Asia and in the South Seas, hoping that in some way the dark world would unite forces and thrust itself across the color bar.[107]

Du Bois's "outside in" perspective on the United States indexes his position as a rapporteur, à la John Reed, from the Russian Revolution back onto his native land. He first recounts the rise of "economic power" in the United States on the backs of slave labor and an "organized anti-slavery movement, helped by fugitive slaves and by white laborers who sought to get rid of slave competition."[108] Then came the war, and emancipation. "What was to be done?" Du Bois wrote, channeling Lenin of 1902 to the United States of 1863.[109] What follows is an "attempt" at adequate employment, civil rights, and minimum land provision, then a Freedmen's Bureau—the edifice of Reconstruction. "This," Du Bois writes, "was a great start toward incipient socialism in the United States, without color caste and with full economic opportunity."[110] As he did in his original account in *Black Reconstruction in America*, Du Bois recounts the "counterrevolution" of property as a deterrent to social progress: "By 1885, the United States had adopted its basic philosophy: Life was Business and Business was Life; Civilization was the product of Industry and Industry was seed and product of Human Culture. . . . The United States entered upon its fabulous modern career as the greatest industrial nation on earth."[111]

Du Bois's experiences in Russia become the basis for interrogating whether Soviet-style socialism can reverse this American counterrevolution. The first chapter thus recounts his earlier, fleeting glimpses and near-misses with both the 1917 revolution and Marxism, leading to his decision to visit Russia to learn "at first hand just what has taken place in Russia and just what the development is at present."[112] Du Bois begins by noting that the Soviet Union nationalized the land after 1917, a far cry from the betrayed promise of forty acres for every freedman during Reconstruction. The state also nationalized industry and invested heavily in education, so that peasants are slowly rising from ignorance and poverty. For Du Bois, raising conditions of the farmer, peasant, and freedman—another challenge of Reconstruction—remains essential to the fulfillment of economic and political democracy: "We must remember that this problem of the farmer in modern life has been neglected to our cost. Here are folk who in every land have been physically by-passed by science, education and technique; they have in all lands been natural victims of exploitation and propaganda and in the automatic world market have been deprived of a decent income. . . .This has stopped democracy in France, Germany, Britain, and the United States."[113]

What does Du Bois mean by democracy in "Russia and America"? In a section of the manuscript devoted to comparing the U.S. and Soviet political systems, Du Bois rejects democracy as electoral polity or parliamentary rule. Rather, democracy is localized political activity in which "matters of vital interest to the people, that is, work and wage and living conditions," are discussed and debated by citizens—emblematized by soviets at the village, farm, and city ward level in the Soviet Union.[114] In comparison, the rollback of voting rights in the American South after Reconstruction delayed what Russia has tentatively achieved. Contemporarily, deferral of U.S. freedom has been further sustained by New Deal programs. Du Bois points out that black farmers and domestic workers have been squeezed out of relief programs. With the New Deal thus stalled, Du Bois proposes, a "Sovietization" of the United States is necessary. As he told an audience of one thousand in Moscow during his visit in 1949, "The cure for this and the way to change the socially planned United States into a welfare state is for the American people to take over the control of the nation in industry as well as government."[115] It is toward this "takeover" that Du Bois's manuscript tentatively proceeds.

At the same time, Du Bois introduces doubts about triumphs of the Soviet experiment. He describes as "savage" Stalin's attacks in January 1933 on the kulaks who resisted liquidation, some of whom "had to be dealt with summarily."[116] "Something like a million out of 2.5 million peasant families were removed," he writes, penciling in the larger figure above the smaller. "Those who refused to cooperate were removed to distant places and put to work at road building, cutting timber or mining. It was hard, poorly paid work, and caused much suffering."[117] Du Bois then writes in and crosses out by hand this paragraph, obviously never intended for publication in the final manuscript: "There were a million kulak families in Russia in 1928, but of 25,000,000 peasant families, and the State proceeded to break their power. The proceedings involved force and cruelty. The kulaks reduced agricultural output, stirred up revolt and slaughtered animals, so as to bring a crisis in 1929 to 1932. But the state persisted. Large numbers were banished to Siberia and the struggle was won by 1934."[118]

Du Bois's distaste for violence and brutality in Stalin's Russia echoes his long-standing expression referenced earlier about what he called Marxist "dogma" about workers' takeover of state power. It kindles memories of his anxieties about African Americans being used as shock troops by the Communist Party in Alabama during the Scottsboro Boys case and his lament in 1940 about preferring the "victim" Radek to the tyrant Stalin. The passage is also a reminder that throughout the 1920s and 1930s, Du Bois described himself generally or specifically as a "pacifist" who was ill at ease with political violence of any kind, a politics codified by his work on the Stockholm Appeal after World War II.[119] Du Bois's contradictory response to Stalinist tactics in the Russian Revolution are foundational to his comparative framework in the text. If real peace and prosperity were to be achieved out of the Cold War and Cold War violence, what tactics and strategies could legitimately be relied on? Du Bois answers the question again by measuring the Russian Revolution in part against America's history:

> We may ask whether or not the Russian Revolution might not have been carried through with less blood and cruelty, with less appeal to brute force. We may believe that with all the gain from the efforts of Lenin and Stalin, most of it might not have been accomplished at lower cost to the decent instincts of mankind. But Russia answers and has right to answer, that this revolution cost less in life and decency than the French Revolution, than the Protestant Reformation, and than the English Civil War; that the chief guilt for the high cost of communism was not the fault of Russia but of America and America which silently condoned the slavery of Russians for centuries and then at fabulous cost tried for ten years to reenslave them to the degenerate Czars and filthy priesthood. If the cost of revolution was excessive and revolting, the fault is certainly not to rest on Russia alone.[120]

Du Bois's description of the Russian Revolution here is intended to recall his description of the African American freedom struggle in *Black Reconstruction in America* as "an upheaval of humanity like the Reformation and French Revolution."[121] Indeed, as noted earlier, Du Bois's interpretation of slaves and white workers simultaneously fleeing the plantation in a "general strike" during Reconstruction was itself retroactively influenced by his interpretation of the Russian Revolution. Du Bois's "comparative" framework in "Russia and America," then, is meant to make explicit a shared history "from below" that constituted an advance for the world's workers: these historical echoes redound in Du Bois's doubling use of the word "slavery" to describe Russian life under the tsars. Here, then, we can understand "Russia and

America" as part of Du Bois's late-in-life revision of revolutionary historiography. In 1951, just after completing "Russia and America," Du Bois published the essay "John Brown Liveth!" in the *West African Pilot*. The essay was part of an ongoing reconsideration of revolution in American history, spurred by Du Bois's sympathy for revolutions in Russia and China. In his additions to *John Brown*, for example, Du Bois revised his argument against Brown's raid on Harper's Ferry in 1909 that revolution is "always a loss and a lowering of ideals." In the 1962 edition of the book, which included revisions undertaken specifically for publication of a Russian edition, Du Bois stated of Brown's rebellion, "If it is a true revolution it repays all losses and results in the uplift of the human race." He continued, "One could wish that John Brown could see the results of the great revolution in Russia. . . . The greatest source of human rejoicing today is the phenomenal rise of the people of Russia. From an ignorant, despised, suppressed peasantry they have in less than a century become in many respects the leading nation of the world." Du Bois's reconsideration of Brown's attack on Harper's Ferry as necessary, despite its violence, for advancing human freedom was a direct consequence of his struggle to understand the Russian Revolution as a template for black (and white) freedom in "Russia and America."[122]

Du Bois's comparative strategy also reflects an attempt to develop in "Russia and America" an interlocking conception of world history, what Trotsky called "combined and uneven development" and what Marx, Engels, and Lenin referred to as capitalism's tendency to unite the world in its predatory grasp. His rationalization of the "high cost" of communism recognized the immense task the working class faced in reversing the course of capitalist history that long predated the Cold War and the appearance of communism on the world stage. It was this process he referred to in 1951 when he declared that he believed in communism but also believed that nations would not achieve it "in the same way or at the same time." In "Russia and America," he thus revisits nineteenth-century American and Soviet history to argue for both as a singular, not binary, strand of capitalist history, as what Marxists call a "totality," a premise already established for the reader in Du Bois's interpretation of Russia in 1917 as a second Reconstruction. A resolution of this interpretive method for the twentieth century is spelled out in the book's later stages and conclusion.

Du Bois casts the challenges of the Depression that brought Roosevelt to power in the United States as analogous to crises in economic conditions that the Bolsheviks sought to overcome in 1917 and the federal government sought to overcome after the Civil War: "restoration of industry; relief distress and reform of the social organization."[123] By analogy, Du Bois renders the New Deal as a second effort at "incipient socialism." In an essay on Paul Robeson dating from March 1950, just months before he completed "Russia and America," Du Bois had written, "All intelligent men . . . know that our New Deal was socialism pure and simple, and must be restored or continued war expenditure will end in worse disaster than the Great Depression."[124] Du Bois's imprecise description of New Deal "socialism" is of a piece with his willful and anachronistic naming of Reconstruction as a proletarian rebellion. Also of a piece with Reconstruction is his interpretation of Roosevelt's installation of bankers and industrialists in his New Deal cabinet as a counterrevolutionary alliance analogous to one made between northern industrialists and southern plantation owners to reverse the popular gains of Reconstruction. Not surprisingly, then, Du Bois turns his attention to African Americans as the historical group for whom the New Deal betrayal is the most significant— black workers:

> The first blow to Negroes came when farm laborers and domestics were not included under the protection of the [National Recovery Administration] codes for industry. Thus three million Negro workers, more than half of the total number who must work for their livelihood, were not covered by the industrial codes. These three million were the backbone of the Negro consumer market. For them an immediate rise in prices meant additional insecurity and suffering. Furthermore, in certain areas where uniform minimum wages were established for black and white workers, employers replaced Negroes with whites rather than pay the same wages.
>
> Thus the New Deal not only met opposition of concentrated wealth based on Negro disenfranchisement, but also increased the opposition of white labor by increasing or failing greatly to decrease the number of poor and unemployed Negroes whose plight threatened the white standard of living. The result was violence and race riots.[125]

To see the historical pattern Du Bois wants us to see repeated, we can simply turn back to the pages of *Black Reconstruction in America*:

> It must be remembered and never forgotten that the Civil War in the South which overthrew Reconstruction was a determined effort to reduce black labor as nearly as possible to a condition of unlimited exploitation and build a new class of capitalists on this foundation. . . .
>
> The lawlessness in the South since the Civil War has varied in its phases. First, it was that kind of disregard for law which follows all

war. Then it became a labor war, an attempt on the part of impover-
ished capitalists and landholders to force laborers to work on the capitalist's own terms. From this, it changed to a war between laborers,
white and black men fighting for the same jobs. Afterward, the white
laborer joined the white landholder and capitalist and beat the black
laborer into subjection through secret organizations and the rise of a
new doctrine of race hatred.[126]

Read dialectically, the Thermidor of counterrevolution—the post–Civil
War rise of the Ku Klux Klan, lynching, the Negro moving "back into slavery"
after a moment in the sun of freedom—is reiterated by the riots in Harlem
and Detroit of 1943, postwar lynchings, New Deal disenfranchisement, and
attacks on returning black soldiers after the war. Soviet citizens, meanwhile,
notes Du Bois, were still faced with the absolutist tactics of Stalinist reforms
described earlier, an economy that still failed to approximate conditions of
real plentitude in the United States, and a hostile American state that sought
to discredit and destroy the gains made by its own working class since 1917.
Over both nations also hung the specter of nuclear annihilation.

Thus, the shared goal of Russians and Americans, Du Bois wrote, had
to be "abolition of war and the abolition of poverty."[127] To this end, Du Bois
asserted that it was the *populaces* of the Soviet Union and United States, not
its states or leaders, that would be the final arbiters of the present. Du Bois's
final chapter, titled "World Peace," describes the United States and the Soviet
Union as bound by a common understanding that "another world war will
fasten poverty on earth for a thousand years."[128] The chapter thus urges the
argument that citizens of the Soviet and U.S. nation-states must recover their
own histories of revolution from below to improve and safeguard the lives of
workers and citizens in both countries:

> Both nations know that in modern days they have led the world in
> realistic attack upon the degradation of the worker. It was revolution
> in the United States against exploitation of colonial labor that led to
> echoing revolution in France and Haiti, and resulted in uplift of labor
> throughout Europe and particularly in the great republic this side of
> the seas, *where the wage and stand of living among the working masses
> today leads the whole world.*
>
> It was revolution in Russia that founded a nation built on the
> determination to abolish poverty in the modern world by equitable
> redistribution of wealth made through the democratic power of an
> intelligent people; *and to start towards this great end by making the
> mass of people intelligent.*[129]

Du Bois's concluding "experiment of Marxism" in "Russia and America" was to imagine the democratic masses of the two antagonistic nations as co-actors and allies in leading a world revolution from below. Their common antagonists—war and poverty—might produce a united front that was more unlikely, but not less effective, than the general populations who had made history in 1776, 1789, 1804, 1867, and 1917: "It is a direct challenge to all men of good will to take firm and open stand not simply against war, but especially against all causes of war. It calls upon intelligent men to admit that the greatest causes of war in the last five hundred years has been the degradation of the worker, especially through the colonial system and the human slavery upon which the colonial imperialism was originally built."[130]

Du Bois here globalizes two lines of "revolutionary" political argument from what he understands as dialectically related national traditions: one the freedom cry from the nineteenth-century United States, and the other from twentieth-century Russia. Russians and Americans must "not forget that the slave system that stifled democracy in the United States for a century after the first brave effort to declare all men equal, is today denying under various guises the equal humanity of the majority of mankind," he wrote, and that "the right of people anywhere to follow their own line of thought and action, in accord with the thought of any nation is sacred so far as there is no attempt to transgress the law."[131] The latter sentiment echoed words used by Du Bois in his testimony to the House Un-American Activities Committee on August 8, 1949, less than a year before he completed "Russia and America." Asked by the committee to assess Soviet socialism, Du Bois responded, "Russia has won the right to conduct her own economy as she wishes."[132] In the final chapter of "Russia and America," Du Bois applied this self-determination thesis equally to the two nations as a language of truce: "Peace and prosperity for all citizens of the state are the objects of both of these nations. They may differ, and have a right to differ, as to the immediate way and means of accomplishing these ends; but there is and can be no question as to the desire of both nations to abolish war and poverty."[133]

It is difficult to assess these conclusions merely, as did Henry Giroux, as an "excessive condemnation of the United States" and "uncritical apologia" for the Soviet Union. Du Bois not only consecrates both the struggle against slavery and national self-determination in the name of a vox populus in "Russia and America" but also invigorates each with democratic fervor. In this regard, "Russia and America" was invested with something like a Popular Front valence: it carried forward to 1950 the optimistic spirit of alliance of the United States and the Soviet Union during World War II into a broad, if unlikely, appeal for peace and prosperity after the war's end. "The American people want Peace," Du Bois wrote. "They want neither to conquer the world nor police it. They have no desire to meddle in other people's affairs, or censor their thought or control their industry. They want to spend the billions now wasting in war on human education and uplift for all men."[134] Du Bois's idiosyncratic application of national self-determination and revolution from below to the Cold War was also partly the result of real political triumphs that were emerging as he prepared the manuscript. India's independence in 1947 and China's liberation in 1949 each registered for Du Bois as a successful national liberation struggle that could rebalance the Cold War. These examples superseded the stalled results of the United Nations meetings to alleviate U.S.-Soviet hostilities and to recognize the full rights of colonized nations. Seen in this light, "Russia and America" was an attempt by Du Bois to destroy twentieth-century antagonism between capitalism and communism through a "third way" solution. This aspect of the book, too, makes it a clear artifact of what is often called the Bandung era of the Cold War. Nehru's theory of "nonaligned" politics balancing between communism and capitalist democracy is reminiscent of Du Bois's strained efforts to make the Soviet Union and the United States equal partners for world peace.

At the same time, the nearly complete blindness of "Russia and America" to disasters of Soviet history shows the constraining limits of Du Bois's "typological" approach to revolution. It is not just the gulags and purges that are missing from his account of the Soviet state but also the alliance with Hitler, the seizure of the Balkans, the repression of dissidents, and Stalin's colonization of Eastern Europe after 1945. Indeed, Du Bois's silence on matters such as drought in Yugoslavia in 1950, the year "Russia and America" was composed, elicited attack from Joseph Hansen of the Socialist Workers Party, who ran against Du Bois that year for a seat in the New York State Senate. "In the twilight of a career of service to the people of America," Hansen wrote, "you have permitted Stalinism, 'the syphilis of the labor movement,' in Trotsky's words, to place its hideous sore on your name."[135] Hansen's accusations foreshadowed a coming period of Du Bois's life in which firmer dedication to defending the Soviet Union would only deepen his resistance to criticism of Stalin. From the vantage point of this study, Du Bois's egregiously narrow readings of Soviet history and idiosyncratic applications of doctrines such as "self-determination" and the Popular Front also reflect contortions of political perspective elicited by Stalinism itself. By 1950, Du Bois had imbibed so strongly of Socialism in One Country theory and practice that defending the Soviet Union became a necessary edifice for preserving—and extending— his confidence in the world revolution concept, even to counterrevolutionary America. Du Bois's "comparative" mode for keeping the concept alive by locating African Americans in Reconstruction or American and Soviet citizens of the Cold War, for example, as revolutionary agents demonstrated a *textualization* of history implicit in his typological mode for reading revolution. To invert James, even if Negroes (and white workers) were *not* rebelling in the real worlds of 1877, 1935, or 1950, they could in the pages of revisionist historiography. Such optimism of the will and stubborn resistance to contravening fact remained a keynote for Du Bois in his support for revolutions elsewhere in the world, tendencies that linked him perpetually to his peers in the diasporic international.

3

INDIA, THE "INDIAN IDEOLOGY," AND THE WORLD REVOLUTION

There is no doubt but that India is a congery [*sic*] of ignorant, poverty-stricken, antagonistic groups who are destined to go through with all the hell of internal strife before they emancipate themselves. But it is just as true that Europe of the sixteenth century was no more ready for freedom and autonomy than India.

—W.E.B. Du Bois, "Prospect of a World without Racial Conflict," 1944

The reaction of the Spanish War on me indicates how, in my mind, the problem of India was tied up with other world problems. More and more I came to think that these separate problems, political or economic, in China, Abyssinia, Spain, Central Europe, India or elsewhere, were facets of one and the same world problem. There could be no final solution of any one of them till this basic problem was solved. . . . As peace was said to be indivisible in the present day world, so also freedom was indivisible, and the world could not continue for long part free, part unfree.

—Jawaharlal Nehru, *An Autobiography*, 1942

The only classes of the Indian people who can lead India to a real victory, to the destruction of British rule and the establishment of an independent India, are those whose interest are in no way bound up with those of England—those who have nothing to lose but their chains, and a world to gain.

—Agnes Smedley, *India and the Next War*, 1928

Even more than in his support for the Russian Revolution, Du Bois's dedication to India's twentieth-century struggle for independence bespeaks the widest field of his ideational attachment to the World Revolution concept. Du Bois was drawn to study and support of Indian national history first by a scholarly endeavor to demonstrate ties in antiquity between the Asian and African worlds. This enterprise prompted a brand of cultural nationalism in his thought suitable to the first wave of Pan-African and Pan-Asian enthusiasm that was coterminous with the founding of the Indian National Congress (INC) and the Pan-African Congress. The confluence of World War I with the Russian Revolution realigned his views. Through association with Indian émigré nationalists such as Lajpat Rai; introduction to the life and careers of Mohandas Gandhi and Jawaharlal Nehru; exposure to the Comintern thesis on national self-determination; and absorption of the influential commitment to Indian independence of American contemporaries such as John Clellon Holmes, Hubert Harrison, and Agnes Smedley, Du Bois gradually "secularized" his view of India as part of a global struggle for working-class emancipation and what the nationalist movement called *swaraj*, or home rule. Once so committed, Du Bois, as was his wont, adapted Indian struggle to an agenda for black freedom: in the 1930s, his black economic cooperative campaign drew directly from Gandhi's *swadeshi* movement, and he would come to near-idolization of Gandhi and Nehru as "great men" leaders whose support for African Americans was a symbiotic call for international affiliation he could hardly refuse. In *Black Reconstruction in America*, India joined Du Bois's pantheon of world revolutions meant to substantiate his interpretation of African American freedom struggle as typological of twentieth-century national uprisings. By the time of formal Indian independence, Du Bois had made India something like the "jewel in the crown" of his idiosyncratic conception of world revolution. August 15, 1947, he would write, "deserves to be remembered as the greatest historical date of the nineteenth and twentieth centuries."[1]

Yet as with Russia's revolution, Du Bois often embraced aspects of India's national liberation struggle that betrayed ignorance of Indian history or reactionary aspects of his increasingly Stalinized conception of revolution. Du Bois's romanticization of Indian nationalism, for example, blended into a mystification of Hindu nationalism inherited from his first mentor (Lajpat Rai) and never expelled. This led to faint demonization and incomplete understanding of caste and especially communalism in India. As late as 1947, Du Bois was denouncing Muhammad Ali Jinna, the architect of Muslim independence in India, for "throwing two great religions into difficult and bitter political competition" and thus blaming the victims of Hindu pogroms after partition.[2] This shortsightedness stemmed from Du Bois's attempts to analogize American race to Indian caste, equating an oppressed national minority with an oppressed national majority. It also spoke to his epidemically weak understanding of class forces and the Indian left. As Sumit Sarkar has noted in his magisterial *Modern India*, the Stalinized Communist Party of India (CPI) in combination with uneven struggle in Indian trade unions created a syncopated modern history in which the nationalist movement and wider class struggles remained hopelessly scheduled to miss each other. Du Bois's narrow attention to top-down nationalisms and figures (Rai, Nehru, Gandhi) obscured these social processes even as Du Bois declared his support for Indian socialism. Blind spots of analysis, as was the case with his fellow travelers Agnes Smedley and Anna Louise Strong, were often compensated for by an equivalence of national self-determination struggle *with* socialism, an error that also beset the most determined Bolshevik aspirant of the Indian world-revolutionary left: Nehru. Indeed, Du Bois's, Nehru's, and, to a lesser extent, Smedley's analyses of the relationship of Indian national struggle to proletarian internationalism, particularly as enunciated by the Communist International after 1928, reveals contradictions at the heart of both the Indian nationalist movement and the Communist International under the influence of Stalin. As the time of Indian independence neared, the world revolution concept had retreated entirely into a defense of the Soviet state and a compensatory idealization of national self-determination, which blunted attention to working-class struggles on the global left. It was this dynamic that Du Bois had tried to identify, belatedly, in the closing pages of "Russia and America,"

In *The Discovery of India* (1946), Nehru posited that a "dream of unity has occupied the Indian mind since the dawn of civilization."[3] Nehru's book, like Du Bois's *Souls of Black Folk* a national history disguised as intellectual autobiography, proposed to shore up from the fragments of India's colonial ruins a metahistorical framing of the nation: "astonishing thought: that any culture or civilization should have this continuity for five or six thousand years or more; and not in a static or unchanging sense, for India was changing and progressing all the time."[4] Nehru sought to impose on the Indian national liberation struggle a teleology, or "fate," endemic to national history: that the idea of the Indian nation, not yet come into being, preceded the nation itself. Perry Anderson has dubbed Nehru's vision a shared "Indian ideology" that has given dominant shape to the country's nationalist formation. It is best captured by the aforementioned Nehruvian sentiment: a "dream of unity has occupied the mind of India since the dawn of civilization."[5] Du Bois's India teleology was likewise grounded in a transhistorical conception of the "souls" of Indian folk constructed in part from Africa's manifest destiny. "There is in this new land, certain great advantages," Du Bois wrote shortly after Indian independence. "They have a spiritual faith; a belief in the inner value of the human being as different from and transcending the matter of wealth and material things."[6] In his research for *The World and Africa*, Du Bois had mined what he thought of as the black gold of India's subcontinental history: "The ethnic history of India would seem to be first a prehistoric substratum of Negrillos or black dwarfs; then the pre-Dravidians, a taller, larger type of Negro; then the Dravidians, Negroes with some mixture of Mongoloid and later of Caucasoid stocks. The Dravidian Negroes laid the bases of Indian culture thousands of years before the Christian era."[7] Du Bois imagined the roots of an Afro-Asiatic nation in his archaeology of India that could flower with independence. It proceeded forward through the history of the Arab slave trade—"Africans were imported into India"—a historical cross-pollination of culture, commerce, and blood that exceeded the grasp of the West: "For a thousand years Asia and Africa strove together, renewing their sprits and mutually fertilizing their cultures from time to time, in West Asia, North Africa, the Nile valley, and the East Coast. But at last Europe encompassed them both."[8] For Nehru, transhistorical Indian sovereignty was also an "impress of oneness" of disparate geographies stretching back six thousand years. "Of the three larger empires it witnessed," writes Perry Anderson, "none covered the territory of Nehru's *Discovery of India*."[9]

I begin with these affiliated conceptions because it is Nehru among twentieth-century Indian political figures whose thought most nearly approximates Du Bois's relationship to the diasporic international and India's place in the world revolution concept. Both came to the revolutionary left via periods of study as students abroad (Du Bois in Berlin; Nehru at Harrow and Cambridge); both were temperamental Brahmins whose intellectual moorings were Western and European civilizationist (each liked to begin and end chapters of their writing with poetic epigraphs from the Western canon). Nehru overcame his self-described bourgeois alienation from the Indian peasantry by traveling the countryside after being drawn by Gandhi into the nationalist upturn after 1917, as Du Bois affected solidarity with southern "folk" after choosing to teach at Fisk and Atlanta universities. During the 1910s and into the early 1920s, each perceived himself as a version of Fabian socialist, with Nehru, like the later Du Bois, heavily influenced by the work of the British radicals Sidney and Beatrice Webb. Both, too, were magnetically drawn to and changed by the Russian Revolution. Much like Du Bois, Nehru took an invited pilgrimage to the Soviet Union in 1927, publishing a seldom studied book on his return titled *Soviet Russia: Some Random Sketches and Impressions*. I discuss the book in more detail later but note here that it served nearly the exact same function in his political evolution as "Russia and America" did in Du Bois's. The book is a comparative study of conditions of workers and peasants in the "new" Russia and India and committed Nehru for the next ten years of his life to an effort to apply Marxist-Leninist analysis to Indian liberation. More specifically, like Du Bois's, Nehru's book insisted that the Soviet Union was for oppressed national minorities across the world a singular political guiding light. "It is difficult to draw any final conclusions about anything Russian at this stage," Nehru wrote, "but it would certainly appear from the progress made in the last five years that the problem of minorities has been largely solved there."[10] And yet by 1949, two years after India's magnificent independence and a lifetime of mutual admiration, including a recurring correspondence during the 1940s, Du Bois would join Alphaeus Hunton, Kumar

Goshal, Howard Fast, and others in sending the new Indian prime minister a letter protesting "wide-spread violation of civil liberties" in India and the mass imprisonment under Nehru's command of progressive trade unionists, peasants, and political leaders.[11] What had gone wrong?

Much as in the case of the Russian Revolution of 1917, India's historic "destiny" as described by Du Bois was determined by national events in push and pull with events worldwide. India first came into Du Bois's political purview around 1914, when he met K. D. Shastri, secretary of the Indian Home Rule League in New York.[12] Du Bois was also early influenced in favor of Indian decolonization by Reverend John Haynes Holmes, a founder and board member of the National Association for the Advancement of Colored People, who in an article in *The Crisis* in 1921 declared Gandhi the "greatest man alive in the world today," a hagiographic view replicated in the title of an article for Du Bois's *Brownie's Book*: "Saint Gandhi."[13] But the overbearing and lasting influence on Du Bois's early analysis of India's national liberation struggle was cast by his relationship beginning in 1916 to Lajpat Rai. Rai was born in 1865, three years before Du Bois, in Dudhike, India. Trained, like Gandhi and Nehru, as a lawyer, Rai was an early convert to Arya Samaj, a Hindu reformist movement that initially cast him against Islam in Indian politics. After joining the Indian National Congress, he went to England in 1905. On his return to India, he took up support for the nascent *swaraj*, or home rule movement, and the *swadeshi*, or boycott campaign that started and spread from Bengal (a movement that preceded Gandhi's widespread popularizing of it some ten years later). By 1907, Rai had become a hot-blooded nationalist—"The tree of the nation calls for blood. It is watered with blood"—and a member of the militant, pro-boycott triumvirate Lal-Bal-Pal.[14] In that year, Rai was deported to Burma for instigating peasants. Despite his election as president of the first All India Trade Union Congress (AITUC), Rai's politics in these years reflected the dual elitism Sumit Sarkar has captured of both professional-class loyalists of the INC and nationalist agitators from upper castes.

Two events in particular broadened this perspective and put Rai on track to become Du Bois's mentor. The first was exposure to African American life in the United States. Rai first visited the country in 1905, traveling to historically black colleges, including Morehouse, and meeting both Booker T. Washington and George Washington Carver.[15] These meetings reflect an Afro-Asian bourgeois alliance also suggested by Gandhi's fascination with Washington's economic uplift program, which was at least one source of his *swadeshi* philosophy.[16] The visit began Rai's longer-term interest in the relationship of American race to Indian caste. When he returned in 1914 to begin a five-year term of exile, this subject became a special focus. His travels across the country produced *The United States of America: A Hindu's Impression and a Study* (1916), which argued that African Americans in the United States represented a "larger proportion of 'untouchables' and a more severe form of untouchability than in India."[17] Rai declared the Negro the "pariah" of America. Yet the book's general use of the U.S. race example was conservative. Rai argued that a flawed American democracy should give hope to the Indian national movement even while leaving uninterrogated his own nationalist sentiments derived from Arya Samaj training that Hindus descended from Aryan stock, an idea Du Bois would imbibe wholesale and that would significantly diminish his ability both to analyze caste and to develop a critical perspective on the defense of the caste system by Indian leaders such as Gandhi.

The second intersectional influence on Du Bois was Rai's contradictory understanding of the Russian Revolution and its support for nationalist movements. Like Du Bois, Rai was drawn to Bolshevism in part because of its overthrow of a feudal order that had diminished illiteracy while increasing compulsory education and economic opportunity for the peasantry.[18] The Soviet Union also provided an attractive alternative to reigning British, French and U.S. imperialism and its history of bourgeois revolutions; even the French Revolution, Rai contended, had erected "Bastilles all over the world in Asia and Africa."[19] But also like Du Bois, Rai, in his early analysis of Bolshevism, reflected a crude Fabian Second Internationalist boosterism. "For the first time in the political history of the world," he wrote, "the Russian Revolutionists have preached the brother-hood of nations."[20] About Trotsky, who in 1919 would meet with Ghadr Party leaders in New York, he wrote, "The truth which he had placed before the world in giving the Persians their liberty and declaring the Anglo-Russian Convention void [a reference to the Soviets' relinquishing Ottoman territory formerly held by the tsars] will stand forever as a monumental step towards true world democracy. So far, there is nothing in the world which equals that."[21] Finally, in an article from 1919 titled, symptomatically, "Bolshevism and Anti-Bolshevism," Rai wrote that Russia "represents that the world is for all and not for the few who happen to be in possession at this minute."[22]

Rai's diffuse and erratic Asian nationalist sympathies for revolution from the east comported easily in the 1910s with Du Bois's analysis in 1915 of the African "roots" of World War I and his Pan-Africanist enthusiasm for the Lenin and Comintern self-determination thesis, particularly its emphasis on the "Eastern" question. Even *Dark Princess* would celebrate the "toilers" of the East, the university established in 1922 to bring Asiatic and Arab nations into the revolutionary fold. Rai helped shape Du Bois's lament that "Egypt, India and Ireland are not free," his general sympathy for the Russian Revolution, and his dedication throughout the 1920s to writing and correspondence with Rai and other anticolonial intellectuals from the subcontinent.[23] In 1925, Du

Bois responded to letters published in *The Crisis* from Banarsidas Chaturvedi
with a message titled "To the People of India" modeled, as Nico Slate notes,
on Marx's letter to Abraham Lincoln during the Civil War. Du Bois parroted
a line from Rai's 1916 book—"If India has her castes, American Negroes have
in their own internal color lines, the plain shadow of a caste system"—and
described the battle for racial justice in the United States as "the same terrible
battle of the color bar which our brothers in India are fighting."[24] Du Bois
became a sometime contributor to the Indian publication *Aryan Path*, where
he called for "colored unity," and corresponded with the secretary of the All
India Congress Committee's Foreign Department, who wrote to him, "We
here attach the highest significance to the Negro Front of anti-Imperialism."[25]

How did this talk of transnational solidarity relate to events on the ground
in India, Russia and black America? As I noted in Chapter 1, the years 1917–
1921 were climactic ones of revolutionary upturn in all three national settings.
Gandhi's campaigns in Champaran in Bihar and Kheda in Gujarat in 1917,
the Ahmedabad strike of 1918 led by Gandhi, and the Bombay textile strike of
January 1919 were the political skeleton on which Rai's and Du Bois's Russian
enthusiasm were in part framed. In the United States, notoriety around the
prosecution of the Ghadr Party for fundraising and treason and inflamma-
tory reports in the U.S. press of a "Hind-German Conspiracy" ratcheted up
imperialist counteroffensives in the United Kingdom and elsewhere that put
even more steam into Du Bois's support for the Indian national movement.
By 1921, disparate black leaders such as Marcus Garvey and Hubert Harrison
were including Indian decolonization in their roster of struggles that required
black unity of support. Under the influence of both Rai's "comparative" para-
digm and the Soviet self-determination thesis, Du Bois would come during
this period to describe African Americans as a "bound colony of the United
States just as India is of England"—possibly the strongest formulation in his
thought to emerge directly from Comintern influence.[26] In 1917, Agnes Smedley also met Lajpat Rai in New York City, where she became the secretary of a
study group he conducted at the Civic Club.[27] Rather quickly, Smedley began
to move from Rai's immediate tutorship into closer affiliation with Bengali
radicals to his left, including Sailendra Nath Ghose. She also moved closer to
M. N. Roy, the former member of the Indian Revolutionary Party in Bengal
and a founder in 1920 of the first incarnation of the CPI (and nearly simultaneously the Mexican Communist Party). According to Ruth Price, Roy raped
Smedley some time in this period, an event she would recount, in trauma-
tized, fictional form, in her novel *Daughter of Earth* (1929).[28] He would also be
the primary political rival to her lover Virendranath Chattopadhyaya in negotiations with the Comintern about Soviet policy toward India.[29] In December
1917, the German-financed Indian National Party, whose members included

Smedley, Ghose, and Bhagwan Singh, drafted a letter to Leon Trotsky asking for his support for Ghadr Party members on trial in San Francisco. Smedley's relationship to Rai would suffer a permanent break when Rai returned to India in 1919 to resume his role in the INC during what was clearly a revolutionary situation at home.

The period 1917–1928 constitutes a radical interregnum in the development of India's place in world-revolutionary thinking that would bring Smedley, Chattopadhyaya, and Du Bois into closer contact both with one another and with a transitional figure in their lives and the national movement itself—namely, Nehru. All would also be drawn tightly into the orbit of the Communist International in this period. Chattopadhyaya, for example, would first come into contact with the Bolsheviks in Sweden in 1917 during the formation of the Swedish Indian National Committee, a counterpart to its Berlin Committee.[30] On November 1, 1917, Chattopadhyaya would submit to the Comintern a memorandum titled "India Work in Russia," contending that because of World War I "the anti-English feeling is very strong now in Russia and propaganda for India (as well as Ireland, Egypt and Persia) will meet with success."[31] In 1919, in turn, Trotsky and Lenin would both single out India's anticolonial struggle as in need of special support from the Communist International.[32] In 1920, the Colonial Theses advocating national self-determination as a step in world revolution was approved by the Comintern. At the same time, Nehru's self-confessed radicalization after the inception of Gandhi's *swaraj* campaign in 1920 survived the Mahatma's controversial decision to call off the noncooperation movement in 1922 after the retaliatory burning alive by angry villagers of twenty-two British police at Chari Chaura. He would shortly serve the first of numerous prison sentences at British hands for distributing notices for a *hartal*, or labor strikes.[33] Mass labor agitation of the early 1920s meanwhile swept many Indian nationalists to the left: by mid-1920, a section of the Ghadr movement had turned communist; communist journals had debuted in Bombay; and communists were newly prominent in labor agitation such as the Kharagpur railway workshop strikes of February and September 1927.[34] Nehru, meanwhile, was in Switzerland in 1926 when the English general strike broke out, about which he commented that the "frightened and terrorized look" in the eyes of British strikers reminded him of Indian workers at home.[35] Also in 1926, Nehru met up with Chattopadhyaya in Berlin, where Chattopadhyaya, at the Comintern's direction, had joined the German Communist Party. The Communist International was in the process of planning its first League against Imperialism meeting to take place in Brussels. Nehru, learning of the meeting, wrote home to suggest that the Indian National Congress take part. "It was felt more and more," wrote Nehru of this moment, "that the struggle for freedom was a common one against the thing that was imperialism, and joint deliberation, and where possible, joint action, were desirable."[36]

Together, Nehru and Chattopadhyaya led the Indian delegation at the First International Congress against Colonial Oppression and Imperialism, held on February 10, 1927, at the Palais Egmont in Brussels. One hundred and twenty-four representatives were present. Nehru was appointed honorary president of the league, and Chattopadhyaya was named to run its office in Berlin, where he was living with Smedley. S. Gopal has called Nehru's work with the league a "turning point" in his political life.[37] Like Du Bois's, Nehru's declarations during this period reflect a turning away from an earlier stage of Fabian socialism initiated by the Comintern commitment to anti-imperialism and national liberation struggles. The record of Second International socialism after the war "filled me with distaste," he wrote, "so I turned inevitably with good will towards Communism, for whatever its faults, it was at least not hypocritical and not imperialistic."[38] Upon his return to India from Europe, Nehru would write, "My outlook was wider, and nationalism by itself seemed to me definitely a narrow and insufficient creed. Political freedom, independence, were no doubt essential, but they were steps only in the right direction; without social freedom and a socialist structure of society and the state, neither the country nor the individual could develop much." He added, "Soviet Russia, despite certain unpleasant aspects, attracted me greatly, and seemed to hold forth a message of hope to the world."[39] Nehru and his father were thus quick to accept an invitation from the Soviet Union to visit the country in November 1927, just over a year after Du Bois's first visit. En route to Moscow, Nehru would visit with Chattopadhyaya and Smedley in Berlin, where, according to Price, Smedley would find Nehru too "female . . . modest and reserved" for her firebrand style of radicalism.[40] Just at the moment of Nehru's mission to Moscow, Smedley's ties to the Communist International were solidifying: her work had put her in contact with the Comintern official Alexander Trachtenberg and with Earl Browder, director of the Pan Pacific Trade Union Secretariat, a subsidiary of the Comintern's trade union arm, the Profintern, and an official with the Communist Party of the USA (CPUSA). "For her," wrote Price about Smedley in this period, "the Comintern was the single most critical weapon in the battle for the freedom of the world's oppressed nations."[41]

From this constellation of events emerged five texts published in 1928 and 1929 that mark an apex of diasporic internationalist thought and advance of the world revolution conception for their authors and, in the case of India especially, constituents. They are Du Bois's reports on his Soviet visit later republished in "Russia and America" and his novel *Dark Princess*; Nehru's *Soviet Russia: Some Random Sketches and Impressions*, published first in 1929 in Bombay; and Smedley's *India and the Next War*, published by the Kirti Office in Amritsar in 1928, and *Daughter of Earth*, published in New York in 1929. In tandem, the texts provide a fond commemoration of ten years of Bolshevik reign in Russia and a vanguard interpretation of a Soviet-inspired future of permanent class uprisings, especially for oppressed colonial nations. The texts also affirm an early canonization on the world left of Stalinism, if not of Stalin. The heir apparent to the Russian Revolution of 1917 is seldom named, but Soviet policy in the areas of economy, agriculture, education, minority rights, and women is generally affirmed. Most important for each writer, the Soviet example as a model for emancipation elsewhere—in China, India, and African America—is rendered as a historical inevitability. For each writer, it is clear that communism and the Communist International have cleared away the primary challenges of civil war, economic catastrophe, and foreign invasion to emerge as the unqualified leader of the world revolution.

Although they visited a year apart, Nehru and Du Bois each participated in the tenth-anniversary celebrations of the Russian Revolution that were the putative rationales for their visits. Du Bois was a witness to "parts of the tenth Celebration of Youth in Moscow," featuring 200,000 children and youth marching through Red Square, including "a hundred or two Chinese, Tarts, Caucasians, Turks, two or three Negroes—an extraordinary demonstration."[42] At Moscow's Grand Hotel, Nehru watched more than a million workers, children, and troops marching past the Lenin Mausoleum. Each was also treated to a visit to the theater—Nehru's visit was to the State Opera House, which was "overflowing with people in their work-a-day attire, sometimes without coats and in their shirt sleeves." The impression signified the democratization of culture.[43] That their tours were orchestrated along parallel celebratory lines is also marked by nearly matching itineraries. Both visited what Nehru called two "communist universities": the Oriental University (or what Du Bois called the "University for Eastern Peoples") and the Sun Yat-sen University. Both were taken to prominent cultural centers: Du Bois to the National Library and the library of the Communist Academy, and Nehru to the Leningrad Academy of Sciences. Each was also provided a similar set of "supporting documentation" of the success of the revolution during their visit: copies of "Soviet Russia Today," a report by a delegation of British trade unionists invited to Russia to take part in tenth-anniversary celebrations prior to their arrival, which was described by Nehru as "valuable and full of information."[44] The British contribution is a reminder that Nehru and Du Bois shared intellectual and political connections to Beatrice and Sidney Webb, who stoked their enthusiasm for the Soviet Revolution for more than a decade.[45]

Other parallels include accounts of arranged visits to prisons meant to demonstrate the superior humanization of crime and punishment under socialism but that for both visitors—Nehru in particular—raised the specter of excess and deception on the part of the Soviets. "Nothing is perhaps more confusing to the student of Russia than the conflicting reports that come of the treatment of prisoners and of the criminal law," Nehru wrote. "We are told of the Red Terror and ghastly and horrible details are provided for our consumption," an echo of Du Bois's allusion to torture and secret police that were whispered about but not represented during his visit.[46] When he went to a former tsarist prison on the outskirts of Moscow and was invited to choose the cells he wanted to visit, Nehru wrote, the insistence was "rather curious and seemed to indicate that the whole prison was more or less of a show place, specifically meant for the education of visitors."[47] After being introduced to a prisoner convicted of spying on behalf of Czechoslovakia who had been made the director of music in the jail, Nehru noted, "We had an impression that we had been shown the brighter side of jail life."[48] Yet as with Du Bois, Nehru's comparative framework, or episteme, drew the observer into deep Soviet sympathy. Nehru concluded that "desired and radical improvements" had been made in incarceration over tsarist rule and that "anyone with a knowledge of prisons in India [Nehru had himself already served the first of numerous terms for his anticolonial agitating] and of the barbarous way in which handcuffs, fetters and other punishments are used will appreciate the difference."[49] Finally, both Du Bois and Nehru were shown the achievements of gender equality in the new Russia: Nehru had a personal meeting with Lenin's widow, Nadezhda Krupskaya, as well as with Madame Sun Yat-sen and Clara Zetkin. Labor laws protecting women, the provision of four months of paid maternity leave, free divorce, Alexandra Kollontai's role as the world's first female ambassador (to Mexico), and the election of 100,000 women to village soviets and 169 peasant women to the All Union Congress of Soviets are all underscored in both Du Bois's more general impression and Nehru's detailed account that women in the Soviet Union had gone leaps and bounds past their counterparts at home.[50]

Yet the most important political conclusions for Nehru, as in Du Bois's account, lay in two areas: comparative assessment of the conditions of workers and peasants, and the treatment of ethnic minorities—the central planks of the Communist International's advertisement for its initial world revolution program. Earlier, I noted Du Bois's reorientation to the Soviet self-determination thesis after 1919, especially in contradistinction to the Western powers' abrogation of colonial rights, earmarked in "The African Roots of War." Nehru's orientation in *Soviet Russia* was nearly identical: early in the book, he calls the self-determination argument of Woodrow Wilson's Fourteen Points the "acid test for the powers" in their relationship to the Soviet Union, a test they have all but failed, given the fourteen-nation attack on the revolution—he cites as example the recent Anglo-French Naval Pact against the Soviets—and the attempts to isolate Bolshevism internationally. Nehru turns Wilson's own words against him in sympathy with the Soviet project, arguing that the Soviet revolution has survived because Russia has the "voices of humanity" with it.[51] Nehru's assessment of the stakes of the Soviet experiment also align with Du Bois's interpretation of the revolution as a litmus test for drawing oppressed nations and peoples into an emancipatory history of their own making. In Du Bois's words, "If Russia fails, reason in industry fails. If Russia succeeds, gradually every modern state will socialize industry."[52] Nehru's first chapter, "The Fascination of Russia," notes that Indians are "always trying to forget our present misery and degradation in vague fancies of our glorious past and an immortal civilization. But the past is dead and gone and our immortal civilization does not help us greatly in solving the problems of today."[53] Soviet communism provides a means to "help us to find some solution for the great problems which face the world today. It interests us especially because conditions there have not been, and are not even now, very dissimilar to conditions in India. Both are vast agricultural countries with only the beginnings of industrialization, and both have to face poverty and literacy. If Russia finds a satisfactory solution for these, our work in India is made easier."[54]

Still other aspects of the revolution instill symmetry of views in the two men differentially positioned in the combined and uneven development of the global capitalist economy. First is the commitment to peasant uplift. As noted earlier, The Colonial Theses of 1920 codified as Comintern policy support for peasant movements in backward countries against landlords and an attempt to conjoin the peasantry to struggles of urban proletariats within the colonies and in Europe.[55] The ideational imprint is clear on both texts. "Never on so broad a side," wrote Du Bois, "has an attempt been made to reach and civilize the country districts of a vast land and raise the rural economy to a level with the urban."[56] Nehru wrote, "Russia, like India, is essentially rural and agricultural. Eighty percent of her population lives in villages, and seventy-five percent of her working population is engaged in the cultivation of the soil."[57] Where Du Bois valorized the role of black slaves and former slaves in creating the temporary "democracy" of Reconstruction, Nehru ticked off signs of a new peasant democracy in Soviet Russia: rural education was on the rise; a *Peasant's Gazette* newspaper, with a circulation of one million, had begun; and village councils, or *mirs*, had emerged as local decision-making bodies, sometimes holding common land, which for Nehru were analogous to *punchayats* (workers' councils) in India. Soviet policy was to keep taxes low for peasants and form cartels, an association of peasants that pooled resources and common land. Agricultural banks and credit societies were also lifting the Soviet Union from the peasant bottom up.

Second, Du Bois and Nehru wrote in accord about the Soviets' commitment to ethnic minority populations. Du Bois expressed elation about the "little nations of nations" at the Soviet print shop and the absence of anti-black racism; Nehru set the Soviet challenge of ethnic harmony in an Indian context: "Many of us are apt to imagine that India is particularly unfortunate in having to face a complicated problem of minorities and different communities. As a matter of fact many other countries have faced and solved this problem. Russia specially is a country with numerous national minorities with different languages and cultures, and it is interesting and instructive for us to study the methods of the Bolsheviks in regard to these minorities."[58] Nehru supportively delineated the four major declarations of the All Russia Congress, which overturned tsarist policy of "pitch[ing] one nationality against the other": equality and sovereignty to the Russian people; the right of self-determination, even to separation and formation of an independent state; abolition of every kind of national, racial, and religious privilege; and free development of national minorities and ethnographic groups.[59] Minorities' autonomy in the development of language and culture now flourishes, he stated. Women in Uzbekistan before the revolution "were mostly purdanashins [living in seclusion]"; they were also seldom literate. Now, however, they were enrolled in 276 women's educational institutions. Although both Nehru and Du Bois acknowledged that problems remained, their comparative scales tipped heavily in favor of the Soviets. "The hundred and fifty years of British rule compare very badly in this respect with the effort," Nehru wrote. "But may we whisper it? The British do not want the problem to be solved."[60]

As noted earlier, the Great Depression, rise in anticolonial struggles, and economic freefall for African Americans were conditions that shaped Du Bois's enthusiasm for the Soviet experiment. What conditions shaped Nehru's? First, the massive upturn in labor strikes and peasants' mass participation in noncooperation after 1917 had made him a reluctant populist, dismantling some of his self-admitted bourgeois orientation to class struggle. Second, by 1927 "Purna Swaraj," a popular anti-imperialist slogan, suffused the nationalist movement and was soon to become the codified cry of independence. Third, Hindu–Muslim communal politics both indigenous to anticolonial debate about representation and fanned by the British were already boding ill for the national movement. Nehru found a possible elixir in Soviet ethnic cooperation. Fourth, Nehru's appointment to serve as the Indian National Congress's representative to the League against Imperialism in February had in fact turned up the political ground of his thinking before his arrival in the Soviet Union in November. Prior to leaving for Soviet Russia, he had become a demonstrative president of the INC, which was now calling for complete independence and close links with the League against Imperialism, and even passed a resolution hailing both Alluri Sitarama Raju, martyr of the so-called Rampa Rebellion against the British Raj in Andhra Pradesh, and the martyred Italian anarchists Nicola Sacco and Bartolomeo Vanzetti.[61]

It is thus not hard to comprehend how in 1926 and 1927, the years of Nehru's and Du Bois's visits, the world revolution concept seemed less than still-born, despite the slings and arrows cast against the Soviet revolution during the lead-up to its anniversary. Indeed, Smedley's *India and the Next War*, published the same year as Du Bois's *Dark Princess*, extracted the political essence of Du Bois's and Nehru's favorable analyses for communism's prospects into a polemic on revolution in India directed against her former mentor Lajpat Rai. The debate opened with an article first published by Smedley, in a sign of their onetime affiliation, in Rai's newspaper, *The People*, in Lahore in October 1927. Smedley, following carefully through Chattopadhyaya and in her Comintern offices the radicalization of the Indian national movement, paraphrased Lenin's foundational writing on imperialism and national-self determination to exhort the Indian nation to break its chains. "Imperialism is the final stage of capitalism," she wrote, "and India is the chief pillar upon which British imperialism rests."[62] Smedley's class analysis of the noncoopera-tion movement pitted peasants against large Indian landowners who "hug the chains of British rule," with the British themselves whipping up the commu-nal differences to which Nehru sought resolution in Soviet Russia. "We find the Indian Muslim being appealed to on the ground that Russia is an enemy of religion and of Islam, and that Hindus are Bolsheviks," she wrote. "On the other hand Hindus are being warned that the Muslims are waiting to unite with the Afghans and the Turks to overrun India and establish Muslim Raj."[63] Smedley's imperial context, however, was not just the iron fist of British man-date but also China: former tsarist troops, she noted, were fighting Chinese alongside English advisers and directors in Shanghai, the site of the largest workers' uprisings in the country. Rai's response to Smedley was a sign of his abandonment of communist analysis and an affirmation of his deep Hindu-tva roots. "We are not . . . convinced that the Bolsheviks are so disinterested friends as Miss Smedley makes them out," he wrote. "The fact of it is that religionism is the curse of India, and no Muslim can to-day be anything but a Communalist. That does not mean that the Hindus can be. But some at least among the latter can rise above religionism, but a Muslim never."[64]

Smedley, never one to shy away from a fight, responded to Rai by wedding her Soviet sympathies to Nehru's. "A subjected India is always in danger," she wrote. "To-day, the Russian menace is nothing but a menace to British rule and prestige in Asia. This viewpoint is also well developed in Jawaharlal Nehru's article in 'Forward.'"[65] Smedley then attacked Rai's Hindu nationalism with a class analysis that was entirely consistent with the Comintern's rejection of bourgeois nationalisms unmoored from proletarian internationalism and in favor of alliance between the proletariat and peasantry: "When the Indian masses enter the national revolutionary movement against British imperialism, they enter the movement also against certain social classes within Indian society itself—landlordism and capitalism. The working and peasant masses, combined with the revolutionary intelligentsia, are the only reliable leaders of the national movement."[66] Finally, Smedley's orientation to self-determination included aspects of analysis of women's oppression championed by the likes of Kollontai and Zetkin, as well as one of her personal mentors, Emma Goldman. Islam, she wrote, was a "class religion like all others, it has subjected women along with the poor, making her a thing of private property."[67] Hinduism has brought women enforced widowhood, child marriage, and suttee "based upon the belief that woman is the private property of a man and that she must remain so in life and an in death."[68] Smedley's embrace of what might be called Third International feminism here also drew her analysis of and support for the Soviet revolution into alliance with Nehru and Du Bois.

What followed immediately from publication of these works for these members of the diasporic international was a rededication to anti-imperialism and commitment to Marxist thought, tempered by pragmatic and often locally determined skepticism about full-scale identification with the Russian Revolution. We have already seen this pattern in the life of Du Bois, who undertook his prolonged self-study in Marxism after writing *Dark Princess*. Nehru, upon his return from Russia, pushed for a snap resolution in the INC calling for complete independence (over Gandhi's caution that he was moving too fast). With communists increasingly penetrating Indian trade unions and a labor upsurge signaled by a huge textile workers' strike in Bombay, Gandhi's acting as a "brake" on mounting pressure for a new round of mass struggle aimed at full independence was all that seemed to stand between India and full-scale revolution. At the Lahore Congress in December 1929, Nehru showed what Sumit Sarkar calls a "new internationalist and socially-radical perspective for the freedom movement."[69] Shortly thereafter, Nehru was jailed for work on an agrarian reform program, where his "intellectual radicalization" continued.[70] Letters to his daughter written from prison and published as *Glimpses of World History*, as well as his *Autobiography*, written in prison in 1934–1935, mark the "height" of Nehru's interest in and partial commitment to Marxist socialist ideas, according to Sarkar.[71] At the same time, when the Uttar Pradesh Congress drew up "A Tentative Socialist Programme for India" in April 1934, Nehru never joined, in part because he was intimidated by Gandhi's strong and persistent animus toward socialism, and in part because of the general weakness, numerically, of the socialist movement and Communist

Party (now made illegal by the British) relative to the growing heft of the INC and the hegemony of a largely bourgeois nationalist movement.[72]

Smedley, meanwhile, found herself in Moscow by 1928, beginning a form of Comintern shuttle diplomacy between Berlin and Shanghai, where she was assigned, covertly, as an agent to monitor and promote workers' uprisings against the Kuomintang. According to Price, Smedley's reaction to Stalin's abandonment of the United Front at the Sixth Soviet Comintern in favor of "class against class" struggle that year was increased skepticism about the future of revolutions outside the Soviet Union. For Smedley, Price writes, the Comintern was increasingly a "monopoly of power exercised by the Russian Communist Party, for whom Soviet example and guidance was paramount and whose directions would be applied without alteration to every other Communist Party in the world."[73] Indeed, a sense of burgeoning disillusionment and increasing powerlessness for the left hangs over the book on which Smedley put the finishing touches that same year: *Daughter of Earth*. The autobiographical novel, as discussed earlier, refracted the long period of Smedley's radicalization dating to the Ghadr Party and International Workers of the World in the United States and ends with the exile of her protagonist Marie Rogers from U.S. shores. Du Bois's *Dark Princess* alludes to the lives of Rai, Smedley, Chattopadhyaya, and the Berlin circle and to prospects for self-determination and world revolution; Smedley's novel is a traumatic account of the place of women within the same political matrix. Du Bois's exoticized and eroticized portrait of Princess Kautilya is answered, figuratively, by Marie Rogers's violent rejection of marriage, men's paternalism, and capitalist love. The book is an "anti-romance" in which Rogers must extricate herself from the institutions of marriage and maternity to achieve a socialism of gender equality. Exile from the nation and the capitalist state's inscription of women's oppression is the price of becoming a revolutionary in Smedley's novel. The book punctures in particular romantic nationalism expressed on the body of working-class women: Juan Diaz's rape of Rogers (Diaz is a composite of M. N. Roy and Herambalal Gupta in the novel). Even Anand, a fictional rendering of Chattopadhyaya, is possessive and paternalistic in the novel, a testament to Price's documentation that he abused Smedley physically in their relationship. "Do you regard a woman who has lived an independent sex life, as I have done, as anti-social?" Rogers asks Anand skeptically.[74] The single constant in Smedley's/Rogers's revolutionary life in *Daughter of Earth* is the absence of a completely revolutionary man, whether Indian or American, to comprehend equality of social relations.

At the same time, *Daughter of Earth* was Smedley's political bildungsroman that forecast both her fealty to Indian decolonization and her support for the Soviet line on self-determination for the rest of her life, as well as her vexed relationship to both Stalinism and the Comintern. This is signaled in at least two ways in the text. Smedley's title invokes the metaphor of "grounding" political movements in indigenous terrain of struggle. In her case, the "earth" is that mined by her working-class family and the land rights of the dispossessed. Rogers's early-in-life identification with the Bedonkohe Apache leader Geronimo's battles against Mexican and U.S. military forces for the expansion of tribal lands is meant to signal her eventual leap into anticolonial struggle with the Ghadr Party: "Together with my comrades, I was speaking and writing, and I felt that I was molding the native earth of America."[75] For Smedley, alliance with anticolonial struggle is symbolized as a marker of an indigenous proletarian solidarity. At the same time, Smedley recounts leaving the U.S. Socialist Party after the "split" between the two wings in the movement over support for imperialist states, joining neither while remaining revolutionary: "The entire ideology of the right wing made no appeal to me, for it had no vitality, no strength; step-by-step progress seemed to me shortsighted. And I did not join the left wing because many of its leaders were those brilliant intellectuals who had formerly so aroused my resentment. They were leaders and I had no use for leaders. I didn't want to be led by them. Nor could I believe that the Russian Revolution was their private property."[76]

Smedley's attempt at independent fealty to the world revolution concept would mark her work of the 1930s and 1940s as she tacked between support for and dissent from Comintern policy toward anticolonial and working-class movements in India and China especially. This was exacerbated by her personal involvement and response to Stalin's terrors: her onetime lover Chattopadhyaya would be executed in Moscow during the purges of 1937. Smedley's entire life was lived on the threshold of a break with Stalinism. In this way, too, *Daughter of Earth* is Smedley's Comintern novel, both an anchoring point in the record of the diasporic international and a crucial text in the lineage of twentieth-century writing on women's oppression and class struggle that I revisit in Chapter 5. Her inclusion of rape, abortion, and sexual autonomy for revolutionary women in her account of coming to political consciousness anticipates the later work of black feminist internationalists attempting to pull Third International feminism forward to a revived Leninism in the postwar period (see Chapter 5). The final lines of Smedley's novel describe her entry into the diasporic international as a violent expulsion into a revolutionary unknown and unmade: "I was cold and numb. Slowly, with difficulty, I arose and began to pack. Out of this house—out of this country."[77] Eventually, as we shall see, China's communist revolution seemed to offer Smedley at least a political habitus where she could hold up half the sky.

In the fall of 1928, the writer and Indian nationalist Sarojini Naidu, Virendranath Chattopadhyaya's sister, arrived in the United States on a campaign to improve American opinion of Mohandas Gandhi and the INC. One year earlier, Naidu had presided over the East Indian National Congress in South Africa. Her visit, according to Nico Slate, influenced Du Bois to begin a closer study of Gandhi's life and methods. In 1930, Du Bois met the Nobel Prize-winning writer and polymath Rabindranath Tagore in New York City, a meeting that prompted Du Bois to say, "Negroes and Indians realize that both are fighting the same great battle against the assumption of superiority made so often by the white race."[78] In the fall of 1931, Du Bois, as a representative of the International Committee for Political Prisoners, wrote a letter to the secretary of India protesting the British charges of treason against the Bengali Marxist nationalist M. N. Roy. In India, meanwhile, in a book titled *Whither India?* a radicalized Nehru sought, without full success, to distinguish his leadership brand from that of his mentor, Gandhi, injecting socialist objectives into a program for national liberation.[79] The communist movement in India, weakened by mass arrests at Meerut in 1929, was suddenly split several ways between the more moderate National Trade Union Movement and the communist Red Trade Union Congress as rivals to the AITUC.[80] Nehru, serving as president of the AITUC, urged it to work together with the INC but was hesitant to align it to the Third International because of the Comintern's mistaken direction to the Chinese Communist Party that it ally with the Kuomintang, advice that dealt a setback to the workers' movement.[81] Indeed, Smedley, now in the full, covert employ of the Communist International, was in Shanghai facing direct consequences of Stalinist policy. The Soviet Union's emerging rivalry with an expansionist Japan began to trump its strategy for supporting workers' revolutions, portending both a prolonged failure to build up a successful revolutionary challenge to the Kuomintang and Smedley's increasing disillusionment with the Stalinist emphasis on defending Socialism in One Country.

These conflicting vectors after 1928 help frame contradictions in India's national liberation struggle and the response of members of the diasporic international to it. In many ways, its twists and turns were perfectly synchronized to world-revolutionary events and the ever changing responses of the Communist International to them. Events that had a particular impact were the Comintern's turn to its Third Period of ultra-leftist proletarian struggle in 1928 and the volte-face reversal to a Popular Front strategy after 1935. As shown earlier, the Communist Party's Third Period turn to a Black Belt thesis polarized members of the diasporic international—for example, Du Bois and

Padmore, who were temporarily estranged over hardline militancy and the expectations for African Americans, especially in the South. In India, after the arrests in Meerut of CPI members in 1929, the party was declared illegal and forced underground. The formation of a new Congress Socialist Party as a rival to the CPI forced the leadership of the national movement to seek reconciliation between them. This became a central task for Nehru, in particular, and secondarily for Gandhi. New mass mobilizations brought about by restricted successes of civil disobedience (including Gandhi's attempts to slow both labor protests and spontaneous demonstrations) brought a new generation of radical nationalists into the movement. By the mid-1930s, writes Sarkar, a new United Front strategy appeared that endeavored to bring radicalizing communists in contact with left-nationalist elements within the Congress Socialist Party and the INC itself.[82]

Attendant to these shifts was the increased prominence, especially for African Americans such as Du Bois, of Gandhi as a putative figurehead of both Indian decolonization and, increasingly, a vaguely conceived program of race solidarity between India and African Americans. As within India, Gandhi's role in shaping the struggle for African Americans was both progressive and reactionary. Even as he continued to valorize Hindu nationalism, the caste system, and, most famously, a defense of private property based on "trusteeship" ("In India, we want no political strikes," he once said), he was increasingly lionized by black leaders as a moral and political compass—and ceiling—for what Afro-India unity could achieve.[83] Du Bois himself fell prey to the spell of Gandhi during this period. By 1936, he was basing much of his program for cooperative economics—his own version of national self-determination—largely on Gandhian *swadeshi* principles. In the essay "The Union of Color," published in the Indian journal *Aryan Path*, Du Bois called for "consumers' co-operation and production" based on Gandhian preachings to "stop the dependence of coloured consumers upon white exploitation."[84] Du Bois's lingering focus on consumption rather than production, on boycott rather than workers' power (though to be challenged by his "Basic Creed," as discussed earlier) was entirely consistent with Gandhi's own hostility to class struggle and attacks on private property. Yet for Du Bois, cooperative economics were also intended to be a nonviolent step toward socialism, at least for the nonwhite citizens of the world. In the same essay, he described his ministrations toward cooperative economics as "a desperate attempt to find a third path—a path that will not necessarily range the forces of the world into 'two camps, sullen, suspicious, and menacing,' but which will aim at inner cohesion and understanding among the coloured peoples, and especially organizations designed to meet and solve their pressing economic problems."[85] For Du

Bois, and for many African Americans, the Gandhian appeal seemed to offer an alternative to Third Period communism's call for revolution and the use of African Americans as "shock troops," on one hand, while fulfilling a publicly stated commitment to represent the "wretched of the earth," on the other. Overlooked or not understood by Du Bois, Howard Thurman, and other black leaders who hitched their support for Indian liberation to his star, was Gandhi's own unpleasant background of animus toward Zulus in South Africa; his calculated appeals to Dalits, which, as Perry Anderson has noted, stripped them of independent political voice; and a moral overlay to anticolonial anti-imperialism suitable to a bourgeois framing of Afro-Asian solidarity.[86]

At the same time, Du Bois's conception of a cooperative socialism "between camps" of capitalism and Sovietized socialism anticipated both the language and the pragmatism that would characterize what has come to be known as "Nehruvian" or Third World socialism. Indeed, Nehru's autobiographical reflections on the implementation of Marxist principles to the Indian national liberation struggle are nearly a perfect mirror in temperament to those of his contemporary fellow traveler, tinged as were the former's, with anxious knowledge—or, at least, suspicions—about Stalinism and the Stalinization of the CPI. "I dislike dogmatism, and the treatment of Karl Marx's writings or any other books as revealed scripture which cannot be challenged, and the regimentation and heresy hunts which seem to be a feature of modern communism," Nehru wrote. "I dislike also much that has happened in Russia, and especially the excessive use of violence in normal times. But I incline more and more towards a communist philosophy."[87] Throughout the mid-1930s especially, Nehru's rhetoric of socialist commitment and philosophy played out in practice in a liberal nationalism increasingly clothed in modernization and developmentalist rhetoric. As Benjamin Zachariah notes, "It was . . . in this period . . . that Nehru became the spokesman for, and the political focal point of, self-proclaimedly 'modern' trends in Indian politics, as opposed to the 'indigenist' trends"—read, Gandhism.[88] Such a politics had a utility especially conducive to the Popular Front turn in the global left after 1935. Nehru's intuition to wed the Indian bourgeoisie to the nationalist movement, to "yoke" class alliances of elites and middle guards over and against the interests of workers and peasants, would propel INC policy and popularity from 1936 forward. As Sarkar notes, "Nehru's vision of a modern industrialized India . . . fitted in much better with bourgeois aspiration than the Gandhian evocation of rural simplicity and handicrafts, and there were enough indications already that the former's socialist flourishes were eminently manageable."[89] The Indian bourgeoisie, Sarkar writes, were happy to support Nehru's socialist rhetoric "so long as socialism did not mean wholesale nationalization along revolutionary lines."[90]

As it did elsewhere in the revolutionary left, the Popular Front turn in India consolidated a new progressive middle domestically against the specter of militancy from below while refashioning the fight against British colonialism into a united front against fascism. The immediate beneficiary was the INC. Its membership rose from a half-million in 1936 to 3.1 million in 1937 and 4.5 million in 1938.[91] The "rise" of the INC made it the new able-bodied spokesperson for India's revolution internationally and for the African American left. Nehru, the party's president, would visit Britain in January 1936 and meet Paul Robeson through the auspices of Cedric Dover, a member of the Congress Socialist Party. Dover was a Eurasian, or "Anglo-Indian," who would also play an intermediary role among Du Bois, the Pan-African Movement, and the Indian national struggle. In 1936, Dover sent Nehru a copy of George Padmore's *How Britain Rules the Blacks* and was constantly attempting to influence Nehru to read more about Soviet policy on national minorities. Dover's first book, *Cimmerli; or, Eurasians and Their Future*, published in Calcutta, was influenced by his readings of Du Bois and brought him to Du Bois's attention. In 1937, Dover would go to the United States to see Howard and Fisk universities and visit with Du Bois, by invitation, at Atlanta University.[92] About this time, according to Gerald Horne, Nehru also discovered one of Du Bois's published essays on African Americans and Indians and began to consider writing something about black Americans. In 1940, he wrote to Du Bois that he was "greatly interested in the future of the American Negroes" and cabled the newly created Council on African Affairs.[93] After visiting Spain during the Civil War there to express solidarity with the International Brigade defending Madrid; condemning Italy's invasion of Ethiopia; declaring support for the Palestinians in their indigenous fight against Zionism; commanding the INC to send a medical mission to China in response to an appeal from Chu The, who was increasingly seen by the Comintern as the "left hand" of China's struggle for national liberation, Nehru rebaptized himself a Popular Front internationalist: "More and more I came to think that these separate problems, political or economic, in China, Abyssinia, Spain, Central Europe, India or elsewhere, were facets of one and the same world problem."[94]

Yet as we saw earlier, world revolution rhetoric around national self-determination and solidarity in the anticolonial struggle, especially during the Popular Front, often served as a surrogate for stalled or aborted working-class struggles. India was no different. Nehru found little support, and had little stomach, for fighting for working-class interests within a largely bourgeois INC. The Indian proletariat remained small and politically disorganized in part because of the fragmented and undersize Indian communist and socialist movements. In contrast, "On international issues . . . the Left clearly set the tone," according to Sarkar. Nehru "in fact increasingly sought in internation-

INDIA, THE "INDIAN IDEOLOGY," AND THE WORLD REVOLUTION

alist gestures a kind of surrogate for effective Left action at home—'I have felt out of place and a misfit. This was one reason . . . why I decided to go to Europe," he wrote to Gandhi on April 28, 1938.[95] We should not underestimate here the opaque solidarity of exilic wanderlust between the lines of this diasporic internationalist's lament. Like Du Bois, Smedley, Strong, Padmore, and James, Nehru was determined to "follow" revolutions worldwide partly because of the difficulty of building one at home, and partly to keep hope and strategy alive for doing so in the long run. Indeed, attempting to describe her own frisson after returning to the United States in 1941 after a long stint in China, Smedley turned to Nehru's expression of displacement: "I am a queer mixture of the East and West, out of place everywhere, at home nowhere. . . . I have an exile's feeling."[96]

From 1938 to 1947, India's anticolonial "fate" would move inexorably toward freedom and popular support globally while jettisoning many of the domestic constituents who were the base of that popular support. This was the devil's bargain struck by Nehruvian "socialism"—a mixed economy, centralized state planning, and limited land redistribution—meant to navigate between a wildly popular INC, on one hand, and, on the other, a Stalinized communist movement that followed to a fault the command of its leaders in both the Communist International in Moscow and, to a lesser extent, the Communist Party of Great Britain. Much like the Popular Front in the United States, which likewise attracted large numbers of African Americans, India's "United Front" produced a giddy alliance of forces around anti-imperialism and antifascism while tamping down the prospects of a unified working-class challenge to those same forces. Anderson has described this general motion this way:

> The wine of electoral success had done what the water of non-violence had failed to do: give Congress a political weight and strength that neither rulers [n]or rivals could henceforward ignore. It would be the last time the party threw itself into a popular campaign with such vigour. . . . "The consensus pursued by the high command in the 1930s," Ian Copland has written, "was at the expense of important sections of Indian political society which were deliberately left out in the cold—the poor peasantry, the tribals, the factory workers, and the people of the princely states."[97]

In short, under Nehru, the INC became the Raj. Yet Nehru and Gandhi, himself largely withdrawn from the foreground of the colonial struggle by the late 1930s, remained the singular figureheads of the movement for men like Du Bois, whose enthusiasm for India's freedom—much like his interpretation of black liberation in *Black Reconstruction in America*—hewed to a vaguely sensed appreciation for the Leninist thesis on self-determination combined with a Pan-Africanist longing for increased Afro-Asian unity (see Figure 3.1). Much as he had done in Soviet Russia, Du Bois looked past or occluded questions of workers' self-emancipation as long as someone like him was representing the workers. That man was in the main Nehru. In his review of *An Autobiography* published in 1942, Du Bois fashioned a portrait of Nehru that was a mirror to his own. He called him the "great democrat of the world," a man who "early sensed the shadow of the color veil" and "sympathized with the Boers in the Boer War and with the Japanese in the Russo-Japanese War." Nehru "began to believe in socialism and even in communism minus its violence."[98] If believing in Nehru meant believing in the "Raj," so be it for Du Bois, just as believing in Stalin required believing in a Stalinized version of "socialism" in the Soviet Union.

Eventually, the Comintern, or the idea of the Comintern, helped to sweep away all doubts for Du Bois, pulling him closer to its bosom even as it marked a fairly catastrophic course for India's revolution. As it did for India's Popular Front, British imperialism heavily determined his analysis and sympathies. Du Bois's dedication to India followed both Stalinist prescription and uncritical support for Soviet resistance to British rivalry before the Stalin-Hitler Pact of 1939 and to the British-Soviet alliance after 1941. Within India, the influence of Stalinism, in retreat during the CPI's period of illegality, resurfaced with a particular vengeance in the critical revolutionary years of 1942–1943. In January 1942, the CPI called for all-out antifascist "people's war" to defend the Soviet Union. The "Quit India" resolution passed by the Bombay session of the All India Congress Committee on August 8, 1942, was followed up by a call for "mass struggle on non-violent lines on the widest possible scale."[99] For the first time since the massive labor strikes of 1919–1921, full-scale revolution seemed a real possibility in India. Even Gandhi would declare, uncharacteristically, "If a general strike becomes a dire necessity, I shall not flinch."[100] Sensing the upturn, and overestimating his own influence, Walter White tried to persuade Franklin Roosevelt to send a delegation of African Americans to meet with Sir Stafford Cripps, the British liaison to India, to negotiate a peaceful settlement.[101] The proposal, much more favorable to Britain than India, drew support from both the CPUSA and CPI because of Britain's wartime alliance with Stalin and the Soviet Union. The INC rejected the proposal. The growth of the CPI during this period, however, was discordant with its actual power. Like wartime Stalinist communist parties worldwide, the CPI continued to subordinate workers' struggles to winning the war. The centralization—if not hegemony—of the INC during this period, riding the wave of

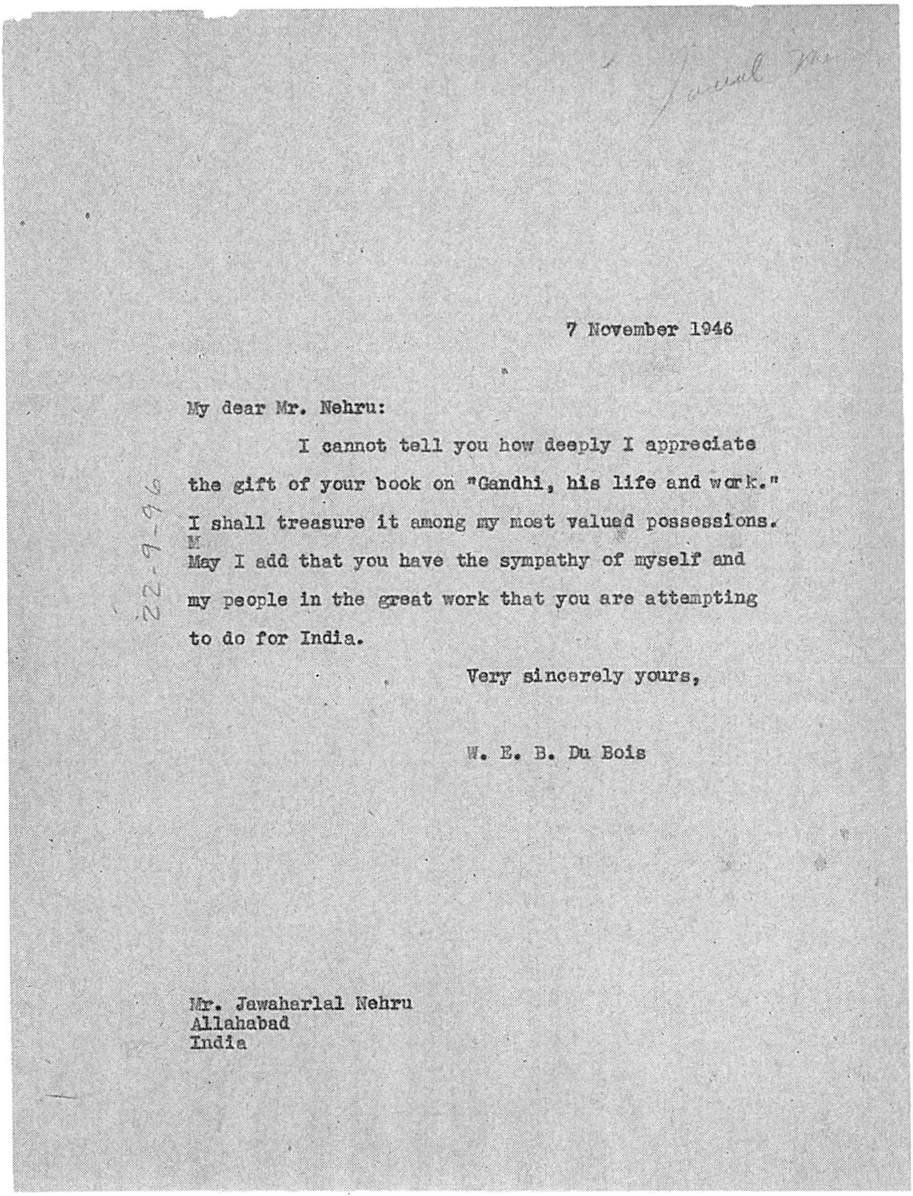

7 November 1946

My dear Mr. Nehru:

        I cannot tell you how deeply I appreciate the gift of your book on "Gandhi, his life and work." I shall treasure it among my most valued possessions. May I add that you have the sympathy of myself and my people in the great work that you are attempting to do for India.

                      Very sincerely yours,

                      W. E. B. Du Bois

Mr. Jawaharlal Nehru
Allahabad
India

Figure 3.1. Letter from W. E. B. Du Bois to Jawaharlal Nehru, November 7, 1946. *(Used with permission of the David Graham Du Bois Trust and the Special Collections and University Archives, W.E.B. Du Bois Library, University of Massachusetts Amherst.)*

"Quit India" and a sense of British power that declined with each day the war was prolonged, further narrowed the horizons of *swaraj*.

Du Bois's horizon on India, meanwhile, remained in the main anti-British and hagiographic. In an essay titled "A Chronicle of Race Relations," published in *Phylon* in 1942, Du Bois alternately cited Nehru's and Gandhi's leadership as the keys to victory. "Despite the slurs of Churchill [who famously called Gandhi a 'naked fakir']," Du Bois wrote, "here is one of the world's great men," and he singularly attributed the "Quit India" resolution to the Mahatma. Du Bois then affirmed in a manner reminiscent of his conclusions to come in "Russia and America" a tempered reaffirmation of the right of self-determination as the crucible of conflict: "The argument that India cannot be allowed freedom until she settles her internal difficulties is astonishing when it comes from Europeans. That there will be innumerable and serious internal problems which a free India will have to settle; that they may even lead to civil war is quite possible; but that Europe or any European nation should be allowed to settle India's problems for her or to say when India shall be allowed to begin her own settlement, is an inadmissible conclusion."[102]

Du Bois's facility of devotion to the self-determination principle here belies unresolved contradictions within it that vexed the world revolution conception from its beginnings and haunted India's moment of independence. The weaknesses in mass struggle were in areas where the Communist International, disposed of in 1943 by Stalin, had once sought to lead—the self-emancipation of the working class and peasantry and the equitable treatment of ethnic minorities, or "coloured people," worldwide. Mirroring the backsliding of the Comintern into irrelevance, India's independence movement quickly ran aground on a Stalinized communist left. Flush with the popularity of its rising membership through the "Quit India" upturn of 1942–1947, the CPI, in one last Stalinist volte-face, first endorsed and then turned against the nation's declaration of independence. The Stalinist "revolution in one country" line came a cropper as the CPI withdrew members from the INC, then declared "Yeh Azadi Jhuta Hai" (This Freedom Is a Farce) in protest of the INC's too conciliatory line with the British imperialists and desire for friendly relations with the United States in the wake of World War II. As Sarkar has written, the slogan and campaign "cut little ice" in a country, no matter the flaws of independence, that was in little mood for deep, self-critical reflection.[103] At the same time, Nehru's hardened position against the CPI, part of his newfound posture as a Third World diplomat and liaison to the "free world," resulted in his declaring the CPI at war with the INC, summarily arresting members, and contributing to a Cold Warriorization of national politics. It was these actions that inspired Du Bois, Fast, and others to harden their support for

Stalin as the Cold War ratcheted up in the United States, writing in denunciation of Nehru's actions and giving him the cold shoulder during his visit to the United States in 1949.

More catastrophic yet was the tragedy of partition and what can best be described as a closing of ranks in the diasporic international around the "Indian ideology." In his essay "The Freeing of India" (1947), Du Bois assigned the ruins of partition and communal violence entirely to Muhammad Jinnah. The "renegade . . . rich land-holder" had divided India on religious lines; "out of that, among the poor and ignorant, rose fanatical fighting among neighbors who had lived in peace for centuries."[104] In fact, the Muslim minority in India had first been used by the British as leverage through divide-and-rule tactics in the nineteenth century; in the twentieth century, shamefully, it was the national leadership, including Nehru and Gandhi, who perceived Muslim equality as incompatible with the national ideal. That ideal, according to Anderson, transformed the INC "from an elite into a mass organization by suturing its appeal with a Hindu imaginary," a tactic that came home to roost in communal violence in 1947 and 1948 for which Gandhi nearly sacrificed his life in noble protest.[105] Throughout the 1930s, Nehru scoffed at Muslim independence and referred to Jinnah as a "paranoid' heading a party of "Hitlerian leadership and policies."[106] Nehru happily sacrificed the Muslim majority in his homeland of Kashmir and expressed doubts about Pakistan's survival after petition, as well as his expectation that it would one day return to India.[107] Thus, although he expressed sadness and sympathy at partition— "Nothing but an India-wide crusade against religious dogma will win here in the end"—Du Bois's conception of an Indian "destiny" and what he called in 1947 a transcendent "Indian philosophy and religion" was beholden to his own misty conception of self-determination that enabled him to close ranks with his anticolonial idols.[108] The Indian ideology that ultimately united them has been ably described by Anderson:

> The ideology and self-conception of [the INC] rested on a set of historical myths that disabled it from taking any sober stock of the political problems confronting the struggle for emancipation from the Raj. Central to these was the claim that India had existed as a nation time out of mind, with a continuous identity and over-arching harmony prior to the arrival of the British. [The INC}, in this outlook, was simply the contemporary vehicle of that national unity, in which differences of religious faith had never prevented ordinary people living peacefully side by side, under the aegis of enlightened rulers. Imperialism had sought to set community against community, and a handful

of self-seeking Muslim politicians had colluded with it, but independence would show the world an India stretching from the North-West to the North-East Frontier Agencies, at one with itself, a democracy governed by a party in the tolerant traditions of the greatest emperors of the past, the modern expression of an ancient civilization six thousand years old.[109]

Despite his criticism of Nehru in 1949, Du Bois was later reflective about the limitations of both his own assessment of Indian independence and the historical conditions under which it was achieved. India's emancipation had, he was confident, raised the bar for racial justice and civil rights across the globe. "We are not yet equal citizens," he wrote to Nehru in 1956, after independence, "but conditions are improving and real emancipation is in sight. For this we have to thank the rise of the Soviet Republics and the rise and growth of free India."[110] Du Bois's confidence was instilled in part by India's role in leading the condemnation of South African apartheid at the United Nations, Nehru's continued expressions of personal support (including a note of appreciation and mutual respect sent for his eightieth birthday), and India's shining example of upending colonialism and ushering in a new era of national independence movements. Like Nehru, Du Bois was typically contradictory in his assessment of prospects for socialism and socialist revolution in India. Nehru "is a socialist but cannot carry out socialism here against capitalists like Patel," he wrote in 1950, referring to one of the INC's most pro-business members.[111] Although he had written in 1947, "All of that drama of the rights of labor, which has been fought out in Europe and America, must be begun and struggled through in India," Du Bois seemed to have no conception of what a workers' revolution in India might look like, what role an international proletariat movement might play in that movement, and how the American working class might relate to it.[112] Similarly, within India the occasional electoral breakthrough of the CPI, as in 1956 in Kerala, did little to challenge the hegemony of INC rule.

These fundamental absences in Du Bois's Indian ideology speak to deficits in the world revolution conception and its Stalinist variants that had congealed and hardened by the time of Indian independence. Other world events, especially the Chinese Revolution of 1949, would temporarily startle the Indian working class and the left into reconsidering what might, indeed, constitute an economic and political alternative to Nehru's "Adavi Resolution" after independence. Nehru's program of a "mixed" economy—part state control, part private sector—was itself much closer to a Stalinized state capitalism, right down to the five-year plans and phrase making in the place of workers' power. Under campaign slogans such as "We Build for Socialism" in

1951, the INC could enact a distinctly Nehruvian "experiment of Marxism." As Nehru wrote, "My idea of Socialism is that every individual in the States should have equal opportunity to progress. I do not at all prefer the States controlling everything because I attach a value to individual freedom."[113]

As for Gandhi, while Du Bois had rejected his program of nonviolence as a strategy for African Americans in 1943—African Americans simply constituted too small a minority to be effective, he thought—by 1957 he recognized Gandhian thought as a thriving undercurrent of mass mobilizations in Alabama during the bus boycott. A "black seamstress" tired of insult refused to give up her seat on a bus, he wrote, and black workers, led by "educated ministers," began a strike that "stopped the discrimination, aroused the state and the nation and presented an unbending front of non-violence to the murderous mob which hitherto had ruled the South."[114] Du Bois called the occurrence "extraordinary" mainly because "the rise and spread of this movement was due to the truth of its underlying principles and not to direct teaching or propaganda. In this aspect it is a most interesting proof of the truth of the Gandhian philosophy."[115] Du Bois ventured further that year, seeing in the reenactment of Gandhian tactics a new iteration of his own "revolutionary typology" for interpreting history. In "Will the Great Gandhi Live Again?" published in the *National Guardian*, Du Bois wrote, "The greatest philosopher of our era [implicitly Marx] pointed out the inherent contradictions in many of our universal beliefs; and he sought eventual reconciliation of those paradoxes."[116] Today, noted Du Bois, one of those paradoxes was President Dwight D. Eisenhower's declaring that expenditures for war were a preparation for peace. The irony threw Du Bois into sober historical reflection on his own relationship to Gandhian nonviolence: "After the depression I sensed recurring contradictions. I saw Gandhi's non-violence gain freedom for India, only to be followed by violence in all the world; I realized that the hundred years of peace from Waterloo to 1914 was not peace at all, but war of Europe on Africa and Asia, with troubled peace only between the colonial conquerors."[117]

Events in Montgomery, Alabama, Du Bois wrote, "tried to show the world the synthesis of this antithesis. These folk, led by a man who had read Hegel, knew of Karl Marx, and had followed Mohandas Karamchand Gandhi, preached: 'Not by Might, nor by Power, but by My Spirit,' saith the Lord."[118] The particular contradiction of the Martin Luther King era, Du Bois noted, was how to bring peace to an ever more violent South that seemed immune to change. "So long as a people insults, murders and hates by hereditary teaching," he wrote, "non-violence can bring no peace."[119] Gandhian nonviolence thus represented an attempt to return dialectics to history, to wrench justice from injustice, love from hate. "If we can, we solve our antitheses: great Gandhi lives again," wrote Du Bois. "If we cannot civilize the South, or will not even try, we continue in contradiction and riddle."[120] In typically revisionist fashion, Du Bois's essay welds together two of his most prescient tropes: the Souls of Brown Folk and the Riddle of the Sphinx. Alabama becomes not only archetypal but also microcosmic, a figure of a persisting Black Belt hatched in the Comintern, animated in the romance of *Dark Princess*, and kept alive by what Princess Kautilya calls "working thinkers and thinking workers"—"not even the black Montgomery of the Negro professional men, merchants, and teachers," according to Du Bois, "but the black workers: the scrubbers and cleaners; the porters and seamstresses."[121] From the shadows of India's struggle for freedom, and for the sake of an imagined place in a world revolution still deferred, Du Bois dialectically fashioned his own midnight's children.

4

WORLD REVOLUTION AT
THE CROSSROADS

Japan, China, and the Long Shadow of Stalinism

It would take a new way of thinking on Asiatic lines to work this out; but there would be a chance that out of India, out of Buddhism and Shintoism, out of the age-old virtues of Japan and China itself, to provide for this different kind of Communism, a thing which so far all attempts at a socialist state in Europe have failed to produce; that is a communism with its Asiatic stress on character, on goodness, on spirit, through family loyalty and affection might ward off Thermidor; might stop the tendency of the Western socialistic states to freeze into bureaucracy.

        —W.E.B. DU BOIS, "RUSSIA AND AMERICA," 1950

One could see the beginnings of that process in feudalism by which the warring barons of the Middle Ages coalesced into nations. But China would not repeat that history; there were new forces in the world. The forces of the world imperialists; the forces of the world revolution.

        —ANNA LOUISE STRONG, *I CHANGE WORLDS*, 1935

I may not be innocent, but I'm right.

        —AGNES SMEDLEY TO FLORENCE KELLEY, LETTER, 1932

The Chinese Revolution of 1949 culminated many of the hopes, ideals, and defeats of the diasporic international. It also reproduced in an instant the contradictions and shortcomings that beset the world revolution conception. The Chinese Communist Party (CCP) that took power in 1949, throwing off a century's yoke of colonial oppression and imperial rule, was a small cadre of military leaders and intellectuals largely divorced from the Chinese peasantry and working class. It was immediately made the bright red star in the mid-century's anticolonial firmament, but it also proclaimed a communism stripped of workers' power, highly dependent on the Soviet state, and largely isolated from socialist movements around the world. It immediately reproduced Stalinist-style state bureaucracy and repression and strong deviations from ideas recognizable as Marxist, or even Leninist. Just before taking power in July 1949, Mao Tse-tung declared, "The democracy of the people and the dictatorship over the reactionaries constitute the dictatorship of the people's democracy."[1] The opaque and contradictory phraseology were signposts of Stalinist sloganeering and violence against principles of workers' control of the state and means of production; indeed, China's revolution was immediately proclaimed by leaders of both the Soviet Union and China as proof positive that Stalinist Sovietism had won the day, even though it had long contributed significantly to setting back prospects for the Chinese working class.

What Harold Isaacs has called "The tragedy of the Chinese revolution," then, is a central narrative of the world revolution and its long twentieth-century history. In this chapter, I examine how members of the diasporic international betrayed their undying fidelity to the world revolution conception by supporting China's national liberation struggle even as they remained largely uncritical of its ossification and devolution. Central to this story is again the competing valence of metonymic nationalism and proletarian internationalism. For Agnes Smedley, W.E.B. Du Bois, and Anna Louise Strong, the allure of self-determination struggle as a Comintern principle obscured destructive premises of China's nationalist movement and Soviet support for it, especially after the 1920s. Their largely uncritical support for what became the CCP under Mao was colored by both theoretical weaknesses in analyses of events on the ground in China and by a tendency endemic to Communist International discourse on the Chinese revolution to weight it with the burden of offsetting failures and setbacks in the Soviet revolution after 1919. By 1927, China had become a "compensatory" revolution in the eyes of the Comintern that merited support at any cost, even when that support contradicted proletarian ascent and workers' interests. Metonymic nationalism emerged as a substitute in Soviet support for the CCP's alignment with the Kuomintang, for example, and in continuous attempts to capitalize on the revolution as a propaganda symbol of the success of Stalinism. For Du Bois, support for China's revolution was also marked by a variety of forms of belatedness: of education about Chinese history, of understanding of Marxism, and especially of a long-nurtured and overtly nationalist sympathy for Japan as a "champion of the darker world," which dated to his enthusiasm of 1904–1905. Indeed, Japan's ongoing territorial and political wars, first with Russia and then with China, became a slow pivot point in Du Bois's interpretation of the twentieth century. Until then, Du Bois perceived Japanese maneuverings to expand its Asian empire and treaty alliances with Western imperialist nations as a necessary and defensible tool for a colored nation seeking to develop economic autonomy and sovereignty. Prior to 1917, and throughout the 1920s, Du Bois forgave or ignored the social inequalities fostered by the development of Japanese capitalism; Japan's repression of its own working class and the working classes in its colonies; and its overt imperial policies toward Korea, China, and other Asian countries. Not until after the Nanjing Massacre, and even then hesitatingly, was he able to shed a romantic Japanese exceptionalism that converted his metonymic nationalism into a version of proletarian internationalism. Yet that conversion was itself belated, purchased at a time that Stalinism had become the stock-in-trade version of world revolution.

These processes are legible as a series of highly self-conscious revisions of world-revolutionary typology in Du Bois's writings, beginning with his earliest essays on the Russo-Japanese war in 1906, running through his journalistic accounts of the China-Japan civil war of the 1930s, and then carrying into three major texts of his late period. They are "Russia and America: An Interpretation," which includes a twenty-seven-page description of Du Bois's episteme-changing trip from Moscow to China and Japan in 1936–1937 and whose material scholars have entirely ignored because of the work's status as unpublished; *Worlds of Color*, book three in Du Bois's Black Flame (Mansart) Trilogy; and *The Autobiography of W.E.B. Du Bois: A Soliloquy on Viewing My Life from the Last Decade of Its First Century*, completed just before his death and published posthumously. Compositely, I show, this trilogy of late works functions intertextually to demonstrate Du Bois's long march toward support, understanding, and misunderstanding of the Chinese Revolution, of Japan's place in twentieth-century history, and of his own twilight relationship to Marxism and the world revolution concept. Indeed, in "Russia and America," Du Bois, like Agnes Smedley and Anna Louise Strong, finally perceived Asia's place in the world revolution as an entire recasting of Western history and historiography. Their barely concealed Orientalist enthusiasm for world-historic change in Asia became its own version of metonymic nationalism, each conceiving Russia, China, Japan, and India as a continuum of Asiatic revolutions that could fulfill the promise of world revolution at least on one side of the globe. By 1949, none of them could retreat from this premise: revolution had become a self-fulfilling idea, with China its world-historical apotheosis.

––––––

In 1936, fresh after publication of *Black Reconstruction in America*, his epochal intervention into world revolution theory, Du Bois set out to learn more about its practice. With the preliminary assistance of an Oberlander Trust fellowship and the planning assistance of Hikida Yasuichi, described by the U.S. State Department as a "point man for Japan's low-budget operation to influence black American public opinion," Du Bois set off to visit four countries in the midst of global political and economic crisis.[2] Germany, the Soviet Union, China, and Japan were each attempting what Du Bois regarded as an "experiment of Marxism" toward resolution. The Japanese dimension of the trip was prominent. Du Bois's still animate phase of planning for black cooperative economics had been inspired, in part, by the Japanese clergyman and Social Gospelist Toyohiko Kagawa, whose collectivist ideas, along with Gandhi's, had been cited by Du Bois as an inspiration. Du Bois had not long before also lectured on Japan at Fisk, Howard, Morehouse, and Tuskegee as part of his efforts in the early 1930s to monitor, and promote, Japan's example of colored self-determination and self-sustaining competition in the capitalist global order.[3] As he noted many times in his writing, Du Bois was still beholden to Japan for its victory over Russia in 1905 and for proposing a racial equality clause to the Covenant of the League of Nations in 1919 (summarily vetoed by Woodrow Wilson and the Anglo imperial powers). For both, Japan was awarded with Du Bois's silent assent, despite its entanglement with those powers at the Washington Conference of 1921. There, Japan entered into the Four-Power Treaty, which replaced the Anglo-Japanese alliance that had been the mainstay of Japanese diplomacy since the Russo-Japanese War.[4] The new treaty, signed by Britain, the United States, and France, was part of the Nine-Power Accord ensuring that each country would have an "open door" and equal opportunity to exploit China's cheap resources and cheap labor.[5] The treaty was also meant to unify the signatories against their primary territorial and political enemy, the Soviet Union, as part of its efforts to surround, and strangle, the revolution of 1917.

Du Bois's Japanese "exceptionalism" would serve as an undercurrent to his politics until World War II. Du Bois was silent about Japan's alliance with Britain after its war with China in 1894–1895, which arguably was its preparatory war for imperial expansion and an event he admitted later that had "puzzled" him in its time.[6] Japan's annexation of Korea in 1910 drew no remark. Although he wrote in favor of the Russian Revolution of 1917 and its defense, Du Bois made no comment on Japan's sending of warships to Vladivostok in 1917 and its dispatching of troops alongside contingents from France, Britain, and the United States to Siberia in 1918.[7] In *Dark Princess*, Du Bois includes an aging Japanese dignitary in his cadre of world revolutionists who, while hostile to Bolshevism, voices support for participation by African Americans in the battle for a colored empire. While he never acceded to the reductive pro-Japanese strain of black nationalism that marked support among contemporaries such as Garvey and the Ethiopian Pacific League, the Japanese incursion into Manchuria in 1931, a logical extension of the Washington Agreement, unleashed a hyperbolic rhetoric of racial unity against white supremacy that pulled forward Du Bois's enthusiasm for Japan's defeat of Russia as a "crossing of the world color line." In an article published in *The Crisis* in 1933 addressing for the first time Japan's ambitions in Manchuria, Du Bois's appeal for peace and unity between the Asian neighbors was cast as a way of staving off a new round of lurking Western imperial reconquest. "The real rulers of the world today . . . are blood-sucking imperial tyrants who see only one thing in the quarrel of China and Japan, and that is a chance to crush and exploit both," he wrote. "Unmask them, Asia," he implored. "Tear apart their double faces and double tongues and unite in pace. Remember, Japan, that white America despises and fears you. Remember China, that England covets your land and labor. Unite! Beckon to the three hundred million Indians; drive Europe out of Asia and let her get her own raped and distracted house in order. Let the yellow and brown race, nine hundred million strong take their rightful leadership of mankind."[8] Eleven issues of *The Crisis* later, Du Bois was doing ideological back flips to welcome Japanese imperialism to Africa. Du Bois characterized a report that Japan was to receive sixteen million acres in Ethiopia for colonization positively as a "rapprochement between yellow and black people. . . . We have no illusions about the Japanese motives in this matter," wrote Du Bois. "They are going to Ethiopia for purposes of profit. At the same time the treatment of Ethiopia by England and Italy and France has been so selfish and outrageous that nothing Japan can do can possibly be worse."[9]

Beyond this "exceptionalism," Du Bois's analysis of events of the 1930s revealed a significant crisis in his analysis of imperialism and capitalism generated by Japan's ascent as an imperial player. Japanese imperialism became a form of metonymic nationalism for Du Bois that conflated capitalism and white supremacy into a single enemy. The confusion was of a piece with Du Bois's simultaneous domestic program for black cooperative economics as a form of "socialism." Black capitalism might indeed be a "transitional" program toward the elimination of white capitalist rule. Testing these perspectives against his deepening enthusiasm for Marxism and the crisis of global capitalism was at the heart of the query he posed to explore, in book form, when he completed his travels abroad in 1936. "A Search for Democracy," he told Harcourt Brace, would be a novel about a "colored professor" on leave from a small, southern Negro college in correspondence with a "woman friend" at home. She writes to him about "democracy in America" while he "writes of democracy in England and France, of Hitler and the Nazis, and of Russia. Then he plunges into the contradictions and implications of the new political and economic revolution in China and Japan and its inevitable extension in other parts of the East. He then comes back to the newer aspects of the African question, disenfranchisement and land monopoly in South and East Africa, the conquest of Ethiopia, industry and raw materials in West Africa and the influence of all of this on incipient war in Europe."[10]

Du Bois's proposal was rejected by Harcourt Brace, and "A Search for Democracy" was never written. Du Bois scholars, however, will recognize his précis as a forerunner of the "plot" that became the late Mansart trilogy. Those books did indeed set forth an esteemed educator into the world and included, especially in book 3, *Worlds of Color*, report backs from Asia, the West Indies, and Africa; a female protagonist and confidante to the protagonist; and an account of World War II. It also included wholesale reproduction of passages about China and Japan previously published in a series of articles written for *The Crisis* on Du Bois's return in 1937, from his manuscript "Russia and America" of 1950, and, finally, from his posthumously published autobiography, each offered in slightly altered interpretative context, with slightly different interpretive results. The obsessive recombination of thought and piecemeal publishing practice suggests the gravitas of Du Bois's 1936–1937 travels as a tipping point in his understanding of what might be called the world system. Indeed, it is safe to say that Du Bois spent much of the rest of his life after 1936–1937 finding ways to accommodate to his worldview and publishing of that worldview the implications of his discoveries.

In a recent provocative and useful study, Yuichiro Onishi has focused attention on Du Bois's Asian writings, especially his travels in Japanese-controlled Manchuria, as formative to what he calls Du Bois's "Afro-Asian Philosophy of World History." Onishi sees Du Bois's favor for Japan's experiment in colonial economics in Manchukuo on his 1936 trip as a continuation of his efforts in *Black Reconstruction in America* to "assign categorical unity to the insurgency of the colored world, which crystallized at the very moment when the oppressed found themselves standing at critical historical conjunctures."[11] Onishi here sees Du Bois in 1935, as I argued earlier, in a midnight hour of reflection on Western Marxism and revolution, assigning a new leadership role to vanguard Asian populations—the imperializing Japanese—while at the same time failing to recognize Japan's role in sustaining capitalist exploitation. The weakness in Onishi's otherwise penetrating study is its failure to set Du Bois's Japanese travels in the context of shifting perspectives on China. Du Bois, I argue henceforth, resolved what he called the "contradictions and implications" of revolution in China and Japan by setting them in dialectical relation. His attempt to transcend the "national" limitations of his own attachment to Japan eventually resolved itself in a new world revolution conception that synthesized "Pan-Asian" Marxism as something concomitant to his Pan-African support for Bolshevism. This formula also carried with it the seeds of what became Maoist and Third World thought planted by the truncating of the first Chinese revolution of the 1920s. Those seeds also carried the fatal imprint of a Stalinized Comintern, which likewise took hold in the assessment of Asian revolutions in the work of Strong and Smedley. Excavating them requires digging up the ground of China's revolution to understand Du Bois's long march to sympathy after 1936.

———————

As I noted in "The Forethought," China's entry point into the world revolution schema was what Harold Isaacs calls the "second Chinese revolution" of 1919, after the formation of the Chinese Republic in 1911. The impetus came from several sources: an elongated colonial history; the Boxer Rebellion of 1900; and the imposition by Japan in 1915 of its "Twenty-one Demands," in which Japanese troops had occupied China's Shantung Province. Two hundred thousand Chinese laborers sent to Europe during the war had also returned by 1919, carrying heightened nationalism and labor consciousness that led to new strikes in Shanghai and other cities. To this kindling, the Treaty of Versailles, which refused to return Manchuria and other territory to China from occupying Japan, was a lit match. Wilsonian, League of Nations, and Versailles faux pronouncements of "self-determination" fell hard on colonized ears in China and reoriented the direction of China's nationalist protests. As Isaacs puts it, "The disillusionment with the West after the Versailles Conference turned popular attention among the students to the Russia revolution."[12] Ground for that turn had been laid by the announcement on July 4, 1918, by Soviet Commissar for Foreign Affairs Georgi Chicherin that Bolshevik Russia had renounced all "unequal" tsarist treaties with China.[13] Student leaders of the May Fourth Movement smitten with events in the Soviet Union who included, most significantly, Ch'en Tu-hsiu' helped form the CCP in 1920. In June 1920, Grigori Voitinsky was sent as a Comintern representative to meet with Li Dazhao and other founding members of the CCP. At the Second Congress of the Communist International that year, mindful of the nationalist upturn in China after May 4, Lenin's "Theses on the National and Colonial Question" defined internationalism as "the subordination of the interests of the proletarian struggle in one nation to the interests of that struggle on an international scale, and the capability and readiness on the part of one nation which has gained a victory over the bourgeoisie of making the greatest national sacrifices for the overthrow of international capitalism."[14] Delegates from the CCP also attended the First Congress of the Toilers of the East at Baku in January 1922 in support of Lenin's theses.

But the dire conditions facing the Soviet revolution, including famine, civil war, and external invasion, colored Comintern contact and direction toward the CCP from the start, as did external pressure from imperial powers. The first Soviet agents and missions sent by the Comintern were thwarted by U.S. and Japanese pressures on the pro-Japanese clique that dominated the government in Peking.[15] Contrarily, Sun Yat-sen, leader of the Kuomintang, soured by the conduct of the Western powers at the Washington Conference, was looking increasingly to the Soviet Union for assistance. Thus, when the Comintern agent known as Maring went to China in the spring of 1921, he decided "that the main stream of Chinese nationalism flowed through Sun's Kuomintang," an impression doubled by evidence of strong Kuomintang links to the Chinese labor movement.[16] In 1922, at the Fourth Comintern in Moscow, a Chinese delegate described the party's decision to form an "anti-imperialist united front" with the Kuomintang to drive imperialism out of China.[17] In the fall of 1923, Michael Borodin arrived as an adviser to Sun delegated by the Politburo of the Communist Party. At the third conference of the CCP in June 1923, the slogan "All Work to the Kuomintang!" was raised and the party was declared "the central force of the national revolution."[18] Almost immediately, the Kuomintang was transformed into "a rough copy" of the Bolshevik party, and the Russians founded the Whampoa Military Academy, operated with Russian funds and advisers. The CCP, meanwhile, became the "left-wing appendage" of the Kuomintang.[19]

In practice, this resulted in the subordination of the CCP to a bourgeois nationalist party "in the interests of the foreign policy pursued by the Russian bureaucracy."[20] As Duncan Hallas explains, the recommendation was part of a "cult of alliances" in the Comintern that justified the "rightist" line of Nikolai Bukharin and Stalin, which aimed to use the Communist International to shore up Soviet diplomatic relations. The foreign policy was a mirror to the rightist line developing domestically as the Soviets turned to the New Economic Policy to right the ship of revolution. "The bureaucracy has allied itself with the forces of petty capitalism in Russia against the oppositions and against the danger of working-class revival—that was the essence of the Bukharin-Stalin bloc," Hallas writes.[21] This was also reflected in the "Russification" of the CCP and Russian domination of the Communist International. These were the ingredients for Stalin's Socialism in One Country policy, which would take an iron grip on the revolution after Lenin's death in 1924.

To these events Du Bois, he later admitted, was entirely ignorant. In "Russia and America," he would write that his main concerns about Asia in the 1920s centered on European efforts to limit the Japanese navy and a continuing nurturing of his Japanese exceptionalism. "I even interpreted [Japan's] pressure on China as an indirect attack on European imperialism in Asia," he wrote.[22] Du Bois's indifference to what in China between 1924 and 1927 were perhaps the ripest conditions for a workers' revolution in the world is thus an important aspect of his belated relationship to China's place in the world revolution conception. By contrast, Strong and Smedley both had front-row seats to a spectacle that would significantly impress their lifelong devotion to China's revolution. As Jean Chesneaux has documented, the plethora of industrial strikes between 1924 and 1927 have led Chinese historians to call the period the "First Revolutionary Civil War."[23] Rolling waves of industrial action across Wuhan, Canton, and Hong Kong culminated in the so-called Shanghai Insurrection of 1926 in which 169 strikes were carried out, affecting 165 factories and companies and more than 200,000 workers.[24] By the spring of 1927, Shanghai seemed to be prepared for any political outcome, including a workers' takeover. Yet on April 12, Chiang Kai-shek, the leader of the Kuomintang, ordered police to smash out at striking workers and communists in the city. Death estimates ran as high as seven hundred. For its part, the Comintern maintained a "conspiracy of silence" around the coup, which had verified Leon Trotsky's analysis that communist alliance with the national bourgeoisie was a disaster for the Chinese working class. Stalin meanwhile urged a continued bloc between the CCP and Kuomintang, and the Chinese revolution, as Isaacs writes, "plunged on towards new defeats."[25]

For Smedley, the defeat of the workers in 1927 symbolized an ongoing push and pull in her relationship to the Comintern and its policies. Smedley was already distressed by the arrests of her longtime friends Alexander Berkman and Emma Goldman by the Soviets, an experience that left her feeling that she would never forgive the Soviet Communist Party, no matter "how revolutionary it pretend[ed] to be."[26] At the same time, Smedley, Virendranath Chattopadhyaya, and M. N. Roy, each committed to the world revolution in India, were convinced of the Comintern slogan "Via Revolutionary China to the Federal Republic of United States of India."[27] In her writing of the period for the International Workers of the World's *Industrial Pioneer* and for *Comrade*, a communist publication in Delhi, Smedley positioned the workers' struggles in China as part of a "united Asia bloc."[28] The hope for the bloc to hold became a long-term aim paramount to the building of workers' unity. Thus, even after the liquidation of the Shanghai workers' movement and the Comintern's silence in its face, Smedley calibrated the event as a politically expedient alternative to European power in the short term. Smedley's confidence that the Chinese Revolution "would extend to India gave her a fresh appreciation of the Russian leaders' seeming willingness to defend Asia against the long arm of British imperialism."[29]

Like Smedley, Strong was directing her attention to revolutionary prospects in the East. She lived and wrote in Baku, where she became convinced that Soviet public ownership would transform the backwardness of Tartars, Persians, and Tyruks in the region. "The oil-workers of Baku—were rulers!" she wrote.[30] In the fall of 1925, in the midst of workers' uprisings across China, she rode the trans-Siberian train from Moscow across the Urals to Harbin and Peking. Her account of Asiatic "fighting tribes" along the way legitimated a teleological version of world revolution in Asia, which Strong imagined as a form of manifest destiny in the East:

I began to see the Russian revolution not only as a pioneer land emerging from chaos but also as first stage in the awakening and industrialization of Asia. . . .

Now this journey of man had come full circle; it was swinging around the world to Asia after three thousand years. It was crashing upon these people of earth's mother continent, huddled in villages, bound in a farm and family routine that had endured through centuries unchanged. To them now were coming the railroad, the factory, the industrial civilization of the west. They came in two forms between which was war irreconcilable: naked exploitation in the south by the world's imperialists and the Russian revolution in the north.[31]

Strong's confidence in Soviet modernization was sustained until her arrival and assessment of workers' strikes in Shanghai and the British port of Hong Kong, for her a metonymy for workers' revolutions in Seattle, Hamburg, and London. The sight of 100,000 workers rising up in Hong Kong undergirded her confidence that "the forces of the world revolution" would prevent a turning back of the clock in China. Strong's and Smedley's indefatigable enthusiasm for Pan-Asian revolution anticipates Du Bois's appeal for Japanese-Chinese unity of 1933 and indicates a still unrepentant and undaunted confidence in the world revolution concept. Indeed, on May Day in 1930, Strong would give voice to this confidence again at the laying of the last railway spike in the Trans-Siberian Railway by Soviet officials and the seventy-year-old Japanese communist Sen Katayama. "This railway," wrote Strong, "was not only a link between wheat and cotton. It was not only the opening of news lands to pioneers. It was not only the weapon of young herdsmen against tribal oppressors. This railway was world revolution marching down through Asia!"[32] Strong's effusive world revolution rhetoric could have been an outtake of dialogue from Du Bois's *Dark Princess*, published two years earlier.

As for Du Bois, his inclusion of a Chinese character among the "Dark Races" of his Comintern novel of 1928, the aforementioned from his 1933 essay on Japan and China, and his listing of Chinese laborers as among those still awaiting freedom in *Black Reconstruction in America* in 1935 indicate his creeping understanding in the early 1930s of China as one of the world's oppressed darker nations. This panoramic background helps explain how Du Bois, like Smedley and Strong, found himself at a crossroads, or midnight hour, in his understanding of the world revolution and Asia's place in it when he began his 1936 trip. Vying for preeminence were questions about the form national self-determination should take and definitions of "socialism" that had become entangled by global events from afar. In reflections from this period, for example, Du Bois wrote that Germany's National Socialist Party and the state's iron grip on power were a mirror of the state-centered planning and one-party rule of Stalin's Russia. Both countries were making what Du Bois inferred were legitimate claims to "Marxian social-ism."[33] Du Bois's failures to distinguish between the Marxist conception of a workers' state and state capitalism or fascism were symptoms of the creeping Stalinization of Du Bois's thought. These weaknesses of analysis were also kindred to Du Bois's lingering attachment to colonial capitalism as a European, or "white," system of rule, a contradiction that is evident in his first descriptions of Japan when he arrived there in late 1936: "The accom-plishment of Japan has been to realize the meaning of European aggression on the darker peoples, to discover the secret of the white man's power, and then without revolutionary violence to change her whole civilization and attitude toward the world, so as to emerge in the twentieth century the equal in education, technique, health, industry and art of any nation on earth."[34] Japan's task therefore was to advance capitalism into socialism by purging it of its "Eurocentric" flaws. "The Europe which she copied," wrote Du Bois, "was no perfect land. The technique of industry that Japan mastered, the capitalistic regime that she adopted so successfully, has, all thinking men see today, threatening if not fatal tendencies. And now with a herculean task just behind her, Japan is called again to lead world revolution, and lead it with the minimum of violence and upheaval. In the nineteenth century, Japan saved the world from slavery to Europe. In the twentieth century she is called to save the world from slavery to capital."[35]

Keynotes of Du Bois's uneven relationship to Stalinism are all here: fidelity to a Soviet-inspired world revolution concept, metonymic nationalism, unease about revolutionary violence. But it is Du Bois's conception of "state capital-ism" as an emancipatory force that is most revealing of what might be called his "Stalinist blind spot" in regard to Japan and, later, to the Soviet Union and China. In Japan, Du Bois reduces the fight against capitalism to the fight against racial/colonial oppression, not exploitation and expropriation of labor. His primary "test case" for this brand of revolution on his visit, as Onishi has argued, is his brief trip to Japanese-occupied Manchuria, where he was treated by colonial bureaucrats to a description of the state-controlled and state-man-aged Southern Manchuria Railroad Company (SMRC). The SMRC was cen-tral to Manchukuo state builders' development of the East Asian Cooperative Body, described by Onishi as guided by "the idea that a collectivized Asian economy provided a step towards a more 'just' social order."[36] That brutal and violent colonization technique, repression of workers, and rampant labor exploitation—also elements of Stalin's Russia—were fundamental aspects of the Japanese project Du Bois was fully prepared to tolerate, at least initially. For Du Bois, the question of the world revolution had been reduced from how best to emancipate the world's working classes to how to build an alternative to something understood as "Western capitalism."

Du Bois's sojourn from Moscow to Japan to China in 1936–1937 would eventually produce a new typological understanding of both world revolution and the place of Asia within it while laying the groundwork for his support of Mao's Stalinist revolution in China. The turning point was Du Bois's visit to Shanghai just before his visit to Tokyo, Osaka, and Manchuria. Du Bois arrived in China via Tientsin (now Tianjin) after visiting Manchukuo not long after Japan had signed the Anti-Comintern Pact, continuing its long cold war with the Soviet Union. He arrived both headstrong and empty-minded. The worst racial and political ignorance and prejudices of Du Bois's career were arguably directed against colonized China, a story that became a visible subplot in the revision of his world-revolutionary typology. I have already documented Du Bois's rationalizations of Japanese "pressure" on China as an "indirect attack on European imperialism in Asia."[37] In *Worlds of Color*, first published by Mainstream Publishers in 1961, some twenty-five years after, Du Bois provides this information as a character sketch of his fictional persona Manuel Mansart:

> He had never studied or read Chinese history or literature. In elemen-
> tary school, China was a joke and its people "queer." In college he
> learned about the kings of England and France but nothing of the
> Han or Ming emperors. At this very moment, in 1936, Mansart had
> no dream of the frightful tragedy playing over China, or the "long
> March" of eight thousand miles, circling from Fukien to Yunnan,
> Szechwan and Shenshi. Just then, Chu The, of whom Mansart never
> heard, fleeing from capture in the freezing snows of Tibet, was start-
> ing out to join Mao Tse-tung in the future Red Capital of Yenan. The
> long-enslaved, raped and murdered peasants of China were at last
> reeling to their feet, covered with blood and lice, to rule a world.[38]

The hyperbolic retrospective rhetoric of China's "ascent" to world power encompasses both Du Bois's post-1936 Maoist enthusiasms, his 1959 visit to China (to be discussed), and the dramatic shift in his worldview once China's history was fully accommodated to it. But this long road was slow to be built. In October 1937, more than a year after his visit to both Japan and China, Du Bois indulged in a garden-variety form of nationalist chauvinism in berating China for remaining the backslider in Pan-Asia's rise, which was being led, as shown earlier, by India and Russia and, now, Japan:

Even while China was licking the European boots that kicked her and fawning on the West; and when Japan was showing her the way to freedom; China preferred to be a coolie for England rather than acknowledging the only world leadership that did not mean color caste, and that was the leadership of Japan. It was Japan's clear cue to persuade, cajole and convince China, but China sneered and taught her fold that Japanese were devils. Thus the straight road to world dominance of the yellow race was ruined in Asia by the same spirit that animates the "white folks' nigger" in the United States. Whereupon Japan fought China to save China from Europe, and fought Europe through China and tried to wade in blood toward Asiatic freedom.[39]

Du Bois's misapprehension of China as the "Uncle Tom" of the East bespeaks both what he knew and what he did not know about China in the Stalin era. His aforementioned ignorance of the formation of the CCP, of the national strike waves of 1924–1927, and of Chinese antipathy to Japanese imperialism and the contours of the anti-imperialist war sketch this out. More egregious was an inability to imagine national self-determination struggles or proletarian internationalism transcending ethno-nationalist objectives. This, too, was a direct result of Comintern failures after 1919. In "Russia and America," Du Bois wrote about Sun Yat-sen's brief dalliance with the Comintern, "Sen's program was Communism; not the complete Russian line, but an extreme socialism which envisaged division of the land, control of industry, ownership of capital in heavy industry, and the welfare state. How interesting it would have been if Russia and China had been able to cooperate in 1936, as in 1926!"[40] Yet Du Bois's subsequent account in the same manuscript ironically fails to comprehend the reasons for that failure. After Sun's death, "Chiang Kai-shek became commander of the Kuomintang army and proceeded to organize the party. The next year he had deserted the Communists, murdered thousands of students and workers, and with the help of rich bankers set up rule in Shanghai, while Borodin and the Communists ruled in Hankow five hundred miles west."[41] The result, Du Bois wrote, was "dictatorship and reaction," a conclusion that absolves the Stalinized Comintern for its supportive silence in the face of the nationalist Kuomintang counterrevolution.[42] Even as late as 1950, Du Bois was asserting his own account of the "tragedy" of the first aborted Chinese revolution while remaining a de facto advocate and, soon, champion for its chief architects in Moscow.

Thus, Du Bois's sojourn to support for China's communist revolution is marked by twists and turns that are contiguous with his dimly lit understanding of the country upon first encounter. Du Bois's first posting in his Forum of Fact and Opinion column for the *Pittsburgh Courier* on March 6, 1937, was a confused attempt to clarify by eyewitness China's place in the scheme of capitalist colonialism. "Three things attract white Europe to China: cheap women; cheap child-labor; cheap men," he wrote. "And these same three things, too, attract and build the power of Chinese and Japanese capitalists."[43] Complicating matters, Du Bois writes, is a political order that comprises "forces and counter-acting efforts. The Kuomintang is a government of one party like communism in Russia, Hitlerism in Germany and Fascism in Italy. But it has peculiar difficulties in Chinese conditions: the immensity of the land and population; the breakdown of all central government for a long series of years, and catastrophes; the retreat of social control to the curious Chinese family unit, perhaps the strongest social unit in the world today. Entrenched here is almost impenetrable walls of custom, religion and industry, the attempts at reform meet a rock wall of opposition and misunderstanding."[44] Du Bois's conflation of multiple state bureaucracies into a single typology is as imprecise as his lack of distinction between socialism and fascism, a confusion supplemented here by an Orientalist reading of China as Japan's docile student in developmental mentorship. Until late 1937, Du Bois held that China had "failed" Japan's lead in demonstrating that "colored nations are going to escape this fate [subjugation to the West] in the future if they organize themselves in self-defense."[45] As he wrote in February of that year, the basis of "trouble" between China and Japan was not Japanese occupation but "China's submission to white aggression and Japanese resistance; Japanese determination to co-operate with Europe even when that involved aggression in China."[46]

What begins to draw Du Bois away from his own, obfuscating interpretation of China's history of imperial subjugation is forced encounter with the Chinese working class during his visit to Shanghai in 1937. Foreign capital flow into China, he wrote, has "put the hardest working people on earth to making goods and rendering services."[47] Here, Du Bois pauses to note something absent entirely from his portraits of Manchukuo and, later, Tokyo and Osaka—namely, labor exploitation. "The profit has been enormous," he wrote. "But not only Europe, but Asia: Japan and China herself has invested in cheap labor and called this Progress." He continued:

> The result is baffling. Always there is this mass of labor. Labor that has never learned to revolt, to demand, and is only beginning to strike in a few mass industries—ideal labor for profits. The wage is low, and only balanced by still lower cost of living. The rickshaw man drags you, running five miles or more in a half hour for a cent and a half or three cents. A gardener gets five dollars a month with room and board, that is rice and a bit else; a factory hand, I have been told, may get 12 cents

a day; a miner's wage of 25 cents a day was cited as high, since he could live on less than 10 cents.[48]

This passage leads immediately into a description of the nearby city of Hangchow (Hangzhou): "Here vestiges and legends carry one back to 200 years before Christ; back to the Wu-Yueh kings who made Hangchow a metropolis in 900 A.D., only to have it destroyed by the Mongols in the thirteenth century. A hundred years later Marco Polo found it a "great and noble city," defended by 13 miles of walls, built in days by Chang Shih Hsin, who used 5,000,000 workers for the task. Today Imperial Industry born in Europe and imitated in Asia is using man-power in China in just this devastating way."[49]

The Communist International's promise to liberate "toilers" of the East became in the framing analysis of the diasporic international its own archetype. On the trans-Siberian train from Moscow over the Urals, Strong described Russians, Tartars, and Chinese as "ancient peasant peoples left behind in the march of the world."[50] She wrote, "The hopeful revolution was in the dark recesses of this sixth of the world's surface, where peasants and workers of more than a hundred tongues and nations were overthrowing the Middle Ages."[51] For Smedley, whose father mined and whose childhood was a choked-out working-class existence, sympathies with the wretched of the earth, especially the peasantry, was a political calling. When CCP members went underground in response to Chiang Kai-shek's "White Terror" and established their Kiangsi Soviet in primal winter, Smedley wanted only to live and be with them. "The men's defiant resistance to crippling conditions made more sense to Agnes," writes Ruth Price, "than the intrigues of Shanghai's impotent leadership."[52]

Du Bois's gradual understanding of the antiquity of China's proletarianization was, as is often the case, autobiographical and historical. In a typically revisionist telling of his Chinese reeducation in the *Autobiography*, Du Bois wrote, "I used to weep for American Negroes, as I saw what indignities and repressions and cruelties they had passed; but as I read Chinese history in these last months and had it explained to me stripped of Anglo-Saxon lies, "I know that no depths of Negro slavery in America have plumbed such abysses as the Chinese have seen for 2,000 years and more. They have seen starvation and murder; rape and prostitution; sale and slavery of children; and religion cloaked in opium and gin. . . . This oppression and contempt came not only from Tartars, Mongolians, British, French, Germans and Americans, but from the Chinese themselves: Mandarins and warlords, capitalists and murdering thieves like Chiang Kai-shek; Kuomintang socialists and intellectuals, educated abroad."[53]

Yet in early 1937, Du Bois was still far from totalizing in his view of China, even its egregious labor exploitation. The process of developing a complete analysis would take the final twenty-six years of his life and would be marked by a self-conscious process of revision, rethinking, and reassessment. A single event and Du Bois's representation of it best helps to explicate this process when viewed in dialectical relationship to events on the ground in China after 1937. What might be called Du Bois's long historical epiphany regarding China's place in the world revolution concept was first recorded in his account in *Forum of Fact and Opinion* in 1937 of a lunch arranged at his request by University President Herman C. E. Liu to discuss "frankly race and social matters." The assembled group was a cross-section of the Chinese bourgeoisie: an editor of the China Press, the secretary-general of the Bank of China, the general manager of the China Publishing Company, the director of the Chinese schools for Shanghai, and the executive secretary of the China Institute of International Relations. Portending his later reassessment of the event, Du Bois wrote, "I plunged in recklessly." He regaled the group with stories of his ancestry, of his education, "of the Negro problem." Then, Du Bois noted, "I turned on them and said: 'How far do you think of Europe as continuing to dominate the world, or how far do you envisage a world whose spiritual center is Asia or the Colored races? You have escaped from the domination of Europe politically since the World War—at least in part; but how do you propose to escape from the domination of European capital? How are your working classes progressing? Why is it that you hate Japan more than Europe when you have suffered more from England, France, and Germany, than from Japan?'"[54]

Once he finished, Du Bois reported, "There was a considerable silence, in which I joined." Then came a response from one of his hosts, paraphrased by Du Bois this way:

> Asia is still under the spell of Europe, although not as completely as a while back. Still it is not simply our ideal to ape Europe. We, however, know little of India or Asia in America. We see the danger of European capital and are slowly extricating ourselves, by the method of establishing our own capitalistic control and the political power of taxation and regulation. . . .
>
> Our wages are too low, but slowly rising; labor legislation is appearing; we have sixteen million children in school—short terms and inadequate provisions, but schools to fight a 90 percent illiteracy, but Japan hinders us.[55]

Du Bois's response was cited earlier: the "basis" of trouble between China and Japan was "China's submission to white aggression and Japanese resistance." He then added, "With China and Japan in rivalry, war and hatred, Europe will continue to rule the world for her own ends."[56] How best can one understand Du Bois's reaction? As Jon Halliday has noted, Japanese capitalism in the twentieth century was "the prodigy of the age of imperialism, the only outsider and late starter to join the leaders of world imperialism."[57] He adds, "The experience of the last century indicates that there is no such thing as peaceful co-existence with imperialism. A non-socialist state has only a choice between attempting to combat other imperialist powers or forming an alliance with one or more of them."[58] In his "belated" encounter with Asian revolution in 1936, Du Bois perceived China and Japan as the crossroads of this dilemma. His appeal to the Chinese bourgeoisie—metonymic nationalism by another name—endeavored to link colonizer and colonized in what might be called a co-prosperity sphere against the encroachment of European capital. The eventual irreconcilability of Du Bois's analysis, which led to his own change of thought, would quickly be borne out by events. Between December 1936, when he arrived in Japan and China, and December 1937, China and Japan would make final their divergence at the crossroads. Japan ramped up wars against both China and the Soviet Union, dedicating troops to battles with Chinese garrison forces at the Marco Polo Bridge in July and against Soviet troops at the Amur River. By August, the "Battle of Shanghai" pitting Chinese air force planes in attack against Japanese troops and naval ships had begun. On December 8, the Japanese Army began its assault on the walled city of Nanking. After it fell on December 13, siege and slaughter continued against the city and six adjacent rural villages for three months. According to Herbert Bix, "General Nakajima's Sixteenth Division, in just its first day in the capital, killed approximately 32,300 Chinese prisoners of war and fleeing soldiers."[59] What became known as the Rape of Nanking would help commit Japan and China to permanent war and, in combination with three years of ongoing battle with the Soviet Union, solidify Japan's place with the Axis powers through World War II.

Concurrently, and dialectically, 1937 was a turning point in China's sweep toward communist victory and revolution. The Communist International's turn to a Popular Front fight against fascism in 1935, after Hitler's victory in 1933, had led to renewed efforts to build a united front between the CCP and Chiang Kai-shek in fighting Japan. Those efforts helped constitute the fighting forces at Amur and other insurgent attacks on occupying Japanese forces in 1936 and 1937. Yet as Harold Isaacs notes, "Chiang continued to fear the Communists more than he feared military defeats. His own position steadily worsened. The Kuomintang leadership split wide open under Japanese attack."[60] Chiang Kai-shek was increasingly caught between carrying out his policy of "propitiating the Japanese while simultaneously attacking his internal enemies."[61] In late 1936, Manchurian troops in Shensi refused to carry out an ordered attack against the communists and demanded a chance to turn their guns on the Japanese.[62] When Chiang flew to Sian in December— Du Bois was still in the country, he would write in late acknowledgement in *Worlds of Color*—he was kidnapped, and anti-Japanese demands were placed on him by the communists. In 1941, Kuomintang troops attacked the communist New Fourth Army as it attempted to cross to the northern bank of the river in the Yangtze Valley. The army's commander, Yeh T'ing, was arrested and held prisoner until the end of the war. The events "to all intents and purposes terminated the Kuomintang-Communist alliance."[63]

These events left conflicting traces on diasporic international support for China while overdetermining support for communism's victory there. Despite her articulations of doubt about Stalinist direction of the Comintern, Strong's *One Fifth of the World* (1938) was a wholesale endorsement of a Chinese Popular Front united front strategy that was already uneasy. Strong referred, for example, to the communists' kidnapping of Chiang Kai-shek and forced support for the fight against Japan as a "turning point" in the *unification* of China's warring parties. She drew parallels between China's fight for liberation and the American Revolution in her opening chapter. Her account of the Eighth Route Army was equally vainglorious. The book condemned Trotskyists in China as the sole opponents of the united front. It provided as evidence of progress toward democracy the presence of seven communists among two hundred delegates to the Kuomintang's sixth congress in March 1938.[64] In short, Strong recast the world revolution concept in terms rigidly typecast from the Comintern's Popular Front turn. "Thus, step by step," she wrote, "the struggle of the Chinese people for freedom from the invader becomes part of the world-wide struggle for the rights of the common people against the fascist oppressors and the makers of war."[65] Strong also reiterated the metonymic nationalism still suffusing the world revolution concept, concluding, "When 450,000,000 Chinese win their freedom, the world will soon be free."[66]

Strong's book drew in part on Smedley's written reports on the "long march" and Kiangsi Soviets, where she hunkered down with the comrades. Her book *China Fights Back*, a diary of her travels with the Eighth Route Army, was released in the United States and Britain in 1938.[67] Smedley's political life in this period is a microcosm of the diasporic international's complex relationship to Stalinism. Even though she continued to be employed as a Far Eastern agent of the Comintern, reporting on labor conditions in Shanghai, her book *Chinese Destinies* was published in the United States by Vanguard Press rather than by the Communist Party, which did not approve of her sharp criticisms of Chiang Kai-shek's betrayals of the Chinese communists, an implicit criticism of the Comintern's line. During the Popular

Front's united front period after 1935, according to Price, Smedley was continuously outraged by Stalin's failure to prioritize support for the CCP over the Kuomintang. In 1937, Earl Browder, chairman of the CPUSA, sought to denounce Smedley for her dissent from Comintern orthodoxy. At the same time, Smedley broke off her personal friendship with Florence Kelley in this period because of Kelley's sympathies for Trotsky, who continued to criticize Stalin's united front direction as a drag on the Chinese working class. Smedley's absolute support for the CCP in the face of a Stalinized Comintern and CPUSA would not relent for the rest of her life; it eventually converged with Du Bois's own, a confluence made more tenable and less strenuous with the dissolution of the Comintern in 1943.

That convergence, meanwhile, was a work in progress over what may be considered a capstone period in Du Bois's revisionist conception of the world revolution idea. From 1937 to 1950, a period that included World War II, China's 1949 revolution, and completion of "Russia and America," Du Bois made Asia generally, and China specifically, a new centerpiece of his revolutionary typology. Du Bois returned from his 1937 trip still holding firm to the thesis that, "with China and Japan in rivalry, war and hatred, Europe will continue to rule the world for her own ends."[68] His Japanese exceptionalism thesis had also been challenged but was intact. "For the first time in my life," he wrote, "I stood in a land which white people did not control directly or indirectly. The Japanese run Japan, and that even English and Americans recognize and act accordingly."[69] His ethno-nationalism, still buoyed by the dazzle of Japan's Manchukuo experience in economic "co-prosperity," also sustained a continuing misequivalence of "cooperative" economics with "communism"—an error we saw in his interpretation of the Soviet revolution, as well. On July 12, 1941, Du Bois mused about the consequences of a German victory in the war for the *Amsterdam News*. One meaning would be Japanese domination of Dutch India, British East India, and Australia. That still left the "puzzle" of the relation of Japan to Hitler and Mussolini. Eventually, Du Bois concluded, Japan "must make a tremendous choice. Outside of her justifiable hatred of Great Britain and suspicion of America, she has got to realize that the new industrial revolution which has already essentially transformed the Western World which she has been imitating, must be yielded to in Japan; that will be easier than it appears; for as Matsuoka, himself, once told me: within and essentially, Japan is already Communistic."[70]

Yet less than a year later, Du Bois was radically reconsidering. Ironically, it was Du Bois's Popular Front enthusiasm for the fight against fascism that sharpened his analysis of Japanese capitalism. "The infinite tragedy of this war is that an oriental nation, wincing under the sting of inferiority imputed to it by the West," he wrote, "should turn in the 19th Century to follow the very path which the West had followed to superiority; namely, conquest and subjugation, economic imperialism by war and military power, on land and sea."[71] This essentially historical materialist analysis replaced Du Bois's prior "exceptionalist" image of a Japan "saving the world from slavery" with an assertion of its fundamentally capitalist character. Hence, the dream of a twentieth-century Japan "saving the world" from capitalism was also revised. Instead, he wrote, "No little voices like ours in that day could warn Japan or much less England, France and Germany, that power politics held the germ of their own overthrow and disaster. In the end, and in the fourth decade of the 20th Century, Europe and America find themselves fighting in Japan the same ideals which they laid down for Japan as the path of progress nearly a century earlier."[72] Du Bois's evolving assessment here of World War II as an inter-imperialist rivalry hinged on a reconsideration of capitalism as white supremacy; under the pressure of Japanese and German atrocities, the Gordian knot of that conception was coming undone. What the world needed now was a colored nation that was clearly committed to smashing capitalism itself. This question was also embedded in Du Bois's exasperated appeal in 1942, "Can we hope in the Orient for a miracle: that in the midst of war and revolution, the program of imperial dominion will be laid aside, and an era of freedom and accommodation among prospective equals be accommodated?"[73]

For Du Bois, that "miracle" of the Orient was to be China's communist revolution, an event that overdetermined both the last stages of his world revolution conception and his break with Cold War America. Typical of his "belated" relationship to it, recognition of its deliverance to his own revolutionary typology was more retrospective than on time. Throughout the 1940s, Du Bois paid little direct attention to the war between China's nationalists and communists, turning to China's successful revolution of 1949 to make final sense of its meaning only after the war had ended.[74] This process of revision is sketched out for us in the major writings of his later period, which retrospectively "returned" Du Bois to his preliminary visit to China of 1936 to recast and reassess its historical significance.

The first public evidence of Du Bois's turn to support for the CCP over the Kuomintang appears in fact in January 1948. In his "Winds of Time" column for the *Chicago Defender*, Du Bois announced the national conference American Policy in China and the Far East. The event was organized by the Committee for a Democratic Far Eastern Policy, a communist front organization chaired by Maud Russell in New York. Agnes Smedley, who joined the committee sometime in the winter of 1947–1948, spoke at the New York conference.[75] Du Bois used the conference to condemn Chiang Kai-shek and U.S. support for him, decrying "methods which he is using to reduce one of the greatest nations in the world into subjection to a venal and selfish set of exploiters."[76] "It is time," wrote Du Bois, "that Public Opinion should array itself on the side of decency and refuse to be stampeded by the silly yell of "communist" and try to give the great and long-suffering Chinese people a chance to have real voice in their own government and to develop their own land."[77] Du Bois's support for and participation in the conference marked his trajectory of alienation from U.S. ascendancy into what in 1945 he called one of the world's three "colonial" rulers, and his concomitant boostering for socialism as a solution to world economic problems in the postwar war period. More specific to the case of China, Du Bois's support applied the victorious logic of national self-determination elevated at the "colonial international" in Manchester in 1945 and the August 15 midnight of 1947 India to China. China was to be the next great test case of the world revolution conception as hinted at in the vaguely proletarianized rhetorical cast of Du Bois's closing exhortation to attend the 1948 conference: "There will be programs and speeches, but chiefly this is to be a real conference where the rank and file are going to talk and carefully consider the present and future."[78]

The wind in Du Bois's red sails also included deepening attacks on new-found China allies such as Smedley. Near the end of the war, Smedley had been identified as a communist by Whittaker Chambers, a former member of the CPUSA and of the Comintern underground, even if she was not a party member.[79] Before being executed as a communist spy, Richard Sorge had likewise identified Smedley as one of his main assistants in his work in Shanghai, a charge that Ruth Price has since shown to be true.[80] A report with Sorge's allegations was publicly released in the United States in 1948. While the CPUSA—still acrimonious over her dissident criticism of Stalin—did not come to her defense, Edgar Snow did. Eventually, Smedley was cleared of the charges by the U.S. War Department. The allegations bolstered Du Bois's developing interpretation of the Cold War as the most recent U.S. "counter-revolution." China and Chinese communism circa 1948 were now to join Reconstruction, Russia of 1917, and Indian independence as nodes in Du Bois's alternative revolutionary typology. "Asia is disappearing as a colonial area" he wrote in November 1948. "Britain has lost India. France cannot hold Indo-China. Holland is losing Indonesia. China is beating Chiang Kai-shek, puppet of the West, to his knees. In the Near East, Arabs and Islam spell a sharp curb to European overlordship."[81]

Surprisingly, the declaration of the People's Republic of China on October 1, 1949, did not elicit direct written comment from Du Bois. But in the interval between October 1949 and June 1950, Du Bois did assemble the manuscript for "Russia and America" and in so doing began his longer recasting of Japan and China in his world revolution conception. In what I have been calling throughout this book revisionist typological fashion, Du Bois reassembled, in a somewhat mix-and-match fashion, passages excerpted from his *Pittsburgh Courier* columns from February and March 1937, cited earlier. They included sections pasted in verbatim from, for example, his column "What Japan Has Done" of March 20, 1937 ("The accomplishment of Japan has been to realize the meaning of European aggression on the darker peoples"), supplemented by retrospective reflections on both his 1937 visits and his prior written accounts. For example, Du Bois retells in the main the story of his lunch visit at the University of Shanghai from the *Courier* column of February 27. He inserts the four paragraphs that represented the first account in its entirety, supplemented by a series of reflections not in the original on the resentment of Japanese intrusion into China, Chinese "exploitation" by Japan under colonization, and a long historical account of China's colonization under the British and European powers. The text then moves toward repetition of passages from Du Bois's 1937 *Courier* columns on Japan, leading to a recounting of Japanese aggression in China in 1932 and 1933 and Japan's withdrawal from the League of Nations in 1936. These reflections lead Du Bois to the heretofore unasked question in his Japan-China portfolio, "What next?" The answer accounts for the first time in equivocal form for China's new communist status. Du Bois calls for China and Japan to work together "as equals" to industrialize in production of goods that "by the pressure of the communist trends in China be distributed upon a new basis."[82] That basis would be "Marxian in its abolition of industrial profit, toward which family and state communism in Asia already tends."[83] Its character and nature also would be "Asiatic in its use of the vertical clan division and family tie, instead of reaction towards a new bourgeoisie along horizontal class layers which must be the temptation of Europe."[84] This, Du Bois avers, might be a "different kind of Communism": "It might through the philosophy of Gandhi and Tagore, of Japan and China, really create a vast democracy into which the ruling dictatorship of the proletariat would fuse and deliquesce; and thus instead of socialism ever becoming a stark negation of the freedom of thought and a tyranny of action and propaganda of science and art, it would expand to a great democracy of the spirit."[85]

It is tempting to accede here to Onishi's reading of Du Bois's revisionist Marxism the mere spirit of "Afro-Asian philosophy." Yet the passage also demands a dialectical understanding of its relationship to the world revolution concept that inspires it. "Stalinism" in this passage becomes the unnamed trope for the ossification of the Western world spirit, on one hand, as well as for the end game of the age of the Comintern, on the other. In classically revisionist fashion, tinged with an Orientalist enthusiasm that itself would not withstand strong critical scrutiny, Du Bois attempts to spin from a web of contradictory histories a Pan-Asian Marxism. Much as he did in the closing pages of the manuscript of "Russia and America," willing the joint "self-determination" of the American and Soviet populaces, Du Bois attempts to inject new life into what has become a "stalemated" world revolution. "Russia and America" thus again serves as revisionist "sequel" to the "experiment of Marxism" that was *Black Reconstruction in America*.

Du Bois's method of ideological and textual revision in "Russia and America" also gave him the raw material and a generic template for what was to become his Mansart, or Black Flame, trilogy. Du Bois closes his "Asia" section of "Russia and America" with two paragraphs that were reproduced in full as the closing section of "Worlds of Asia," in *Worlds of Color*, book three of the trilogy. There, Du Bois would do even more revision to his analysis of his Asian excursions. The most strenuous was again to his account of his visit to the University of Shanghai. Mansart becomes the fictional Du Bois, traveling from Moscow to Manchuria, then on to Shanghai. The account proceeds according to the original, except for the out-of-order addition of material from another section of the same *Courier* account. The original story is an anecdote related prior to his arrival at University of Shanghai. Du Bois recounts seeing "a little white boy of perhaps four years order three Chinese out of his imperial way on the sidewalk of the Bund, and they meekly obeyed: it looked quite like Mississippi."[86] In *Worlds of Color*, that story is retold directly from the lips of the protagonist Mansart to his astonished guests:

> I saw today something on the streets of your city which reminded me of America. A well-dressed English child of perhaps six years was walking with his nurse along the Bund when he met some Chinese children, small, poorly dressed and dirty. With a gesture he ordered them off the sidewalk; they meekly obeyed and walked in the gutter. In general the whites here treat the Chinese just as we Negroes are treated in the Southern United States. I hear that only recently have Chinese been admitted to the Race Track which is the fashionable amusement center of your city. The white foreigners rule your city, force your children into separate schools and in general act as though they owned China and the Chinese. Why do you permit this?[87]

There is no record to substantiate whether Du Bois in fact omitted this account from his original column, but the effect of placing it in the Black Flame Trilogy is clear and polemical: it is to punish the earlier Du Bois for his misreading of history. "In later years," Du Bois writes, "Mansart was deeply ashamed of calling this conference and asking these questions because he came to realize how abysmally ignorant he was of China and her history. . . . They must have wondered whether he was fool or spy."[88] The text of the trilogy then proceeds to an elongated account of Western colonialism in China and a sharpened, even defiant, response from his audience that was not included in the 1937 original. The school superintendent remonstrates, "We are, sir, as you say, in a sense strangers and outcasts in our own land. That we realize each day. But are not sitting supinely by and doing nothing. Oh, no! Europe is not always going to own and rule Asia."[89] Chastened, Mansart prefaces a presentation by the president about Japan with this self-conscious caution: "He probably sensed that Mansart had the Western prejudice in favor of the Japanese and knew nothing of recent occurrences." That is a precise summary of Du Bois's later self-declarations.[90]

The net effect of Du Bois's textual revisions is to reorder history. China moves from the back of the bus to the driver's seat in the world revolution conception. The final textual and political revisions in Mansart complete this circle of revision by knocking down Du Bois's formerly pristine portrait of Japan as the champion of the darker world. Du Bois's original account, from March 20, 1937, stated:

> There is poverty in Japan; there is oppression; there is still ignorance. But nowhere in the modern world is there such a high literacy, as newspaper circulations of three, and even five million prove; the Japanese laborers is probably the most contented in the world, and this is not the content of stupor, but rather of simple wants and joys.[91]

The revised version read:

> There is poverty in Japan; there is oppression; *there is no democratic freedom.* But nowhere in the modern world is there higher literacy, as newspapers circulation *of one,* three and even five millions prove. The Japanese laborer *is not happy but he is not hopelessly discontented, for he belongs to the same class and family as the highest Japanese. They will guide and protect. He will obey.*[92]

Du Bois's downgrading of Japan in the world revolution schema is given an exclamation point by these revisions that massage the contours of his formula for "Pan-Asian Marxism" from 1950 onto a changeable past. What Du Bois called the "vertical clan" structure of Asian societies acts as a buffer here against class stratification and alienation. At the same time, the passage re-mediates Du Bois's Japanese exceptionalism to make it suitable for final conversion to Asiatic socialism now operant in the neighboring People's Republic of China. Du Bois's last additive comment in *Worlds of Color* on the saga of twentieth-century Japan is this appended statement on the "tragedy" of its own attempt to lead an Asian revolution grafted from Russia and America:

> To me the tragedy of this epoch was that Japan learned Western ways too son and too well, and turned from Asia to Europe. She had a fine culture, an exquisite art, and an industrial technique miraculous in workmanship and adaptability. The Japanese clan was an effective social organ and her art expression was unsurpassed. She might have led Asia and the world into a new era. But her headstrong leaders chose to apply Western imperialism to her domination of the East, and Western profit-making replaced eastern idealism. If she had succeeded, it might have happened that she would have spread her culture and achieve a co-prosperity sphere with freedom of soul. Perhaps![93]

This long emotional and ideological goodbye to Japan achieved real finality and closure in Du Bois's autobiography: he exiled his account of his visit to Japan from the book. The country's national arc of the twentieth century could no longer be accommodated by or to the world revolution concept. Instead, Du Bois revised and rewrote yet again his visit to China of 1937, this time supplemented by an account of his second visit with Shirley Graham Du Bois to the country just before he completed the manuscript for *The Autobiography of W.E.B. Du Bois*. Once again, Du Bois centered his revision on his visit to the University of Shanghai, now the equivalent of a Wordsworthian trauma or rupture in his life story. Fully two paragraphs of his account from 1937 are repeated verbatim, supplemented by this final reflection and evaluation of the moment:

> We talked three hours but it was nearly a quarter of a century before I realized how much we did not say. The Soviet Union was scarcely mentioned, although I knew how the Soviet Union was teaching the Chinese. Nothing was said of the Long March which had just ended its 6,000 miles from Kiangsi to Yenan, led by Mao Tse-tung and Chu The. We mentioned America only for its benefactions and scarcely for its exploitation. Of the Kuomintang and Chiang Kai-shek, almost nothing was said, but hatred of Japan for its betrayal of Asia was amply pointed out.[94]

As he did in *Black Reconstruction in America*, "Russia and America," and the Black Flame Trilogy, Du Bois embraced historical anachronism and revision as an objective correlative for his revolutionary consciousness. "Time, in other words, shifts—future is partly the past and the past is future," he wrote.[95] Du Bois's supplement of historical events with posterior history and consciousness are indices of his leap twenty-five years after the fact into the "open sky" of China's revolution. Indeed, the passage just cited is the bridge or transition in the autobiography to Du Bois's account of his visit in 1959, where all prior doubts and historical gaps are filled with the certainty of revolutionary commitment, just as the "China" chapter of the autobiography concludes with this apocalyptic passage of return and rebirth as a lead-in to the interlude titled "Communism." In its backward and forward movement of time and space, Du Bois attempts to reveal his encounter with his own agonized rendition as Benjamin's messianic Angel of History: "Fifteen times I have crossed the Atlantic and once the Pacific. I have seen the world. But never so vast and glorious a miracle as China. This monster is a nation with a dark-tinted billion born at the beginning of time, and facing its end; this struggle from starved degradation and murder and suffering to the triumph of that Long March to world leadership. Oh beautiful, patient, self-sacrificing China, despised and unforgettable, victorious and forgiving, crucified and risen from the dead."[96]

The Chinese Revolution of October 1949 expressed the Stalinization of the world revolution conception in several ways. The setbacks to workers' uprisings in 1927 detached the Chinese proletariat for nearly two decades from membership and leadership in the CCP. This mirrored the trajectory within the Soviet Union, where the Chinese defeats of 1927 persuaded Stalin to liquidate his opponents once and for all and begin the deproletarianization of the Soviet Communist Party.[97] Second, the defeat of urban proletariat uprisings drove the party into what the CCP called "Chinese Soviet Republics" like Kiangsi, where, largely isolated and under attack, they were unable to carry out any consistent program of agrarian reform.[98] Third, the Popular Front's united front strategy after 1935, which the Comintern intended mainly as protection of the Soviet Union against fascist threat, resulted in a protracted destructive alliance with the Kuomintang. This alliance gave fatal shape to the Communist Party that emerged triumphant in 1949. As Harold Isaacs notes, "The regime created by the Communists upon their conquest of power was represented to be a resurrection of the same "bloc of classes" that had featured the initial Communist-Kuomintang alliance, with the difference that it was now "under the special leadership of the working class," which in turn was "exemplified" by the position of the Communist Party itself in the commanding role. It was, therefore, a "people's democracy" in which the power to define the "people" remained with the communist leadership. It was, in a word, a "dictatorship of the party itself."[99]

Operating over rather than within the mass of workers and peasants, the CCP resorted to terror in the face of inevitable dissent. On February 20, 1951, the communist government in Peking proclaimed the death penalty for "counterrevolutionary offenses."[100] Purges and executions of internal enemies began forthwith. These events not only repeated the pattern of the Stalinized Soviet bureaucracy but also helped to legitimate its tactics and techniques. China, Isaacs writes, "became part of the Russian national power orbit in the midst of an acute world power struggle. Its fate, like that of the rest of the world, was linked in large measure to the ultimate resolution of that struggle."[101] Thus, despite the fact that the actual influence of the Soviet Union on China's 1949 revolution was small (the Comintern having been disbanded six years earlier), "The victories of the Chinese communists brought Western influence in China to an end and automatically moved the entire country into the new Eurasian empire ruled by Russia."[102] As a result, "The Chinese Communists seized power in China and yoked themselves to the Russian drive to win power in the world. Together they plunged on down the dark road of totalitarianism."[103]

In this, the Chinese Revolution was the quintessence of contradictions in the world revolution concept for members of the diasporic international. For the vast majority of the revolution's unfolding, their support for it coincided and overlapped with a U.S. alliance with the Chinese independence struggle. Until 1946, the "Stalinist" stamp on the revolution was a bipartisan consensus manufactured by the Popular Front united front against fascism that Du Bois had attempted to resurrect in "Russia and America" to end the Cold War impasse. China's revolution also held for Du Bois, Smedley, and Strong, each committed to antiracist politics formed in the crucible of America, the luster of a revolution by what Du Bois called a "dark-tinted billion." Russia may have refused to be "white" in its Comintern support for anticolonial struggles in Asia and Africa and in proclamations for ethnic equality in state, but China fulfilled the historical archetype of the "wretched of the earth" coming into full self-determination, a reputation that would animate Maoist enthusiasm among a broad range of ethnic nationalist movements of the 1950s and 1960s.

China also bore the weight of two distinctive aspects of the Cold War that were constituent of Stalinism's legacy. First, support for China's revolution carried with it by default the glory and advance of Soviet communism, even in the face of often strong disagreement with Soviet treatment of the Chinese liberation struggle. Most emblematic here is Anna Louise Strong. In the fall of 1948, she and Du Bois would appear together at Carnegie Hall, at a meeting called by the National Conference on American Policy in China, where she was withering in her criticism of Stalin for failing to provide material support to communist forces in their war with the nationalists. In early 1949, Strong was expelled from the Soviet Union for "spying," a cover for her public criticism. Only after the rapprochement that followed communist victory in October 1949 would she return to favor in the Soviet Union. Indeed, just six days before Du Bois's eighty-second birthday in 1950, and just months after the October Revolution, China and the Soviets would sign an alliance formally wedding their revolutions and putting in place an official plank of the Cold War. Throughout this period, regardless of her position on the Soviet Union, Strong was a declared enemy of both the American state and the Stalinist Communist Party and an uneasy ally of the Soviets.[104]

Second, Du Bois's support for China's 1949 revolution was arguably as much a response to the ravages of U.S. anticommunism after 1946 as it was to any understanding of or support for the meaning of the revolution itself. Between 1948 and 1950, a hard anticommunist rain fell across the United States, leaving Du Bois a drowning man: his own NAACP severed ties with the communist front Civil Rights Congress and expelled communist branches and members from its ranks.[105] The Council on African Affairs, which Du Bois had joined in 1946, was targeted for Red influence. Du Bois's close friend Paul Robeson was tagged the "Black Stalin" by the anticommunist Manning Johnson for his pro-Soviet remarks at the World Partisans for Peace conference in Paris in 1949. Twelve members of the Communist Party USA were found guilty on October 14, 1949, of trying to overthrow the U.S. government under the Smith Act.[106] On August 8, 1949, Du Bois himself was called to testify before the House Committee on Foreign Relations. About widespread fear of a Soviet attack on the United States, Du Bois remarked, "We did not believe this when we asked ten million Russians to die in order to save the world from Hitler. We did not believe it when we begged Russian help to conquer Japan.... We want to rule Russia and we cannot rule Alabama."[107] In November 1949, Agnes Smedley sailed for Europe, exhausted by the prolonged public defense against allegations of spying and having lost audiences for her lectures.[108] "Under no condition," she wrote, "shall any American claim my body or any of my personal possessions, save the sum I leave to my small niece, and except for my executors, or the friends who are to receive my manuscript. Should I die, it will be with a curse on American Fascism, as represented by the American government, the American Congress, and all the armed forces and official representatives on my lips."[109]

Smedley's letter makes clear that by 1950 her enthusiasm for the Soviet and Chinese revolutions was constituted in large part out of domestic animus against them. It was, to return to an earlier conception in this book, a negative dialectics already cast in the dark hues of internal and external exile. Indeed, Du Bois's open, *public* support for the Chinese Revolution was belated to the last four years of his life, as recorded in his writings undertaken after his second and third visits to the country in 1959 and 1962; in the books of the Black Flame Trilogy; and in his final, posthumously published autobiography. By that time, China had also become part of a new world revolution concept for Du Bois that functioned as a bridge between the age of the Communist International and that of the Colonial International, between 1917 and 1949 and the new world to which it seemed to be giving birth. Sometimes called the "Bandung," or postcolonial, era, this, too, should be understood as a revised typology of the century of world revolution. It is to its contours and dimensions that I now turn.

5

MAKING PEACE

Gendering the World Revolution/ Reckoning the Third World

In this struggle, Communist women, by their leadership among the masses of women, and learning from them to fight for their demands, will fuse the women's peace movement under the leadership of the working class and will thereby help to change the relationship of forces in our land in such a way as to make for a new anti-fascist, anti-imperialist people's coalition, advancing through this struggle to Socialism.

—CLAUDIA JONES, "FOR THE UNITY OF WOMEN IN THE CAUSE OF PEACE," 1951

I do not believe that, in the economic revolution through which the present world is bound to go, force or violence is necessary. Mankind surely is coming to the stage when great and revolutionary change can be brought about by reason and peace.

—W.E.B. DU BOIS, "THE AMERICAN NEGRO IN MY TIME," 1956

Today we see how Africa is moving forward. And although in Congo the heart of Africa is still bleeding, and although madmen in the South of Africa are still keeping their power, our peoples are full of confidence in their ultimate victory. They have leaders who possess courage and wisdom. Noble ideas and commandment of Vladimir Ilyich Lenin shine for us, as the morning of a new day.

—W.E.B. DU BOIS, "UTRO NOVOGO DNIA," APRIL 22, 1963

Mansart opened his eyes and whispered, "It was a nightmare. I know it now. I am back from a far journey. I saw China's millions lifting the soil of the nation in their hands to dam the rivers which long had eaten their land. I saw the golden domes of Moscow shining on Russia's millions, yesterday unlettered, now reading the wisdom of the world. I saw birds singing in Korea, Viet-Nam, Indonesia and Malaya. I saw India and Pakistan united, free; in Paris, Ho Chi Minh celebrated peace on earth; while in New York—"

—W.E.B. DU BOIS, *WORLDS OF COLOR*, 1961

The Chinese Revolution of 1949 and the beginning of the Cold War forced W.E.B. Du Bois to again revise his typology of world revolution. Asia's string of anticolonial successes beginning with India (1947), Burma (1947), and China (1949), he predicted, would reorient global imperialism back to the African continent and thus necessitate new linkages between national liberation struggles across the capitalist colonial world. From 1949 to 1963, Du Bois rededicated himself to drawing together the bilateral strands of his thought: Pan-Africanism (and now Pan-Asianism) and global socialism. The urge to sustain a world revolution conception still beholden to the dream of Communist Internationalism put him temporarily at odds with what Vijay Prashad has aptly called the "internationalist nationalism" of the postwar Third World.[1] Internationalist nationalism was the shared ideology of decolonizing nations in Africa and Asia seeking solidarity based on anti-imperialism and the often deformed adaption of Marxist and socialist principles to national liberation struggles. Throughout the 1950s, for example, George Padmore's growing conviction that Pan-Africanism was an "ideology" capable of replacing Marxism completed the succession of the "Comintern" by the "colonial international" articulated at the Pan-African Congress in Manchester in 1945. Du Bois initially chafed at this conception, as he did at doctrines of "African socialism" that were proliferating in decolonizing African states. Still beholden in name to a Leninist conception of nationalism as a step toward proletarian internationalism, Du Bois insisted that decolonizing African countries model their revolutions on workers' states in Russia and China, even when those states had badly forestalled workers' takeover of state power. Du Bois relented, slightly, after Nikita Khrushchev's revelations of Stalin's atrocities at the twentieth Soviet Congress in February 1956 and the Soviet invasion of Hungary in November of that year. Throughout the anticolonial period, the valence of nationalist ideologies as surrogates for proletarian internationalism also carried the legacy of Stalinism's Socialism in One Country program.

Du Bois's second typological revision was a nearly obsessive new commitment to global peace activism. From the time of his participation in peace conferences in Moscow, Stockholm, and Paris in 1949 to the end of his life, Du Bois perceived the threat of a third world war as a global "counterrevolution" facing all of humanity. As he wrote in the closing pages of "Russia and America," the discovery in 1949 that the Soviet Union had joined the United States in holding the "secret of the atom bomb" meant that "evidently the world must disarm or go bankrupt or infinitely worse than either go to war."[2] For Du Bois, the threat of nuclear war and competitive global expansion between the superpowers consummated an era of capitalist modernity predicated on the "degradation of the worker, especially through the colonial system and the human slavery upon which the colonial imperialism was originally built."[3] Thus, combating nuclear war became an essential step to unite the world's working class against its own extinction. Here, Du Bois's political allies and mentors became a wide network of women affiliated with the Communist Party and broad U.S. left headed by his final life partner,

Shirley Graham Du Bois. Graham Du Bois has rightly been credited with moving Du Bois closer to eventual membership in the Communist Party in 1961, which she had joined years earlier. Less heralded is Graham Du Bois's influence on what might be called the "gendering" of Du Bois's world revolution conception. Graham Du Bois, along with her friends and associates, many of them communists or fellow travelers, including Louise Thompson Patterson, Esther Cooper Jackson, Charlotta Bass, Vicki Garvin, and Claudia Jones, pulled Du Bois decisively in the direction of antinuclear work that foregrounded the impact of Cold War and world war especially on women. Jones in particular led theoretical innovation on the left in the United States and the United Kingdom that peace work and working-class women's lives were central to building a sustainable proletarian internationalism. China's slogan "Women Hold Up Half the Sky" became in Jones's hands the revised slogan "Half the World," the title of a column she published in the 1950s in the "Woman Today" section of the Sunday edition of the *Daily Worker*. Jones argued that working-class unity and victory depended on the role of women as leaders of the class. Du Bois's close political and personal affiliations with Graham Du Bois, Jones, and Jackson thus both pulled forward and refreshed prior commitments of the diasporic international to resolution of what the Communist Party called the "woman question" by centering African American women's political work and leadership. By his death in 1963, "making peace" would become for Du Bois both a personal metaphor and a political strategy for capstoning a lifetime commitment to world revolution.

———

The doubled direction of Du Bois's late-life theory and practice were anticipated by his meeting in London in 1945 with Esther Cooper Jackson in the wake of the Pan-African Congress (PAC) in Manchester. Jackson was in London as a delegate of the Southern Negro Youth Conference (SNYC) to the Soviet-sponsored World Youth Congress. Jackson and her husband, James, had revered Du Bois since they had moved to the left and joined the Communist Party in the 1930s. Jackson's meeting with Du Bois began a long political collaboration. They worked together in the 1950s on *Freedom*, the political journal started by Du Bois and Robeson; in 1961, Jackson would cofound and become managing editor of its successor, *Freedomways*. Jackson, like Du Bois, would become an ardent supporter of the Soviet Union and Stalin during the 1950s, traveling to the Soviet Union immediately after their meeting in London in 1945. In 1947, Du Bois accepted Jackson's invitation to deliver the keynote speech to the SNYC in Columbia, South Carolina. While the address became well known for its assertion of interracial working-class militancy in the South and the southern United States as a "straight path" to the colonized world, the significant role of black women in the SNYC's leadership and its featuring of several black female speakers (including Dorothy Burnham, Modjeska Simkins, and Charlotte Hawkins Brown) foreshadowed Du Bois's involvement with a new network of activists who would reorient both his world revolution conception and his deepening commitment to a Stalinized Communist Party of the USA (CPUSA).[4] As Erik McDuffie points out, the World War II–era communist left "remained the primary site from which black women radicals agitated for black rights and forged transnational political alliances with women and men across the Global South."[5] What this meant in practice was developing new political lines of argument in the post-Comintern period that might reconstitute world revolution. Two of those lines were emphases on the role of women in building proletarian internationalism and the importance of fighting for world peace. A third, intimately related line was continuous defense of the Soviet and Chinese revolutions. All three would significantly affect Du Bois and the new postwar diasporic international's reckoning of Cold War politics in the Third World.

Events of 1951 help constellate this turning point. Du Bois's arrest and indictment for violation of the Smith Act for his role in the Peace Information Center less than a year after completing his peace opus "Russia and America" hastened a hard redirection of his thought and political orientation. Du Bois understood his arrest as an attempt to expel him from the diasporic international. As he later wrote in his autobiography, "The real object was to prevent American citizens of any sort from daring to think or talk against the determination of big business to reduce Asia to colonial subservience to American industry; to re-weld the chains on Africa; to consolidate United States control of the Caribbean and South America; and above all to crush socialism in the Soviet Union and China."[6] Indeed, Du Bois had just watched Agnes Smedley, with whom he had spoken at a solidarity meeting on China, dragged through public colloquy for her Chinese and Soviet sympathies. A political pariah at home, Smedley applied for a passport and left the United States for England later that year. In early 1950, she became a subject of inquiry by the House Un-American Activities Committee; the Federal Bureau of Investigation (FBI) would declare her case a matter of "urgent and . . . great importance."[7] In April 1950, Smedley wrote in a letter from exile, "I have had but one loyalty, one faith, and that was to the liberation of the poor and oppressed; and, within the framework, to the Chinese revolution as it now materialized."[8] Less than a month later she was dead, her ashes scattered in Beijing. Du Bois also had the painful experience of watching Anna Louise Strong expelled from the Soviet

Union for spying in February 1949 (she had not been sufficiently adulatory toward Stalin in some of her journalistic accounts), only to be accused by the United States of spying for the Soviets when she returned to the country. Defiantly, she, too, left the United States, never to return.

His arrest in 1951 drove Du Bois into a similarly intransigent corner of *internal* exile, formalizing his un-Americanness as a collaborative work in progress between his self-image and the image in legal and bureaucratic production by the state. One immediate result was the essay "I'll Take My Stand," published in *Masses and Mainstream* in 1951, which might be considered an early manifesto of his late world revolution typology. In it, Du Bois redefines capitalism as what Michael Kidron would later call a "permanent arms economy."[9] The thesis, first put forward on the left in 1944 by Ed Sard (under the aliases Frank Demby, T. N. Vance, and Walter Oakes), offered that U.S. capitalism would by necessity depend on continuous war expenditures and threats of war to sustain growth. Rolling wartime production fueled by taxes and extraction of surplus value from labor simultaneously moved profits to the top of the economy and expanded American empire abroad.[10] Du Bois's argument thus retrofitted and revised for the geopolitical dynamics of the Cold War aspects of his thesis in "African Roots of War" (1915) that capitalist imperialism's primary purpose was redistribution of wealth from the global South to the global North:

> The powerful who today own the earth and the fullness thereof; who monopolize its industry and own its press and screen its news ... order us to fight an Idea, to "contain" and crush any dream of abolishing poverty, disease and ignorance; and to do this by organizing war, murder, and destruction on any people who dare to plan plenty for all mankind. From the nineteenth century, the attempt to take over imperialism to bribe the workers and thinkers of the powerful countries by high wage and privilege, in order to build a false and dishonest prosperity on the slavery and degradation, the low wage and disease, of Africa and Asia and the islands of the sea; and to pay the price for this, they demand that you, yours sons and daughters, in endless stream, be murdered and crippled in endless wars.[11]

Du Bois here retypifies a central argument of the diasporic international: the capitalist colonial complex now uses communism as the common enemy to mutually exploit and oppress workers of the world: "This is why we are fighting in Europe, Asia and Africa—not against an enemy, but against the Idea—against the rising demand of the working classes of the world for better wage, decent housing, regular employment, medical services and schools for all."[12] Thus, in the face of state intimidation—"swear to God that never, never did you ever sympathize with the Russian peasants' fight to be free"—Du Bois enumerates a world revolution conception pitched first to global peace:

> I want progress; I want education; I want social medicine; I want a living wage and old age security; I want employment for all and relief for the unemployed and sick; I want public works, public services and public improvements. I want freedom for my people. And because I know and you know that we cannot have these things, and at the same time fight, destroy and kill all around the world in order to make huge profit for big business; for that reason, I take my stand beside the millions in every nation and continent and cry *Peace—No More War!*[13]

Du Bois's declaration of peace principles aligned him both to the "official" Soviet line in support of nuclear disarmament and global peace work and to the CPUSA's new emphasis on connecting the violence of U.S. imperialism to domestic attacks on African Americans. Yet to understand fully the contours of "peace politics" in his shifting revolutionary typology, we must also attend to the political distance between Du Bois's "formal" account of his peace work in this period and the more complete record filled in by contemporary scholars of that same work. For example, in his autobiography and in *In Battle for Peace*, Du Bois describes his "connection with the movement" as dating to his attendance at peace society meetings in St. Louis in 1913; attendance at various international conferences, including the Cultural and Scientific Conference for World Peace in March 1949 at the Waldorf Astoria Hotel, and a subsequent meeting in Paris in 1949; and the all-Soviet peace conference in Moscow in August 1949, which provided material for the last sections of "Russia and America." At the Moscow conference, Du Bois delivered a long address whose fundamental theme was the interrelation of capitalist development with race and caste in the United States, and which included an appeal for an American "takeover" of the nation in industry and government cited in Chapter 2. The speech gestured toward socialism as an alternative to exploitative capitalist relations and the redistribution of wealth as a beneficent deviation from private profit. It ended with a somewhat quiescent nod to the 1948 Progressive Party campaign of Henry Wallace as a "challenge" to these tendencies and protests against war organized by the Council of Arts, Sciences, and Professors and the Quakers. This account of Du Bois's Moscow address leads immediately in *The Autobiography of W.E.B. Du Bois* to the creation of the Peace Information Center in the United States, the issuing of "Peacegrams," and the reporting on and circulation of the "Stockholm Appeal" that brought the center, and Du Bois, into the glare of state persecution. In Du

Bois's account of his trajectory into peace work, a variety of individuals are named as primary spurs and collaborators, including the former ambassador O. John Rogge, the communist journalist Albert E. Kahn, Linus Pauling, John Clark, Uta Hagen, the Dean of Canterbury, and Pablo Picasso.[14]

Missing from Du Bois's retrospective account of his peace work is the prominent network of black female activists who helped give clear political shape and direction to that work. Indeed, it is not until near the end of his account of his trial as a "foreign agent" that Du Bois acknowledges "the collaboration of Shirley Graham" and his "open thanks to the Communists of the world" for their help in his defense.[15] Beyond mere help, Graham Du Bois, Claudia Jones, Esther Cooper Jackson, Charlotta Bass, and other African American women of the left provided important political arguments that enabled Du Bois to conceive of his "peace" strategy as the most effective way to reckon a new conception of world revolution for the postwar Third World. As Gerald Horne notes, Shirley Graham's peace work preceded her marriage to Du Bois in 1951 by at least two years; in 1949, she attended the World Peace Conference in Paris where Robeson made his notorious declaration that African Americans would not fight the Soviets.[16] She also played a prominent role, as did Du Bois, at the World Conference for Peace at the Waldorf Astoria in 1949. In December 1950, two months before her marriage to Du Bois, she wrote to an Indian friend describing a speaking engagement that night against the new U.S. war in Korea. Graham Du Bois emphasized women's special role in peace work: "Unless women everywhere come out very strong in the struggle for *peace* selfish men are going to drag us into war. And the heaviest responsibility lies on the women of America. We are the only women in the world who have not suffered horribly in wars."[17]

By the time Graham wrote the letter, the notion of a "special burden" on women living under U.S. imperialism was a well-established theme among her circle of black women activists on the communist and noncommunist left. Charlotta Bass, too, attended the peace conferences in Paris and Prague in 1950 as a member of the Peace Committee of the World Congress. She likewise attended the World Student Congress in Prague and visited the Soviet Union, writing articles for *Soviet Russia Today* praising the lack of racial discrimination in the United States.[18] Du Bois's "I'll Take My Stand" was also published within months of Claudia Jones's "For the Unity of Women in the Cause of Peace" and the communist fellow traveler Beulah Richardson's influential poem "A Black Woman Speaks of White Womanhood, of White Supremacy, of Peace." The speaker in Richardson's poem is a black woman who describes brothers, husbands, and sons: "their blood chilled in electric chairs, / Stopped by hangman's noose, cooked by lynch mob's fire."[19] As McDuffie notes, the poem "placed special emphasis on the social consequences of being a black woman in a historically violent, racist, sexist society and understood black women as key agents for human rights and world peace."[20] Richardson's poem would become a key inspiration in the formation in 1951 of a new black women's social justice group, Sojourners for Truth and Justice. Leaders of the group included the long-time activist and Du Bois admirer Louise Thompson Patterson and Shirley Graham Du Bois. Graham had married Du Bois in February 1951, after a long courtship that culminated in Graham's public defense of Du Bois during his arrest and trial. Seven months later, Sojourners for Truth and Justice held its inaugural convention in Washington, DC, at the meeting hall of the Cafeteria Workers Union.[21]

What connected Graham to Du Bois, the Sojourners to both, and all to the world revolution conception was the battle for peace against Cold War violence. The Sojourners called simultaneously for the end of Jim Crow attacks in the American South and an end to the Korean War.[22] The linkage of southern violence and American imperialism—a keynote of Du Bois's "Behold the Land" speech to the SNYC and an inspiration to the Sojourners—was revised now as a tool to fight black women's oppression. Precursive to the formation of the Sojourners, for example, had been work by its founding members on the case of Rosa Lee Ingram, a Georgia sharecropper, widow, and mother facing a death sentence (along with her two sons) for killing a white man in self-defense after he tried to rape her. Beginning in 1949, Claudia Jones, Eslanda Robeson, and Shirley Graham Du Bois organized a defense of Ingram framed as a violation of international human rights. The Ingram defense committee argued that the United States chose "to pardon hundreds of Nazis responsible for" the Holocaust rather than Ingram, and in the spring of 1949 they sent President Truman ten thousand Mother's Day cards and a petition with twenty-five thousand signatures seeking Ingram's freedom. One of the signatories was W.E.B. Du Bois.

The Ingram campaign became a template and test case for Du Bois's political orientation to new tactics and strategies for orienting peace activism to the world revolution conception. By 1949, Du Bois was showing impatience with signs of stalled progress across various fronts of the diasporic international. In that year, for example, Du Bois made no effort to see Jawaharlal Nehru on his U.S. visit, joining Howard Fast and others in sending him a letter protesting his jailing of trade union, peasant, and communist leaders.[23] Nehru, it seemed to Du Bois, was already foreclosing possibilities for real socialism in India, a development, as we have seen, that should not have been unexpected. Gandhi's assassination in 1948 had also been a blow to optimism about an easy transition to a postcolonial state, as had the genocidal division of India and Pakistan. The Soviet Union's announcement in 1949 that it had discovered the "secret" of the atomic bomb galvanized Du Bois's preservation sympathies for the revolution of 1917, on one hand, but also doubled down on the counter-revolutionary prospects of another world war, on the other. Finally, after the magnificent flurry of activity in Manchester, the PAC had dispersed, with no clear direction. Plans for a sixth congress, in Liberia in 1947, proved short-lived; by 1948, the PAC had "lost its way," according to Immanuel Geiss.[24] Pan-Africanism was also coming under steady Cold War attack. In October 1949, George Padmore attended a Congress of Peoples against Imperialism in London, where he criticized the newly seated Labour Party for indifference to the fight against imperialism and colonialism. Labour Party members in turn accused Pan-Africanists of being "communist."[25]

In this context, the proletarian militancy of the Ingram campaign and the new, energetic leadership of Graham Du Bois, Jones, Eslanda Robeson, and others in linking the fight against racism and sexism at home to violence and imperialism abroad struck Du Bois as a necessary, if not sufficient, mode of new militancy. As Cheryl Higashida has argued, the black feminist left played a central role in revising Leninist principles and tactics during the Cold War. Especially after his arrest in 1951, Du Bois found these revisions newly conducive to his thought and his plight. For example, in 1946 the CPUSA repudiated its allegiance to the last vestiges of the Popular Front by removing Earl Browder as head of the party, vanquishing its wartime designation as the Communist Political Association. The party's left turn included a revival of the so-called Black Belt thesis from the Sixth Communist International of 1928. Queen Mother Audley Moore and Harry Haywood, both Comintern veterans and the latter an original architect of the 1928 resolution, were prominent in leading this charge.[26] Although Du Bois never fully embraced the Black Belt thesis, as we have seen, the party's turn to focus on black proletarian internationalism comported with his frustrations with the National Association for the Advancement of Colored People (NAACP) for back-burnering questions of African freedom (he would resign from the organization again in 1948), his enthusiasm for classical tenets of diasporic internationalism that had turned him to the left to begin with, and his insistence on the role of the black (especially African) working class in building proletarian internationalism. An example of this new set of principles was his work on the "We Charge Genocide" petition to the United Nations. That document, officially the work of the CPUSA's Civil Rights Congress, used the political logic, though not the framework, of the party's rededication to a national self-determination perspective. Invoking the United Nations' recently passed charter on genocide to describe crimes of violence against African Americans, "We Charge Genocide" animated human rights discourse and international law to tacitly identify African Americans (like the Jews of World War II) as a specially oppressed national minority. Thus, not only the CPUSA's lead attorney and organizer

William Patterson but also the party members Claudia Jones, Charlotta Bass, and several other members of the Sojourners for Truth and Justice counted themselves as signatories to the petition when it was presented to the United Nations in 1951. "We Charge Genocide" was also an implicit attempt both to criticize the United Nations for its failure to commit clearly to a right of self-determination for the colonies and to bring international attention to violence as a permanent structural element of U.S. imperialism and domestic racism.[27]

Du Bois also turned to the United Nation and a strategy for peace because he saw in its operative politics a violent political partitioning of the modern world that was a sequel to both the Berlin Conference of 1884 and the colonial debacle of 1919 that was the League of Nations. In his reporting on the United Nations meetings in San Francisco in June 1945, Du Bois dissected the creation of "strategic areas" such that the "United States proposed in her own right to police the Pacific bases with her right wing on Australia and using the Union of South Africa to protect her rear. In this way she proposed to keep the Asiatic peoples in her places."[28] Du Bois likened the process to the handing over of mandates to imperial powers during World War I: "Thus, the United States with her territories and quasi-colonies in the Pacific under the guise of strategic areas, becomes one of the three colonial powers—Great Britain, France and the United States."[29] Alternatively, the United States could have been, along with Russia and China, a decisive voice in "ruling the future world with three nations which did not depend upon the exploitation of colonies for their future development. . . . Here, then, I seem to see outlined a third World War based on the suppression of Asia and the strangling of Russia."[30] As to Africa, through his work with the Communist Party front organization Council on African Affairs and in numerous columns for the *Chicago Defender*, *March of Labor*, *People's Voice*, and *National Guardian*, Du Bois hammered away at the economic inequalities across the continent and their relationship to the "combined and uneven" development of global peace and prosperity. "No fight for the eventual improvement in equality of the workers in the United States, France and Great Britain will be successful until they [cease] to be pulled down and kept back by the conditions in Africa, Asia and the West Indies and by conditions in our own South," he wrote in 1954.[31] Still later he wrote, "We must realize that there can be no world peace which is not peace for and in Africa."[32] For Du Bois, resistance to colonialism, slavery, and capitalist exploitation was to be understood as the simultaneity of workers' power from below and the demilitarization—and deimperialization—of the planet, a virtual reset of the Leninist thesis of 1917 and of his own "The African Roots of War" of 1915: "The reason that modern European civilization descended so disastrously into the hell of war in the twentieth century was because of their determined and continuous war in Asia and Africa, their theft of raw materials which belonged to other peoples and their exploitation and enslavement of coloured human labor. In a world effort to stop this method of forwarding modern culture to realize liberty, equality and brotherhood, the peace movement has begun and is showing itself most effectively in the upsurge of nationalism in Asia and Africa."[33]

Yet the woman who provided the strongest theoretical foundation on which Du Bois, Shirley Graham, Bass, and others approached peace work against the capitalist colonial complex was Claudia Jones. In three essays published in 1946, 1949, and 1950, she reoriented the CPUSA and the broader American left to a new conception of gender, Leninism, and imperialism and their relationship to peace work. She concurrently articulated an internationalism typologically figured on Leninist and Stalinist ideas regarding national self-determination and women's oppression that both harked back to and pulled forward arguments Du Bois had made, in a different register, years earlier in his seminal essays "The African Roots of War" and "The Damnation of Women."[34] While Carole Boyce Davies has demonstrated that Jones considered Du Bois her "teacher" at this time and after, a reciprocal influence is evident in the trajectory of Du Bois's work during this period.

Like those of so many figures of the diasporic international, Jones's life was one of continuous movement, exile, and pursuit—"roving to revolutions," as her contemporary Anna Louise Strong described her own life's work. Jones was born in 1915 in Trinidad and came to the United States after her parents had emigrated in 1934. She lived first in a working-class home in Harlem, where she joined the Young Communist League in 1936, having first been attracted to the Communist Party because of its International Labor Defense campaign on behalf of the Scottsboro Boys. In Harlem, she worked as a staff writer for the *Daily Worker*, edited the YCL's newspapers, and served as Harlem organizer for the YCL and then on its National Council. She also worked with the National Negro Council, a communist-backed organization, and the SNYC with Esther Cooper Jackson. In 1945, she "graduated" from the YCL to the CPUSA.[35] In 1947, she was reassigned to work among women as executive secretary of the National Women's Commission of the Community Party. In 1948, she was elected to the party's National Committee and later became editor of its journal *Negro Affairs Quarterly*.[36]

As scholars have recently pointed out, Jones entered a communist milieu in the 1930s significantly imprinted by the work of black women such as Maud White, Louise Thompson Patterson, Dorothy West, and Grace Campbell.[37] By 1940, Jones was contributing essays and pamphlets about African Americans and reports on the "Negro Youth Movement" of the CPUSA. She participated in debates within the organization about "revisionism" and sided with the leftist current that expelled Browder and arranged for the return of William Z.

Foster as chair. Her first major published theoretical contribution to these debates was the discussion article "On the Right to Self Determination for the Negro People in the Black Belt" (1946). The essay cites Lenin's writings of 1913 on the right of nations to self-determination as the basis of the argument that "taught Negro workers to fight against petty-bourgeois nationalism—a result of white chauvinist ideology—and to have both Negro and white workers form strong bonds of unity with each other."[38] The essay argued that Negro oppression was a "national question" of oppression under U.S. imperialism "in the ultimate sense as India is oppressed by British imperialism and Indonesia by Dutch imperialism"—a position noted in Chapter 3 that Du Bois also articulated during the wave of Comintern self-determination pronouncements of the 1920s.[39] Jones was also careful to delineate radical nationalism as "working class" in character: "The extension of the working-class base in the oppressed Negro nation is fundamentally the guarantee of the successful forward movement of the national liberation cause of the entire Negro people."[40] This difference was meant, first, to mark national liberation struggle as a step toward proletarian internationalism, and second, to distinguish its "radical" character from bourgeois nationalisms emblematized for Jones by anticommunist organizations such as the NAACP.

Jones's "An End to the Neglect of the Problems of Negro Women" was first published in *Political Affairs*, the premiere theoretical journal of the Communist Party, in June 1949. Fundamentally, the essay builds on and revises Jones's self-determination essay of 1946. Where the former identified African Americans as an "oppressed nation" and thus uniquely in need of support for self-determination, the latter argued that "it is necessary to have a special approach to Negro women workers who, far out of proportion to other women workers, are the main bread winners in their family."[41] Jones challenged progressive unionists and fellow communists to recognize disproportionately low wages for black female industrial and domestic workers as the basis for organizing them into trade unions. Attention to black women's oppression, Jones argued, should be constitutive of the black self-determination struggle, not antithetical to it: "A developing consciousness on the woman question today, therefore, must not fail to recognize that the Negro question in the United States is prior to and not equal to the woman question; that only to the extent that we fight all chauvinist expressions and actions as regards the Negro people and fight and fight for the full equality of the Negro people, can women as a whole advance their struggle for equal rights."[42]

Jones's considered formulation of the fight against chauvinism and for full equality for women and for black self-determination as coequal was her first major endeavor to reconceive originary Leninist and Stalinist principles for a new historical moment. The Black Belt thesis was to be "gendered" just as women had to play a leading role in the struggle for self-determination. This was a question not just for the class but for the party. "Who, more than the Negro woman, the most exploited and oppressed, belongs in our Party?" she asked. "Negro women can and must make an enormous contribution to the daily life and work of the Party."[43] Three months later, in an essay for the *Daily Worker* titled "We Seek Full Equality" Jones strove to root her argument more deeply in Marxist thought. "Marxism-Leninism," she wrote, "views the woman question as a special question which derives from the economic dependence of women upon men. The economic dependence as Engels wrote over 100 years ago, carries with it the sexual exploitation of women, the placing of woman in the modern bourgeois family, as the 'proletariat' of the man, who assumes the role of 'bourgeoisie.'"[44] Jones's summary of Engels's *The Origins of the Family and Private Property* is the key to what others scholars have called black radical feminism's "familial" discourse on emancipation.[45] The defense committee's argument in 1949 that Rosa Lee Ingram was a "widow, sharecropper, and mother" had challenged black feminists to reconceive terms of exploitation and oppression relevant to domestic structures under capitalism. Jones's essays were the theoretical responses to the call of the Ingram case and others like it. Jones's 1949 essay thus referred to the "triply-oppressed status of Negro women" as a "barometer of the status of all women and that the fight for the full, economic, political and social equality of the Negro woman is the in the vital self-interest of white workers, in the vital interest of the fight to realize equality for all women."[46] The argument that black women were essential to the health of the entire working class in turn inspired Jones to revise and reconceive Georgi Dimitrov's theoretical doctrine of 1935 that helped to initiate the Seventh Congress Soviet Popular Front. In "The United Front against Fascism," Dimitrov wrote, "While fascism exacts most from youth it enslaves women with particular ruthlessness and cynicism, playing on the most painful feelings of the mother, the housewife, the single working woman, uncertain of the morrow. . . . We must spare no pains to see that the women workers and toilers fight shoulder to shoulder with their class brothers in the ranks of the united working-class front and the anti-fascist people's front." In turn, Jones concluded, "Let us rededicate ourselves to the fight for the complete equality of women."[47]

Several keynotes merit mention here. Jones's revisionist typology perceives a new "Popular Front" not of working class and bourgeoisie but men and women "standing shoulder to shoulder" within the working class. She reroutes a gendered fight against women's oppression back into the "class against class" politics of the Third Period via the Popular Front. Second, Jones's invocation of women under "fascism" slides ideologically into Du Bois's loose formulation in 1940 of "fascist capitalism"—another political blurring wrought by the

Popular Front. Indeed, the political slippage is significant, as it would later tilt Jones, Graham Du Bois, and other former Communist Party members (such as Harry Haywood) into a version of what Gerald Horne and Margaret Stevens call "left nationalism" manifested in later strong support for "colored" socialist regimes such as China over the Soviet Union.[48] Mainly, however, Jones's essay should be understood as a stage in her influential development of a new world revolution typology. Black women and white women were to be seen as new "coequals" to men in building both proletarian internationalism and national self-determination struggles—the twin streams in the twentieth-century world revolution conception. That argument would come to full fruition in her important essay "International Women's Day and the Struggle for Peace" (1950).

Jones's essay was originally written as a speech to be delivered on International Women's Day, March 8, 1950. As Jones cites in her essay, Women's Day, first celebrated by American working women in 1908, was designated "International Working Women's Day" by the International Socialist Conference (ISC) in 1910 at the initiative of the German communist leader Clara Zetkin. Zetkin initially sought to call attention to expansion of the franchise, but as the Soviet feminist Alexandra Kollontai pointed out in 1920 in an essay explaining the day's origins, rising costs of bread and other household goods forced "even the most peaceful housewife to take an interest in questions of politics and to protest loudly against the bourgeoisie's economy of plunder. 'Housewives' uprisings' became increasingly frequent, flaring up at different times in Austria, England, France and Germany."[49] As Jones also points out in her essay, in attendance at the ISC meeting was Lenin, who in 1907 had insisted that the "women question be specifically mentioned in Socialist programme because of the special problems, needs and demands of toiling women."[50] International Women's Day entered a new typological narrative in 1917 when Soviet women took to the streets on March 8 in St. Petersburg to protest prices and tsarist rule. The protests launched the Russian Revolution and replaced the "reformist" cries of the Second International with the slogans of the Third Communist International. As Kollontai argued, the streets were now filled with the cries, "Working women of all countries! Organize a united proletarian front in the struggle against those who are plundering the world! Down with the parliamentarism of the bourgeoisie! We welcome Soviet power! Away with inequalities suffered by the working men and women! We will fight with the workers for the triumph of world communism!"[51]

For Jones, March 8, 1950, was meant to be the starting point of a new world revolution. In conjunction with the Women's International League for Peace and Freedom and the Soviet-sponsored Women's International Democratic Federation, more than fifty demonstrations across the United States for "peace, freedom and women's rights" were to be linked "in solidarity with the anti-imperialist women, united, 80 million strong in 59 lands . . . who are in the front ranks of the struggle for peace and democracy."[52] International Women's Day was to be a new "united front" against U.S. imperialism and hydrogen bomb production, and for U.S. negotiations with the Soviet Union on disarmament. As in 1917, female workers who "still find a large gap between their wages and those of men . . . while wages of Negro women are particularly depressed" were to be the "vanguard" of this global rebellion.[53] Jones's interpretation of women as the leading edge of the revolution was rooted citationally in the argument in *The Communist Manifest* that "by the action of modern industry, all family ties among the proletarian are torn asunder . . . and has reduced the family relation to a mere money relation."[54] The essay invoked female warriors from America's own "1848"—Harriet Tubman and Sojourner Truth—and "militant women proletarians of the textile workers."[55] Communist revolutionaries such as Zetkin, Lenin, and Stalin were thus part of a historical pedigree in which working-class women announced women's equality as attainable only under socialism. Jones's essay quoted Stalin's words as formative of her argument: "There has not been a single great movement of the oppressed in history in which working women have not played a part. Working women, who are the most oppressed of all the oppressed, have never stood aloof and could not stand aloof from the great match [*sic*] of emancipation."[56] They "may and should become . . . a regular army of the working class . . . fighting shoulder to shoulder with the great army of the proletariat."[57]

Yet like that of Du Bois, Strong, Smedley, and other members of the diasporic international, Jones's "Stalinism" bore traces of both fealty and dissent. Jones would have known, as did all members of the communist left, about Stalin's rollbacks of women's rights in the Soviet Union in the 1930s. Thus, in discussing the position of women in the Soviet Union, Jones is careful to state that women's attainment of "equal rights with men in all spheres of economic, state, cultural, social and political life" owes to "Marxism-Leninism," which "rejects as fallacious all petty-bourgeois equalitarian notions."[58] The essay also cites Stalin only after delineating a history of women's self-activity dating to 1848. In Jones's typology, Lenin and Stalin "*restored and further developed the revolutionary Marxist position on the woman question.*"[59] This subtle distinction is part and parcel of Jones's efforts to center women—not the Soviet state—in peace work. In the essay, she cites "anti-fascist women" who "collect millions of signatures for the outlawing of the A-bomb," just as in her essay "For the Unity of Women in the Cause of Peace," published in *Political Affairs* in 1951, Jones emphasized that "the outstanding peace heroines of the Stockholm Peace Petition campaign were Negro women—Molly Lucas of Illinois and Jackie Clark of California—who were sent as delegates to the Warsaw

Peace Congress and had the opportunity to visit the USSR."[60] Conspicuously
absent from Jones's account were "race men" leaders of the Stockholm campaign, such as Du Bois. In fact, the larger argument of Jones's essay is to call
for a "distinct women's peace movement" led by "millions of women workers."[61] She wrote, "No labour peace movement is possible without the millions
of women workers decisively represented in the textile, garment, needle, laun-
dry, packinghouse, food and other industries. No working class base can be
secured without the organization of seamen's wives, railroad workers' wives,
longshoreman's wives, wives of steel workers, miners, etc. No movement for
peace can be secured unless large masses of national group and farm women
are organized for peace, as well as the specially oppressed Mexican-American
and Puerto Rican women."[62]

The PAC in Manchester in 1945 produced the "colonial international"
revision to the world revolution conception; here, Jones was generating what
Higashida has called a black feminist internationalism that attempted to fuse
proletarian internationalism and peace politics. In ways Jones could not have
predicted, her essay was both prophetic and conclusive. The essay was the
immediate cause of her indictment by the FBI and was subsequently included
in her FBI files. It is important to note that she was indicted under the Internal Security Act of 1950, itself a typological amendment of section 20 of the
Immigration Act of February 5, 1917, in response to the first red scare of Russia's first revolution that year. The Internal Security Act spelled out the threat
of a "World Communist movement which in its origins, its development, and
its present practice, is a world-wide revolutionary movement."[63] Politically, the
essay helped to galvanize the formation of the Sojourners for Truth and Justice
and committed Jones, Graham Du Bois, Eslanda Robeson, and an increasingly wide range of black female activists to peace work in support of the
Soviet Union and for the fight for socialism. By the end of the 1950s, Lorraine
Hansberry, Alice Childress, and a host of other black women would constitute
something like the black feminist international.

Significant for this study, Jones and the Communist Party's reconstitu-
tion of peace work as central to twentieth-century Leninism also came at a
crucial moment in the life of Du Bois. I have already noted their collaborative
efforts on the "We Charge Genocide" petition to the United States and the
Rosa Ingram case. Du Bois appeared before the United Nations Commission
on Human Rights on behalf of the National Negro Congress—the progenitor
of "We Charge Genocide"—in 1946, the same year that Jones's essay on self-
determination was published. Jones's vanguard prescriptions for a revisionist revival of classic world-revolutionary tenets encouraged Du Bois to make
"peace work" a new home front in the diasporic international. Du Bois wove
this geographical and political dilemma directly into his refashioned con-

ception of world revolution. This was most evident in a speech he delivered repeatedly across American cities in 1953 as he traveled with Shirley Graham in his own defense after his indictment and acquittal:

> When, then, modern world revolution started of which that of Russia is but a part, revolution which has changed the face of industry in every modern nation, here in America there has started a desperate effort to lead this nation into witchhunting and world war, to stop this world trend toward abolition of labor exploitation and a real brotherhood of man, and to abolish forever the vulgar role of private wealth. Thus the Peace movement epitomizes in itself the world uplift today and of this the American Negroes must become increasingly aware if they do not want to fall behind progress and hold back the march of mankind.[64]

As he did in "Russia and America," Du Bois here renders explicitly the American counterrevolution of McCarthyism and the militarized Cold War as brakes on a century's aspiration toward world revolution. His comments distill from Jones's analysis of militarized capitalism as imperialism's engine an argument for disarmament as a first step in the socialist redistribution of wealth and resources. Du Bois's arrest, trial, and alienation from former sources of support also put him in league with a new social class of political dissidents populated by black women that centered peace work in his response. For example, Graham Du Bois and Du Bois recruited Alice Citron, a veteran schoolteacher in Harlem, to become the executive secretary of the defense committee formed to raise funds on his behalf. Citron had been suspended without pay and then dismissed by the superintendent of New York City schools for refusing to answer the question, "Are you or were you ever a member of the Communist Party?" As Du Bois recounts, Citron "threw herself into the work with unfaltering sacrifice and at a nominal salary."[65] From 1951 onward, Du Bois also shared the political stage with Graham Du Bois; by the end of the 1950s, she would even be reading his speeches because of his declining health. Their piece/peace work became a collaboration between peers and a rebalancing of Du Bois's autocentric and largely androcentric life as he navigated personal attacks and assaults during internal exile. Some sense of the personal and palliative compensations he associated with the stresses of this period is evident in his poem "The Rosenbergs" (1953), written just after their execution. The poem, published in *Masses and Mainstream*, is dedicated to the two agents of espionage and their children. It is a litany and lament for the historic dead, a typology of martyrdom: "Crucify us, Vengeance of God / As we crucify two more Jews, / Hammer home the nails, thick through our skulls, / Crush down the thorns, / Rain red the bloody sweat / Thick and heavy, warm and wet." The poem moves to a citational catalogue of martyrs past and present, including "Sacco and Vanzetti, John Brown and Willie McGee," the latter the subject of an intense defense campaign by both the Civil Rights Congress and, later, the Sojourners for Truth and Justice. Rosalie McGee, the wife of Willie McGee, was on the initiating board with Shirley Graham Du Bois for an event called Sojourners for Truth and Justice in defense of victims of "legal lynchings."[66] Du Bois's poem winds up with an exhortation, "Hope of the Hopeless / Hear us pray!" and a question for "America the Beautiful": "Who was enthroned in sunlit air? / Who has been crowned on yonder stair? Red Resurrection / Or Black Despair?"[67]

As Gerald Horne underscores in his book on Du Bois and the Cold War, Du Bois's life of internal exile in the mid-1950s was rendered sustainable, even endurable, mainly by the close attention of Shirley Graham and a strong supporting cast of black communist women and fellow travelers who would pass in and through their Brooklyn home that included Vicki Garvin, Esther Cooper Jackson, and Eslanda Robeson. For this group, defense of the Soviet Union had become synonymous with a self-defense campaign to protect black women, black workers, and Du Bois himself, now in his eighties, from the slings and arrows of the state; they perceived one another as "pressed to the wall, dying, but fighting back," as Claude McKay had once said. Making peace was a politics of mutual survival in what seemed like an ideological and political war without end. Du Bois put it as follows in his essay "On the Future": "Progress is *peace*, and peace is time for food, homes for love, health for happiness, and books to read."[68]

———

On December 7, 1955, Claudia Jones was deported from the United States to London. The deportation was the culmination of seven years of state surveillance and harassment in which Jones was arrested four times and charged with violating both the Smith Act and the McCarran-Walter Internal Security Act. On the day of her deportation, more than three hundred people gathered at Harlem's Hotel Theresa to bid her farewell. W.E.B. and Shirley Graham Du Bois, traveling, sent a telegram. Just two years earlier, the United States had also deported C.L.R. James, ostensibly for overstaying his visa. James spent his last days in the United States on Ellis Island furiously composing *Mariners, Renegades and Castaways*, his brilliant extended essay on Herman Melville. The essay, he told George Padmore in a letter, was in part an allegory for Cold War anticommunism. In London, James and Claudia Jones would begin a new chapter in the diasporic international dedicated to building political and cultural institutions for an expatriate West Indian community. In 1959, Jones launched the newspaper *West Indian Gazette and Afro-Asian Caribbean News.* The first issue was emblematic of its anticolonial emphasis: reports on the visit by Sekou Toure, president of the newly independent Guinea, to London, sponsored by the National Council for Civil Liberties at Friends House (opened by Eslanda Robeson); a profile of Jomo Kenyatta, later to become the president of Kenya; and a debut editorial entitled "Support South African Boycott." The *Gazette* also developed Jones's black feminist internationalism in a new diasporic setting. Amy Jacques Garvey, the widow of Marcus Garvey, was a member of the *Gazette*'s editorial board. The inaugural issue included a report by Toure titled "The Place of Women Mirrors a Free Society," a report on the formation of an Afro-Asian West Indian Nurses Association, and "Appeal to Women: Help Shape West Indian Nationhood."

Du Bois's internal exile within the Cold War United States would come to something of an end in 1958, when he and Shirley Graham Du Bois had their passports returned. During their domestic captivity, the work of the diasporic international toward world revolution had born strange and ample fruit. Decolonization movements begun in India, China, Burma, and Malaysia were rapidly followed by the emancipation of Libya, Sudan, Morocco, Tunisia, and, in 1957, Ghana. The applied fervor of the "colonial international" reached apotheosis in the years 1945–1948 as depleted European states lost the will (and the means) to sustain empire; the dismantling of the Communist International and calculated caution of the Soviet state toward decolonization fostered greater autonomy for independence movements, helping to invigorate and emancipate national bourgeoisies as their leaders; and new anticolonial formations and organizations emerged to coordinate and support these activities. The conference held in Bandung, Indonesia, in 1955 that brought together heads of twenty-nine decolonizing states is the best known of these. In combination, these events generated a number of new ideological and political formations, which are best understood as typological revisions of the world revolution conception.

For example, what Vijay Prashad calls the "internationalist nationalism" of the Bandung era made emancipatory nationhood rather than proletarian internationalism the "common coin" of anticolonial struggle. Across much of Africa and Asia, the emphasis in anticolonial struggle lay on what might be called a "developmentalist" internationalism reflective of economic challenges facing decolonizing states entering suddenly into a postwar capitalist order, what the *Gazette* called "From the Frying Pan into the Fire."[69] "Nationalism has a place in each country and should be fostered," wrote Nehru, "but it must not be allowed to become aggressive and in the way of international development. Asia stretches her hand out in friendship to Europe and America as well as to our suffering brethren in Africa. We of Asia have a special

responsibility to the people of Africa."[70] Nehru's notion of Panchsheel, or Five
Principles of Coexistence between decolonizing states, was a "soft" reiteration of the self-determination principle of the Communist International now
fitted to a program of intercolonial cooperation that stressed economic viabil-
ity rather than proletarian power. An editorial in the journal *United Asia*, a
prominent theoretical organ for Afro-Asian political and economic interac-
tion after 1948, built from these Nehruvian principles a communalist version
of the world revolution in which a globalized metonymic nationalism directly
replaced workers of the world. "The problem of peace is nothing less than the
problem of creating a world community," the editorial said. "Peace today more
than ever is matter of peace between nations. . . . Classes are not so acutely
in conflict as the Marxists, to suit their own ends, imagine. Races are living
together in peace, and come into conflict only on questions of nationhood. In
other words it is only on the national level that man has failed to reconcile his
differences and live in peace."[71] As Partha Chatterjee has remarked, such for-
mulations "produced a discourse in which, even as it challenged the colonial
claim to political domination, . . . [it] also accepted the intellectual premises of
'modernity' on which colonial domination was based."[72] Fundamental tenets
of Nehruvian nationalism, including nonalignment, self-determination, and
even anti-imperialism, preserved the fundamental "bases" of modernity as
long as they remained separate from open support for communism interpreted as workers' control of the state. Internationalist nationalism was also
a byproduct of the limited role of communist and socialist parties in newly
decolonizing states brought on by forcible repression (Nehru, Gamal Nasser of
Egypt, and Kwame Nkrumah all arrested or excluded communists from state
positions after taking power) and the Stalinization of socialist practice. Nehru's version of Indian socialism included a "mixed economy," five-year plans,
trade agreements, and technology training from the Soviets. As a former
Soviet "technical expert" and member of Nehru's National Planning Committee put it, "'Industry and technique solve all problems rightly' said Com-
rade Stalin."[73] The Chinese Revolution of 1949, itself modeled closely on the
Stalinized Soviet model, also fractured the Indian left. The revolution split the
Indian communist movement into two Stalinized camps: the Andhra group,
which asserted that Mao's "New Democracy" campaign should be followed in
India, and Soviet loyalists.[74] Nehru, hewing to his own mixed economy and
Panchsheel, would have neither. In 1956, in turn, the Chinese delegation at the
Twentieth Congress of the Soviet Union called Nehru the leader of the Indian
bourgeoisie. The attack anticipated the coming splits within the Indian Com-
munist Party (the leftists going in a Maoist direction in 1959) and between
India and China in its clash over Tibet in October of the same year.[75] These
schisms were the political underbelly of what became Nehruvian bureaucratic

hegemony in the 1950s, described by Pranab Bardhan as a coalition of capitalists, landowners, bureaucrats, intellectuals, and technocrats.[76]

Nehru did perceive the form of internationalist nationalism correctly when it confronted him elsewhere. On his first trip to the United States
in October 1949 (when he was boycotted by Du Bois), Nehru predicted to
U.S. officials that nationalism would supersede socialism in China after the
revolution.[77] Nehru correctly perceived the small working-class base of the
Communist Party, relatively weak proletariat, and deep-rooted nationalism
nurtured by the anti-Japanese war as the strongest constituent elements of
China's revolutionary victory. In the immediate aftermath of the revolution,
approximately one-half of China's communist elite were from upper-class and
middle-class families, and a quarter were from prosperous sections of the
peasantry.[78] The Chinese Communist Party line was by necessity improvised
out of the objective conditions of the war with the Kuomintang and Japanese
up to 1949 and shaped by the war's own nationalist objectives: two-stage revolution, or, as Mao called it, democracy followed by socialism; so-called New
Democracy, agrarian reform, and the "united front of four classes."[79] Each of
these steps was, in Mao's own words, an attempt to build a "new China, . . . a
national, scientific and mass culture—such is the anti-imperialist and anti-
feudal culture of the people, the culture of New Democracy, the new culture
of the Chinese nation."[80] In practice, Maoist New Democracy meant a reorientation of the world revolution concept to fit national needs rather than the
other way around, a variation of Stalin's Socialism in One Country. Thus,
Shoa Chuan Leng could write about China in 1954, "Asian Communism is
a part of international Communism especially adapted to the Asian scene,"
and "one of the major attractions of Communism in Asia is its alliance with
nationalism."[81] To M. N. Roy, these prescriptions constituted a defeat of proletarian internationalism and the supersession of "bourgeois nationalism" over
its proletarian adversary—a debate Roy fiercely engaged with Lenin at the
1920 Comintern. Thus, Roy could write in the journal *Pacific Affairs* in 1951,
"Communism in Asia, essentially, is nationalism painted red."[82] Roy's words
would ring prophetic by the end of the decade as China, India, and the Soviet
Union would endure nationalist fractures and splits wrought beneath the surface of Bandung era unity in the Sino-Soviet contest of 1960 (India would side
with China) and China's border war with India over Tibet and Kashmir.

The inherent contradictions in internationalist nationalism also provided
the ideological horizons for the Bandung Conference in Indonesia in 1955,
an event that, like the events in Russia in 1917, the League against Imperialism meeting in Brussels in 1927, the PAC in Manchester in 1945, and events
India in 1947 and in China in 1949, must be understood within twentieth-
century world revolution typology. The extraordinary fact of the leadership of

Asian and African worlds aligning themselves against their colonial masters instantiated a diasporic international from above. Symbolically, the national bourgeoisies of the anticolonial world consecrated metonymic nationalism as the victorious wing of the world revolution movement. That metonymic nationalism and not proletarian internationalism was on the ascent is evident in the proclamations Bandung produced. China's Chou En-lai, perhaps the single most important individual representative at the meeting, enumerated the goals of the conference as "opposition to colonialism and striving for and safeguarding national independence in opposition to aggressive war and upholding world peace, and the promotion of friendly co-operation of the Asian and African countries on these bases, form the common desires and demands of the peoples of the Asian and African countries."[83] Chou articulated the nationalist base of these internationalist tenets: "The principles underlying the foreign policy of the People's Republic of China are the defence of its national independence, freedom, sovereign rights and territorial integrity, supporting a lasting international peace and friendly co-operation of all countries, and opposition to the imperialist policy of aggression and war. These principles are at one with common desires and demands of the peoples of the Asian and African countries."[84] In Chou's conception, Stalin's Socialism in One Country had now become the "minimal demand" for anticolonial states measured out in the language of bourgeois modernity: freedom, sovereignty, peace, and cooperation. "Cooperation" rhetoric in this scenario could also serve to both buttress and mask an emerging postcolonial order destined to replicate exploitative features of the old. As Antoinette Burton has written, Nehru's response to the question "Was India part of Afro-Asia?" was that "it was *prima inter pares* in civilizational terms, and he arguably viewed a decolonizing Africa as a set of successor states to the Raj over which independent India would seek market advantage and to which it would offer geopolitical tutelage."[85]

Finally, Bandung's practical achievements underscored the precarious economic circumstances shared by former and soon-to-be-independent colonies. Unanimous resolutions based on support of peaceful coexistence and mutual cooperation papered over what Dipesh Chakrabarty calls the "deep and irreconcilable differences among the nations represented."[86] These refer particularly to the radically unstable economic positions of countries thrust by decolonization into new states of mutual and global economic competition and interdependence unprotected from the vicissitudes of capitalist markets. As Giovanni Arrighi and John Saul have argued, "formal decolonization" brought with it "liberalizing economic access to the erstwhile colonies. If, as must have seemed a good bet, trustworthy indigenes were those likely to seize and hold the reins of power, a neocolonial solution then seemed an acceptable answer to the growth of nationalist pressure."[87] Perhaps the most egregious examples were to be found in Africa. Capitalist penetration of Africa even before decolonization had generated an "undevelopment . . . as a whole relative to the industrial centers of the west . . . accompanied and mediated by uneven development as between regions, states, tribes and races within Africa itself."[88] For example, U.S. direct investment in South Africa rose from $50 million in 1943 to $140 million in 1950 and $286 million in 1960.[89] Huge upturns in foreign investment in Africa in the 1950s generated cycles of low-wage, high-turnover jobs; massive gaps among skilled, unskilled, and semi-skilled labor; and a migrant labor system between countries that weakened workers' capacities for industrial conflict.[90] Across Africa from 1950 to 1965, real production grew at a lower rate than the rate of export, conditions manufactured by and profitable to multinational investors, but generative of widening gaps in wages between urban and rural workers. In short, as numerous scholars have written, what critics called then (and call now) "neocolonialism" in Africa merely reproduced many of the capitalist features of imperial rule and "served to obscure the realities of international capitalism's involvement on the continent."[91] As Abdul Babu has argued, these problems were not necessarily mitigated by the investment of putatively socialist states such as China and the Soviet Union. "A change of trading partners from capitalists to socialists," he has written of his period, "without changing the internal basis of the economy, would mean only shifting our dependency from one camp to another; only a change of masters."[92] With periodic exceptions—the Nigerian miners' strike of 1945, the South African miners' strike of 1948, and the union militancy of the African National Congress, these conditions also hindered and dampened the organizational unity of national working classes.

W.E.B. Du Bois was precluded from attending Bandung by his confiscated passport, but his thesis that the beginnings of decolonization would only intensify the exploitation of Africa by imperial states was first sharply stated in a column in the *National Guardian* of January 3, 1949, titled "Watch Africa." Du Bois wrote, "Today there are "signs of international conspiracy to make the countries of Africa the slums of the world; to steal their land and materials and get power of life and death over millions of blacks."[93] Du Bois singled out Ethiopia's economic isolation by the imperial powers, Britain's and Egypt's struggle to control "the black labor of the Sudan," and the U.S. use of military force in Liberia as examples. "The world is trying to keep Ethiopia choked in her mountains away from commerce on the high seas," he wrote. "Egypt and Great Britain are rivals in trying to control the black labor of the Sudan. The United States is bribing Liberia and strengthening her grip by army, navy and investment."[94] In a 1953 letter to Dean Pruitt, Du Bois complained, "The money which we have furnished the [D. F.] Malan government of the Union of South Africa is larger in amount that that of the British Empire. Our largest industries have been investing great sums and building large plants in South Africa since the Second World War."[95] In other *Guardian* columns published in the early 1950s, Du Bois referred to Africa as the new "El Dorado" of the West, describing African extraction (cobalt, diamonds, coffee) and ever spiking U.S. investments especially in South Africa, where General Motors, Goodyear, and Firestone were making extraordinary profits while paying "black labor 45 cents a day."[96] Du Bois's analysis comported with Nkrumah's description of "neocolonial" postwar foreign investment especially by multinationals as generating a "balkanization of Africa . . . that makes it impossible for individual nations to cope with the bargaining power of the international corporations, by means of interlocking directorships, cross-shareholding, and other devices, effectively . . . on a pan-African scale."[97]

In many ways, then, the Bandung era was a grand repeat of world revolution contradictions and alignments. Where World War I–era capitalism had grown wars, imperial expansion, and capitalist exploitation from "African roots," generating both the diasporic international and its dedication to a new world order, postwar "neo-colonialism" would reunite many of its national actors on a new anti-imperialist stage armed with hard-won sovereignty and "national self-determination" but still beggared by capital. Forty years later, development was still combined, still uneven. In accordance with the scaling back of the Communist International and the emergence of China's "colored" revolution, these were the conditions that generated the Hundred Flowers period of so-called Third World liberation ideologies and yet another new alignment of the world revolution conception. In Africa, as Ali Mazri has noted, Leninist (and by implication, Stalinist) analysis of national liberation and self-determination was married to indigenous, Pan-Africanist, or otherwise non-Western historical social formations.[98] Julius Nyerere's response to Tanzanian underdevelopment was socialism rooted in traditional communal Tanzanian society, "socialist characteristics" carried out by people who did "not call themselves socialists, and they were not socialist by deliberate design."[99] Nyerere's *Ujamaa* was fashioned from a Maoist conception of theory springing spontaneously from historical circumstances rather than textual doctrine: "It is not part of the job of a socialist . . . to worry about whether or not his actions or proposals are in accordance with what Marx or Lenin wrote. . . . The task of a socialist is to think out for himself the best way of achieving desired ends under the conditions which now exist."[100] Nyerere's socialism also indexed the attempt to braid together the strands of Pan-Africanism and Marxism. To talk as if "Marx invented socialism, is to reject both the humanity of Africa and the universality of socialism."[101]

For Abdul Babu, Nyerere's *Ujamma* more closely approximated Narodnik socialism, conceiving development rooted in the material conditions of national peasantry rather than in proletarian internationalism.[102] *Ujamaa* endeavored to solve the problem that, as Abdul Babu has written, "Since we (Africa) have not developed a capitalism of our own, we suffer from all the ills of world capitalism from the receiving end."[103]

Ujamaa was one constituent consequence of the revised "colonial international" logic developed out of Manchester in 1945 as it attempted to navigate a path between Communist Internationalism and national self-determination. As George Padmore had cautioned Du Bois about African anticolonial leaders in a letter dated August 1945, "Even those who call themselves Communist are nationalist. That is to say, they realize that their countries must first be nationally free before they can begin to practice their Communism."[104] It is fitting and ironic, then, that Du Bois wrestled through these contradictions of the Bandung era with Padmore himself. Where twenty years earlier the Comintern loyalist had accused Du Bois of "petty-bourgeois" radicalism and helped pull him farther to the Marxist left, now Du Bois, in 1955, challenged his comrade's orientation to Pan-Africanism as a stand-alone ideological surrogate for the world revolution conception. After Manchester, Nkrumah and Padmore became the architects of Gold Coast independence. Padmore became Nkrumah's close adviser and in many ways replaced Du Bois as his left-hand aide in the diasporic international. Nkrumah's People's Convention Party also wedded Leninism to collectivism supported by international investment. By 1954, in the wake of independence for Liberia and Uganda, Padmore was convinced that the liberation of the continent was a historical inevitability. Padmore wrote to Du Bois from London, "Believe me, dear Dr., no force on earth can now hold back the forward march of Africa."[105] Padmore also asked Du Bois whether he had read Richard Wright's recently published book *Black Power*, an enthusiastic journalistic account of the rise of the Convention People's Party to state power. Wright's book was shot through with contradictions of the Bandung era, on the one hand advocating a "developmentalist" approach to African decolonization (Wright cautioned African leaders that they might need to accept money from imperial powers, a process that was already under way) while on the other emphasizing the need for national self-determination. Wright's book was also unequivocally cynical about communist support for African decolonization. Wounded by 1954 by the Stalinization of the Soviet Union, Wright advocated a "secular" Pan-Africanism that would adapt the best of the West, mainly science and technology, to national liberation struggles.[106]

Du Bois's response to Padmore reflected his strong political reorientation during his peace-building years toward support for and defense of the Soviet Union. His confidence in the Soviet Union's commitment to anti-imperialism was bolstered by China's victory and its refusal to play the "great game" in Asia and Africa. (As for Eastern Europe and the Balkans, Du Bois continued to include them as "defensive" fronts for the Soviets and "real" socialist states.) Du Bois was thus skeptical of Padmore's nationalist enthusiasms and Wright's investment portfolio for African nations. "I am very glad to hear about Africa," he wrote back to Padmore. "I understand the policy of you and Dr. Nkrumah, although I am a little afraid of it. The power of British and especially American capital when it once gets a foothold is tremendous. But of course I realize that once political power is in your hands you can curb capital, providing your own bourgeoisie permits it. I am watching the struggle with great interest." About Wright, Du Bois wrote, "He starts out to save Africa from Communism and then makes an attack on British capitalism which is devastating. How he reconciles these two attitudes I cannot see."[107] Du Bois also characterized Wright as jaded by his experiences of the American Communist Party: "But because of that to slur Communism as such, to slander Russia and above all, to spit on American Negroes is too much for an honest artist. Wright has great talent and his descriptions of West Africa are literature; but to write a book to attack Communism in Africa when there has been no Communism in Africa, and when the degradation of Africa is due to that Capitalism which Wright is defending—this is sheer contradiction."[108]

Du Bois had aptly if unwittingly described a corner into which the world revolution concept had been driven by both the Cold War and the Stalinization of the Soviet Union. His challenge to Padmore was sedimented with contesting the degraded *meaning* of communism after Stalinism. Du Bois's reference to Wright's slander of "communism *as such*" was a verbal index to this contestation. Within a year's time, Du Bois would reprise and deepen this argument upon the publication of Padmore's *Pan-Africanism or Communism? The Coming Struggle for Africa*, published in 1956. Du Bois's *National Guardian* review of the book highlighted several claims by Padmore in order to debunk them. "Pan Africanism," wrote Padmore, "sets out to fulfill the socioeconomic mission of Communism, under a libertarian political system." While communists had "never faltered" in supporting African rights, they had made "tactical mistakes and psychological blunders."[109] The answer to Africa's plight therefore was nationalism, described this way: "Economically and socially, Pan-Africanism subscribes to the fundamental objectives of democratic socialism, with state control of the basis of production and distribution." Padmore's resolution of a long struggle with Stalinized communism took the form of a program of communism without communism—or, as Roy put it, nationalism "painted red." (In his response to the book, Padmore's friend Daniel Guerin would tell Padmore he had simply confused Stalinism with Marxism.) Initially, Du Bois would have none of it:

I have great regard for Padmore's scholarship and character. But I fear that here his logic slips a cog. How can a national African socialism meet the danger of a rising black bourgeoisie associated closely with foreign investors? Padmore wants "an American Marshall Plan" for Africa; he welcomes British capital for the Volta dam. He thinks the Philippines are free. This seems to be dangerous thinking. . . .

[W]ith a mass of sick, hungry and ignorant people, led by ambitious young men, like those today supporting tribalism on the Gold Coast and Big Business in Liberia, under skies clouded by foreign investing vultures armed with atom bombs—in such a land, the primary fight is bound to be between private Capital and Socialism, and not between Nationalism and Communism. It may be in Africa, as it was in Russia, that Communism will prove the only feasible path to Socialism.[110]

Backed into his own corner by Padmore—Pan-Africanism *or* communism—Du Bois resorted to a "totality" of vision meant to reconcile once again a feasible typology of world revolution. His suspicions about the role of national bourgeoisies in African decolonization would prove prophetic of their role not only in the eventual corruption and downfall of the Nkrumah regime but also, more broadly, in relation to Franz Fanon's famous declaration in *Wretched of the Earth* that nationalist elites can become a "new class" for themselves.[111] "The national middle class discovers its historic mission" [after decolonization]: that of intermediary," wrote Fanon, which "consists, prosaically, of being the transmission line between the nation and capitalism, rampant though camouflaged, which today puts on the mask of neo-colonialism."[112] By emphasizing the "fight between private Capital," Du Bois also meant to animate the African working class as the agent of anticolonial transformation, a confidence more easily abstracted by the time and space between him and Nkrumah's advisers on the ground in Gold Coast. At the same time, Du Bois's distance from the scene and his domestic detention prevented the excess of nationalist enthusiasm that might have been more easily felt in Accra. But that enthusiasm was still to come in the final leg, and revision, of his vision for a new day.

––––––––––

Du Bois's review of *Pan-Africanism or Communism?* was published in the *National Guardian* on October 29, 1956, six days into the Soviet invasion and occupation of Hungary. The workers' uprising against Soviet rule was the first prolonged strike against Hungary's deeply repressive Stalinist state. As with the revelations by Nikita Khrushchev at the twentieth Soviet Congress in February of that year of the catastrophic and inhumane crimes of Joseph Stalin, Du Bois was "publicly unmoved," although events of 1956 caused onetime intimates of Du Bois such as Howard Fast (who claimed to have recruited Shirley Graham Du Bois to the Communist Party) to resign their membership.[113] Du Bois's initial silence was consistent with his hagiographic tribute "On Stalin," published in the *National Guardian* on March, 16, 1953, upon the Soviet leader's death. It is, along with Du Bois's essays on Gandhi and Nehru, an example of Du Bois's Stalinist historiography. Du Bois invests and invents a "hero" for his world revolution conception modeled from an inventory of characteristics he partly attributes to himself. Stalin is "one of the despised minorities of man" who "first set Russia on the road to conquer race prejudice." Stalin's application of the Leninist "self-determination" thesis to Russia's 140 national groupings is "perhaps his greatest feat," according to Du Bois. Stalin was the "son of a serf but stood calmly before the great without hesitation or nerves."[114] Stalin rose to the three great decisions of his life magnificently: the problem of the peasants, Western European attack, and World War II. After helping the allies to defeat fascism, Stalin was at his best in the resolution of peace, demanding in concession to Winston Churchill and Franklin D. Roosevelt only the return of the "cordon sanitaire" to the Soviets and that the "Balkans were not to be left helpless before Western exploitation for the benefit of land monopoly. The workers and peasants there must have their say."[115] Stalin, unlike U.S. liberals, saw through Leon Trotsky's lies and "continued to advance toward a real socialism."[116] Implicit throughout the essay is Du Bois's tacit acceptance of Stalin's Socialism in One Country doctrine as what he called, metonymically, in his 1953 essay cited earlier, "one part" of the world revolution conception.

Less than a year after the Hungarian rebellion, and in response to it and Khrushchev's speech, Anna Louise Strong's *The Stalin Era* was published. Du Bois's review, published in *Mainstream*, presents a slight shift in both hagiographic tone and substance. While recommending that the book be "required reading for all confused and frustrated commentators on socialism in this day," Du Bois foregrounds less a unilateral interpretation of Stalin's greatness than accomplishments of the revolution itself. Strong's affirmation of Stalinist policy—Socialism in One Country and the first Five-Year Plan—not surprisingly are summarized without much embroidery. The violent overthrow of the kulak system and forced collectivization is treated by both Strong and Du Bois as a necessary entrée for a "new people . . . national cultures developed; women emerged from subjection; the power of the church was overthrown; . . . [a] girl won the world record in parachute jumping and cried: 'The sky of our country is the highest sky in the world!'"—details in Strong's book trained to Du Bois's eye by his past and present relationship to the "woman question" and black feminist international. Du Bois also alludes to both Hungary and

Khrushchev's speech, the latter in reference to his account of the murder-ous purges of 1936–1938.[117] Du Bois calls this point in Soviet history "reac-tion"; Strong calls it the "Great Madness." She writes, "I do not think anyone anywhere knows the full story of the excesses that occurred in the USSR in 1936–1938," a tacit denial of the details of Khrushchev's speech, and that she regards the purges "as only the Russian phase of a world-wide sickness: the Spanish war; the capitalist depression; the Hitler Fifth Column." Strong also rebuts Khrushchev's account of the murder of Sergei Kirov as paranoia "due to the knowledge that the enemy had penetrated" into the inner circles of the Soviet state.[118] In the postwar world, Du Bois affirms the Soviet Union mainly as a victim of Western manipulation, "frozen out of the Far Eastern peace-making" and refused a $6 billion loan expected from the United States. "The dream of alliance and peaceful cooperation died in the Cold War," writes Du Bois in summary. "The Korean War began the new policy of 'contain-ing' Communism by force." Du Bois's most finite assessment of Strong and her book is delivered less as a defense of Stalin the leader than of the ideal of revolution itself: "That many persons including herself suffered in this process was regrettable and in some cases terrible, but the total result was a glorious victory in the uplift of mankind."[119]

The wavering tone of endorsement of Strong's book in 1957 is legible as Du Bois's anxieties about Stalinism only in a careful reading of the fine details of Du Bois's last years. The final act of Du Bois's dedication to the world revo-lution conception is both a gathering and a coming undone. Events of 1956 forced Du Bois to improvise once again on the world revolution theme, revis-ing political (and national) distinctions coterminous with the final geographi-cal legs of his diasporic internationalism. This "wordliness" also took the form of what Walter Benjamin conceived as "revolutionary nostalgia," described by Terry Eagleton as "the power of active remembrance as a ritual summon-ing and invocation of the traditions of the oppressed in violent constellation with the political present." As Eagleton puts it, for Benjamin "how we act in the present can change the meaning of the past. The past may not exist (any more than the future does), but it lives on in its consequences, which are a vital part of it."[120] For Du Bois, revolutionary nostalgia meant reckoning directly and indirectly with all of the ghosts of the century past, including the loom-ing shadows of Stalin's crimes, Cold War repression, atomic war, the uphill push of revolution, exile, death. Approaching his own final midnight hour, the challenge after events of 1956 was reconceiving a historiography (and autobi-ography) in which these events could still foretell human emancipation.

We can see this process beginning with his response to Nkrumah's invita-tion to attend state ceremonies for Ghana's independence in January 1957, less than two months after the invasion of Hungary. Du Bois and Shirley Graham were forced to decline the invitation because the United States refused to grant Du Bois a passport. As he recounts in his autobiography, Du Bois responded to Nkrumah with "advice for the future of Ghana and Africa" based on their twelve-year relationship dating back to Manchester. Today, wrote Du Bois, "when Ghana arises from the dead and faces this modern world," it should "seek to develop a new African economy and cultural center standing between Europe and Asia, taking from and contributing to both."[121] It must "avoid subjection to and ownership by foreign capitalists," and, most important, it "should try to build a socialism founded on old African communal life, rejecting the exaggerated private initiative of the West, and seeking to ally itself with the social program of the Progressive nations; with British and Scandinavian Socialism, with the progress toward the Welfare State in India, Germany, France and the United States; and with the Communist States like the Soviet Union and China, in peaceful cooperation and without presuming to dictate as to how Socialism must or can be attained at particular times and places."[122]

Three significant revisions to Du Bois's prior conception of world revolution in October 1956 leap forward here. Where Du Bois had previously scorned Padmore's "national African socialism" in favor of Soviet-model communism, he now advocated a socialism grounded in "old African communal life." Du Bois's confidence that Africa could replicate Russia's lead in developing communism was also attached to an internationalism that was coterminous with, not opposed to, "Pan-Africanism." Du Bois blurred traditional national and categorical distinctions (peasant and proletariat, First World and Third World) and temporalities (welfare state and African communal life) into a revolutionary worldliness that forces into dialectic reconciliation hard oppositions to progress. Finally, Du Bois's caution to Nkrumah of "peaceful cooperation" goes beyond Bandung logic of coexistence and nonalignment to a caveat not to "dictate" how socialism must or can be attained—an obvious echo of the guns of Budapest. This is both revolutionary worldiness and revolutionary weariness, a forced march to make peace with counterrevolution in the name of sustaining a typology of revolution itself.

The stress marks of this endeavor and the pursuit of relief from them dot virtually every gesture of Du Bois's life in his final years. Du Bois's Fifth Act constitutes a continuous struggle to revise into a "totality" the events of his own life as a legible map of the possibility of world revolution. In so doing, Du Bois was forced to account more and more for its brutalities. Only ten months after his response to Nkrumah, in November 1957, Du Bois was invited to write an essay for the Soviet journal *Literaturnaya Gazeta* to commemorate the fortieth anniversary of the October 1917 revolution. After defending the achievements of the revolution as "an unprecedented leap," an obvious allusion to China, Du Bois wrote, "It is not a surprise that all these great achievements cost a lot of blood and tears to the Soviet people—because it was tormented not only by foreign aggressors but by internal enemies as well. It is not a surprise that in the periods of this superhuman exertion Russia experienced starving, discord and hunger. Because Russians are not angels and they were never angels; they were ordinary people who were for many centuries humiliated and exploited by the same countries that now try to destroy them."[123] As for Stalin, he wrote: "I am fully ready to believe that Stalin was cruel and there are no doubts that in the Soviet Union there was a place for an excessive suspicion and the cases of persecution of the innocent when tolerance and justice would give more results." The essay concludes with an ode to a new political mode, what might be called Pan-Sovietism: "I greet you comrades and thank you for becoming the first of all countries of the modern world who accepted equality of colored people of Africa and Asia America and Oceania with white people of the earth."[124]

Du Bois wrote a series of article for the Soviet press in the last four years of his life. They included "Nevidannyi Skachok" (An Unprecedented Leap) in *Literaturnaya Gazeta*, "Bortsy za Mir" (Fighters for Peace) in the May 10, 1959, issue of *Ogonek*; "Triumf Sotsializsma" (The Triumph of Socialism) in the November 7, 1959, issue of *Izvestia*; and "The Morning of a New Day," his response to winning the Laureate of the international Lenin Peace Prize. The keynote of these addresses was the triumph of socialism for the working masses of the Soviet Union and standard boilerplate declarations about the shape of the new Soviet society. Lenin and Khrushchev replace Stalin in these essays as Du Bois's touchstones for the revolution. About his personal meeting with Khrushchev and Khrushchev's speech for peace at the United Nations General Assembly in 1959, Du Bois wrote, "He is a communist and never denied this fact and was never sorry for it. . . . He made thousands of Americans stop looking at communism through dark glasses and begin to learn about this great system of thought and action."[125] To some extent, Stalin's disappearance from Du Bois's public writing and his "making peace" with the man who had at least symbolically expelled him from the Soviet pantheon was Du Bois soldiering forward with the party line. Du Bois also never veered even in his final visits from a blind misrecognition of the Soviet bureaucracy as brutalist state capitalism either in the Soviet Union or in its satellites states in Eastern Europe.[126] At the same time, even as he praised Khrushchev, Du Bois strove to reconcile Soviet socialism of the day with what he understood to be its *originary* world revolution conception. In "The Morning of a New Day," for example, he turns to citing Lenin's essay on Italian imperialism published in *Pravda* in 1912, a seedling of what became "Imperialism: The Highest Stage of Capitalism" (1917). He recuperates Lenin's opposition to war as the basis for his (and Du Bois's own) lifetime fight against imperialism, for peace, and for national self-determination. "He consistently and firmly spoke out for peace," he wrote, "and at the same time he called for free peoples to support by any means the national emancipation movements of the colonized peoples."[127] He also showed lingering anxiety about the cost of the Soviet revolution. In what is most likely a veiled reference to Stalin, Du Bois wrote, "A manifestation of human nature at times can be disgusting, but the world incessantly improves; stumbling and falling a human being continues to go further. Never in human history was the world witness of such a brave and successful struggle as the struggle in the Soviet Union from the revolution of 1917."[128]

Revising and sustaining world revolution typology also reinitiated DuBois's links to the diasporic international after the return of the Du Boises' passports in August 1958. Du Bois and Graham Du Bois immediately set out for Eastern Europe, the Soviet Union, and China. Du Bois gave one speech in the Soviet Union at Tashkent, where he exhorted decolonizing African states to boycott big capital from the "exploiting world, led by America," and to "buy of the Soviet Union and China as they grow able to sell at low prices. Save thus your own capital and drive the imperialists into bankruptcy or into Socialism."[129] After being advised by doctors not to travel, Du Bois sent a speech with Shirley Graham Du Bois to be read at the All-Colonial Peoples Conference organized by Kwame Nkrumah. Du Bois again conjoined the two strands of his revolutionary typology. Africa must "forget nothing but set everything in its rightful place: the Glory of the six Ashanti Wars against Britain; the wisdom of the Fanti Confederation; the unity of Nigeria . . . the rebellion of the Madhi and the hands of Ethiopia . . . the revenge of Mutessa, and many other happenings and men."[130] Africa's "bond," he wrote, is with the "white world . . . closest to those like the Union of Soviet Socialist Republics . . . no mere color of skin but the deeper experience of wage slavery and contempt."[131] Waxing now archetypal as well as typological, both nostalgic and forward-looking, Du Bois exhorted:

> *Awake, awake, put on thy strength, O Zion . . .*
> *Africa awake, put on the beautiful robes of Pan-African Socialism.*
>
> *You have nothing to lose but your Chains!*
> *You have a continent to regain!*
> *You have freedom and human dignity to attain!*[132]

Similarly, three major textual revisionist projects occupied Du Bois in the Soviet Union. The first was preparation of a Russian edition of his autobiography. That text, a compilation and mash-up of portions of Du Bois's life and writings, including a newly penned "Postscript," would appear in 1962, six years before an English-language edition in the United States. The second was the preparation of a book, *Africa: Towards a History of the Continent*, also published in Russian in the Soviet Union. The third was the revision of his biography *John Brown*, originally published in 1909, for Soviet publication, as discussed briefly in Chapter 2. In December 1959, Du Bois published "The Crucifixion of John Brown" in the Soviet journal *New Times*, a commissioned essay on the hundredth anniversary of Brown's death. The essay is a précis of the larger book and an introduction for Soviet readers to Brown's life. In the essay, there is only one hint of the longer revisions to the book's final chapter that Du Bois was preparing for republication. Du Bois concludes, "So was American slavery clothed in 1859, and it had to die by revolution, not by milder means. And this men knew. They had known it a hundred years."[133] Du Bois's odd conception of "prefigurative" revolutionary consciousness was historicized for readers in the revised text for *John Brown*. Where the original final chapter ended with Du Bois's "Revolution is not a test of capacity; it is always a loss and a lowering of ideals," the revised text began with this new sentence: "But if it is a true revolution it repays all losses and results in the uplift of the human race."[134] Then, as he did in *Black Reconstruction in America*, Du Bois provided an "anachronistic" typology of Brown's rebellion akin to his "Sovietized" rendition of the "general strike" of American slaves and workers described in Chapter 2. Du Bois retrospectively referenced the Russian Revolution of 1917 and the "resurrection of China" as an anticipation of the new revolutionary typology of Brown's rebellion. Among the "dates whose events conditioned John Brown and his acts" were the Battle of Plessy in 1757, the French Revolution, the Haitian Revolution, the terminus of the slave trade in the United Kingdom in 1808, and, finally, their analytical synthesis by Marx and Engels in the publication of *The Communist Manifesto* (1848). Of these events, Du Bois writes, "John Brown never read the *Communist Manifesto* and knew little of the rise of Socialism. But he did realize that a suppressed and exploited part of the laboring class in America—the Negroes—had been deprived by capitalists and land monopolies of the freedom to earn a living and to direct their lives which was vital in John Brown's mind to human being."[135] Similarly, the capitalist scramble for the colonies born *after the end* of Reconstruction—what Du Bois called earlier the "modern world system" of capital that has held back Asia, Africa, and the American Negro—were now precursive to Brown's resistance. This led to Du Bois's conclusion, cited earlier, that "all this John Brown did not know and yet his life's work was in consonance with it."[136] Hence, Brown's "crucifixion" is made "resurrection" in Du Bois's anachronistic typology. The present remakes the past. Du Bois here carries out the revolutionary historiographical function he insisted should be the *political* task of "Mother Africa" to sustain world revolution: "Forget nothing but set everything in its rightful place."

I have discussed earlier how Du Bois's follow-up visits to China in 1959 (he arrived in February) and 1962 generated significant revision to both his personal historiography and China's and Japan's place in the world revolution conception. The 1959 visit was a one-month stay in Beijing at the invitation of the Chinese Peace Committee spent in a "ceremonial cocoon," as aptly described by David Levering Lewis.[137] It was during this visit that Du Bois was reunited with Anna Louise Strong at Mao Tse-tung's villa; Strong also attended Du Bois's state-sponsored ninety-first birthday celebration where she was "looking happy, busy and secure," by his account.[138] Strong had arrived in Beijing via Moscow in late 1958, her first return to China since 1947, when she conducted what became a well-known interview with Mao at Yenan. Strong was told by Chinese officials when she arrived that her book *The Stalin Era* had sold 110,000 copies in China, although she was pushed to explain what she meant by her designation the "Great Madness" of 1936–1938.[139] Within two years of her arrival, China and the Soviet Union would be in conflict over Khrushchev's "revisionism," which Mao would call in his later book "Khrushchev's Phony Communism," a designation that could have applied to both country's bureaucratic suppression of workers. Strong was in fact in China to write a book about that country's push to collectivize agriculture and create communes as part of the disastrous Great Leap Forward, details of which neither she nor Du Bois referenced in their accounts of their visits. Strong did caution the Chinese to avoid the speed-up of collectivization, which she told Chinese officials had caused "great dislocation and misery" thirty-five years earlier, an assessment that had helped lead to her expulsion by Stalin. Strong arrived biased to favor China's revolution over the errors of the Soviets; she hoped to participate in steel work to test the mettle of the "Great Leap."[140]

Strong had sent a welcoming letter to Shirley Graham and W.E.B. Du Bois when they arrived in China but did not see them in person until she attended a dinner party in their honor on March 7. Shortly thereafter, she joined them in Wu-ch'ang, Hupeh Province, at a resort where Du Bois and Strong were to be granted a formal interview with Mao. Du Bois wrote little about the event in his accounts of the visit. Strong's published account of the interview session was mainly idolatrous. Strong's biographers Tracy Strong and Helene Keyssar report that Du Bois was irritated by the levity with which Mao discussed the policy of John Foster Dulles's State Department and for underestimating the threat of U.S. capitalism to African Americans. "Many of my family have been exterminated," he complained—a pulling forward of the arguments from the Civil Rights Congress's "We Charge Genocide" pamphlet of 1951.[141] By Du Bois's account from his autobiography, based partly on his decision to republish a large section of the speech there, the most significant event on his visit was the speech "China and Africa" delivered at his ninety-first birthday celebration. The speech, rapidly published in *Peking Review* on March 3 and republished in *New World Review* in April, reprised arguments from his earlier Accra speech that Africa must turn to China and the Soviet Union and not the West for support. Consistent with the almost manic revisionist impulse now driving his work and thought, Du Bois's essay was deeply anachronistic: it made no mention of or reference to the sharp tensions that existed between the Soviet Union and China by early 1959 or to Khrushchev's warming to the West, for which Mao would develop his attacks on Soviet "revisionism." Like "Russia and America," the essay looked backward ideologically to an era of rapprochement between countries where unity around the world revolution concept was everything. "The *essence* of the revolution in the Soviet Union and China and in all the 'iron curtain' nations," wrote Du Bois, "is not the violence that accompanied the change—no more than starvation at Valley Forge was the essence of the American revolution against Britain. The real revolution is the acceptance on the part of the nation of the fact that here-after the main object of the nation is the welfare of the mass of the people and not the lucky few."[142] Du Bois's attempt to distill the meaning of socialism into typological form was an attempt to reconcile the spirit of world revolution with the violently deformed letter of its practice he refused to acknowledge publicly in Eastern European states (Hungary, Poland, East Germany), as well as the increasing ideological fractures in Marxism in the form of Maoism, Stalinism, Khrushchevism, and Pan-African socialism.

The Du Boises returned home in mid-1959. In 1960, Du Bois published the essay "Africa and the French Revolution" in *Freedomways*, with which I began this study, suturing into a totalized whole the work of C.L.R. James, now in Trinidad; that of Herbert Aptheker, his close friend and soon to be his executor; and his own earlier work. On July 1, 1960, he flew to Accra to take part in ceremonies establishing the Republic of Ghana. Not long after his return to the United States, the Supreme Court upheld the McCarran Act of 1961 requiring registration of "communist action" and "communist front" organizations.[143] On October 1, 1961, he applied for membership in the Communist Party. Fearing that the state might again restrict his ability to travel, he made plans to move to Accra, a decision Levering Lewis described as the most difficult of his life. On his ninety-fifth birthday in February 1963 (see Figure 5.1), he became a citizen of Ghana, as Levering Lewis writes, "largely because the American embassy refused to renew his passport."[144] Du Bois's formal un-Americanism was complete. Ideologically, Du Bois reconstituted his exilic end as a new beginning. The final section of his late revised *Autobiography* included a postscript written after his return to American soil. In it he revised one last time his revolutionary typology while providing a hermeneutic "coda" to the meaning of the revision. Du Bois at once proclaimed the

Figure 5.1. W. E. B. Du Bois on his ninety-fifth birthday, with President Kwame Nkrumah and Madame Fathia Nkrumah, Accra, Ghana, February 23, 1963. *(Used with permission of the Special Collections and University Archives, W.E.B. Du Bois Library, University of Massachusetts Amherst.)*

United States "a land of magnificent possibilities" that was "selling its birthright" to war, poverty, and exploitation while "systematically distorting the truth about socialism."[145] Du Bois then offered a summary of his own personal history—"The day after I was born, Andrew Johnsons was impeached"—to the arc of his present: "I believe in socialism. I seek a world where the ideals of communism will triumph—to each according to his need, from each according to his ability. For this I will work as long as I live. And I still live."[146] And then he provided this final rumination on history:

> You are not and yet you are: your thoughts, your deeds, above all your dreams still live. So, too, your deeds and what you forgot—these lived as your bodies died. With these we also live and died, realize and kill. . . . Suffer us not, Eternal Dead, to stew in this Evil—the Evil of South Africa, the Evil of Mississippi; the Evil of Evils which is what we hope to hold in Asia and Africa, in the southern Americas and islands of the Seven Seas. Reveal, Ancient of Days, the Present in the past and prophesy the End in the Beginning. For this is a beautiful world; this is

a wonderful America, which the founding fathers dreamed until their
sons drowned it in the blood of slavery and devoured it in greed. Our
children must rebuild it. Let then the Dreams of the Dead rebuke the
Blind who think that what is will be forever and teach them that what
was worth living for must live again and that which merited death
must stay dead. Teach us, Forever Dead, there is no Dream but Deed,
there is no Deed but Memory.[147]

Du Bois is, of course, signifying here on Marx's own conjuring of the
dead of world history in "The Eighteenth Brumaire of Napoleon Bonaparte."
Marx's most famous essay on the dialectics of history insists first and foremost that the revolutions of the present always inhere in revolutions of the
past: "The tradition of all dead generations weighs like a nightmare on the
brains of the living. And just as they seem to be occupied with revolutionizing
themselves and things, creating something that did not exist before, precisely
in such epochs of revolutionary crisis they anxiously conjure up the spirits
of the past to their service, borrowing from them names, battle slogans, and
costumes in order to present this new scene in world history in time-honored
disguise and borrowed language."[148] It was this conception that Benjamin, to
return to our own beginning, transfigured as *Jetztzeit*, the here and now, the
prophetic Angel of History in the midnight hour always running forward
into the past to fashion a new human future. Du Bois's "Dreams of the Dead,"
which rebukes the Blind "who think that what is will be forever," was no less
than Benjamin's messiah come home, even from exile, to reanimate the dream
and the deed of revolution, the souls of the whole world made flesh.

CODA: THE AFTERLIVES OF WORLD REVOLUTION

These are revolutionary times. All over the globe men are revolting
against old systems of exploitation and oppression, and out of the
wounds of a frail world, new systems of justice and equality are being
born. The shirtless and barefoot people of the land are rising up as never
before. The people who sat in darkness have seen a great light. We in the
West must support these revolutions.
—MARTIN LUTHER KING JR. "BEYOND VIETNAM,"
RIVERSIDE CHURCH, NEW YORK, APRIL 4, 1967[149]

By the time of Du Bois's death in Ghana on August 28, 1963, world revolution
was becoming the new common coin of an international left both shaped and
cleaved by its long and winding evolution. The many-vectored lives of individual members of the diasporic international who helped birth it provide a
provisional map of its numerous legacies. For Mohandas Gandhi and Agnes

Smedley, the former murdered by a Hindu extremist in 1948 and the latter interred in Beijing, the legacy was martyrdom in service to polarized ends. Gandhi's methodical projection of a predominantly Hindu-centric national state and public declamations against socialism shadowed post-Indian national governments and Nehru's careful cultivation of nonalignment internationally and bureaucratic normalization domestically. Gandhi also functioned as a talisman for a range of African American conceptions of Third World solidarity, from Du Bois's late memorial essays discussed earlier to Martin Luther King Jr.'s well-known commitment to nonviolence and Countee Cullen's poetic tribute republished in the Afro-Asia journal *United Asia* in 1953. Titled "Karenge ya Margene" (Do or Die), Cullen's poem links the Mahatma retrospectively (and typologically) to both the American Revolution and an unfinished struggle for the darker nations; Gandhi's freedom cry, the poem insists, must not be weighted less by history than Patrick Henry's "Give me liberty or give me death!"[150]

For Smedley, commemoration after her death in 1950 for her role in the diasporic international came from enemy camps: at memorial services to scatter her ashes at the Youth Palace in Beijing, the writers Mao Dun and Ding Ling testified to her role in supporting the Chinese Revolution and building the League of Revolutionary Writers. In 1953, her books *Daughter of Earth* and *Battle Hymn over China* were burned as part of a "cleansing campaign" of U.S. Information Agency libraries abroad ordered by Joseph McCarthy.[151] Revelations of Smedley's role in the Stalinization of the Comintern has been a constant theme from the time of a Communist Party operative (and FBI informant's) testimony in 1951 that she was a Soviet agent to the unearthing of that information to the public in Ruth Price's biography *The Lives of Agnes Smedley* (2005).[152]

The political trajectory of Gandhi and Smedley's one-time collaborator Jawaharlal Nehru roughened under the contradictions of internationalist nationalism. At the Belgrade Conference of nonaligned countries in 1961, Nehru found his own, once revered principles of nonalignment in conflict with emerging Pan-Africanism and Indian border skirmishes with China in 1959, followed by the "China War" of 1962. China's denunciation of Nehru as representative of the major Indian bourgeoisies was followed by India's providing free rein to the U.S. Central Intelligence Agency to use Indian territory in its war against China in Tibet.[153] A further rightward tilt in the direction of the post-independence revolution was the passage in 1963 of the Official Language Act, making Hindi the sole official language of India. Nehru's supremely nationalist role in the repression of Kashmiri rebels might also be seen as a predictor not only of the perpetual calamity of Kashmir as the "Palestine of South Asia" but also of the intensifying Hindutva cast of the Indian polity, as evident in the rise of the Bharatiya Janata Party years later.[154] India's backsliding place in the world revolution conception can, in retrospect, be seen as a tantalizing and unfulfilled postscript to Du Bois's claim for August 15, 1947, as one of the most important dates of the twentieth century.

Strong's lifetime of attraction to and disdain toward Stalinism and the Stalinization of the Russian Revolution helped tip her sympathies to China during its conflict with the Soviet Union over the Soviets' expulsion of Albania from the Warsaw Pact. Her memory of ignoring (and misrepresenting) the Soviet famines during the 1930s informed her favorable reporting on the development of farm communes in China in the 1960s. Strong generally supported Mao's claims to her that China remained a Marxist-Leninist state "promoting world revolution" while the Soviets had become "revisionists who fear imperialism and try to make a deal with imperialism"—a criticism of Khrushchev's efforts to warm relations with the United States.[155] In response to the United States' sending advisers to Laos to put down the Pathet Lao insurgents, Strong traveled to Vietnam and Laos for three weeks and wrote a short book, *Cash and Violence in Laos and Vietnam*, in which she used the words "American imperialism" for the first time.[156] She met with Che Guevara when he went to Beijing seeking support for the Cuban Revolution and asked to translate Strong's book on Chinese Communes into Spanish.[157] Eleanor Roosevelt took time out to excoriate Strong in her newspaper column for Strong's criticism of U.S. militarism in Korea. Strong never returned to the United States or to the Soviet Union after 1959. When the Cultural Revolution erupted in China, she was critical of the Maoist cult of personality and the abandonment of what she understood as democratic centralism. She joined the Red Guard but also wrote, "All that one knows of Mao indicates that he appreciates dissent. But the drift in China is towards a religion, a deity, whose every word is of equal weight. This may be needed by people faced by a big possible war. But it leaves me a heretic, and hence restless and even unsafe."[158] Strong died in Beijing in 1970 and was interred in the Babaoshan Cemetery of Revolutionary Martyrs on the city's outskirts. Her gravestone was inscribed "Progressive American Writer and Friend of the Chinese People."[159]

The lives of George Padmore, Kwame Nkrumah, and C.L.R. James were so tightly braided before and after 1945 that, in hindsight, they almost seem to be a single presence in the grand narrative of the diasporic international. James, who had introduced Nkrumah to Padmore through letters in 1945, had known Nkrumah since he was a student at Lincoln University in Pennsylvania and had known Padmore since childhood in Trinidad; he was reunited with both on an itinerant basis after his deportation to London from the United States in 1952. Between 1952 and 1957, when Gold Coast declared independence, Padmore was the primary adviser to Nkrumah in building the Convention People's Party, negotiating relationships with socialist and capitalist states (always advising against relations with the Soviet Union, a lingering legacy of his anti-Stalinism) and arguing for the development of Pan-African socialism. Padmore's *The Gold Coast Revolution: The Struggle of an African People from Slavery to Freedom* (1953) was an ideological handbook for the revolution, proposing Gold Coast nationalism as an inheritance of both the Ashanti Confederacy and European imperialism "coming home to roost." The book also cited Du Bois's *Pittsburgh Courier* pamphlet *The Century of the Color Line* to argue that the future world would be largely "what the coloured men make it."[160] In 1957, at Gold Coast's independence as Ghana, C.L.R. James visited for the first time. Ghanaian freedom persuaded James, too, to revise his world revolution typology. As Robin D. G. Kelley notes, "The level of militancy and self-organization he observed challenged earlier theories of revolution, including some of the ideas put forth in his own *Black Jacobins*. Now he questioned the extent to which revolutions in Western Europe and African revolutions were interdependent. . . . By making Ghana the center of a continent-wide African liberation movement, James surmised, Nkrumah would keep the revolution permanent. And by moving immediately to socialism through state intervention and 'initiating new social relations from below,' Ghana could make the revolutionary transition that neither the USSR nor Eastern Europe was capable of making."[161]

Put in terms of this study, James's revisions were typological, rooted in questions about the world revolution dating to his book on the Comintern during the midnight hour of the mid-1930s. Indeed, James chose to express revisions to that period of his thought in an updated, expanded edition of *A History of Negro Revolt*, originally published in 1938. The changes attempted to reconcile yet again the two dominant ideological streams of world revolution thought: Pan-Africanism and Communist Internationalism, leaning toward increased sympathy and tolerance for the former. James made small revisions to the text, providing a slightly less hostile portrait of Marcus Garvey, and added an epilogue, "The History of Pan-African Revolt: A Summary, 1939–1969." Between 1957 and 1969, James had soured on the bureaucratic corruption and failures of the deposed Nkrumah regime. He now offered Tanzania and Nyerere's *Ujamaa* as an alternative to the failed socialisms of Russia and Eastern Europe, praising "cooperative villages" as a "whole new attempt to create a new society."[162] For James, Tanzanian socialism was also a return not just to African "communalism" but to "real" Marxism after Stalin. He assessed Nyerere's dedication to rural agriculture as an inspired variation on Lenin's insistence that "the Soviet official leave high-flown theorizing and personally go to work among the backward Russian peasants."[163] This idea— better characterized by Babu as Narodnism than Leninism, nonetheless sustained James's late-in-life faith that the originary fountain of world revolution might still nourish the planet: "It is sufficient to say that socialist thought has been nothing like this since the death of Lenin in 1924, and its depth, range and the repercussions which flow from it, go far beyond the Africa which gave it birth. It can fertilize and awaken the mortuary that is socialist theory and practice in the advanced countries."[164] James's optimism of the will contrasts sharply with Babu's much more viable assessment of Tanzania (along with Nigeria, Kenya, Ivory Coast, and Egypt) as a "mish-mash collection of comprador capitalist states—the weak appendage of a dying imperialism."[165]

Esther Cooper Jackson, Shirley Graham Du Bois, and Claudia Jones likewise form a powerful troika who, as much as any three figures, carried forward the legacy of the diasporic international. In 1961, Jackson became the co-founder and managing editor of *Freedomways: A Quarterly Journal of the Negro Movement*. Before leaving for Ghana, Du Bois provided advice on the journal's formation, and Graham Du Bois agreed to be general editor even in exile. A successor to *Freedom*, on which Jackson had worked for nearly a decade with Du Bois, Graham Du Bois, Eslanda Robeson, and others, *Freedomways* was its own typological revision on the world revolution conception. In its premiere editorial published in April 1961, the editors proclaimed, "*Freedomways* offers a means of examining experiences and strengthening the relationship among peoples of African descent in this country, in Latin America, and wherever there are communities of such people anywhere in the world."[166] The journal's Pan-Africanist and Bandung tilt was an editorial manifestation of objective conditions of mass African decolonization: Kwame Nkrumah, Julius Nyerere, and Jomo Kenyatta were among its contributors. But the journal's deeper roots were in the communist left. In addition to Jackson, Louis Burnham, Dorothy Burnham, Augusta Strong, Edward Strong, and James Jackson, the contributors all had met in the SNYC. An early issue of *Freedomways* reprinted Du Bois's "Behold the Land" speech. Like the PAC in Manchester in 1945, the double currents of *Freedomways* reflected the long imprint of the Communist International on both Popular Front–style politics carried forward into the journal and "deviations" from the Stalinist legacy in Pan-African socialism. Both shaped the editorial contours of *Freedomways* through at least the 1960s.

On February 23, 1968, Jackson and *Freedomways* organized a centennial celebration for Du Bois's birth at Carnegie Hall in New York. Just six weeks before he made his speech at Riverside Church opposing the war in Vietnam, Martin Luther King gave another speech there, "Honoring Dr. Du Bois," which was also published in *Freedomways*. It endeavored to link King's new dedication to anti-imperialism to an appeal for tolerance for Du Bois's communist commitments. King invoked a diasporic international of communists among whom the un-American Du Bois might be favorably viewed: "In contemporary life the English speaking world has no difficulty with the fact that Sean O'Casey was a literary giant of the twentieth century and a Communist or that Pablo Neruda is generally considered the greatest living poet though he also served in the Chilean Senate as a Communist. It is time to cease muting the fact that Dr. Du Bois was a genius and chose to be a Communist. Our irrational obsessive anticommunism has led us into too many quagmires to be retained as if it were a mode of scientific thinking."[167] In addition, *Freedomways* pulled forward and foregrounded black feminist writers, activists, and theory. Angela Davis and Dorothy Burnham published reconsiderations of black women, race, and class self-consciously beholden to Claudia Jones's groundbreaking essays on black women's "triple oppression" years earlier. Jackson remained the editor-in-chief of *Freedomways* through its demise in 1985.

During her time as editor, Jackson maintained a steady if uneven relationship to Shirley Graham Du Bois. Jackson was the still point of the black feminist triad of the diasporic international, while Graham Du Bois was its moving leg, "roving to revolutions." According to Gerald Horne and Margaret Stevens, while living in Ghana Graham Du Bois solicited articles for the journal from Tom Mboya of Kenya, Oliver Tambo of South Africa, and Julius Nyerere of Tanzania.[168] After Du Bois's death, Graham Du Bois was appointed by Nkrumah to direct the television industry in Ghana because of her background in theater and writing. Horne and Stevens describe as "left nationalist" Graham Du Bois's strong tilt to support for China in the Sino-Soviet split and her staunch advocacy for Nkrumah until she was placed under house arrest during the 1966 coup that brought him down.[169] Detached from her CPUSA setting where members remained loyal to the Soviet Union, and in need of a new revolutionary home, she set out for Beijing, a trajectory also being pursued by a new wave of black internationalists following in Graham Du Bois's footsteps. They included Vicki Garvin; Jack O'Dell, another *Freedomways* editor and contributor; and Robert F. Williams, whom Graham Du Bois had turned down for a job with the Nkrumah administration and who ended up in Cuba before going to Beijing. En route, Graham Du Bois lived briefly in Cairo, supporting Nasser's nationalism even as he repressed Egyptian communists and developing (along with her son David) an affinity for Arab nationalism that would reverse Du Bois's sympathies for Israel up to the Suez Canal incident in 1956. Both Shirley and David Graham Du Bois would become pro-Palestinian and strongly anti-Zionist by the end of their lives, especially after the Six Day War in 1967 and Israel's annexation of parts of Jordan, Syria, and the West Bank. Shirley Graham Du Bois eventually returned to the United States, delivering lectures on relationships of Africa and China and attending meetings in Oakland, California, sponsored by the Black Panther Party. A diasporic internationalist to the end, she was buried in China as a citizen of Tanzania when she died of cancer in April 1977.

Claudia Jones arrived in London in December 1955 and joined the Communist Party of Great Britain (CPGB). In 1956, she joined the Caribbean Labor Congress and the West Indian Students and Workers Association. Jones's frustrations with inattention within the CPGB to anti-imperial anti-colonial struggles at their high point tilted her decidedly in the direction of "leftist nationalism." At the twenty-fifth Congress of the CPGB in 1957, Jones said, "The backward peoples of China and backward people of Czarist Russia were the first to throw off the old regimes, and are now going forward with the most advanced ideology—the ideology of socialism—while the technically advanced peoples of the Western bourgeois democratic tradition are still stepped in the mire of backward imperialist ideology. And now India is following suit. The anti-imperialist struggles of the backward Afro-Asian nations, from Egypt to Ghana, are today leading the progressive anti-imperialist ideological struggle."[170] Jones weighed on the CPGB to revise its British Road to Socialism to call for the British labor movement to "fight against the colour bar and racial discrimination, and for full social, economic and political equality of colonial people in Britain."[171]

A turning point in Jones's life came in December 1958 with the Notting Hill riots in London's largest West Indian community, a response to attacks on West Indian homes and an interracial couple living there. Jones founded in rapid succession the Committee of Afro-Asian Caribbean Organizations and the newspaper originally named the *West Indian Gazette*. In January 1959, Jones founded London's Carnival. But it was the *Gazette* that functioned as a powerful sign of the persistence of the world revolution concept. Jones sought to use the paper to sustain both a Stalinized Communist Internationalism, heavily tipped toward support for China after 1961, and a triumphalist anti-colonialism. The paper alternated profiles of Eric Williams ("Conscience of Caribbean Nationalism") and exhortations to "Free Jomo Kenyatta" with reports on Pete Seeger's Anniversary Concert with Paul Robeson and warning articles of "U.S. Task Ships in Caribbean Waters." Cuba's revolution was a running narrative: reports were published on Castro's nationalization of oil in August 1960, as was the "Eye Witness in Cuba" report by Eric Hobsbawm, who wrote, "If the rest of the Caribbean is anything like Cuba's that's the place for me."[172] The paper reprinted "The Last Letter of Patrice Lumumba" from the Tunisian weekly *Afrique Action* and a long poem from the rising Caribbean literary star Jan Carew about his murder. The paper also led and reported on protest marches against the Commonwealth Immigrants Bill, published a report from Shirley Graham Du Bois in January 1962 on the All-African

Peoples Conference in Accra, and reported favorably on Nkrumah's designation of the European Common Market as a "Neo-Colonial Plot," calling it in an editorial "A Collective-Colonial Cold-War Monster."[173]

In December 1962, Jones visited the Soviet Union as an invited guest of the editors of the magazine *Soviet Woman*. Although her reports on the lives of women were glowing, in general, the *Gazette*'s coverage was outweighed editorially by affirmative reporting on the Caribbean, India, and China (although Soviet support for Cuba was noted by Jones). As Marika Sherwood has noted about Jones's writings on her Soviet trip, "She did not raise issues of democracy, or whether all or a majority of the people had consented to the politics of the communist regime. Nor did she apparently question whether all the policies and practices were in essence 'communist.'"[174] Jones's political persona in the diasporic international by this time was capable of simultaneous leftist nationalism and support for competing Chinese and Soviet revolutions, no matter their socialist content—a blend of metonymic nationalism and Stalinized communism. On August 31, 1963, the *Gazette* carried coverage of a march of 750 people organized largely by Jones to commemorate the March on Washington and the death of W.E.B. Du Bois. The same issue of the paper reprinted part of Mao's public statement "Support for Negro Rights," a legacy of Du Bois's final appeal on his visit in 1962. In May 1964, the *Gazette* warned, "Vietnam War May Spread," and predicted victory for the guerrilla opposition. In August–September, Jones reported as a delegate at the tenth World Conference against Hydrogen and Atomic Bombs in Japan under the title "Anti-Bomb Meeting Blow to Imperialism."[175]

From Japan, Jones flew to China and wrote, "What China Means to U.S. Africans." She visited Yenan, the site of a Red Army encampment and of Mao's address on revolutionary culture of 1942. Inspired on August 28, 1964, the first anniversary of Du Bois's death, Jones wrote the poem "Cradle of the Revolution" in an airplane flying from Yenan. The poem conjures generations of revolutionaries "who fashioned from soil / Of centuries, crude weapons" of rebellion: "No idle dreamers these— / And yet they dared to dream."[176]

Five months later, in January 1965, Jones died in her sleep. Official tributes poured in from the world-revolutionary left: from China, Cuba, Japan, the Soviet Union. Messages of love and support came from the U.S. actors Ruby Dee and Ossie Davis and from Gus Hall, chairman of the CPUSA. In her honor, the *Gazette* reprinted "Limits of Tyranny Are the Measure of Our Resistance," Jones's public statement of February 2, 1953, read out before she was sentenced in the United States for violating the Smith Act. A photograph of Jones with W.E.B. Du Bois was offered to readers as a memorial and paper shrine. Shirley Graham Du Bois, Jones's onetime sister and still a comrade, the *Gazette* reported, was sending a letter from Africa, and grieving.

THE AFTERTHOUGHT

In one sense, we know more about the French Revolution or the Stalinist reign of terror than those who were involved in them, because we know what they led to. With the privilege of hindsight, we can inscribe these events in a broader narrative, making more sense of them than Robespierre or Trotsky were ever able to do. . . .

It is up to us to ensure that Michelangelo and Thomas Mann, say, did not belong to a race that ended up destroying itself. They themselves, being dead, are powerless to prevent that tragic denouement, whereas we are not. We can make a difference to their stories. We cannot undo the fate of those in the past who fought for justice and were murdered for their pains. But we can rewrite their narratives by our own actions in the present, and even give them a classical happy ending.

—Terry Eagleton, "Waking the Dead," 2009

In the summer of 2013, the Italian autonomist Ferruccio Gambino published "Reading *Black Reconstruction* on the Eve of 1968" in a special issue of the *South Atlantic Quarterly* dedicated to Du Bois's book. Gambino describes himself in the essay as a searching young activist of the 1960s European left living in a world divided. The Cold War partition into "two Europes" separated with a "line of barbed wire from the Baltic to the Black Sea" was haunted by the specter of Hungary's failed workers' uprising against Stalinist rule in 1956, leaving a generation of leftists "even more divided and more closed in on themselves."[1] The malaise made it difficult for radicals in Europe to assess relationships to events worlds away, including African and Asian decolonization struggles and a southern U.S. Civil Rights Movement whose religious orientation, he suggests, made it "pallid" to a generation of historical materialists.

In the spring of 1967, Gambino was a student staying in the United States under the mentorship of the historian George Rawick. As he recounts it, Rawick strongly advised Gambino to read two books: W.E.B. Du Bois's *Black Reconstruction in America* and C.L.R. James's *The Black Jacobins*. Suddenly, for Gambino, the "gray North Atlantic shroud of the early 1960s" was rent. "It was easy to see," wrote Gambino, "that *Black Reconstruction* cast a bright light on crucial developments that were scarcely known or completely negated in the history books. Du Bois's book put the slaves at center stage and sought to over-turn the dominant opinion that continued racist prejudice and the consequent intellectual laziness."[2] More important for Gambino, Du Bois's book seemed to "rend" a historical impasse plaguing his own political generation's capacity to relate to struggles beyond the pale of home. The recognition that American slaves in 1848 had protested the U.S. invasion of Mexico became for a genera-tion steeped in another, European trajectory from that year a global license to dream: "Du Bois's move seemed to be in tune with the anticolonial revolts in Asia and Africa in the 1920s more than with the interclass politics of the popular fronts, the alliance with colonial powers, and the abandonment of the anticolonial struggles, positions officially adopted by the Third International in the same year as the publication of *Black Reconstruction*. In other words, Du Bois's book was a milestone of historiography for all those whose history had been denied or stolen."[3] Gambino's potent account animates a central theme of this book—namely, the recursive power of the world revolution conception. The emphasis on black self-determination in *Black Reconstruction in America* redeems for Gambino a prior narrative of Third International history seem-ingly emptied out by years of Stalinist betrayal and Socialism in One Country doctrine. Thus, much as James had complained that until his (and Du Bois's) scholarship the only place Negroes were *not* revolting was in the pages of his-tory books, "so the youth of the 1960s" who became the generation of 1968, writes Gambino, "instead of limiting themselves to the assigned textbooks, were violating with their internationalism the old gentlemen's club."[4]

Gambino's memory of political awakening also speaks to the inevita-ble relationship between thought and practice, historiography and history making. The capacity to "rewrite . . . narratives by our own actions in the present"—what, in the case of Du Bois and the diasporic international, I have been calling a revolutionary typology—animates the core radicalism of Du Bois's work long after its expiration date. Yet this moment of backward glance also indexes roots of a recurring problem in Du Bois scholarship, or what we might more broadly call commemoration. Rawick notwithstanding, 1967 was a "low tide" in public appreciation for Du Bois's legacy; it was, after all, the same year that Martin Luther King Jr. made his desperate, and futile, appeal to Americans that they accept once and for all Du Bois's final turn to member-ship in the Communist Party. Were it not for the dogged efforts of Herbert Aptheker and International Publishers, it is possible that Du Bois's autobiog-raphy would not have seen the light of day in the United States in 1968, some six years *after* its international publication. In the same year that Du Bois's book did appear, as Amy Bass has documented, a broad alliance of groups in his hometown of Great Barrington, Massachusetts, that included the Ameri-can Legion, Knights of Columbus, and Daughters of the American Revolution, worked to oppose an emergent campaign to construct a memorial in his honor.[5] Du Bois's letters, newspaper columns, and secondary writings, especially those published after his more open turn to socialist thought, appeared intermittently in collections—mostly by small leftist publishers and mostly shepherded single-handedly by Aptheker—only in the 1970s and 1980s, well after his death. Until 1995, Du Bois's Comintern novel *Dark Princess*, first published in 1928, remained out of print and virtually unread. Meanwhile, Du Bois's blacklisted manuscript "Russia and America" remains unpublished to this day, despite efforts by scholars and publishers to bring it into print.

It was also *this* "shroud" that was rent for Gambino by his chance encounter with Du Bois in 1967. Yet the persistence of rigid classification of Du Bois's career and thought—the benevolent, soulful early work and the later dogmatic period; the "scholarly" Du Bois and the "polemical" Du Bois; the Du Bois of "racial uplift" and the "transnational" Du Bois; the "humanist" Du Bois and the "Stalinist" Du Bois—are categories that themselves reflect what Alan Wald has called the "polarized thinking" of scholarship and commemoration generated under the influence of the Cold War.[6] In the case of Du Bois, an obsessive conflation of Stalin and Stalinism with the *idea* of communism in the twentieth century finds its mirror in an obsessive conflation of Du Bois with American (and African American) cultural and political history and an unnerving anxiety about miscegenating the two. Great man narratives of each have helped hold in place ossified, unnuanced analyses of the history of communism and revolutionary thinking within and outside the United States (the general absence, for example, of Trotskyist scholarship on the U.S. cultural and political left), reflected in ossified and unnuanced analysis of Du Bois's body of thought on questions of Marxism and revolution.[7] This frozen dialectic has taken the place of the kind of fluid, aspirational, and transformative approach to history and politics captured in the "doubling" of history and historiography in Benjamin's (and Du Bois's) work that I have attempted to use as inspiration for my efforts in this study. It has also "provincialized" Du Bois, a latent anticommunism holding back detailed study and reflection of his relationship to the world revolution concept, privileging American nationalism, disciplinary boundaries, and the preservation of reputation as part of an effective strategy of commemorative "containment."

In this context, this book might be seen as an effort to uncongeal political and analytical categories; to examine their interlocking, contradictory, and self-contradictory associations; and to sweep aside hagiographical and biographical impulses that have narrowed our understandings of both history and biography. In large part, the generation of scholars and memorializers of Du Bois born well after the "Stalin era" have begun that work, and it is in some ways on their methodological shoulders and insights that this study stands. This scholarship is unified by its own revisionist impulses dedicated to creating what Eagleton calls a "broader narrative" of history, which throws into relief essential elements of diasporic internationalism such as cross-border solidarity; collaborative and collective political struggle; interrogation of gender roles; and the search for a redemptive, and often revisionist, relationship to both Marxism and its practice. In general, this scholarship has confronted directly questions of political successes and failures of the revolutionary left in the twentieth century by detaching from Stalinist—or what is better called "Stalinized"—historiography. I have already indicated the drift of this scholarship in the previously cited claim by Eric Porter that "Du Bois might have praised Stalin, for example, but he was not a Stalinist in any systematic way."[8]

Porter's insights clear the way in his important book *The Problem of the Future World* (2010) for study of Du Bois's late, more explicitly anticapitalist work, not just unto itself but in relationship to the moment of our time. In the wake of the collapse of state capitalist communism in the Soviet Union and China, and in the face of current global neoliberal devastations to workers, social welfare, and the environment, Porter offers the following quote from David Levering Lewis's *W.E.B. Du Bois: The Fight for Equality and the American Century, 1919–1963*: "It may be suggested that Du Bois was right to insist that to leave the solution of systemic social problems exclusively to the market was an agenda guaranteeing obscene economic inequality in the short run and irresoluble political calamity in the long run."[9] Like the current study, Porter's book links the de-Stalinization of scholarship on Du Bois to a recovery of his radical internationalism. Socialism, Porter writes, became the "vehicle" by which Du Bois could "partially detach from domestic political imperatives and answer to a higher cosmopolitan calling."[10] Porter's ambitious attempt to read the present into the past via Du Bois's attempts to negotiate a "middle way" between capitalism and communism also corresponds to what Wald has called a need to "decolonize" Cold War scholarship, in part by reexamining the political questions of that sometimes ossified genre from the perspective of our own midnight hour.[11] This does not necessarily mean giving the previous era or our own a "classical happy ending" as much as it means studying afresh the residual pastness of the present in order to change it. Porter ends his book, for example, by writing, "While the historically specific state socialist project through which Du Bois hoped his reconstruction of democracy would happen founders on the ruins of the Soviet Union and on Russia's and China's free market and imperialist adventures in the present, the project of transforming the state to better promote economic and racial justice remains a necessity."[12]

Scholars who identify with postcolonial studies, especially in South Asian and East Asian American studies, have also accelerated the "decolonization" of Du Bois studies. Among them are Yuichiro Onishi, Dohra Ahmed, Nico Slate, and Etsuko Taketani.[13] Their studies of twentieth-century leftist internationalism and Du Bois's place in it are united by an endeavor to reframe African American political and cultural history within two broader twentieth-century narratives: anticolonial struggles in Asia and diasporic international solidarity. Among the significant and original aspects of Taketani's book, for example, is that it is one of the first to examine the Japan and China sections of Du Bois's "Russia and America" to interpret Du Bois's support for twentieth-century Asian national liberation struggles.[14] These studies also recover a century of collaboration between South Asian and East Asian revolutionaries and African Americans in the West, a turn Onishi calls "Du Bois's challenge" to scholars of the twenty-first century. In turn, these studies span the globe to *name* this diasporic internationalism. Ahmad titles it "anticolonial utopianism"; Onishi, "colored internationalism"; Taketani, a "black Pacific narrative"; and Nico Slate, "colored cosmopolitanism." While none of these studies, in my thinking, gives sufficient space to the catalytic role of Communist Internationalism, they are all fellow travelers to my own, particularly in their desire to link the present to its own pastness. They represent an effort to create a history of U.S. colonial and postcolonial history of a piece with scholarship influenced by the South Asian subaltern school: Partha Chatterjee, Dipesh Chakrabarty, Sumit Sarkar, Gayatri Spivak, and other scholars cited in this book.[15] The simultaneity of this body of scholarship across the globe is also a function of revolutionary typologies: the successes and defeats of the twentieth-century global left, particularly in the wake of anticolonial liberation and communist defeat, have taken on the sweet and sour tang of historical necessity for assessing the present. The cast of global figures meeting at historical crossroads of collective anti-imperialist struggles in these scholarly works, from Lala Rai to James Weldon Johnson, suggests many still untraveled roots and routes for scholars seeking to map diasporic internationalism in the century of world revolution.

The decolonization of scholarship on the twentieth-century revolutionary left has also, not surprisingly, deposed conventional, and masculine, biographical means of commemoration. Hagiographic studies of Du Bois as a "race man" directing black intellectual traffic across the color line have faded as quickly as the anticommunist historiography that cast numerous key figures into the shadows. That many of these figures were women who are now emerging as historical protagonists and movement builders, well beyond the scopic and intellectual influence of great man leaders, is itself a historical revision of a narrative embedded deep in the century of world revolution— namely, the fight against women's oppression. The simultaneous recovery, for example, of Agnes Smedley's literary career by figures such as Tillie Olsen, the Old Left Communist Party member, and by Alice Walker, a civil rights activist of the 1960s, shows a deep debt to the left's treatment of the "woman question" dating to Alexandra Kollontai, Clara Zetkin, and others.[16] Walker's identification of Smedley as a literary foremother in her foreword to the Feminist Press's republication of *Daughter of Earth* has also helped make clear lineages of revolt between the Old Left's apprehension of the "Negro question" and its legacy for a postwar generation.[17] In addition to biographies of Smedley, Barbara Ransby's recent biographies of Ella Baker and Eslanda Robeson, Carole Boyce Davies and Marika Sherwood's separate biographies of Claudia Jones, and Gerald Horne's biography of Shirley Graham Du Bois are important for throwing into relief some of the most important figures of the twentieth-century diasporic international while providing a *subordinated* perspective on a figure such as Du Bois, who connects to all of them.[18] These works have enabled us to see political influence on the left and on the African American left as bidirectional, fusing anticolonial, antiracist struggles to the gender equity these struggles strove to produce. In recent years, scholars such as Lise Vogel, Angela Davis, Martha Jimenez, Susan Ferguson, David McNally, and Tithi Bhattacharya have also plumbed the line on the woman question back to the early twentieth (and nineteenth) century to extraordinary revisionist effect. Debates on the Marxist left, and on the academic left, about women's oppression and how to fight it have rarely been as robust as they are now.[19]

An even more complete decolonization of scholarship on Du Bois and the twentieth-century left must also entail a reconsideration of academic disciplinary boundaries. Du Bois's monumental standing as a paternal figure of African American studies and American studies, for example, has generated overtly or covertly nationalist paradigms for considering crucial questions of political internationalism. To cite one example, scholarship on "whiteness studies" that center narrowly on close readings of select passages from *Black Reconstruction in America* have totally obscured more internationalist readings of the meaning of race in Du Bois's work provided by scholars such as Cedric Robinson and Paul Gilroy, on one hand, and Ferruccio Gambino, on the other. This owes to what Du Bois himself would have called an American "racial provincialism," which his quest for an international perspective, as demonstrated throughout this study, was meant to contravene. It was not just the Soviets' "refusal to be white" but the world's refusal that drew Du Bois well beyond the cramped and narrow confines of U.S. color line discourse well before the end of his life. The desire to force his thinking and career backward on questions of race is a sign of the narrowing tendency in U.S. political discourse that he resisted all of his life. In recent years, gender studies scholars such as Alys Weinbaum and scholars of diaspora such as Paul Gilroy have done much to enhance an internationalist frame of Du Bois's racial thinking by locating it in the currents of biopolitics, or planetary humanism.[20] Eric Porter has even argued that the mid-twentieth century in the United States was "the first post-racial moment" in his analysis of Du Bois's work, not to diminish race's centrality, but to explain why other, more worldly—and revolutionary—frames powered Du Bois's thinking as he approached the end of his life, frames that, as I have argued, in turn reframed what had come before.[21] Efforts to broaden and internationalize African American studies scholarship and Du Bois's place in leftist anticolonial movements have also benefited from exemplary studies by Penny Von Eschen, Kevin Gaines, and Gerald Horne. Horne's *The Counter-Revolution of 1776* (2014) self-consciously deploys the Du Boisian notion of an American "counterrevolution" to describe the role and effects of 1776 on American slaves, a perspective that winds backward to what remains a still undervalued classic of Du Bois scholarship, Horne's *Black and Red* (1985).[22]

This process of "reframing" both Du Bois and American radicalism should also take its lead from a vanguard of scholars who have filled a gaping void in attention to black women's proletarian internationalism. Recent books by Cheryl Higashida, Dayo Gore, Carole Boyce Davies, Marika Sherwood, and Erik McDuffie on black women and the global left constitute a generational recovery and typological revision of the twentieth-century world revolution conception.[23] Higashida's notion of "black feminist internationalism" as a centerpiece of mid-century revolutionary thought comes closest to embodying the practice of diasporic internationalism that I have located in a wide-ranging group of revolutionary affiliates in this book. Higashida's study of predominantly working-class black women of the First World and the Third World in the 1930s–1950s demonstrates how black women linked the fight against women's oppression and racism to the Leninist thesis on national self-determination. While the figures in her book remained nominally committed to the Soviet revolution through 1953—and hence to Stalinism—they also produced an independent body of thought that looked forward to black feminism. Higashida has also mined more carefully than any other scholar the lineage of Claudia Jones's "triple oppression" thesis with later intersectionality theory, a critical linkage for connecting the Old Left and the New Left and mainstream and dissident revolutionary feminism in the twentieth century. As Higashida writes, Jones's feminism is "intersectional, but not in the sense espoused by cultural critics who value non-hierarchical conjunctions of different modes of resistance. In specifically giving precedence to national liberation, Jones demonstrates that it is necessarily transformed by centering black women's struggles within it instead of focusing exclusively on men."[24] While I differ with Higashida's general characterization of this feminism as "post-nationalist," her attention to a crucial advance in leftist political theory that is beholden to, yet in creative tension with, Third Internationalist thought is a model for the kind of dialectical reframing of world revolution theory I have aspired to in this study.

Similarly, McDuffie and Gore have significantly broadened our understanding of African American women on the U.S. left. McDuffie recounts the communist Williana Burroughs's ten-year stay in the Soviet Union, from 1935 to 1945, as an early point on a century-long trajectory of black women's expatriatism that Gore punctuates with an account of the life of Vicki Garvin.[25] Garvin was drawn to the leftist circle around *Freedom* (and the Du Boises) in the 1950s. In 1961, she moved to Nigeria after she was offered employment by her fellow leftist Thelma Dale Perkins. After experiencing what she called two years of "neocolonialism-disillusionment," she moved to Ghana, meeting up briefly with Shirley and W.E.B. Du Bois. In 1964, she went to China, where she lived in exile for six years.[26] She was what Gore describes as a "behind-the-scenes" strategist in supporting both China's Cultural Revolution and black liberation, the two conjoined, however crudely, after Mao's declaration of support for Negro liberation in 1963. The experience of exile and affiliation with a diasporic revolutionary left (her stay in China overlapped with those of Shirley Graham and Robert F. Williams) left Garvin describing herself as certainly an offspring of the twentieth-century world revolution: a "Pan-Africanist" and "proletarian, working-class, internationalist."[27] Cumulatively, these works on black female radicals have helped achieve a fresh perspective on the U.S. left and, especially, on the complex legacy of Stalinism. As Wald notes, the books "confirm the intellectual shallowness of overarching applications of the political category of 'Stalinism,'" especially when applied to a broad range of political thinkers and activists.[28]

Similarly paradigmatic of decolonizing Cold War scholarship are biographies of Claudia Jones by Sherwood and Boyce Davies. Both offer reflective accounts of the life of their subject steeped in political moments of the present. Sherwood's *Claudia Jones: A Life in Exile*, for example, consists of seven chapters based almost entirely on primary source documents excavated after her death, supplemented by transcripts of a Claudia Jones Symposium in London organized in 1996 by friends and former colleagues. The symposium included sessions on four aspects of Jones's life: "My Friend Claudia," a roundtable discussion by, among others, Rajana Ash, who recounted Jones's formation of the Committee of Afro-Asian and Caribbean Organization; "The Political Activist," with reflections by former comrades in the British Communist Party; "The West Indian Gazette"; and "Carnival."[29] Sherwood's book is the best extant account of Jones's place in the wider postwar British left and the local activists who built it. Its combination of scholarly interpretation and commemoration make it an important model for understanding and applying the lessons of diasporic internationalism to our present. Similarly, Boyce Davies locates the repression, surveillance, and deportation Jones suffered during the 1950s in the context of post–9/11 U.S. homeland security. She compares the Smith Act and McCarran-Walter Acts to the Illegal Immigration Reform and Immigrant Responsibility Act of 1997 and USA Patriot Act of 2001, both of which increased deportation, surveillance, and the political demonization of dissidents and immigrants, especially from Arab states. Boyce Davies challenges romantic paradigms of transnational and diasporic scholarship to include deportation and involuntary migration (political refugeedom) as a central category of "mobility," a particularly apt trope for understanding figures in this study such as Smedley, Strong, the Du Boises, James, and Jones herself, whose "diasporic" internationalism was induced in part by the dialectics of state repression and political dissidence.[30]

Finally, the "decolonization" of twentieth-century scholarship is an ongoing project enabled in part by the decolonization and de-Stalinization of the last century's archives. This study benefits from that process in several ways, including having had access to both primary and second source interpretations made possible only by texts that have surfaced for public view in the wake of the post-1989 collapse of the Soviet Union. For example, Du Bois's contributions to the Soviet press (*Pravda, Literaturnaya Gazeta, Izvestia*),[31] as well as Soviet commentary on his visits and publication, affirm, complicate, and refute scholarly portraits of him as an "unrepentant Stalinist."[32] Ruth Price's magisterial biography of Agnes Smedley, which includes definitive revelations about her career as a Comintern agent, has likewise been made available by the opening up of the Comintern archives. Kate Baldwin's *Beyond the Color Line and the Iron Curtain* (2003) was one of the first books to take advantage of the opening of Soviet archives to reinterpret the relationship of Du Bois, Paul Robeson, and Langston Hughes to the Soviet Union.[33] Baldwin also remains one of the few scholars to seriously engage Du Bois's unpublished manuscript "Russia and America." Another is Taketani, whose *The Black Pacific Narrative* also takes up documents related to Chinese suspicions that Langston Hughes was operating as a Soviet Comintern agent during his time in Shanghai in the 1930s. (He was not.) John Riddell's magnificent restoration of the transcripts of the Communist International of 1922, published in 2011 under the title *Toward the United Front*, provides an indispensable record and interpretation of what James in 1935 called the "rise and fall" of the world revolution. Finally, Sobhanlal Datta Gupta's study *Comintern and the Destiny of Communism in India 1919–1943* draws on extensive Comintern archives to revise entirely the relationship of the Indian communist left to the Comintern. Gupta's first chapter, "Comintern: The New Historiography," is essential reading. These works of scholarship also provide an emerging tip of the iceberg that scholars continue to construct of the global dynamics of world revolution, the political horrors and errors of Stalinism, and the tendrils that connected many members of the diasporic international in a shared project. Collectively, too, this scholarship is motivated by political crises of the present. As Gupta writes, historical recovery of Comintern records is vital "because the Left in India is still heavily dominated by the spirit of Stalinism, the consequence of which has been the persistence of a fundamentalist mindset." His book, he writes, "is addressed to all those who are prepared to rethink the history of Indian communism by going back to the basics, with the openness to look back at what happened and consider what could have possibly happened."[34]

Gupta's admonition that acts of recovery in the present can foretell a future world is finally thrown into relief by the very moment of our own living. On August 28, 2013, hundreds of thousands gathered in Washington, DC, to commemorate the fiftieth anniversary of the March on Washington, an event that famously coincided nearly to the hour with Du Bois's death in Accra, Ghana. People who marched in the event's sequel carried their own ghosts of history. Everywhere were T-shirts and handmade placards featuring images of two people: Dr. Martin Luther King Jr. and Trayvon Martin. The event seemed saturated with the memory of George Zimmerman's shooting of Martin on the enclaved streets of a Florida gated community in March 2012, a perverse footnote to and echo of King's assassination in a Memphis hotel forty-four years earlier. In the aftermath of the day's events, three black activists and a spillover crowd gathered in the dusk to reflect on time and history. None of the three speakers who took the podium had been invited to speak by organizers of the official commemorative march—all were beyond the pale of the official event's formal political aspirations: the British-based journalist Gary Younge, who had come to remember the masses of people themselves—not the leaders—who made the March on Washington the archetypal event it has become in collective memory; Cornel West, formally ostracized by the Obama administration for his criticism of the first African American president and his minions, including those who organized the march; and Keeanga Yamahtta-Taylor, a scholar, activist, and rising presence on the stage of a rejuvenated American left.

Their joint appearance as self-proclaimed radicals and revolutionaries on the margins of lived American history stirred a pathos of exclusion that is, still, part of the drama of political commemoration in our time. Indeed, others compelled by world-historical events around 1963 that kept them elsewhere that day—Claudia Jones, Shirley Graham Du Bois, Anna Louise Strong—seemed to be standing in the wings of a history now occupied by intransigent descendants. Yet of the day's speakers, it was Yamahtta-Taylor who most stirred the crowd's capacity for typological revision and revolutionary dreaming. After cataloguing a long list of the declining conditions for African Americans in the United States under the first black president and scolding those who would blame the victims of racism and capitalist exploitation for their diminished state, Yamahtta-Taylor turned to a late speech by King, rarely remembered as much as his "I Have a Dream" speech, titled "Where Do We Go from Here?" Delivered in Atlanta, on August 16, 1967, the speech was part of King's thematic turn to his developing "Poor People's Campaign" focused on redistributive economic justice. Organized to respond to his own question, "Why are there 40 million poor people in America?" King's call pushed to the brink limits of his public commitments to reform, asking for a "higher synthesis" of Cold War oppositions between capitalism and communism in the name of something larger: "But one day we must come to see that an edifice which produces beggars needs restructuring. It means that questions must be raised. And you see, my friends, when you deal with this you begin to ask the question, 'Who owns the oil?' You begin to ask the question, 'Who owns the iron ore?' You begin to ask the question, 'Why is it that people have to pay water bills in a world that's two-thirds water?' These are words that must be said."[35] Yamahtta-Taylor's public reading, and rereading, of King's words were intended to reshape the day's march into a more strident, and transformative, iteration of its original. As she spoke, it was difficult not to remember August 28, 1963, as its own typological moment in world-revolutionary history, an instant in which one diasporic internationalist fell and another seemed to rise from his ashes. In the dusk that day, ceremonial reiteration of time and place summoned its own Angel of History, coming around again to wake the living and the dead.

NOTES

THE FORETHOUGHT

1. "Spanish Miners Dig in against Budget Cuts," *New York Times*, July 28, 2012, A4; Ter Garcia, "Miners' Protest Revives Anti-austerity Movement in Spain," *Tucson Citizen*, available at http://occupiedtucsoncitizen.org/?p=983. Media coverage of the Tunisian protests widely reported the reemergence of Echebbi's poem in the demonstrations that launched the Arab Spring: see, e.g., the website at http://aasilahmad.net/abu-al-qasim-al-shabi-the-poet-of-the-tunisia-and-egyptian-revolution. The lines from the poem "The Will to Live" are also included in the Tunisian national anthem.

2. For Tagore, see Pankaj Mishra, *From the Ruins of Empire: The Revolt against the West and the Making of Asia* (New York: Penguin, 2012), 225. The poem, originally in Bengali and titled "Sunset on the Century," is included at the end of Tagore's *Nationalism* (London: St. Martin's Press, 1917). The book and poem are available at http://www.gutenberg.org/files/40766/40766-h/40766-h.htm.

3. Trotsky's argument stemmed from analysis of the "backward" economic conditions in Russia that produced the revolution of 1905 in a nonindustrialized, semifeudal country. Trotsky specifically defined permanent revolution as tactics of workers in underdeveloped countries such as Russia to "destroy the barriers between the minimum and maximum programme of Social Democracy, go over to more and more radical social reforms and seek direct and immediate support in revolution in Western Europe": Leon Trotsky, *The Permanent Revolution and Results and Prospects* (New York: Pathfinder Press, 1969), 31. Marx and Engels had first used the phrase "permanent revolution" in *The Holy Family* in 1844 in reference to Napoleon and the French Revolution: see Karl Marx and Frederick Engels, *Collected Works*, vol. 4 (New York: International Publishers, 1978), 123. Marx and Engels used a variant of it again in 1850 in "Address to the Central Authority of the Communist League" to refer to a proletarian revolution as a complete political revolution that would exceed a "bourgeois" revolution by bringing the working class to state

power—a "Revolution in Permanence": Karl Marx and Frederick Engels, *Collected Works*, vol. 10 (New York: International Publishers, 1978), 287. As Peter Camejo has noted, Marx thought that a socialist society "presupposed the development of the highly industrialized and mechanized production fostered by capitalism" and hence predicted that socialist revolution "would most likely begin in those countries where such preconditions for socialism as a powerful industry and a well-organized proletariat had already been created": Peter Camejo, Introduction to Trotsky, *The Permanent Revolution and Results and Prospects*, 9. Marx did not foresee how what Trotsky called capitalism's "combined and uneven development" could possibly advance a revolution in a "backward" state.

4. W.E.B. Du Bois, Alexander Walters, Henry B. Brown, and H. Sylvester Williams, "To the Nations of the World," in *Report of the Pan-African Conference*, July 23–25, 1900, Headquarters 61 and 62, Westminster Hall, London, 10–12, reprinted in *W.E.B. Du Bois: A Reader*, ed. David Levering Lewis (New York: Henry Holt, 1995), 641.

5. Mishra, *From the Ruins of Empire*, 1–11.

6. See Glenda Gilmore, *Defying Dixie: The Radical Roots of Civil Rights, 1919–1950* (New York: W. W. Norton, 2008). Living in the Yucatán in 1915 when the revolution arrived there, Fort-Whiteman became a syndicalist and socialist in the anarcho-syndicalist Casa del Obrero Mundial (House of the World Worker): ibid., 33–34.

7. Sobhanlal Datta Gupta, *Comintern and the Destiny of Communism in India, 1919–1943: Dialectics of a Real and Possible History* (Kolkata: Seribaan, 2011), 50.

8. Tariq Ali, ed., *The Stalinist Legacy: Its Impact on Twentieth-Century World Politics* (Chicago: Haymarket, 1984), 9.

9. Sumit Sarkar, *Modern India, 1885–1947* (New Delhi: Macmillan, 1983), 189.

10. See Anton Pannekoek, "World Revolution and Communist Tactics," available at http://www.marxists.org/archive/pannekoe/tactics (accessed April 21, 2014).

11. Gorter's essay argued that the Soviet revolution was already in decline. It was, he wrote, "a bourgeois-democratic one, that is today only a capitalist revolution." The countries that remained "truly proletarian" were "England and Germany, and parts of the USA." Gorter argued that the Paris Commune was a better exemplar of proletarian revolutions than the Soviet Union: see Herman Gorter, "The World Revolution," *Workers' Dreadnought*, 1923, available at http://www.marxists.org/archive/gorter/1923/world-revolution.htm (accessed January 23, 2015).

12. C.L.R. James provides powerful accounts of the setbacks and failures of the revolutions in Germany (1923) and China (1926) especially in *World Revolution 1917–1936: The Rise and Fall of the Communist International* (Atlantic Highlands, NJ: Humanities Press, 1993), esp. chaps. 7, 9. Also see Duncan Hallas, *The Comintern* (London: Bookmarks, 1985); Jean Chesneaux, *The Chinese Labor Movement, 1919–1927* (Stanford, CA: Stanford University Press, 1968).

13. Alex Callinicos, *Making History: Agency, Structure and Change in Social Theory* (Chicago: Haymarket Books, 2009), 207.

14. W.E.B. Du Bois, "Africa and the French Revolution," *Freedomways* 1 (Summer 1961): 136.

15. Ibid.

16. Walter Benjamin, "On the Concept of History," https://www.marxists.org/reference/archive/benjamin/1940/history.htm (accessed February 12, 2015).

17. Eric Porter, *The Problem of the Future World: W.E.B. Du Bois and the Race Concept at Midcentury* (Durham, NC: Duke University Press, 2010), 165.

18. W.E.B. Du Bois, *The Souls of Black Folk* (1903; repr., Boston: Bedford Books, 1997), 38.

19. Patterson develops the concept of "natal alienation" in *Slavery and Social Death: A Comparative Study* (Cambridge, MA: Harvard University Press, 1985).

20. W.E.B. Du Bois, *The Autobiography of W.E.B. Du Bois: A Soliloquy on Viewing My Life from the Last Decade of Its First Century* (New York: International Publishers, 1968), 108.

21. Ibid., 57.

22. W.E.B. Du Bois, *Dusk of Dawn: An Essay toward an Autobiography of a Race Concept* (New York: Schocken, 1968), 321.

23. For example, in *The Black Atlantic*, Gilroy declares a "degree of convergence" between his conceptions of a counterculture of modernity with Marxism, only to argue, "Their convergence is . . . undercut by the simple fact that in the critical thought of blacks in the West, social self-creation through labor is not the center-piece of emancipatory hopes": Paul Gilroy, *The Black Atlantic: Modernity and Double Consciousness* (Cambridge, MA: Harvard University Press, 1993), 40.

24. Quoted in Ali, *The Stalinist Legacy*, 7.

25. Alan Wald, "From 'Triple Oppression' to 'Freedom Dreams,'" *Against the Current* 162 (January–February 2013): 24; Ali, *The Stalinist Legacy*, 13.

26. W.E.B. Du Bois, "Russia and America: An Interpretation," unpublished draft ms., 1950, W.E.B. Du Bois Papers, University of Massachusetts Amherst, 65.

27. See Robin D. G. Kelley, *Freedom Dreams: The Black Radical Imagination* (Boston: Beacon, 2003), 570; Porter, *The Problem of the Future World*, 10.

28. James accused Aptheker of presenting African Americans as "following docilely behind the Abolitionists," just as the Stalinists view them "following docilely behind" the Communist Party: see C.L.R. James, "Herbert Aptheker's Distortions," *Fourth International* 10, no. 11 (1949), available at http://www.marxists.org/archive/james-clr/works/1949/12/aptheker.htm (accessed April 21, 2014).

29. Benjamin, "On the Concept of History."

30. Karl Marx, "'The Eighteenth Brumaire of Louis Bonaparte," in *The Portable Karl Marx*, ed. Eugene Kamenka (New York: Viking, 1983), 287.

31. This view structured much Du Bois criticism during the Cold War and was concordant with blacklisting of his late work, as I discuss in "The Afterthought" in this volume. It lingers in major scholarship. For example, in his otherwise extraordinary biography of Du Bois, Levering Lewis dedicates a mere sixteen of his 1,400 pages to the last eight years of Du Bois's life, which included his final travels to the Soviet Union, China, and Ghana; his decision to join the Communist Party; publication of his *Autobiography*; and the publication of numerous other essays in the Soviet and Chinese press. Levering Lewis also gives short shrift to Du Bois's late, unpublished manuscript "Russia and America." Recent scholarship by Eric Porter and Yuichiro Onishi, for example, has been much more reflective and considering of Du Bois's late work, largely because it is detached from Cold War and anticommunist paradigms for assessing it.

32. Mary Frances Fahey, "Allegorical Dismemberment and Rescue in Book III of 'The Faerie Queene,'" *Comparative Literature Studies* 35, no. 1 (1998): 49. Neil Davidson refers to what I call Benjamin's "typology" of revolution as a political consciousness that "every moment in history is potentially of use to revolutionaries": Neil Davidson, "Walter Benjamin and the Classical Marxist Tradition," in *Holding Fast to an Image of the Past: Explorations in the Marxist Tradition* (Chicago: Haymarket, 2014), 224. This means not "that revolutionaries should be declaring a state of permanent insurrection" but, rather, "that they should behave in the knowledge that we are in the period where revolution is historically possible and necessary": ibid., 221.

33. C.L.R. James, *The Black Jacobins: Toussaint L'Ouverture and the San Domingo Revolution* (1938; repr., London: Allison and Busby, 1980), 81.

34. Ibid.

35. C.L.R. James, "Revolution and the Negro," in *C.L.R. James and Revolutionary Marxism*, ed. Scott McLemee and Paul LeBlanc (Atlantic Highlands, NJ: Humanities Press, 1994), 77.

36. More evidence that James considered *The Black Jacobins* a response to Stalinist influence on the world revolution comes in his preface. "It was in the stillness of a seaside suburb that could be heard more clearly and insistently the booming of Franco's heavy artillery, the rattle of Stalin's firing squads and the fierce shrill turmoil of the revolutionary movement striving for clarity and influence. Such is our age and this book is of it, with something of the fever and the fret": James, *The Black Jacobins*, xi. This statement obviously alludes to both Marx's "Eighteenth Brumaire" thesis on history and Du Bois's method as he described it in *Black Reconstruction in America*. "Great men make history, but only such history as it is possible for them to make. Their freedom of achievement is limited by the necessities of their environment. To portray the limits of those necessities and the realization, complete or partial, of all possibilities, that is the true business of the historian": W.E.B. Du Bois, *Black Reconstruction in America, 1860–1880* (1935; repr., New York: Free Press, 1992), x.

37. Herbert Aptheker, *American Negro Slave Revolts, 50th Anniversary Edition* (New York: International Publishers, 1993), 13.

38. Ibid., 383.

39. Karl Marx, *Capital*, vol. 1 (New York: Penguin, 1990), 414. Aptheker also owes this argument in part to Herman Schlüter, *Lincoln, Labor and Slavery: A Chapter from the Social History of America* (New York: Socialist Literature, 1913). Schlüter argued that the Civil War was a test of interracial unity in the United States and reported on the history of the development of the International Workingmen's Association in the United States and Europe and on Marx's correspondence with Lincoln. Aptheker included the book in the bibliography of *American Negro Slave Revolts*. Du Bois likewise included Schlüter in his bibliography for *Black Reconstruction in America* under books classified as "Fair to Indifferent on the Negro." I discuss Schlüter's influence on *Black Reconstruction in America* in Chapter 3. In general, Du Bois's emphasis on white working-class cooperation (or lack thereof) with slaves before and after emancipation, his class analysis of northern capital's role in the war, and his insistence on application of Marxian terms such as "black proletariat" and "white proletariat" demonstrate an endeavor to develop a Marxist analysis of the Civil War and Reconstruction.

40. W.E.B. Du Bois, *Black Folk Then and Now: An Essay in the History and Sociology of the Negro Race* (1939; repr., Millwood, NY: Kraus-Thomson, 1975), 230.

41. Ibid.

42. In volume 1 of *Capital*, Marx explains "primitive accumulation" as the starting point of the capitalist mode of production. It includes slavery, the seizure of gold from the Americas, and dispossession of peoples from colonized lands. For Marx, primitive accumulation must be distinguished from later forms of accumulation, such as "surplus value," that occur after the fact of capitalism's establishment: see Marx, *Capital*.

43. Du Bois, *Black Folk Then and Now*, 383.

44. See Du Bois et al., "To the Nations of the World."

45. See W.E.B. Du Bois, "The Color Line Belts the World" and "The World Problem of the Color Line," in *W.E.B. Du Bois on Asia: Crossing the World Color Line*, eds. Bill V. Mullen and Cathryn Watson (Jackson: University Press of Mississippi, 2005), 33–34,

35–36. Du Bois also uses it in the conclusion to "Worlds of Color," *Foreign Affairs* 3 (April 1925): 442.

46. Karl Marx and Frederick Engels, *Manifesto of the Communist Party*, in *The Portable Karl Marx*, ed. Eugene Kamenka (New York: Penguin, 1983), 241.

CHAPTER 1

1. David Levering Lewis, *W.E.B. Du Bois: The Fight for Equality and the American Century, 1919–1963* (New York: Henry Holt, 2000), 203.

2. Quoted in Kevin Anderson, *Marx at the Margins: On Nationalism, Ethnicity, and Non-Western Societies* (Chicago: University of Chicago Press, 2010), 221.

3. Anderson's *Marx at the Margins* is a singularly useful study of how Marx's writings on colonialism can be used to interpret twentieth-century debates about race and ethnicity and how Marx's own writings on colonialism show an evolving understanding of the centrality of anticolonial and antiracist movements to the fight against capitalism.

4. See, e.g., Levering Lewis, *W.E.B. Du Bois: The Fight for Equality*, 15. For more on Du Bois and his changing relationship to Second International and Third International socialism in this period, see Mark W. Van Wienen, *American Socialist Triptych: The Literary-Political Work of Charlotte Perkins-Gilman, Upton Sinclair and W.E.B. Du Bois* (Ann Arbor: University of Michigan Press, 2012), especially chap. 4; Barbara Foley, *Specters of 1919: Class and Nation in the Making of the New Negro* (Urbana: University of Illinois Press, 2003).

5. W.E.B. Du Bois, "The African Roots of War," in *W.E.B. Du Bois: A Reader*, ed. David Levering Lewis (New York: Henry Holt, 1995), 645.

6. Vladimir Ilyich Lenin, "Imperialism: The Highest Stage of Capitalism," available at http://www.marxists.org/archive/lenin/works/1916/imp-hsc/pref02.htm. (accessed April 22, 2014).

7. Du Bois, "The African Roots of War," 650.

8. Lenin, "Imperialism."

9. John W. Steinberg, "Was the Russo-Japanese War World War 0?" *Russian Review* 67, no. 1 (January 7, 2008): 1–7.

10. Gerald Horne, *The End of Empires: African Americans and India* (Philadelphia: Temple University Press, 2008), 35. See also Pankaj Mishra, *From the Ruins of Empire: The Revolt against the West and the Remaking of Asia* (New York: Allen Lane, 2012), 1–11.

11. W.E.B. Du Bois, "The Color Line Belts the World," in *W.E.B. Du Bois on Asia: Crossing the World Color Line*, ed. Bill V. Mullen and Cathryn Watson (Jackson: University Press of Mississippi, 2005), 35.

12. Two important studies of the intersection of early twentieth-century nationalist and communist movements are Minkah Makalani, *In the Cause of Freedom: Radical Black Internationalism from Harlem to London, 1917–1939* (Chapel Hill: University of North Carolina Press, 2011), and Yuichiro Onishi, *Transpacific Antiracism: Afro-Asian Solidarity in 20th Century Black America, Japan, and Okinawa* (New York: New York University Press, 2013). W.E.B. Du Bois, "The World Problem of the Color Line," in Mullen and Watson, *W.E.B. Du Bois on Asia*, 35–36.

13. Onishi, *Transpacific Antiracism*, 48.

14. Lars Lih, *Lenin* (London: Reaktion, 2011), 291.

15. Ibid., 96.

16. William Walling, *Russia's Message: The True World Import of the Revolution* (New York: Doubleday, Page, 1908).

17. See Van Wienen, *American Socialist Triptych*, 137–138.

18. W.E.B. Du Bois, "Worlds of Color," *Foreign Affairs* 3 (April 1925): 442.

19. W.E.B. Du Bois, *John Brown* (New York: Modern Library, 2001), 233. Du Bois revised the 1909 edition for International Publishers' 1962 edition, adding favorable comments on the Russian Revolution and making Brown a forerunner of that revolution. On this subject, see David Roediger, "Note on the Text," in Du Bois, *John Brown*, 257–258, and Chapter 5 herein.

20. See, e.g., W.E.B. Du Bois, "A Field for Socialists," *New Review* 1 (January 11, 1913): 54–57; W.E.B. Du Bois, "Socialism and the Negro Problem," *New Review* 1 (February 1, 1913): 138–141; W.E.B. Du Bois, "Socialism and the Negro," *The Crisis* 22 (October 1921): 245–247.

21. Anna Louise Strong, *I Change Worlds* (1935; repr., Seattle Seal, 1979), 58.

22. Ibid., 251.

23. Ibid., 68.

24. Ibid., 68–69.

25. Levering Lewis, *W.E.B. Du Bois: The Fight for Equality*, 343.

26. Tracy B. Strong and Helene Keyssar, *Right in Her Soul: The Life of Anna Louise Strong* (New York: Random House, 1983), 236.

27. Herbert Aptheker, ed., *The Correspondence of W.E.B. Du Bois, Volume 1: Selections from 1877–1934* (Amherst: University of Massachusetts Press, 1973), 315.

28. Dohra Ahmad makes a case that *Dark Princess* is modeled in part on the Universal Races Congress of 1911 attended by Du Bois. Textual and historical evidence, especially the Berlin setting and preeminence of Indian radical nationalism, point more to the Comintern period as likely influences on the novel's main action: see Dohra Ahmad, *Landscapes of Hope: Anti-Colonial Utopianism in America* (New York: Oxford University Press, 2009), 152.

29. See ibid., 123.

30. As I discuss in Chapter 3, Smedley also wrote for Rai's newspaper, *The People*, published in India.

31. Du Bois, quoted in Horne, *The End of Empires*, 77.

32. W.E.B. Du Bois, "The Freeing of India," in Mullen and Watson, *W.E.B. Du Bois on Asia*, 145.

33. Du Bois, quoted in Nico Slate, *Colored Cosmopolitanism: The Shared Struggle for Freedom in the United States and India* (Cambridge, MA: Harvard University Press, 2012), 123.

34. W.E.B. Du Bois, "Gandhi and the American Negroes," in Mullen and Watson, *W.E.B. Du Bois on Asia*, 155.

35. Slate, *Colored Cosmopolitanism*, 42.

36. W.E.B. Du Bois, "The Clash of Colour: Indians and American Negroes," in Mullen and Watson, *W.E.B. Du Bois on Asia*, 73.

37. W.E.B. Du Bois, "Nehru," in Mullen and Watson, *W.E.B. Du Bois on Asia*, 144.

38. Horne, *The End of Empires*, 125.

39. Duncan Hallas, *The Comintern* (London: Bookmarks, 1985), 123.

40. James R. Hooker, *Black Revolutionary: George Padmore's Path from Communism to Pan-Africanism* (New York: Frederick A. Praeger, 1967), 17.

41. George Padmore, "The Life and Struggles of Negro Toilers," available at http://www.marxists.org/archive/padmore/1931/negro-toilers/index.htm (accessed April 22, 2014).

42. Hooker, *Black Revolutionary*, 24.

43. Ibid., 33.

44. Penny Von Eschen, *Race against Empire: Black Americans and Anticolonialism, 1937–1957* (Ithaca, NY: Cornell University Press, 1997), 12. See also George Padmore, "An Open Letter to Earl Browder," *The Crisis*, October 1935, 302, 315. The letter details Padmore's complaints against the Comintern in explanation of his decision to resign from the Communist Party.

45. Hooker, *Black Revolutionary*, 33. That Padmore's departure from the Comintern was acrimonious is not in dispute. Earl Browder claimed that Padmore was expelled because he felt the road to proletarian internationalism ran a "race war" between blacks and whites: Von Eschen, *Race against Empire*, 12.

46. Foley, *Specters of 1919*, 114.

47. Ibid., 120.

48. Hooker, *Black Revolutionary*, 44, 64.

49. Kwame Nkrumah, quoted in Hakim Adi and Marika Sherwood, *The 1945 Pan-African Congress Revisited* (London: New Beacon, 1995), 56.

50. W.E.B. Du Bois, *Dusk of Dawn: An Essay Toward an Autobiography of a Race Concept* (New York: Schocken, 1968), 285.

51. Sumit Sarkar, *Modern India, 1885–1947* (New Delhi: Macmillan, 1983), 60.

52. Nell Irvin Painter, *Standing at Armageddon: The United States, 1877–1919* (New York: W. W. Norton, 1987), 139.

53. Good accounts of the split between the Second and Third Internationals include Lih, *Lenin*, and Hallas, *The Comintern*. Regarding black internationalism, see Makalani, *In the Cause of Freedom*; Foley, *Specters of 1919*; Anthony Dawahare, *Nationalism, Marxism, and African American Literature between the Wars: A New Pandora's Box* (Jackson: University Press of Mississippi, 2003).

54. W.E.B. Du Bois, "Close Ranks," in Levering Lewis, *W.E.B. Du Bois: A Reader*, 697–698. See also Levering Lewis, *W.E.B. Du Bois: The Fight for Equality*, 470.

55. Hallas, *The Comintern*, 29–30.

56. Nigel Harris, *The Mandate of Heaven: Marx and Mao in Modern China* (London: Quartet Books, 1978), 3.

57. Sarkar, *Modern India*, 188.

58. Ibid., 177.

59. Foley, *Specters of 1919*, 9.

60. Ibid., 46.

61. Ibid., 8.

62. David Levering Lewis, *W.E.B. Du Bois: Biography of a Race, 1868–1919* (New York: Henry Holt, 1993), 577.

63. Ibid., 578.

64. W.E.B. Du Bois, "Let Us Reason Together," *The Crisis* 18 (September 1919): 232.

65. Ibid.

66. Ibid., 234–235.

67. Ibid., 240.

68. Sarkar, *Modern India*, 189.

69. See David Arnold, *Gandhi: Profiles in Power* (Essex, UK: Pearson Education, 2001), 111; Sarkar, *Modern India*, 193.

70. Jawaharlal Nehru, *The Discovery of India* (New Delhi: Oxford University Press, 1985), 29.

71. Ahmad, *Landscapes of Hope*, 171.

72. Karuna Kaushik, *Russian Revolution and Indian Nationalism: Studies of Lajpat Rai, Suhas Chandra Bose and Rammanohar Lohia* (New Delhi: Chanakya, 1984), 46.

73. Horne, *The End of Empires*, 72.

74. Strong, *I Change Worlds*, 60.

75. Ibid., 71.

76. Foley, *Specters of 1919*, 39–40.

77. Strong, *I Change Worlds*, 82.

78. See Hallas, *The Comintern*, 13; Harris, *Mandate of Heaven*, 13; Sarkar, *Modern India*, 247.

79. Hallas, *The Comintern*, 71.

80. Ibid., 71–72.

81. Immanuel Geiss, *The Pan-African Movement: A History of Pan-Africanism in America, Europe, and Africa* (New York: Africana, 1974), 244.

82. Ibid., 247.

83. Levering Lewis, *W.E.B. Du Bois: The Fight for Equality*, 78.

84. Geiss, *The Pan-African Movement*, 339.

85. Levering Lewis, *W.E.B. Du Bois: The Fight for Equality*, 302, 306.

86. Du Bois, quoted in ibid., 310.

87. W.E.B. Du Bois, *Black Reconstruction in America, 1860–1880* (1935; repr., New York: Free Press, 1992), 704, 708.

88. C.L.R. James, *World Revolution 1917–1936: The Rise and Fall of the Communist International* (Atlantic Highlands, NJ: Humanities Press International, 1993), 36–37.

89. Robin D. G. Kelley, Introduction to C.L.R. James, *A History of Pan-African Revolt* (Oakland, CA: PM Press, 2012), 16.

90. Hooker, *Black Revolutionary*, 48.

91. Padmore, quoted in ibid., 52, 55.

92. See Barbara Foley, *Spectres of 1919: Race and Nation in the Making of the New Negro* (Champaign-Urbana: University of Illinois Press, 2008), 162. Foley's term is meant to signal the contending forces and ideas often embedded within the concept of the nation and nationalism. In particular, Foley uses the term to describe what she calls the "essentialization of race, the fetishization of place, and the organic character of the trope mediating between the two": ibid., 161–162). See also Leon Trotsky, *The Permanent Revolution and Results and Prospects* (New York: Pathfinder, 1969), 280.

93. Padmore, quoted in Hooker, *Black Revolutionary*, 71.

94. Ibid., 72.

95. George Padmore, *How Russia Transformed Her Colonial Empire: A Challenge to the Imperialist Powers* (London: Dennis Dobson, 1946), xii.

96. Hallas, *The Comintern*, 160; italics added.

97. "World Trade Union Conference: A Call to All the Peoples," available at http://www.unionhistory.info/timeline/Tl_Display.php?irn=3000094&QueryPage=. ./AdvSearch.php, 1 (accessed April 22, 2014).

98. Hakim Adi and Marika Sherwood, *The 1945 Manchester Pan-African Congress Revisited* (London: New Beacon, 1995), 17.

99. Ibid., 19.

100. Ibid., 12.

101. Ibid., 21.

102. Ibid., 20.

103. Ibid.

104. Padmore, quoted in ibid., 18.

105. *Paris 1945: Report of the World Trade Union Conference Congress, September 25–October 8, 1945*, World Trade Union Congress, 1945, 1.

106. Ibid., 172.

107. Annan, quoted in ibid., 179.

108. Nkrumah, quoted in Hooker, *Black Revolutionary*, 95.

109. See Adi and Sherwood, *The 1945 Manchester Pan-African Congress Revisited*, 150–161.

110. Ibid., 113.

111. Ibid., 80.

112. Ibid., 103–108.

113. Ibid., 112.

114. Ibid., 115.

115. Du Bois, quoted in ibid., 56.

116. Ibid., 54.

117. Du Bois, quoted in ibid., 62.

118. Appiah, quoted in ibid., 33.

119. Levering Lewis, *W.E.B. Du Bois: The Fight for Equality*, 518.

CHAPTER 2

1. W.E.B. Du Bois, *In Battle for Peace: The Story of My 83rd Birthday*, rep. ed. (1952; repr., Millwood, NY: Kraus-Thomson, 1976), 163.

2. See Adolph Reed, *W.E.B. Du Bois and American Political Thought: Fabianism and the Color Line* (New York: Oxford University Press, 1999).

3. Mark W. Van Wienen, *American Socialist Triptych: The Literary-Political Work of Charlotte Perkins Gilman, Upton Sinclair and W.E.B. Du Bois* (Ann Arbor: University of Michigan Press, 2012), 5.

4. Quoted in David Levering Lewis, *W.E.B. Du Bois: The Fight for Equality and the American Century, 1919–1963* (New York: Henry Holt, 2000), 4.

5. See Vladimir Ilyich Lenin, "The State and Revolution," available at http://www.marxists.org/archive/lenin/works/1917/staterev (accessed November 29, 2014). In a letter to George Streator dated April 24, 1935, Du Bois wrote, "I am a pacifist. I regard with astonishment militarists who agitate against violence; and lovers of peace who want the class revolution immediately." In a letter to Mary White Ovington dated March 21, 1938, he wrote, "Communism is the hope of us all but not the dogmatic Marxian program with war and murder in the forefront. Economic communism by the path of peace is possible": see W.E.B. Du Bois, "Letter to George Streator," April 24, 1935, in *The Correspondence of W.E.B. Du Bois, Volume 1: Selections from 1877–1934*, ed. Herbert Aptheker (Amherst: University of Massachusetts Press, 1973), 92, 163.

6. W.E.B. Du Bois, "The Negro and Socialism," in *Writings by W.E.B. Du Bois in Periodicals Edited by Others, Volume 1: 1891–1909*, ed. Herbert Aptheker (Millwood, NY: Kraus-Thompson, 1982), 6.

7. Ibid.

8. W.E.B. Du Bois Papers on Microfilm, UMI, reel 1, frame 1119, W.E.B. Du Bois Papers, University of Massachusetts Amherst.

9. Du Bois, quoted in Van Wienen, *American Socialist Triptych*, 138.

10. Ibid., 244.

11. Ibid., 131.

12. See, e.g., W.E.B. Du Bois, "Socialism and the Negro Problem," *New Review* 1 (February 1 1913): 54–57.

13. Du Bois wrote, "I find, curiously enough then, that my experience in the fantastic accusation and criminal process is tending to free me from that racial provincialism which I always recognized but which I was sure would eventually land me in an upper realm of cultural unity, led by 'My People'": Du Bois, *In Battle for Peace: The Story of My 83rd Birthday* (1952; repr., Millwood, NY: Kraus-Thomson, 1976), 107–108. In *The Autobiography of W.E.B. Du Bois*, as noted earlier, he demarcates his international travels as central to his conversion to international socialism. "Provincialism" generally should be understood in Du Bois's work as the political limitations of holding an exclusionary ethno-national identity.

14. W.E.B. Du Bois, "Russia and America: An Interpretation," unpublished draft ms., 1950, W.E.B. Du Bois Papers, University of Massachusetts Amherst, 9.

15. Ibid., 10.

16. Ibid.

17. Ibid., 12.

18. Ibid., 13.

19. W.E.B. Du Bois, "Opinion," *The Crisis* 22, no. 3 (July 1921): 114.

20. Du Bois, "Russia and America," 15.

21. Duncan Hallas, *The Comintern* (London: Bookmarks, 1985), 84.

22. Ibid., 105, 110.

23. Tariq Ali, *The Stalinist Legacy: Its Impact on Twentieth-Century World Politics*, ed. Tariq Ali (Chicago: Haymarket, 1985), 12.

24. Levering Lewis, *W.E.B. Du Bois: The Fight for Equality*, 202.

25. Du Bois, "Russia and America," 19.

26. Two important artifacts of this support are Du Bois's essay "On Stalin" (1953), written to commemorate his death, and Anna Louise Strong's book *The Stalin Era* (1956): see Chapter 5 in this volume.

27. Levering Lewis, *W.E.B. Du Bois: The Fight for Equality*, 203.

28. Du Bois, "Russia and America," 201.

29. W.E.B. Du Bois, "As the Crow Flies," *Amsterdam News*, February 24, 1940, in *Newspaper Columns by W.E.B. Du Bois, Volume 1: Selections from 1883–1944*, ed. Herbert Aptheker (White Plains, NY: Kraus-Thomson, 1986), 286.

30. Du Bois, "Russia and America," 286.

31. Ibid., 19.

32. Ibid., 18.

33. Ibid., 20.

34. Ibid., 18.

35. Ibid., 27.

36. Ibid., 24.

37. Ibid., 25.

38. Vladimir Ilyich Lenin, "The Right of Nations to Self-Determination," available at http://www.marxists.org/archive/lenin/works/1914/self-det (accessed April 27, 2014).

39. W.E.B. Du Bois, *Dark Princess: A Romance* (Jackson: University Press of Mississippi, 1995), 29.

40. Ibid., 20.

41. Ibid., 16.

42. Claude McKay, "Soviet Russia and the Negro," *The Crisis* 27 (December 1923): 61–65.

43. Du Bois, *Dark Princess*, 29.

44. See Harry Haywood, *A Black Communist in the Freedom Struggle: The Life of Harry Haywood* (Minneapolis: University of Minnesota Press, 2012).

45. See Agnes Smedley, *Daughter of Earth* (New York: Feminist Press, 1987). For a more detailed discussion of Smedley and *Daughter of Earth*, see Chapter 3 in this volume.

46. Du Bois, *Dark Princess*, 286.

47. See Van Wienen, *American Socialist Triptych*, 270–271.

48. Du Bois, "Russia and America," 39.

49. Ibid., 37.

50. W.E.B. Du Bois, "Letter to Algernon Lee," February 15, 1929, in Aptheker, *The Correspondence of W.E.B. Du Bois*, 1:389.

51. Levering Lewis, *W.E.B. Du Bois: The Fight for Equality*, 250–251.

52. W.E.B. Du Bois, "Letter to Edward Clarke," in Aptheker, *The Correspondence of W.E.B. Du Bois*, 1:418.

53. See Levering Lewis, *W.E.B. Du Bois: The Fight for Equality*, 260; Glenda Elizabeth Gilmore, *Defying Dixie: The Radical Roots of Civil Rights, 1919–1950* (New York: W. W. Norton, 2008), 101.

54. Gilmore, *Defying Dixie*, 71.

55. Ibid., 99.

56. DuBois, quoted in ibid., 264–265.

57. W.E.B. Du Bois, "The Negro and Communism," *The Crisis* 38 (September 1931): 313.

58. Levering Lewis, *W.E.B. Du Bois: The Fight for Equality*, 302.

59. Van Wienen, *American Socialist Triptych*, 281.

60. Du Bois, "Russia and America," 40–41.

61. W.E.B. Du Bois, "Reply to George Streator," April 17, 1935, in Aptheker, *The Correspondence of W.E.B. Du Bois*, 1:87.

62. Van Wienen, *American Socialist Triptych*, 278.

63. Ibid., 283.

64. Quoted in Levering Lewis, *W.E.B. Du Bois: The Fight for Equality*, 281.

65. Quoted in ibid., 308.

66. Quoted in ibid., 309, 308.

67. Quoted in ibid., 309.

68. W.E.B. Du Bois, "Forum of Fact and Opinion," *Pittsburgh Courier*, August 21, 1937, in Aptheker, *Newspaper Columns by W.E.B. Du Bois*, 1:230.

69. Ibid., 229–230.

70. Quoted in Levering Lewis, *W.E.B. Du Bois: The Fight for Equality*, 301.

71. Quoted in ibid., 335; italics added.

72. George Streator, "Letter to W.E.B. Du Bois," April 8, 1935, in Aptheker, *The Correspondence of W.E.B. Du Bois*, 90.

73. Ibid.

74. W.E.B. Du Bois, "Letter to George Streator," April 24, 1935, in Aptheker, *The Correspondence of W.E.B. Du Bois*, 92.

75. Ibid., 95.

76. W.E.B. Du Bois, "The Negro and Communism," in *The Oxford W.E.B. Du Bois Reader*, ed. Eric Sundquist (New York: Oxford University Press, 1996), 79.

77. Ibid., 409.

78. W.E.B. Du Bois, "A Negro Nation within the Nation," in Sundquist, *The Oxford W.E.B. Du Bois Reader*, 435–436.

79. Ibid., 437.

80. Ibid., 438.

81. Ibid., 435; italics added.

82. See W.E.B. Du Bois "Forum of Fact and Opinion," in Aptheker, *Newspaper Columns by W.E.B. Du Bois*, 1:82–83, and, later, W.E.B. Du Bois, *Dusk of Dawn: An Essay toward an Autobiography of a Race Concept* (New York: Schocken, 1968), 320–322.

83. Du Bois, "Letter to George Streator," 90.

84. Van Wienen, *American Socialist Triptych*, 278.

85. Quoted in Levering Lewis, *W.E.B. Du Bois: The Fight for Equality*, 363.

86. Quoted in ibid., 376.

87. Cedric J. Robinson, *Black Marxism: The Making of the Black Radical Tradition* (Chapel Hill: University of North Carolina Press, 1983), 236.

88. Du Bois, *Black Reconstruction in America*, 708.

89. See Algernon Lee, "Herman Schlüter: The Man and His Work," *New York Call*, vol. 12, no. 29, January 29, 1919, 29, available at http://www.marxisthistory.org/history/usa/parties/lfed/german/1919/0129-lee-hermanschleuter.pdf.

90. Quoted in W.E.B. Du Bois, *Black Reconstruction in America, 1860–1880* (1935; repr., New York: Free Press, 1992), 354, 357.

91. Herman Schlüter, *Lincoln, Labor and Slavery: A Chapter from the Social History of America* (New York: Socialist Literature, 1913), 9.

92. Ibid., 59, 90.

93. Robinson, *Black Marxism*, 236. The full quote from Du Bois's book about southern whites is, "This attitude of the poor whites had in it as much fear and jealousy of Negroes as disaffection with slave barons. Economic rivalry with blacks became a new and living threat as the black became laborers and soldiers in a conquering Northern army. If the Negro was to be free where would the poor white be? Why should he fight against the blacks and his victorious friends? The poor white not only began to desert and run away but thousands followed the Negro into the Northern camps": Du Bois, *Black Reconstruction in America*, 81.

94. Du Bois, *Black Reconstruction in America*, 15.

95. Ibid.

96. Ibid., 16.

97. Robinson, *Black Marxism*, 239; italics added.

98. Ibid., 240; italics added.

99. Du Bois, "Russia and America," 83. The idea of black workers leading white workers to freedom was first articulated Du Bois when he wrote, "He [the Negro] is beginning to say to these workingmen that, so long as black laborers are slaves, white laborers cannot be free": W.E.B Du Bois, *The Negro* (New York: Henry Holt, 1915), 145–146. *Black Reconstruction in America* was the culmination of this idea in Du Bois's thought. On this theme, see also Ferrucio Gambino, "W.E.B. Du Bois and the Proletariat in Black Reconstruction," available at https://libcom.org/library/w-e-b-du-bois-proletariat-black-reconstruction-ferruccio-gambino (accessed February 23, 2015).

100. Du Bois, "Russia and America," 296.

101. W.E.B. Du Bois, "A Pageant in Seven Decades 1868–1938," W.E.B. Du Bois Papers, University of Massachusetts Amherst, reel 86, no. 987.

102. Du Bois, "Russia and America," 83.

103. Quoted in Kate Baldwin, *Beyond the Color Line and the Iron Curtain: Reading Encounters between Black and Red, 1922–1963* (Durham, NC: Duke University Press, 2002), 367.

104. Levering Lewis, *W.E.B. Du Bois: The Fight for Equality*, 557. Works that discuss the manuscript include Baldwin, *Beyond the Color Line and the Iron Curtain*; Gerald Horne, *Black and Red: W.E.B. Du Bois and the Afro-American Response to the Cold War, 1944–1963* (Albany: State University of New York Press, 1986), 267; Levering Lewis, *W.E.B. Du Bois: The Fight for Equality*. Horne's brief account includes excerpts from correspondence between Du Bois and Herbert Aptheker about the manuscript. Aptheker was critical of individual arguments in the book but contended, "As for the work as a whole, my one fear is that it is much too good and clean to gain publication in our country today. I hope I'm wrong": Horne, *Black and Red*, 267.

105. Levering Lewis, *W.E.B. Du Bois: The Fight for Equality*, 557.

106. W.E.B. Du Bois, *John Brown* (New York: International Publishers, 1996) 300.

107. Du Bois, "Russia and America," 157.

108. "Russia and America," 158.

109. See Lenin's "What Is to Be Done: Burning Questions of Our Moment." The essay, written in 1901 and published as a pamphlet in 1902, argued that the working class needed to form a vanguard party to carry out a successful proletarian revolution. The essay contributed to the eventual split between the Bolsheviks and Mensheviks. Du Bois's playful allusion to the title signifies his historical "quest" in "Russia and America" to locate a vanguard in history and in the Cold War. Lenin's title was drawn from the novel *What Is to Be Done?* (1863), by Nikolai Chernyshevsky, which was a favorite of his. Lenin's essay is in Vladimir Ilyich Lenin, *Essential Works of Lenin: "What Is to Be Done?" and Other Writings* (New York: Dover, 1987).

110. Du Bois, "Russia and America," 159.

111. Ibid., 151.

112. Ibid., 16.

113. Ibid., 78.

114. Ibid., 270.

115. W.E.B. Du Bois, *The Autobiography of W.E.B. Du Bois: A Soliloquy on Viewing My Life from the Last Decade of Its First Century* (New York: International Publishers, 1968), 355.

116. Du Bois, "Russia and America," 76.

117. Ibid, 77.

118. Ibid. 77.

119. The Stockholm Appeal was an international petition calling for the abolition of atomic weapons. Du Bois gathered signatories for the petition, for which he was charged by the United States for not registering as a foreign agent in 1951. He was acquitted after trial. The Peace Information Center was a group of Americans formed in 1950 whose work was, in part, gathering signatures for the Stockholm Appeal. In July 1950, U.S. Secretary of State Dean Acheson publicly accused the Peace Information Center and Stockholm Appeal of serving as a "propaganda trick" for the Soviet Union: see Du Bois, *The Autobiography of W.E.B. Du Bois*, 33, 258. For a more detailed discussion of Du Bois's peace politics, see Chapter 5 in this volume.

120. Du Bois, "Russia and America," 77–78.

121. Du Bois, *Black Reconstruction in America*, 727.

122. "John Brown Liveth!" *West African Pilot*, November 10, 1951, second reprint as "John Brown: God's Angry Man," in *Newspaper Columns by W.E.B. Du Bois, Vol. 2, Selec-*

tions from 1945–1961, ed. Herbert Aptheker (White Plains, NY: Kraus-Thomson, 1986), 1108–1109. See W.E.B. Du Bois, *John Brown* (New York: International Publishers, 1996), 296. As William F. Cain rightly notes, Du Bois invoked Brown's raid on Harper's Ferry as a renewed call for revolution in 1909, the year he published his biography of Brown. For Du Bois, Brown, along with the slaves and white workers of *Black Reconstruction in America*, became a typological touchstone for an American Revolution: see William F. Cain, "Violence, Revolution and the Cost of Freedom: John Brown and W.E.B. Du Bois," in *Revisionist Interventions into the Americanist Canon*, ed. Donald Pease (Durham, NC: Duke University Press, 1994), 305–330.

123. Du Bois, "Russia and America," 171.

124. See W.E.B. Du Bois, "Paul Robeson, Right or Wrong? Right, Says W.E.B. Du Bois," *Negro Digest* 7 (1950): 14.

125. Du Bois, "Russia and America," 183–184.

126. Du Bois, *Black Reconstruction in America*, 670.

127. Du Bois, "Russia and America," 300.

128. Ibid.

129. Ibid.; italics added.

130. Ibid., 301.

131. Ibid., 305.

132. Quoted in Murali Balaji, *The Professor and the Pupil: The Politics of W.E.B. Du Bois and Paul Robeson* (New York: Nation Books, 2007), 300.

133. Du Bois, "Russia and America," 300.

134. Ibid., 314.

135. Horne, *Black and Red*, 315.

CHAPTER 3

1. W.E.B. Du Bois, "The Freeing of India," in *W.E.B. Du Bois on Asia: Crossing the World Color Line*, ed. Bill V. Mullen and Cathryn Watson (Jackson: University Press of Mississippi, 2005), 145.

2. Ibid., 153.

3. Jawaharlal Nehru, *The Discovery of India* (New Delhi: Oxford University Press, 1985), 50.

4. Ibid., 37–38, 40.

5. In *The Indian Ideology*, Anderson elaborates this conception as constituted by four "couplets": "of antiquity-continuity; diversity-unity; massivity-democracy; [and] multi-confessionality-secularity." These define the core of Indian nationalism as articulated by both Nehru and Gandhi in their leadership of the anticolonial struggle. For Nehru, the "discovery" of India is the argument that these characteristics inhere in the nation and need only to be formalized through statehood. As Anderson notes, and as Du Bois suggests, the "Indian ideology" is fundamentally a Western, if not a European, conception: see Perry Anderson, *The Indian Ideology* (London: Verso, 2013), 9, 1–11.

6. Du Bois, "The Freeing of India," 153.

7. W.E.B. Du Bois, *The World and Africa: An Inquiry into the Part Which Africa Has Played in World History* (New York: International Publishers, 1965), 176.

8. W.E.B. Du Bois, "Asia in Africa," in Mullen and Watson, *W.E.B. Du Bois on Asia*, 31.

9. Anderson, *The Indian Ideology*, 10.

10. Jawaharlal Nehru, *Soviet Russia: Some Random Sketches and Impressions* (Mumbai: Chetana, 1929), 83.

11. Nico Slate, *Colored Cosmopolitanism: The Shared Struggle for Freedom in the United States and India* (Cambridge, MA: Harvard University Press, 2012), 197.

12. Ibid., 39.

13. Ibid.

14. Karuna Kaushik, *Russian Revolution and Indian Nationalism: Studies of Lajpat Rai, Suhas Chandra Bose and Rammanohar Lohia* (New Delhi: Chanakya, 1984), 39.

15. Slate, *Colored Cosmopolitanism*, 69.

16. For example, in an essay published in 1903, Gandhi referred to Washington's Tuskegee Institute as an "ideal college." He also considered Washington's theory of "racial uplift" by vocational training an impetus for village-level *swadeshi* (self-sufficiency) production: see Slate, *Colored Cosmopolitanism*, 21.

17. Ibid., 72.

18. Kaushik, *Russian Revolution and Indian Nationalism*, 43.

19. Ibid., 44.

20. Ibid.

21. Ibid., 45.

22. Ibid., 46.

23. Du Bois's complaint about the colonies was in reference to failures of Woodrow Wilson and the League of Nations: see W.E.B. Du Bois, "Opinion," *The Crisis* 19, no. 1 (November 1919): 337.

24. Slate, *Colored Cosmopolitanism*, 79, 74.

25. Ibid., 82.

26. Dohra Ahmad, *Landscapes of Hope: Anti-Colonial Utopianism in America* (Oxford: Oxford University Press, 2009), 172.

27. Ruth Price, *The Lives of Agnes Smedley* (Oxford: Oxford University Press, 2005), 59.

28. As Price tells it, Smedley initially met Roy's physical advance "with ardor" but then "froze, convinced that no decent woman experienced sexual desire or accepted responsibility for such feelings. Then, she would write, she allowed Roy to physically overpower her as she had permitted others in the past": Price, *The Lives of Agnes Smedley*, 61. In Agnes Smedley's *Daughter of Earth* (New York: Feminist Press, 1987), the encounter with Juan Diaz, a fictionalized version of Roy, sends Marie Rogers plummeting into depression and eventually is an incitement for her to leave the United States.

29. An indispensable account of this and the Comintern relationship to the Indian anticolonial struggle is Sobhanlal Datta Gupta, *Comintern and the Destiny of Communism in India, 1919–1943: Dialectics of Real and a Possible History* (Kolkata: Seribaan, 2011).

30. Ibid., 63.

31. Ibid., 64.

32. Ibid., 51–52.

33. See Sumit Sarkar, *Modern India, 1885–1947* (New Delhi: Macmillan, 1983), 225; Jawaharlal Nehru, *An Autobiography* (1942; repr., Oxford: Oxford University Press, 1988), 80.

34. Sarkar, *Modern India*, 250.

35. Nehru, *An Autobiography*, 156.

36. Ibid., 161.

37. Sarkar, *Modern India*, 253.

38. Nehru, *An Autobiography*, 163.

39. Ibid., 166.

40. Price, *The Lives of Agnes Smedley*, 159.

41. Ibid., 161.

42. W.E.B. Du Bois, "Russia and America: An Interpretation," unpublished draft ms., 1950, W.E.B. Du Bois Papers, University of Massachusetts Amherst, 30.

43. Nehru, *Soviet Russia*, 15.

44. Nehru, *An Autobiography*, 51.

45. The Webbs' books on the Soviet Union of the 1930s especially influenced Du Bois's accounts of the Soviet economy in "Russia and America." See esp. "Planned Production for Community Consumption in Sidney and Beatrice Webb," in *Soviet Communism: A New Civilisation?* vol. 2 (New York: Charles Scribner's Sons, 1936), 602–696. In the manuscript, Du Bois mentions reading the book before his second visit in 1936.

46. Nehru, *Soviet Russia*, 62.

47. Ibid., 70.

48. Ibid., 74.

49. Ibid., 75.

50. Chapter 15 of Nehru's book is titled "Women and Marriage." A Russian woman, Nehru writes, is "not a chattel or plaything of man. She is independent, aggressively so, and refuses to play second fiddle to man": Nehru, *Soviet Russia*, 111.

51. Jawaharlal Nehru, Foreword in ibid, xii.

52. Du Bois, "Russia and America," 27.

53. Nehru, *Soviet Russia*, 2.

54. Ibid., 3.

55. Gupta, *Comintern and the Destiny of Communism in India*, 71.

56. Du Bois, "Russia and America," 37.

57. Nehru, *Soviet Russia*, 101.

58. Ibid., 79.

59. Ibid., 80.

60. Ibid., 84.

61. Sarkar, *Modern India*, 266.

62. Agnes Smedley, *India and the Next War* (Amritsar: Kirti Office, 1928), 14.

63. Ibid., 11.

64. Rai, quoted in ibid., 15, 17.

65. Ibid., 31.

66. Ibid., 35–36.

67. Ibid., 44.

68. Ibid., 45.

69. Sarkar, *Modern India*, 281.

70. Ibid., 331.

71. Ibid.

72. Ibid., 332.

73. Price, *The Lives of Agnes Smedley*, 168.

74. Smedley, *Daughter of Earth*, 377.

75. Ibid., 358.

76. Ibid., 345.

77. Ibid., 406.

78. Quoted in Slate, *Colored Cosmopolitanisms*, 99.

79. Sarkar, *Modern India*, 331.

80. Ibid., 334.

81. Benjamin Zachariah, *Nehru* (London: Routledge, 2004), 65–66.

82. Sarkar, *Modern India*, 335.

83. Anderson, *The Indian Ideology*, 33.

84. W.E.B. Du Bois, "The Union of Color," in Mullen and Watson, *W.E.B. Du Bois on Asia*, 67.

85. Ibid., 66.

86. As Anderson reports, Gandhi feared that granting Untouchables "the right to their own electorates" would subtract them from the Hindu bloc in India and weaken its "predominance over the Muslim community." Untouchables were thus "bundled back in to the Hindu electorate. . . . A 'Pact' was reached to give a larger number of reserved seats to Untouchables elected, not by their own kind, but by Hindus at large." Anderson sees this as Gandhi's capitulation to Hindu nationalism as a dominant form of the "Indian ideology": Anderson, *The Indian Ideology*, 40–41.

87. Nehru, *An Autobiography*, 591.

88. Zachariah, *Nehru*, 81.

89. Sarkar, *Modern India*, 361.

90. Ibid., 360.

91. Ibid., 358.

92. Slate, *Colored Cosmopolitanisms*, 76, 83–84.

93. Ibid., 141.

94. Jawaharlal Nehru, *An Autobiography* (1942; repr., Oxford: Oxford University Press, 1988), 601.

95. Sarkar, *Modern India*, 371.

96. Quoted in Price, *The Lives of Agnes Smedley*, 347.

97. Anderson, *The Indian Ideology*, 46.

98. W.E.B. Du Bois, "Nehru," in Mullen and Watson, *W.E.B. Du Bois on Asia*, 144.

99. Sarkar, *Modern India*, 388.

100. Ibid., 388–389.

101. Murali Balaji, *The Professor and the Pupil: The Politics and Friendship of W.E.B. Du Bois and Paul Robeson* (New York: Nation Books, 2007), 159.

102. W.E.B. Du Bois, "A Chronicle of Race Relations [II]," in Mullen and Watson, *W.E.B. Du Bois on Asia*, 125.

103. Sarkar, *Modern India*, 453.

104. Du Bois, "The Freeing of India," 152.

105. Anderson, *The Indian Ideology*, 94.

106. Ibid., 65.

107. Ibid., 89.

108. The strongest statement of this is Du Bois's "The Freeing of India," which prophecies that, owing to its "spiritual faith," India "may become dominant over Europe" and foresees in Afro-Asian unity a possible new anticolonial world order: "The sun of the colored man has risen in Asia as it will yet rise in Africa and America and the West Indies": Du Bois, "The Freeing of India," 145–153. In Chapter 4, I discuss how this Asiatic, and vaguely Orientalist, enthusiasm was buttressed and culminated by China's revolution of 1949.

109. Anderson, *The Indian Ideology*, 96.

110. W.E.B. Du Bois, "Letter to Jawaharlal Nehru," December 26, 1956, W.E.B. Du Bois Papers, University of Massachusetts Amherst, reel 72, no. 1.

111. Slate, *Colored Cosmopolitanisms*, 97.

112. Du Bois, "The Freeing of India," 153.

113. Nehru, *An Autobiography*, 52.

114. W.E.B. Du Bois, "Gandhi and the American Negroes," in Mullen and Watson, *W.E.B. Du Bois on Asia*, 157.

115. Ibid.
116. W.E.B. Du Bois, "Will the Great Gandhi Live Again?" in Mullen and Watson, *W.E.B. Du Bois on Asia*, 184.
117. Ibid.
118. Ibid., 185.
119. Ibid., 186.
120. Ibid.
121. Ibid., 185.

CHAPTER 4

1. Quoted in Harold R. Isaacs, *The Tragedy of the Chinese Revolution* (1938), 2d rev. ed. (Stanford, CA: Stanford University Press, 1961), 312.
2. David Levering Lewis, *W.E.B. Du Bois: The Fight for Equality and the American Century, 1919–1963* (New York: Henry Holt, 2000), 390.
3. Ibid., 391.
4. Herbert P. Bix, *Hirohito and the Making of Modern Japan* (New York: Perennial, 2000), 147.
5. Ibid.
6. W.E.B. Du Bois, "Russia and America: An Interpretation," unpublished draft ms., 1950, W.E.B. Du Bois Papers, University of Massachusetts Amherst, 126.
7. Jon Halliday, *A Political History of Japanese Capitalism* (New York: Pantheon Books, 1975), 96–97.
8. W.E.B. Du Bois, "Listen, Japan and China," in *W.E.B. Du Bois on Asia: Crossing the World Color Line*, ed. Bill V. Mullen and Cathryn Watson (Jackson: University Press of Mississippi, 2005), 74.
9. W.E.B. Du Bois, "Japan and Ethiopia," in Mullen and Watson, *W.E.B. Du Bois on Asia*, 75.
10. Quoted in Yuichiro Onishi, *Transpacific Antiracism: Afro-Asian Solidarity in 20th Century Black America, Japan, and Okinawa* (New York: New York University Press, 2013), 86. The letter describing the project was written by Du Bois to his publisher just after he returned from his trip.
11. Ibid., 69.
12. Isaacs, *The Tragedy of the Chinese Revolution*, 55.
13. Ibid., 60.
14. Ibid., 40.
15. Ibid., 61.
16. Ibid., 62.
17. John Riddell, ed., *Toward the United Front: Proceedings of the Fourth Congress of the Communist International*, 1922 (Chicago: Haymarket, 2012), 713.
18. Isaacs, *The Tragedy of the Chinese Revolution*, 63.
19. Ibid., 64.
20. Duncan Hallas, *The Comintern* (London: Bookmarks, 1985), 10.
21. Ibid., 123.
22. Du Bois, "Russia and America," 127.
23. Jean Chesneaux, *The Chinese Labor Movement, 1919–1927* (Stanford, CA: Stanford University Press, 1968), 237.
24. Isaacs, *The Tragedy of the Chinese Revolution*, 130.
25. Ibid., 199.

26. Ruth Price, *The Lives of Agnes Smedley* (Oxford: Oxford University Press, 2005), 99.

27. Ibid., 146.

28. Ibid., 132.

29. Ibid., 155.

30. Anna Louise Strong, *I Change Worlds* (1935; repr., Seattle: Seal, 1979), 178.

31. Ibid., 228.

32. Ibid., 281.

33. The full quotation about Hitler's Germany in comparison to the Soviet Union is as follows: "With unreasonable bitterness he and his followers denounce communism, recount its crimes and foretell its inevitable failure; and at the same time imitate nearly every method and adopt theoretically nearly every goal that Russia has followed or announced. Germany today is, next to Russia, the greatest exemplar of Marxian socialism in the world, and at the same time posing as the bulwark of Europe against the Red Menace!" W.E.B. Du Bois, "Forum of Fact and Opinion," in *Newspaper Columns by W.E.B. Du Bois, Volume 1: Selections from 1883–1944*, ed. Herbert Aptheker (White Plains, NY: Kraus-Thomson, 1986), 152.

34. W.E.B. Du Bois, "What Japan Has Done," in Mullen and Watson, *W.E.B. Du Bois on Asia*, 78.

35. Ibid., 78.

36. Onishi, *Transpacific Antiracism*, 76.

37. Du Bois, "Russia and America," 127.

38. W.E.B. Du Bois, *Worlds of Color*, Black Flame Trilogy, book 3 (1961; repr., Oxford: Oxford University Press, 2007), 40.

39. Du Bois, "Forum of Fact and Opinion," 245.

40. Du Bois, "Russia and America," 142.

41. Ibid.

42. Ibid.

43. W.E.B. Du Bois, "Man Power," in Mullen and Watson, *W.E.B. Du Bois on Asia*, 76.

44. Ibid.

45. W.E.B. Du Bois, "China and Japan," in Mullen and Watson, *W.E.B. Du Bois on Asia*, 90.

46. Du Bois, "Forum of Fact and Opinion," 174.

47. Ibid., 172.

48. Ibid.

49. Ibid., 173.

50. Strong, *I Change Worlds*, 228.

51. Ibid., 270.

52. Price, *The Lives of Agnes Smedley*, 189.

53. W.E.B. Du Bois, *The Autobiography of W.E.B. Du Bois: A Soliloquy on Viewing My Life from the Last Decade of Its First Century* (New York: International Publishers, 1968), 50.

54. Du Bois, "Forum of Fact and Opinion," 174.

55. Ibid.

56. Ibid.

57. Halliday, *A Political History of Japanese Capitalism*, 3.

58. Ibid., 130.

59. Bix, *Hirohito and the Making of Modern Japan*, 334.

60. Isaacs, *The Tragedy of the Chinese Revolution*, 304.

61. Ibid.

62. Ibid.

63. Ibid., 305.

64. Anna Louise Strong, *One Fifth of the World* (New York: Modern Age, 1938), 200.

65. Ibid., 202.

66. Ibid., 215.

67. Smedley's book was attacked by the communist left, which disapproved of her negative portrait of the Nationalists as contravening its "united front" Popular Front line. Smedley claimed that Earl Browder read and censored her manuscript when it was sent to Vanguard Press. She also accused Anna Louise Strong, who helped with the revisions, of editing "everything vital from it." In 1938, Strong was still more beholden than Smedley to Stalinism and Popular Front politics: see Price, *The Lives of Agnes Smedley*, 330.

68. Du Bois, "Forum of Fact and Opinion," 174.

69. Ibid., 182.

70. W.E.B. Du Bois, "As the Crow Flies," in Aptheker, *Newspaper Columns of W.E.B. Du Bois*, 1:376.

71. Ibid., 475.

72. Ibid.

73. Ibid.

74. Du Bois did organize a conference at the Schomburg Center for Research in Black Culture, New York Public Library, held on April 6, 1945, that featured Kumar Goshal and Bhold D. Panth of India and Msung Saw Tun of Burma among the speakers. Included in the conference resolutions was a call for "Restoration of Manchukuo and Formosa to a democratic China and the independence of Korea"—both aspects of which were directed at Japan: see Gerald Horne, *Black and Red: W.E.B. Du Bois and the Afro-American Response to the Cold War 1944-1963* (Albany: State University of New York Press, 1986), 29.

75. Price, *The Lives of Agnes Smedley*, 384.

76. W.E.B. Du Bois, "The Winds of Time," in *Newspaper Columns of W.E.B. Du Bois, Volume 2: Selections from 1945-1961*, ed. Herbert Aptheker (White Plains, NY: Kraus-Thomson, 1986), 754.

77. Ibid.

78. Ibid.

79. Price, *The Lives of Agnes Smedley*, 375.

80. Ibid.

81. W.E.B. Du Bois, "Africa Today," in Aptheker, *Newspaper Columns of W.E.B. Du Bois*, 2:855.

82. Du Bois, "Russia and America," 150.

83. Ibid.

84. Ibid.

85. Ibid., 151.

86. Du Bois, "Forum of Fact and Opinion," 172.

87. W.E.B. Du Bois, *Worlds of Color*, 40.

88. Ibid.

89. Ibid., 41.

90. Ibid.

91. Du Bois, "What Japan Has Done," 81.

92. Du Bois, *Worlds of Color*, 43.

93. Ibid.

94. Du Bois, *The Autobiography of W.E.B. Du Bois*, 46.

95. Du Bois, *Worlds of Color*, 136.

96. Ibid., 53.

97. Isaacs, *The Tragedy of the Chinese Revolution*, 300–301.

98. Ibid., 302.

99. Ibid., 311.

100. Ibid., 313.

101. Ibid.

102. Ibid., 317.

103. Ibid., 309.

104. Strong, *I Change Worlds*, 236–238.

105. Murali Balaji, *The Professor and the Pupil: The Politics and Friendship of W.E.B. Du Bois and Paul Robeson* (New York: Nation Books, 2007), 223, 305.

106. Ibid., 268, 289.

107. Quoted in ibid., 300.

108. Price, *The Lives of Agnes Smedley*, 407.

109. Ibid., 412.

CHAPTER 5

1. Vijay Prashad, *The Darker Nations: A People's History of the Third World* (New York: New Press, 2007), 12.

2. W.E.B. Du Bois, "Russia and America: An Interpretation," unpublished draft ms., 1950, W.E.B. Du Bois Papers, University of Massachusetts Amherst, 311.

3. Ibid., 301.

4. W.E.B. Du Bois, "Behold the Land!" *New Masses* 62 (1947): 20.

5. Erik S. McDuffie, *Sojourning for Freedom: Black Women, American Communism, and the Making of Black Feminism* (Durham, NC: Duke University Press, 2011), 159.

6. W.E.B. Du Bois, *The Autobiography of W.E.B. Du Bois: A Soliloquy on Viewing My Life from the Last Decade of Its First Century* (New York: International Publishers, 1969), 388.

7. Ruth Price, *The Lives of Agnes Smedley* (Oxford: Oxford University Press, 2005), 410.

8. Ibid., 415.

9. See Michael Kidron, "The Permanent Arms Economy," available at https://www.marxists.org/archive/kidron/works/1967/xx/permarms.htm (accessed November 19, 2014). Kidron first published his essay in *International Socialism* in spring 1967. Attempting to explain the long post-war "boom" of capitalism, Kidron contended that capitalist states were reinvesting surplus value in military build-up in order to sustain capitalist growth.

10. See Walter J. Oakes, "Towards a Permanent War Economy," *Politics*, February 1944, available at http://www.marxists.org/history/etol/writers/vance/1944/02/pwe.htm (accessed November 19, 2014).

11. W.E.B. Du Bois, "I'll Take My Stand," *Masses and Mainstream* 4, no. 4 (1951): 14–15.

12. Ibid., 15.

13. Ibid., 16.

14. Du Bois, *The Autobiography of W.E.B. Du Bois*, 354–356.

15. Ibid., 394.

16. Gerald Horne, *Race Woman: The Lives of Shirley Graham Du Bois* (New York: New York University Press, 2002), 122.

17. Ibid., 122–123.

18. Carole Boyce Davies, *Left of Karl Marx: The Political Life of Black Communist Claudia Jones* (Durham, NC: Duke University Press, 2007), 213.

19. McDuffie, *Sojourning for Freedom*, 172.

20. Ibid., 171.

21. Ibid., 175.

22. Ibid.

23. Nico Slate, *Colored Cosmopolitanism: The Shared Struggle for Freedom in the United States and India* (Cambridge, MA: Harvard University Press, 2012), 197.

24. See W.E.B. Du Bois, "The Winds of Time," *Chicago Defender*, November 17, 1945, 15; Immanuel Geiss, *The Pan-African Movement: A History of Pan-Africanism in America, Europe and Africa* (New York: Africana, 1974), 415.

25. James R. Hooker, *Black Revolutionary: George Padmore's Path from Communism to Pan-Africanism* (New York: Frederick A. Praeger, 1967), 113.

26. See, esp., McDuffie, *Sojourning for Freedom*, chaps. 4–5; Harry Haywood, *A Black Communist in the Freedom Struggle: The Life of Harry Haywood* (Minneapolis: University of Minnesota Press, 2012), chap. 13, epilogue.

27. See *We Charge Genocide: The Historic Petition to the United Nations for Relief from a Crime of the United States Government against the Negro People* (New York: Civil Rights Congress, 1951).

28. W.E.B. Du Bois, "The Winds of Time," in *Newspaper Columns by W.E.B. Du Bois, Volume 2: Selections from 1945–1961*, ed. Herbert Aptheker (White Plains, NY: Kraus-Thomson, 1986), 644.

29. Ibid.

30. Ibid., 645.

31. W.E.B. Du Bois, "A Decent World for All," *March of Labor*, vol. 6, no. 2, 1954, 23.

32. W.E.B. Du Bois, "Africa and World Peace," *Bulletin of the World Council of Peace*, June 1960, 16.

33. Ibid.

34. "The Damnation of Women" was first published in *Darkwater: Voices from within the Veil* in 1920. The essay is Du Bois's single most forceful declaration against women's, and especially black women's, oppression: "To no modern race does its women mean so much as to the Negro nor come so near to the fulfillment of its meaning." Though this piece was not cited by her biographer as a specific influence, Claudia Jones's claim that Du Bois was her "teacher" strongly suggests its impact on her work: see Eric J. Sundquist, ed., *The Oxford W.E.B. Du Bois Reader* (Oxford: Oxford University Press, 1996), 564–580.

35. Marika Sherwood, *Claudia Jones: A Life in Exile* (London: Lawrence and Wishart, 1999), 21.

36. Ibid.

37. See, e.g., Boyce Davies, *Left of Karl Marx*; McDuffie, *Sojourning for Freedom*.

38. Claudia Jones, "On the Right to Self-Determination for the Negro People in the Black Belt," in *Claudia Jones: Beyond Containment*, ed. Carole Boyce Davies (Oxfordshire: Ayebia Clarke, 2011), 62.

39. Ibid.

40. Ibid., 70.

41. Claudia Jones, "An End to the Neglect of the Problems of Negro Women," in Boyce Davies, *Claudia Jones*, 78–79.

42. Ibid., 83.

43. Ibid., 85.

44. Claudia Jones, "We Seek Full Equality," in Boyce Davies, *Claudia Jones*, 87.

45. In *Sojourners for Peace*, Erik S. McDuffie ascribes politics rooted in women's domestic concerns to what Amy Swerdlow has called "familial" politics in her analysis of women's peace activism of the 1960s. Given her background in Marxist-Leninism and her citations of Marx on the family, this seems a more likely source for Jones. For more on "familial" discourse, see Amy Swerdlow, *Women Strike for Peace: Traditional Politics and Radical Motherhood in the 1960s* (Chicago: University of Chicago Press, 1993); McDuffie, *Sojourners for Peace*, 250, n. 26.

46. Jones, "We Seek Full Equality," 87.

47. Ibid., 89.

48. See Gerald Horne and Margaret Stevens, "Shirley Graham Du Bois: Portrait of the Black Woman Artist as a Revolutionary," in *Want to Start a Revolution? Radical Women in the Black Freedom Struggle*, ed. Dayo F. Gore, Jeanne Theoharis, and Komozi Woodard (New York: New York University Press, 2009), 95–115.

49. Alexandra Kollontai, "A Militant Celebration," in *Mezhdunarodnyi den' rabotnitz*, Moscow, 1920, available at http://www.marxists.org/archive/kollonta/1920/womens-day.htm (accessed August 1, 2014).

50. Claudia Jones, "International Women's Day and the Struggle for Peace," in Boyce Davies, *Claudia Jones*, 98.

51. Kollontai, "A Militant Celebration."

52. Jones, "International Women's Day and the Struggle for Peace," 90–91.

53. Ibid., 94.

54. Ibid., 96.

55. Ibid., 98.

56. Ibid.

57. Ibid., 99.

58. Ibid.

59. Ibid., 98; italics added.

60. Claudia Jones, "For the Unity of Women in the Cause of Peace" (1951), in Boyce Davies, *Claudia Jones*, 111.

61. Ibid., 107.

62. Ibid., 106.

63. Boyce Davies, *Left of Karl Marx*, 151.

64. W.E.B. Du Bois, "On the Future of the American Negro," *Freedomways* 5, no. 1 (Winter 1965): 124.

65. Du Bois, *The Autobiography of W.E.B. Du Bois*, 376.

66. Dayo F. Gore, *Radicalism at the Crossroads: African American Women Activists in the Cold War* (New York: New York University Press, 2011), 85.

67. W.E.B. Du Bois, "The Rosenbergs," *Masses and Mainstream* 6, no. 7 (1953): 10–11.

68. Du Bois, "On the Future of the American Negro," 124.

69. Editorial, *West Indian Gazette and Afro-Asian Caribbean News*, vol. 5, no. 7, December 1962, 4.

70. Jawaharlal Nehru, "No Narrow Nationalism," *United Asia: International Journal of Asian Affairs* 1, no. 1 (May–June 1948): 20.

71. *United Asia: International Journal of Asian Affairs* 2, no. 1 (May–June 1948): 8.

72. Partha Chatterjee, *Nationalist Thought and the Colonial World: A Derivative Discourse?* 2d ed. (London: Zed, 1993), 30.

73. Benjamin Zachariah, *Nehru* (London: Routledge, 2004), 192–193.

74. Sohail Jawaid, *Socialism in India* (New Delhi: Radiant, 1986), 92.

75. Ibid., 93.

76. Zachariah, *Nehru*, 228.

77. Ibid., 199.

78. Shao Chuan Leng, "Nationalism and Communism in Asia," *United Asia: International Journal of Asian Affairs* 6, no. 5 (November 1954): 214.

79. Ibid., 214.

80. Mao Tse-tung, "On New Democracy," available at http://www.marxists.org/reference/archive/mao/selected-works/volume-2/mswv2_26.htm (accessed August 1, 2014).

81. Shao Chuan Leng, "Nationalism and Communism in Asia," 213, 214.

82. Ibid., 229.

83. Chao En-lai, "On the Asian-African Conference at Bandung," *United Asia: International Journal of Asian Affairs* 7, no. 6 (December 1955): 308.

84. Ibid.

85. Antoinette Burton, "The Sodalities of Bandung: Toward a Critical 21st-Century History," in *Making a World after Empire: The Bandung Moment and Its Political Afterlives*, ed. Christopher Lee (Athens: Ohio University Press, 2010), 354.

86. Dipesh Chakrabarty, "The Legacies of Bandung: Decolonization and the Politics of Culture," in Lee, *Making a World after Empire*, 50.

87. Giovanni Arrighi and John S. Saul, *Essays on the Political Economy of Africa* (New York: Monthly Review Press, 1973), 53.

88. Ibid., 45.

89. Ibid., 48.

90. Ibid., 122, 124.

91. Ibid., 27.

92. Abdul Rahman Mohamed Babu, *African Socialism or Socialist Africa?* (London: Zed, 1981), 40.

93. W.E.B. Du Bois, "Watch Africa," in Aptheker, *Newspaper Columns by W.E.B. Du Bois*, 2:863; alterations to italics mine.

94. Ibid.

95. W.E.B. Du Bois, "Letter to Dean Pruitt," in *The Correspondence of W.E.B. Du Bois, Volume 3: Selections from 1944–1963*, ed. Herbert Aptheker (Amherst: University of Massachusetts Press, 1978), 341.

96. W.E.B. Du Bois, "The Wealth of the West versus a Chance for Exploited Mankind," in Aptheker, *Newspaper Columns by W.E.B. Du Bois*, 2:941.

97. See Arrighi and Saul, *Essays on the Political Economy of Africa*, 107; Kwame Nkrumah, *Neocolonialism: The Last Stage of Imperialism* (London: Thomas Nelson and Sons, 1965), 107.

98. Ali A. Mazrui, *Towards a Pax Africana: A Study of Ideology and Ambition* (Chicago: University of Chicago Press, 1967), 97.

99. Julius K. Nyerere, *Freedom and Socialism/Uhuru na Ujamaa: A Selection from Writings and Speeches, 1965–1967* (Dar es Salaam, Tanzania: Oxford University Press, 1968), 16.

100. Ibid., 15.

101. Ibid.

102. Babu, *African Socialism or Socialist Africa?* xv.

103. Ibid., 64.

104. George Padmore, "Letter to WE.B. Du Bois, August 17, 1945," in Aptheker, *The Correspondence of W.E.B. Du Bois*, 3:78.

105. George Padmore, "Letter to W.E.B. Du Bois," December 3, 1954, in Aptheker, *The Correspondence of W.E.B. Du Bois*, 3:374.

106. See Richard Wright, *Black Power: A Record of Reactions in a Land of Pathos* (New York: HarperCollins, 1995).

107. W.E.B. Du Bois, "Letter to George Padmore," in Aptheker, *The Correspondence of W.E.B. Du Bois*, 3:375.

108. Ibid.

109. W.E.B. Du Bois, "Africa's Choice," *National Guardian*, October 29, 1956, in Aptheker, *Newspaper Columns by W.E.B. Du Bois*, 2:973.

110. Ibid.

111. Arrighi and Saul, *Essays on the Political Economy of Africa*, 161.

112. Quoted in ibid., 168.

113. David Levering Lewis, *W.E.B. Du Bois: The Fight for Equality and the American Century, 1919–1963* (New York: Henry Holt, 2000), 557.

114. W.E.B. Du Bois, "On Stalin," *National Guardian*, March 16, 1953, 1.

115. Ibid., 2.

116. Ibid., 1.

117. W.E.B. Du Bois, "World Changer," review of Anna Louise Strong, *The Stalin Era*, *Masses and Mainstream*, January 1957, 3.

118. Ibid., 4.

119. Ibid., 5.

120. See Terry Eagleton, "Capitalism, Modernism and Postmodernism," in *Against the Grain: Essays, 1975–1985* (London: Verso, 1986), 136; Terry Eagleton, "Waking the Dead," *New Statesman*, November 12, 2011, available at http://www.newstatesman.com/ideas/2009/11/past-benjamin-future-obama (accessed May 5, 2014).

121. Du Bois, *The Autobiography of W.E.B. Du Bois*, 400.

122. Ibid.

123. W.E.B. Du Bois, "Nevidannyi Skachok" [An Unprecedented Leap], *Literaturnaya Gazeta*, November 5, 1957, 5.

124. Ibid.

125. W.E.B. Du Bois, "Triumf Sotsializma" [The Triumph of Socialism], *Izvestia*, November 7, 1959, 5.

126. For example, as Gerald Horne notes, while he admitted that Stalin was a "hard dictator," Du Bois insisted as late as 1956 that Poland was experiencing "progress, contentment and peace." Du Bois also criticized critics of the Soviet repression of the workers' uprising in Hungary as "American capitalists seeking to sink their claws again into the mines and oil wells, soil and serf labor of ten million Hungarians": see Gerald Horne, *Black and Red: W.E.B. Du Bois and the Afro-American Response to the Cold War, 1944–1963* (Albany: State University of New York Press, 1986), 317–381.

127. W.E.B. Du Bois, "Utro Novogo Dnia" (The Morning of a New Day), *Pravda*, April 22, 1963, 3.

128. Du Bois, "Nevidannyi Skachok," 5.

129. Du Bois, *The Autobiography of W.E.B. Du Bois*, 402.

130. Ibid., 404.

131. Ibid.

132. Ibid.

133. W.E.B. Du Bois, "The Crucifixion of John Brown," *New Times* (Moscow), vol. 49, December 1959, 28.

134. W.E.B. Du Bois, *John Brown* (New York: International Publishers, 1996), 295, 296.

135. Ibid., 297.

136. Ibid., 299.

137. Levering Lewis, *W.E.B. Du Bois: The Fight for Equality*, 563.

138. W.E.B. Du Bois, "The Vast Miracle of China Today," in *W.E.B. Du Bois on Asia: Crossing the World Color Line*, ed. Bill V. Mullen and Cathryn Watson (Jackson: University Press of Mississippi, 2005), 191.

139. Tracy B. Strong and Helene Keyssar, *Right in Her Soul: The Life of Anna Louise Strong* (New York: Random House, 1983), 292.

140. Ibid., 293.

141. Ibid., 301.

142. W.E.B. Du Bois, "China and Africa," in Mullen and Watson, *W.E.B. Du Bois on Asia*, 200.

143. Levering Lewis, *W.E.B. Du Bois: The Fight for Equality*, 567.

144. Ibid., 569.

145. Du Bois, *The Autobiography of W.E.B. Du Bois*, 419.

146. Ibid., 422.

147. Ibid., 423.

148. Karl Marx, "The Eighteenth Brumaire of Napoleon Bonaparte," in *The Portable Karl Marx*, ed. Eugene Kamenka (New York: Viking Penguin, 1983), 287–288.

149. Martin Luther King Jr., "Beyond Vietnam," in *A Call to Conscience: The Landmark Speeches of Martin Luther King, Jr.*, ed. Clayborne Carson and Kris Shepherd (New York: Time Warner, 2001), 140.

150. Countee Cullen, "Karenge Ya Margene," *United Asia: International Journal of Asian Affairs* 5, no. 3 (1953): 170.

151. Price, *The Lives of Agnes Smedley*, 420.

152. See ibid., 452, n. 28.

153. Zachariah, *Nehru*, 249.

154. In the "Republic" chapter of *The Indian Ideology*, Anderson avers, "What is hidden within India is Hindustan. It is that which tacitly shapes the state and determines the frontiers between freedom and expression, what is allowed and what is forbidden." Anderson argues that the breakthrough of the Bharatiya Janata Party in 1992, during its national campaign to demolish the mosque at Ayodhya, was the beginning of a rise of Hindu nationalism that is bearing on Indian elections as I write: see Perry Anderson, *The Indian Ideology* (London: Verso, 2013), 145–155.

155. Strong and Keyssar, *Right in Her Soul*, 321.

156. Ibid., 312.

157. Ibid., 307.

158. Ibid., 337.

159. Ibid., 349.

160. George Padmore, *The Gold Coast Revolution: The Struggle of an African People from Slavery to Freedom* (London: Dennis Dobson, 1953), 12.

161. Robin D. G. Kelley, Introduction to C.L.R. James, *A History of Pan-African Revolt* (Oakland, CA: PM Press, 2012), 27–28.

162. James, *A History of Pan-African Revolt*, 131.

163. Ibid., 135.

164. Ibid., 136.

165. Babu, *African Socialism or Socialist Africa?* 63.

166. Esther Cooper Jackson, Introduction to *Freedomways Reader*, ed. Esther Cooper Jackson (Boulder, CO: Westview, 2001), xx.

167. Martin Luther King Jr., "Honoring Dr. Du Bois," in Jackson, *Freedomways Reader*, 37.

168. Horne and Stevens, "Shirley Graham Du Bois," 108.

169. Ibid., 110.

170. Sherwood, *Claudia Jones*, 75.

171. Ibid.

172. Eric Hobsbawm, "Eye Witness in Cuba," *West Indian Gazette and Afro-Asian Caribbean News*, vol. 3, no. 4, December 1960, 3.

173. "A Collective-Colonial Cold-Monster," *West Indian Gazette and Afro-Asian Caribbean News*, vol. 5, no. 5, 1962, 4.

174. Sherwood, *Claudia Jones*, 82.

175. "Vietnam War May Spread," *West Indian Gazette and Afro-Asian Caribbean News*, vol. 6, no. 4, May 1964, 4.

176. Claudia Jones, "Cradle of the Revolution," in Boyce Davies, *Claudia Jones*, 202.

THE AFTERTHOUGHT

1. Ferruccio Gambino, "Reading *Black Reconstruction* on the Eve of 1969," *South Atlantic Quarterly* 112, no. 3 (Summer 2013): 530.

2. Ibid., 531.

3. Ibid., 532.

4. Ibid., 530.

5. Amy Bass, *Those about Him Remained Silent: The Battle over W.E.B. Du Bois* (Minneapolis: University of Minnesota Press, 2009), 47.

6. Alan Wald, "From 'Triple Oppression' to 'Freedom Dreams,'" *Against the Current* 162 (January–February 2013): 24.

7. In addition to examples cited in this chapter, exceptions would include the scholarship of Paul LeBlanc, Scott McLemee, Robin D. G. Kelley, James Smethurst, Mark Naison, Rachel Rubin, William Maxwell, Winston James, Keeanga Yamahtta-Taylor, Chris Vials, and Alan Wald. While some of these scholars, such as LeBlanc, McLemee, and Wald, openly identify with Trotskyism, others here have generated important analyses of strengths and weaknesses of the American left by carefully examining contradictions and difficulties of maintaining communist and socialist allegiance in the United States before and after the Cold War.

8. Eric Porter, *The Problem of the Future World: W.E.B. Du Bois and the Race Concept at Midcentury* (Durham, NC: Duke University Press, 2010), 10.

9. David Levering Lewis, *W.E.B. Du Bois: The Fight for Equality and the American Century, 1919–1963* (New York: Henry Holt, 2000), 570; quoted in Porter, *The Problem of the Future World*, 5.

10. Porter, *The Problem of the Future World*, 166.

11. Wald, "From 'Triple Oppression' to 'Freedom Dreams,'" 24.

12. Porter, *The Problem of the Future World*, 178.

13. See Yuichiro Onishi, *Transpacific Antiracism: Afro-Asian Solidarity in 20th Century Black America, Japan, and Okinawa* (New York: New York University Press, 2013); Dohra Ahmad, *Landscapes of Hope: Anticolonial Utopianism in America* (Oxford: Oxford University Press, 2009); Nico Slate, *Colored Cosmopolitanisms: The Shared Struggle for Freedom in the United States and India* (Cambridge, MA: Harvard University Press, 2012); Etsuko Taketani, *The Black Pacific Narrative: Geographic Imaginings of Race and Empire*

between the Wars (Hanover, NH: Dartmouth University Press, 2014). See also Robeson Taj Frazier, *The East Is Black: Cold War China in the Black Radical Imagination* (Durham, NC: Duke University Press, 2015).

14. See Taketani, *The Black Pacific Narrative*, chap. 5.

15. See as examples Partha Chatterjee, *The Nation and Its Fragments: Colonial and Postcolonial Histories* (Princeton, NJ: Princeton University Press, 1993); Partha Chatterjee, *The Black Hole of Empire: History of a Global Practice of Power* (Princeton, NJ: Princeton University Press, 2012); Partha Chatterjee, *Provincializing Europe: Postcolonial Thought and Historical Difference* (Princeton, NJ: Princeton University Press, 2000); Sumit Sarkar, *Beyond Nationalist Frames: Postmodernism, Hindu Fundamentalism, History* (Bloomington: Indiana University Press, 2002); Gayatri Spivak, *A Critique of Postcolonial Reason: Toward a History of the Vanishing Present* (Cambridge, MA: Harvard University Press, 1999). An important analysis of the relationship of Marxism to subaltern studies scholarship is Vivek Chibber, *Postcolonial Theory and the Specter of Capital* (London: Verso, 2013). Chibber's book is of a piece with Gupta's attempt to analyze Indian historiography in light of real political gains and losses of the Indian left in the contemporary period. Finally, although it is not located in the tradition of postcolonial studies, one might add Perry Anderson, *The Indian Ideology* (London: Verso, 2013), for providing a refreshed historiographical view of modern Indian scholarship and for its thought-provoking assessment of the rise of Hindu nationalism, culminated in India's recent election of Narendra Modi of the Hindutva Bharatiya Janata Party as prime minister.

16. Olsen, who joined the Young Communist League in 1931, was raised by socialist parents; charted working-class women's oppression in her fiction; and, according to Florence Howe, publisher at Feminist Press, was instrumental in the republication of Agnes Smedley's *Daughter of Earth* (New York: Feminist Press, 1987). Howe wrote that Olsen "insisted" on the book's republication in 1971 and that no gesture was "more significant" in the press's history than Olsen's, as it helped to spearhead the press's efforts to recover other women writers: see Florence Howe, Preface to *Almost Touching the Skies: Women's Coming of Age Stories*, ed. Florence Howe and Jean Casella (New York: Feminist Press, 2000), ix.

17. See Alice Walker, Foreword to *Daughter of Earth*, 1–4. Walker calls Smedley a "poor white woman who, all her life, continued to act, to write like one. I recognize in her a matriot of my own country."

18. See Barbara Ransby, *Ella Baker and the Black Freedom Movement: A Radical Democratic Vision* (Chapel Hill: University of North Carolina Press, 2005); Barbara Ransby, *Eslanda: The Large and Unconventional Life of Mrs. Paul Robeson* (New Haven, CT: Yale University Press, 2013); Carole Boyce Davies, *Left of Karl Marx: The Political Life of Black Communist Claudia Jones* (Durham, NC: Duke University Press, 2007); Marika Sherwood, *Claudia Jones: A Life in Exile* (London: Lawrence and Wishart, 1999); Gerald Horne, *Race Woman: The Lives of Shirley Graham Du Bois* (New York: New York University Press, 2002).

19. See Lise Vogel, *Marxism and the Oppression of Women: Toward a Unitary Theory* (1983; repr., Chicago: Haymarket Books, 2014); Angela Davis, *Women, Race and Class* (New York: Vintage, 1983); Martha Gimenez, "Global Capitalism and Women," in *Globalization and Third World Women: Exploitation, Coping and Resistance*, ed. Ligaya Lindio-McGovern and Isidor Wallimann (Farnham, UK: Ashgate, 2009), 35–48. See also Susan Ferguson and David McNally, Foreword to Vogel, *Marxism and the Oppression of Women*; Susan Ferguson, "Canadian Contributions to Social Reproduction Feminism, Race and Embodied Labor," *Race, Gender and Class* 15, nos. 1–2 (2008): 42–57; Tithi Bhattacharya,

"Explaining Gender Violence in the Neoliberal Era," *International Socialist Review*, no. 91 (Fall 2013): 25–47.

20. See Alys Weinbaum, "Reproducing Racial Globality: W.E.B. Du Bois and the Sexual Politics of Black Internationalism," *Social Text 67* 19, no. 2 (Summer 2001): 15–41; Susan Gillman and Alys Weinbaum, eds., *Next to the Color Line: Gender, Sexuality and W.E.B. Du Bois* (Minneapolis: University of Minnesota Press, 2007); Paul Gilroy, *Against Race: Imagining Political Culture Beyond the Color Line* (Cambridge, MA: Harvard University Press, 2001).

21. Porter, *The Problem of the Future World*, 3.

22. See Penny Von Eschen, *Race against Empire: Black Americans and Anti-Colonialism, 1937–1957* (Ithaca, NY: Cornell University Press, 1997); Kevin Gaines, *African Americans in Ghana: Black Expatriates and the Civil Rights Era* (Chapel Hill: University of North Carolina Press, 2007). Gerald Horne's corpus of scholarship has been dedicated to study of black radicalism and black internationalism and constitutes a canon unto itself. In addition to *Black and Red: W.E.B. Du Bois and the Afro-American Response to the Cold War 1944–1963* (Albany: State University of New York Press, 1985), important books by Horne include *Black Liberation/Red Scare: Ben Davis and the Communist Party* (Dover: University of Delaware Press, 1994); *Black Revolutionary: William Patterson and the Globalization of the African American Freedom Struggle* (Champaign: University of Illinois Press, 2013); and *The Counter-Revolution of 1776: Slave Resistance and the Origins of America* (New York: New York University Press, 2014).

23. See Cheryl Higashida, *Black Internationalist Feminism: Women Writers of the Black Left, 1955–1995* (Champaign: University of Illinois Press, 2013); Dayo F. Gore, *Radicalism at the Crossroads: African American Women Activists in the Cold War* (New York: New York University Press, 2011); Erik S. McDuffie, *Sojourning for Freedom: Black Women, American Communism and the Making of Black Left Feminism* (Durham, NC: Duke University Press, 2011); Carole Boyce Davies *Left of the Color Line: The Political Life of Black Communist Claudia Jones* (Durham, NC: Duke University Press, 2007); Sherwood, *Claudia Jones*.

24. Higashida, *Black Internationalist Feminism*, 20.

25. McDuffie, *Sojourning for Freedom*, 151.

26. Gore, *Radicalism at the Crossroads*, 145.

27. Ibid., 151.

28. Wald, "From 'Triple Oppression' to 'Freedom Dreams,'" 24. An even more recent complication of the relationship of Stalinism and anticommunism to the U.S. African American literary left is Mary Helen Washington's stellar *The Other Blacklist: The African American Literary and Cultural Left of the 1950s* (New York: Columbia University Press, 2014). In individual chapters, Washington takes up studies of the writer Lloyd Brown, the painter Charles White, the playwright and author Alice Childress, the poet Gwendolyn Brooks, and the novelist Frank London Brown.

29. Sherwood, *Claudia Jones*, 178–215.

30. See Boyce Davies, *Left of Karl Marx*, chap. 4.

31. Among the pieces published by Du Bois in the Soviet press and in need of further scholarly attention are "Etapy Izucheniia Negrov v SSHA" [The Stages in the Study of Negroes in the USA], *Voprosy Antropologii* 6 (1961): 92–99; "Bor'ba Polya Robsona" [The Battle of Paul Robeson], *Literaturnaya Gazeta*, April 10, 1958, 4; "V Soedinennykh Shtatakh Neobhodimo Vosstanovit Demokratiu" [In the United States It Is Necessary to Reconstruct Democracy], *Pravda*, June 17, 1960, 3–4; "Nevidannyi Skachok" [An Unprecedented Leap] *Literaturnaya Gazeta*, November 5, 1957, 5.

32. The phrase is Kevin Gaines's: see his *Uplifting the Race: Black Leadership, Politics, and Culture in the Twentieth Century* (Chapel Hill: University of North Carolina Press, 1996), 155.

33. See Kate Baldwin, *Beyond the Color Line and the Iron Curtain: Reading Encounters between Black and Red, 1922–1963* (Durham, NC: Duke University Press, 2002).

34. Sobhanlal Datta Gupta, *Comintern and the Destiny of Communism in India, 1919–1943: Dialectics of a Real and Possible History* (Kolkata: Seribaan, 2011).

35. Martin Luther King Jr., "Where Do We Go from Here?" in *A Call to Conscience: The Landmark Speeches of Martin Luther King, Jr.*, ed. Carson Clayborne and Kris Shepherd (New York: Time Warner, 2001), 172.

INDEX

Bill V. Mullen is a Professor of American Studies at Purdue University. He is the author of *Afro-Orientalism* and *Popular Fronts: Chicago and African-American Cultural Politics, 1935–46.* He is the co-editor (with Fred Ho) of *Afro Asia: Revolutionary Political and Cultural Connections between African Americans and Asian Americans* and (with Cathryn Watson) of *W.E.B. Du Bois on Asia: Crossing the World Color Line.*